Advances in Electronic Business
Volume II

Eldon Y. Li
National Chengchi University, Taiwan &
California Polytechnic State University, USA

Timon C. Du
The Chinese University of Hong Kong, Hong Kong, China

CYBERTECH PUBLISHING
Hershey • London • Melbourne • Singapore

Acquisitions Editor:	Michelle Potter
Development Editor:	Kristin Roth
Senior Managing Editor:	Jennifer Neidig
Managing Editor:	Sara Reed
Copy Editor:	Nicole Dean
Typesetter:	Jessie Weik
Cover Design:	Lisa Tosheff
Printed at:	Integrated Book Technology

Published in the United States of America by
    CyberTech Publishing (an imprint of Idea Group Inc.)
    701 E. Chocolate Avenue
    Hershey PA 17033
    Tel: 717-533-8845
    Fax: 717-533-8661
    E-mail: cust@idea-group.com
    Web site: http://www.cybertech-pub.com

and in the United Kingdom by
    CyberTech Publishing (an imprint of Idea Group Inc.)
    3 Henrietta Street
    Covent Garden
    London WC2E 8LU
    Tel: 44 20 7240 0856
    Fax: 44 20 7379 0609
    Web site: http://www.eurospanonline.com

Advances in Electronic Business is part of the Idea Group Publishing series named *Advances in Electronic Business Series* (ISSN: pending).

ISBN: 1-59140-678-1
Paperback ISBN: 1-59140-679-X
eISBN: 1-59140-680-3

British Cataloguing in Publication Data
A Cataloguing in Publication record for this book is available from the British Library.

All work contributed to this book is new, previously-unpublished material. The views expressed in this book are those of the authors, but not necessarily of the publisher.

Advances in Electronic Business Volume II

Table of Contents

Preface

In the past decade, the boom of Internet technology has encouraged vast ranges of information be created and shared among peoples, organizations, and enterprises. Most of the information has been written in hypertext markup language (HTML), which mainly follows certain format to express the contents. However, this well-formatted information is normally written for human comprehension. When the information volume grows, the time to locate and to digest the information that fits users' needs increases exponentially. There are many possible solutions to the problem and the attentions are drawn to the data and the meaning of data. The XML (extensible markup language) provides the independence between applications and data, allowing the data to be shared among applications. But, what kinds of information can be shared and how to share the information remain as unsolved problems. This brings the attention to the semantic Web. The semantic Web has rules to automatically reason the needs of information and has XML/RDF (resource description framework) to define the meaning and relationship of data. The new phenomenon provides the possibility of having diversified and machine-processable Web services over Internet, intranet, and extranet. We therefore devote the second volume of the book series, *Advances in Electronic Business*, to the issues of *Semantic Web* and *intelligent Web services*.

The mission of *Advances in Electronic Business* book series is to foster the understanding of management methods, information technology, and their joint application in business processes. The subject coverage includes theories and practices of business technologies, enterprise management, public policies, logistics, privacy and law, business ethics, and information technologies that are related to electronic business. The audience of this book series is to be broadly-based, including professionals, policymakers, academics, researchers, and managers in IT, business and commerce. The first volume of this book series focusing on the issues of *collaborative commerce* has been published in 2005. This second volume is to address the issues of *Semantic Web and intelligent Web services*. The organization of this book is as follows.

Chapter I, "From World Wide Web to Semantic Web" by Charles Ling-yu Chou, introduces the incentives for the creation of the Semantic Web, the methodology for its development, and the current status of its development.

Chapter II, "Semantic Descriptions of Web Services" by Farshad Hakimpour, Suo Cong, and Daniela E. Damm, covers the semantic description of Web services. It concentrates on two prevalent specifications in this domain, namely OWL-S (Ontology Web Language for Services) and WSMO (Web Services Modeling Ontology). This chapter briefly introduces Web Services and Semantic Web, the two main technologies underlying the Semantic Web Services technology, and then explains most of the key features of this technology together with simplified examples.

Chapter III, "Developing Intelligent Semantic Web Services" by Sam Lee, presents an approach to the development of intelligent semantic Web services, which are envisioned as system cells that actively discover, learn, and communicate knowledge on the Web.

Chapter IV, "Semantic Web Support for Customer Services" by Quan Thanh Tho, Hui Siu Cheung, and A. C. M. Fong, focuses on the semantic Web support for customer services. It discusses semantic Web support for customer services in which the Web service support is an important operation for most multinational manufacturing companies.

Chapter V, "A Tutorial on RDF with Jena" by Wan-Yeung Wong, Tak-Pang Lau, Irwin King, and Michael R. Lyu, provides a tutorial on resource description framework (RDF), the language (RDF/XML) used by RDF, and a Java API (Jena) for manipulating RDF/XML. RDF is a W3C standard which provides a common framework for describing resources in the World Wide Web and other applications.

Chapter VI, "A Semantic Web Service Architecture for Learning Object Repositories" by José-Manuel López-Cobo, Sinuhé Arroyo, Miguel-Angel Sicilia, and Salvador Sánchez Alonso, aims to describe an architecture of semantic Web service for learning object repositories. In this chapter, provision of computational semantics to metadata is addressed from the perspective of the concept of Semantic Web Service. An architecture based on the specifications of the WSMO project is described, including the definition of an ontology for learning object metadata, and issues of mediation, all under the perspective of the Learning Object Repository as the central entity in learning object reuse scenarios.

Chapter VII, "Using Semantic Web to Facilitate Agent-to-Agent Argumentation for E-Commerce" by Shiu-li Huang and Fu-ren Lin, uses semantic Web to facilitate agent-to-agent argumentation for e-commerce. This study aims to design a multi-agent argumentation system for e-commerce. In this system, buyer and seller agents can argue over product attributes and understand arguments. This study adopts OWL, a Web ontology language, to clearly express arguments and uses a dialectical game approach to support defeasible reasoning. Using this system, a buyer can delegate a buyer agent to search products that exactly match his/her needs, and a seller can delegate a seller agent to present products and persuade buyer agents into believing that the products can satisfy their masters' needs.

Chapter VIII, "Building Dynamic Business Process in P2P Semantic Web" by Timon C. Du and Eldon Y. Li, builds dynamic business process in a P2P semantic Web. It proposes a framework to implement a dynamic business process in the P2P semantics Web, which provides the flexibility to dynamically alter business process and to take semantic data into consideration. The system is demonstrated by a case of order processing of a manufacturer.

Chapter IX, "An Intelligent Metasearch Engine with Link Prediction and Page Clipping Generation Capabilities" by Cheng-Jye Luh and Lin-chih Chen, presents an intelligent metasearch engine that can recommend a user's next hyperlink access and relevant paragraphs extracted from metasearch results. The authors implemented three search methods based on the assumption that users prefer top ranking items in search results.

Chapter X, "Access Control for Web Service Applications: An Example in Collaborative Auditing" by Timon C. Du, Richard Hwang, and Charles Ling-yu Chou, proposes a role-based Chinese Wall model, which organizes the corporate data into four different types of control groups with different access control policies, for the auditors to access the data among collaborating enterprises.

Chapter XI, "Semantics and the Medical Web: Towards Effective Medical Healthcare Search" by Amanda Spink, Robert M. Wolfe, and Bernard J. Jansen, illustrates the semantics and the medical Web. This chapter discusses issues related to semantics and the medical Web, in which much health information is available on the Web, but not always effectively found by users. This chapter examines various aspects of medical Web searching and shows that searchers do not always use correct medical terminology.

Chapter XII, "Web Mining for Protein-to-Protein Interaction Information" by Hsi-Chieh Lee, Szu-Wei Huang, and Eldon Y. Li, introduces a Web mining system finding protein-to-protein interaction literatures. It develops mechanisms for protein name identification and databases for protein names. The experimental results indicate that by using the proposed mining system, a researcher can find protein-to-protein literatures from the overwhelming piece of information available on the biomedical databases over the Internet.

Chapter XIII, "SWAP: A Framework for Ontology Support in Semantic Web Applications" by Arijit Sengupta and Henry Kim, presents Semantic Web Application Pyramid (SWAP) which is a framework for incorporating ontologies in data-oriented semantic Web applications with measurement ontology for a quality management Web service. SWAP facilitates data exchange between these Web services with vendor data stored in databases, and the processing of the data using a combination of RuleML and SQL.

The 13 chapters included in this book cover from basic to advanced concepts of semantic Webs and intelligent Web services. The applications stem from order process to medical diagnosis. A beginner could walk through the first few chapters and become familiar with the subjects. An experienced reader could study the technical details in the last few chapters to implement application systems. The broad spectrum of subjects covered in this book makes it a valuable reference book in your library. We sincerely hope that it could be beneficial to your professional career as well as research endeavour.

Eldon Y. Li,

National Chengchi University, Taiwan & California Polytechnic State University, USA

Timon C. Du, The Chinese University of Hong Kong, Hong Kong, China

Acknowledgments

This book has been prepared in close cooperation with academicians and practitioners who are experts in the area of Web services and Semantic Web from 16 universities and two companies over eight counties or regions. The editors would like to thank all the chapter authors, including Charles Chou, Wan-Yeung Wong, Tak-Pang Lau, Irwin King, Michael R. Lyu, Farshad Hakimpour, Suo Cong, Daniela E. Damm, Sam Lee, Thanh Tho Quan, Siu Cheung Hui, A C M Fong, Amanda Spink, Robert M. Wolfe, Bernard J. Jansen, Jose-Manuel Lopez Cobo, Sinuhe Arroyo, Miguel-Angel Sicilia, Salvador Sánchez, Shiu-li Huang, Fu-Ren Lin, Cheng-Jye Luh and Lin-chih Chen, Richard Hwang and Charles Chou, Hsi-Chieh Lee and Szu-Wei Huang, Arijit Sengupta and Henry Kim for their tireless effort in preparing the manuscripts.

We would like to express our gratitude to the many reviewers for their assistance in reviewing the chapters to assure the quality of this book. Special thanks to Idea Group Inc. who published the book with clear guidelines over the whole process. Last but not the least, we would like to thank Kristin Roth who helped to organize the book and provided all the professional assistance in the past year.

Eldon Y. Li,

National Chengchi University, Taiwan & California Polytechnic State University, USA

Timon C. Du, The Chinese University of Hong Kong, Hong Kong, China

Chapter I

From World Wide Web to Semantic Web

Charles Ling-yu Chou,
The Chinese University of Hong Kong, Hong Kong, China

Abstract

This chapter introduces the incentives for the creation of the Semantic Web, the methodology for its development, and the current status of this development. In contrast to the human function of understanding, the author summarizes four major steps in creating the ability for machines to understand Web content and generate responses. The semantics in the Semantic Web should be explicitly declared in a form that can be operated by a machine, knowledge organization should be provided to support semantic interpretation, software agents must rely on automatic reasoning ability to obtain implied knowledge, and procedural knowledge should be accessed in a community to generate response behavior. Through illustration of the anticipated research efforts in this technology, the author hopes to provide a clear picture of the current status of emergent Semantic Web technology and a suitable direction for its future development.

Introduction

The World Wide Web is an information universe, in which countless nodes of Web content that provide links to online and off-line resources are connected together. Although this information universe tends to be unbounded, the technology that supports it is simple. The World Wide Web is constructed using just three fundamental standards: the uniform resources identifier (URI), the hyper text transfer protocol (HTTP), and the hyper text markup language (HTML). These three standards perform different functions individually, but serve collaboratively to enable information consumer to access remote resources by retrieving Web content from remote nodes and presenting them on local machines.

The URI that is given to each document is a unique address on the World Wide Web, and is the universal identification of the node that is sought. HTTP is one of the communication protocols for information transmission between two participating applications, with which the requesting application can send enquiries to remote applications to retrieve Web content. The requested application then responds with Web content, which is usually packaged as documents in a message body, to the requesting applications.

Upon receiving the requested Web content, the receiving application launches a corresponding display device on the local machine to present the Web content. To be expressible, the Web content must be specified with some demonstrating properties that configure the expected presentation effects for the respective video or audio devices on which the content will be displayed. Content designers use HTML to annotate their configuration of content, which works like a markup that highlights elements of the content with explanatory notion. Thus, two different kinds of information, the main content and the annotated configuration, are synchronized in the same HTML document. Generally, an application that is specifically for remote resource access and Web content display is called a Web browser. When a Web browser receives a document, it knows which part of the document is the main content and how to display the main content with the expected effects using the configuring information that is provided by the other parts of the document. General presentation effects include control of the size, the color effect of the textual content, and the invoking of the configuration for specific devices to display images, videos, or audio files. The annotations that are marked in HTML allow the Web content to be presented in a flexible way by various media, as long as the host machine is properly installed with the necessary devices for presentation. Often the annotation may also include links to other relevant information that allows information consumers to "navigate" the information universe among relevant pages. Through years of effort, the World Wide Web can now be considered as the most influential technology of the late 20th century. Its widespread use among the general public has changed modern life in the developed world in many ways.

Changes in the channels of messages exchange. One of the most significant changes that have been caused by the World Wide Web is that people now increasingly rely on this new message exchange channel to discover and disseminate information. For example, academic scholars rely on the World Wide Web to search for literature. They can complete a comprehensive search for the digital images of journal papers, which cover almost all of the results of research that has been carried out in the last few decades in their field. Usually the number of returns from searches is much more than can be digested. For instance, one of provider of the digital image repository service, ProQuest Company, already provides links to more than ten million full-text items from periodicals and newspapers. Another example is the recently announced digital library project from the Internet search engine Google. The project intends to provide information explorers with comprehensive searching privileges to publicly accessible materials and the copyrighted items that are stored in university libraries. For those who intend to explore new business opportunities, the World Wide Web can be used to collect relevant links to corporate Web sites to obtain detailed product information by using the services of commercial directories, such as Yahoo and Google.

The World Wide Web at one pole demonstrates its dominance in information exploration; and at the other pole, it is a universal platform that people can use to promote their beliefs. As long as Web content is well formatted and is linked to the Internet, any information can be posted and people have an equal opportunity to speak out over the World Wide Web. Moreover, through the collection and dissemination of information, huge business opportunities can be created, such as occurred with the well-known case of Yahoo.com, which took the simple concept of a Web page directory that was originally created by two PhD candidates two years ago, all the way to a public offering that was worth 33.8 million dollars in 1996 (docs.yahoo.com/info/misc/history.html).

Changes in the pattern of collaboration. The World Wide Web also facilitates new forms of collaboration. In a highly differentiated society, most tasks must be done with collaboration among resources. It is almost impossible for a single organization, not to mention a single operator or knowledge worker, to complete a noteworthy task. Collaboration among a team of people requires coordination and communication to guarantee that the team is working in the same direction toward the same goal. Before networks become popular at the late 20th century, coordination and communication among people on a project was often implemented through a series of regular meetings of team members, piles of circulated documentations, and travel between distant cities. Since the appearance of the World Wide Web, the patterns of collaboration have changed, and new patterns have emerged that provide better synergy, efficiency, and convenience in the execution of teamwork. For example, a new car model can be developed over the World Wide Web by the simultaneous collaboration of engineers who are distributed across different locations and different time zones. New product data management (PDM) tools provide Web-enabled virtual working platforms that work with integrated digital vaults for engineering data and project documents, and allow remote design meetings to take place over the World Wide Web. Thus, the people who are working on the project are ensured access to the same version of the data, and the Web-enabled design meetings allow people in various locations to edit the same engineering components on a 3-D visual model. In the design meeting, one person rotates a component by a certain degree and marks a comment on a specific position of the component, while persons who are situated at distant places can see the rotation and the notes at their panel as soon as they are made. Similarly, the World Wide Web can enhance product data sharing in a supply chain. Using product data that are retrieved from a Web-enabled electronic catalogue on the supplier side, a designer can construct a 3-D visual model of the components that are needed and can simulate the assembly process virtually to decide the feasibility of using the components from the suppliers.

The Challenges

The deployment of the World Wide Web was constrained in the early stages by its presentation specification. Web content is designed for human consumption, and the presentation of Web content can only be interpreted and understood by human users. Unfortunately, this rudimentary characteristic of Web content has become a major limitation to the World Wide Web today.

According to an Internet domain survey by the Internet System Consortium, the number of hosts that advertised on DNS was 317,646,084 in January 2005 (www.isc.org). Hosts serve as gateways to Web pages, and the number of Web pages that are maintained by each host may range from tens to millions of Web pages. The huge volume of information and resources that are becoming available over the World Wide Web has exposed the limited ability of humans to screen information for relevancy. In other words, information overload has become a serious problem for humans in locating useful information for their own purposes. For example, a person searching for the lyrics to the song "Yesterday" by John Lennon could easily identify the right song from dozens of lyrics simply by searching using a few words from the song that they might be able to remember. However, if the searcher does not recall that the song was written by John Lennon or any of the words and initiates a search using the keywords "lyric" and "yesterday" in Google, the search will respond with 759,000 links to what it considers to be relevant pages. This creates a problem. How can a human being screen all of the pages to find the specific lyrics to the song?

The limits of human ability also prevent Web-enabled collaboration from becoming widely adopted in practice. As has been stated, Web-enabled collaboration is a new pattern of communication that participants from multiple corporations can use to form virtual corporations. However, this new pattern is currently only deployed among organizations that maintain a tight relationship with their various arms or that are targeting projects with long lifecycles. This is because the implementation of a virtual corporation relies on the deep integration of business data and enterprise applications, which ensures that virtual meetings are supported by seamless intra-operations among different proprietary systems, such as PDM and CAD. This integration also assures that message exchanges among organizations are not confused by ambiguous data definitions. To provide support in such level, the parties that are involved in a virtual corporation are required to make a huge investment of human effort to guarantee the successful integration of data and applications. This requirement has become the major barrier to the deployment of Web-enabled collaboration as a means of seizing contingent opportunities in the dynamic business environment.

The Vision

In identifying the improvements that need to be made to the present World Wide Web, several leading scholars have envisioned a new generation of the World Wide Web and the collaboration patterns therein (Berners-Lee, Hendler, & Lassila, 2001). In their vision, humans in the near future will rely on intelligent software agents to search and interact with Web resources (including Web content and automated services) over the World Wide Web. These software agents are software objects that operate autonomously in a software environment to achieve certain predefined goals (Du, Li, & Wei, 2005; Fuggetta, Picco, & Vigna, 1998). Actually, using software agents as performers over the World Wide Web has already been carried out on a limited scale. A practical example is the software robot that helps marketers to collect and compare book prices over several specified online bookstores (Uschold, 2003). However, these shopping robots normally only surf specified routes and visit predetermined types of Web content, and the information that is being compared is easy to identify because unambiguous terms, such as the international library book code, quantity, and price, are used. Software agents in the future will be very different from their current incarnation, and will be empowered with humanlike intelligence. Typical humanlike intelligence will use practical logical reasoning to deduce and induce, and will recognize patterns through environmental stimulation to determine contextual influence, learn from previous experience, and find adjusting strategies to adapt to environmental changes (Croft, 1997). Software agents that have humanlike intelligence can navigate over World Wide Web, and operate with other automated Web resources on behaves of the humane being. In order to entertain the demand of the visiting software agents, the information being published over World Wide Web must be articulated with intended meaning in a way that machine can recognize and interpret. Such demand for information representation is not supported by current Web specifications, but it will be supported by new generation of Web, called "Semantic Web". Moreover, semantics will become a searchable, portable, and reusable object to assist software agents to cooperate with other automated Web resources to complete sophisticated tasks without human intervention (Berners-Lee et al., 2001).

What is the Semantic Web?

The Semantic Web is defined as "the extension of the current Web in which information is given well-defined meaning, better enabling computers and people to work in cooperation" (Berners-Lee et al., 2001). In this definition, two views are highlighted. The first relates to the meanings of the Semantic Web, and the second relates to the functions of the Semantic Web.

First, the emergence of the Semantic Web does not entail the replacement of the existing World Wide Web. Instead, the Semantic Web will be implemented on current networked information space, and will utilize HTTP to transport messages. The difference is that the Semantic Web requires an unprecedented descriptive structure for content description to cater to the demands of the software agents (Goble, 2003). This does not mean that the conventional expression of the content of the World Wide Web for human consumption will be discarded, but rather that Web content will be expressed simultaneously in a way that machines can also understand.

Second, the newly established Semantic Web is expected to explore the collaboration of humans through software agents and automated Web services. In light of this expectation, scientists and industrial practitioners have invested much effort into constructing an infrastructure to facilitate the expected collaboration among humans and commissioned software forces.

Two questions arise from this definition of the Semantic Web. How do machines do to behave like it understand Web contents, and what should we do to make machines behave in that way? The following elaboration attempts to provide answers to these two questions, and is followed by a review of the current status of Semantic Web technology.

What is Semantics?

Semantics is the "meaning" of expression. As we use a symbolic system to represent the real world or the conceptual phenomenon thereof, semantics is the meaning of these symbols and sets of symbols. If relationships are implied between meanings, then semantics also refers to inference, that is, the transition of the meanings from one meaning to another one (Merriam Webster Online dictionary, www.m-w.com). People usually use many symbolic systems simultaneously to help communicate their thoughts to others. Some typical symbolic systems are natural language, mathematical and chemical formula, and programming languages for software programming. Each symbolic system has its own semantic system. And people usually know how to use them, when they decide to use that language system in communication. Additionally, there are multiple types of semantic contribute, either implicitly or explicitly, to successful communication. Let us take communication over the World Wide Web as an example. Obviously, natural written and spoken languages are the most common symbolic systems to express opinions. The meaning of the terms and the relationship between the terms defined in the natural language are the most basic type of semantics contributing to our communication. Machine communication protocols are also symbolic languages, but they are designed for communication between machines, rather than humans. As machine behavior is hard-coded by human programmers, such semantic types are also predefined and limited by the programmers. Another kind of semantic is generally needed when people make logical conclusions. People can read more meaning between the lines, which is known as referred meaning. Semantics that guides people, either explicitly or implicitly, to imply meaning from assertions is another type of semantics, and is sometimes called *rules* or *logic*. This type of semantics can be generally found in symbolic languages, such as mathematical formula and programming languages.

Beyond symbolic expression, background knowledge is also an important source of meaning. Such knowledge usually aids the inference of assertions by the receivers of expression, and sometime provides procedural knowledge to generate interacting patterns in the deliverers of expression. Procedural knowledge helps us to meet expectations when we interact with others in a specific process. For example, when we transfer an amount of money between accounts through an online banking service, procedural knowledge guides us through the process step by step, and we can anticipate that the amount will be deducted from our account accordingly once the process has been completed.

In the work of categorizing the general semantics that are used in human life, Uschold proposed a general framework for the analysis of semantics that employs three categories: implicit versus explicit, formal versus informal, and intended for humans versus intended for machine processing (Uschold, 2003).

1. **Implicit vs Explicit.** Explicit semantics differ from implicit semantics in that there is an explicit declaration of the specification of the symbolic system. In contrast, the meaning of the symbolic system in implicit semantics is normally conveyed based on a shared understanding that is derived from consensus. For example, when a shopping agent encounters price information, it will implicitly be aware that it may refer to the amount that we need to pay for the acquisition of certain goods. Although the definition of "price" is defined in certain dictionaries, it is seldom as clearly defined on a Web page or related pages in a corporate Web site.

    In contrast with this intuitive conception, Sheth proposed an innovative perspective for the interpretation of "implicit semantics" (Sheth, 2005). Sheth argued that implicit semantics can be implied not only from a shared consensus on the communicating content, but also from undiscovered knowledge from all kinds of data. From this perspective, "implicit" refers to intangible or undiscovered knowledge that cannot be transformed into explicit knowledge. For example, the attempt to allow marketers to extract information on consumer behavior from a marketing data set is a process of extracting so-called implicit knowledge and turning it into explicit knowledge. This interpretation implies that in the future, as we rely more and more on statistical analysis in our decision making, implicit semantics may be hidden in the process. And never may we know that this kind of semantics is being extracted from the data set and used to determine a decision, although we benefit from the operations.

2. **Formal vs Informal.** The difference between these two types of semantics lies in whether they are ambiguous or not. Semantics should be specified clearly through formal documentation or the specification of meaning. A formal language is often used to reduce ambiguity and avoid inconsistent and incompatible implementation. Examples such as Modal logic are used to define the semantics of ontological categories (Guarino, Carrara, & Giaretta, 1994). The articulation in the documentation helps humans to reduce ambiguity while using the idea of rigidity and identity in communication (Uschold, 2003). Modal logic is also used in agent communication language (Smith, Cohen, Bradshaw, Greaves, & Holmback, 1998) to define the semantics of performatives, such as informing and requesting. Such formal definition helps humans to hardcode software agents that can properly understand, evaluate, and compare exchanged messages with others using alternative agent communication languages (Uschold, 2003).

    Informal semantics are defined in an informal notation or natural language. For example, a glossary or a text specification document can explicitly denote certain concepts, but cannot infer decisive or determined assertions by a strict process of deduction. Therefore, this kind of semantics can rarely be understood and processed for further use by a machine.

3. **Intended for Human Processing vs Intended for Machine Processing.** Although all formal languages offer specific semantic meanings to disambiguate subtle

differences, not all formal specifications can be adopted by machines for the purpose of inference. Whether the semantics that is defined in formal languages can be simulated by machine calculation and processed to generate sound and useful inferential results thus marks the difference between these semantic types. The development of the enterprise ontology has provided many clear axioms and definitions (Uschold, King, Moralee, & Zorgios, 1998), but at the time of its development it was not expected to be used as the foundation for automated inference, and therefore further securitization should be undertaken before its adoption as a machine-processable semantic system.

Uschold points out that the semantic language of the Semantic Web should be machine understandable and explicitly specified, formal language (Uschold, 2003). However, no approach to the development of this kind of semantics has been developed. Therefore, in the following sections, I try to make an analysis based on the human operation of "understanding" to derive a proper approach for the development of explicit, and machine understandable semantics.

How do Humans Understand Expression?

Having explored the meaning of semantics, we can start to consider questions about the "understanding" of semantics. We can start with the question of what it means for humans to understand expressions, which is naturally followed by the question of how can we replicate the same behavior in a machine, and finally leads to the question of how we should adopt what we know about the process of human understanding to program a machine to "understand" semantics.

In a normal communication scenario, the "understanding" of a discourse is conceived as the activity of digesting the meaning of the discourse and then generating an appropriate reply to the issuer of the discourse. The digesting process is a procedure of reconstructing either the opinions of the author or speaker, or the statements of facts about the world (Russell, 2003). For example, while listening to a speech, we will try to capture the facts about the world that are revealed in the textual expressions and the opinions or belief that the speaker is trying to convince the audience to believe.

The reconstruction process actually involves several consecutive information processing procedures. These procedures are performed in sequence to achieve the sub-consequences of perception, analysis, disambiguation, and incorporation (Russell & Norvig, 2003).

- **Perception.** Perception is the incipient stage of the understanding process. A person who receives some forms of discourse through various external and physical forms, such as images, printed materials, and voice, first recognizes the symbols through the functions of the brains and the sensory receivers, and then transfers them into internal data correlations that can be analyzed in further processes. For example, if the medium is printed material, then the receiver first recognizes and interprets the markings of the texts into words in the sentences, and then puts them in a similar correlation of textual sequences in the memory. When listening to a speech, in contrast, we need to recognize the materials that are represented by the voice.

- **Analysis.** The analysis on the receiving discourses can be divided into two main portions: syntactical interpretation and semantic interpretation. Syntactical interpretation generally refers to the parsing process, in which a unit of a continuous stream of expression is decomposed into atomic components with meaning to determine the grammatical structure of the parsed elements with respect to a given set of grammar rules. Semantic interpretation, then, represents the process of associating the knowledge that we have in the memory of symbols and patterns with the parsed components and grammatical structure.

- **Disambiguation.** Ambiguity in the analysis results is a common phenomenon in most languages. For instance, a sentence in the discourse expressed in natural language may be analyzed with multiple interpretations, all of which are legal and can be alternative readings, of the same expression. This can cause ambiguous understanding, although that may not have been the speaker or author's intention. However, in considering other environmental determinants, humans can usually decide on the correct interpretation that best reflects the speaker or author's intention and the facts of the world. When humans practice this disambiguation process, domains of interest, the context of communication, and temporally related factors, among others, contribute to making the best decision as to meaning (Wittgenstein, 2001; Staab, Santini, Nack, Steels, & Maedche, 2002; Baader, 1999).

- **Incorporation.** After obtaining a direct interpretation from these processes, a receiver will incorporate their knowledge and the collected information into a set of confidential conclusions about the incoming discourse. This extra effort on the part of receivers generally includes drawing inferences from new assertions, and validating the plausibility of the conclusions that are explicitly stated in the discourse or are implied by inference.

The ability of humans to draw a new conclusion or to evaluate a proposed conclusion from information that has already been collected is generally referred to as "reasoning" (Wason & Johnson-Laird, 1972). Reasoning is usually either deductive or inductive. Deductive reasoning is the process of reasoning based on logical principles that lead us from known assertions to determined conclusions (Williams, 2000; Johnson-Laird, 2000). Deductive reasoning does not increase our knowledge to help us to interpret the world or discourses; it merely uncovers implicit facts that are not disclosed in the discourse. In contrast, inductive reasoning is the process of using specific facts to generalize a likely conclusion that may explain the facts. The conclusions that are generated from inductive reasoning may become a new axiom that enhances our knowledge base for future understanding (Johnson-Laird, 2000). The reasoning process takes all conclusions as legal inferences according to the principles of logic, yet we will not admit the truth of all of the conclusions that we derive from expressions and inference. Some opinions may not be true, and some of the implications of expression may contradict our beliefs and observations in a specific domain or certain circumstances. Therefore, humans may need to make subjective or objective judgments on the portions of the conclusion that are not acceptable to their knowledge. This authentication process, which is termed "proofing," is the process of weeding out less plausible conclusions and accepting the most convincing conclusions. This process is carried out by taking facts or observations as evidence to validate the plausibility of a proposal from conclusions that are inferred from the aforementioned understanding processes. After the authentication process, the validated conclusions that are left at the end of the procedure become the set of propositions that represent what we know and believe about the intention of the speaker or author or the projection of the phenomenon from the expression.

- **Reply.** In a common communication scenario, the activity of "understanding" incoming message is normally followed by corresponding reactions. The reaction may be another expression that is generated to reply to the original author or speaker, or a series of operations that are correlated with the instructions that are given in the expression. To generate these reactions, people take the proofed conclusions as the premise and figure out how they will react. At this point, people deploy a special kind of knowledge, known as procedural knowledge, to govern the implementation of the replying processes (Sternberg, 2003). Normally, a task is done by a sequence of several operations. Procedural knowledge keeps information about the operations under consideration in specific step of the sequence, and information about the rules governing the determination of operations. The rules are contained in terms of causal relationships, which involve putting certain factual statements as the premise and then deriving the solution and action to take.

In our everyday lives, simply a tiny task would involve complicated engagement of multiple rules and determinations. These self-related rules exist in a natural structure correlated by the common factual states of the world in the causal relationships. Cognitive psychologists have found that these modules are normally recalled and implemented unconsciously in groups (Sternberg, 2003). By the same token, these patterns are adopted by computer engineers to group rules into subroutines and modules of operations. It is interesting that the deployment of procedural knowledge in the process of generating corresponding response behavior can be likened to the utilization of predetermined modules of procedures in a computer application, in that each module of procedural knowledge is prepared to cope with a specific operational demand. These may be formed by common norms, special regulations, or agreement among groups. Once the demand is identified, the module will be brought up as the proposed piece of corresponding behavior to be enacted.

Efforts to make machines or applications understand instructions from humans have been made since machines were found to be an efficient and effective way to execute repeated tasks. Generally, applications and machines are programmed in the following methods. While an instruction is input through interface, the machines know how to parse the instructions, and then interpret the meaning of the parsed tokens, invoke relevant modules for operations, and finally generate responses to humans to show they have understood the instructions well and can carry out requested tasks. For example, most general Database Management System (DBMS) provide database administrators with a common communication option to interact with the system using a special query language, which is called structural query language (SQL). Database administrators use SQL to issue their orders to query and update data sets that are stored in the database and that are maintained by the DBMS. A general SQL instruction appears in a similar format to the following example:

> **Select** *Part_No, Product, Price*
> **From** *price_list*
> **Where** *Product = Digital_Camera*

The process of understanding an instruction can be elaborated as follows. First, the DBMS invokes a parsing program to parse the instruction. In this specific example, the parser separates the instruction into three sets of tokens series and then translates the three series into grammatical structures by associating the relationships between the parsed keywords (typed in bold italics in the scripts) and the roles of the parameters (typed in normal italics in the scripts). After parsing the instruction, the DBMS will look in its command dictionary for the semantics of the keywords and the roles of the parameters. Through the identification of the keywords and the roles of the parameters, the DBMS is able to understand the intention of the administrators. The intention here is to request the DBMS to retrieve several records from the table "price_list" that satisfy certain requirements in the "product" column and then list out the value of the named features in the retrieved records. The intention is thus executed by the DBMS through the invocation of a series of routine modules using the parameters that were assigned in the instructions. Finally, the DBMS reports the results of the work to the terminal device for review in a predefined format that is understandable to the administrators.

The same approach in the example is generally adopted in the development of many languages for communication between humans and machines, as well as in many of the protocols between two applications, such as HTTP on the World Wide Web. Yet, the common strategy is taken under several presumptions that prevent it from becoming a solution to demand from Semantic Web. First of all, the responsibilities of the applications or machines are contained in specific domains, and the knowledge that is required to assure successful communication is of a limited scale. Secondly, since that the knowledge domain in use is easily predicted, the keywords and syntax are simple and barely ambiguous so as that the analysis of the semantics can be carried out by simple parsers. Thirdly, the semantics of the symbolic system is shared in an implicit consensus among the users of the application. Application programmers hardwire the semantics into the application procedures, and the application users should learn to communicate with the application using the same agreed-upon semantics. Since the semantics is specifically contained in the agreed keywords and syntax. No ambiguous expressions are allowed in the instruction; otherwise the parsers will deny the orders for further interpretation. Fourthly, it is clear that both disambiguation and reasoning are unnecessary in the understanding procedure. Lastly, the procedural knowledge always pertains to the domains of the application, and its operation is also hard coded as modules in the application.

Requirements for the Semantic Web

I would now like to conclude this section by looking at how software agents can be made to understand Web content. There are several requirements that need to be fulfilled in the development of this capability.

The semantics should be declared explicitly. Humans use natural languages and other complex symbolic systems that possess complicated syntax and ambiguous semantics to format their Web content. The convenience of language selection makes it impossible for software agents to ascertain the meaning of such Web content using parsers, each of which represents the articulation of knowledge in a particular domain. Additionally, it is less likely that software agents will be able to negotiate in advance with the potential information providers to identify the relevant parsers that would be needed to analyze the semantics in specific domains. Taking these concerns into consideration, the first breakthrough in the development of Semantic Web will be the presentation of semantics in a form with which machines are familiar. This breakthrough could be implemented in two ways: through the transformation of Web content to a form that software agents can process, and by providing software agents with clues as to the semantics that occur on the World Wide Web.

Normally, software agents can recognize data, which is complied with a predefined data schema, and propositions. A typical example of the data in a schema is a set of records of personal information. A schema, such as (Personal_ID, Name, Birthday, Gender, Nationality, Address, Phone_number), reveals the important information of a residence registry. A proposition, in the view of cognitive psychologists and artificial intelligence experts, is a factual assertion that reveals a determined relationship between two or multiple concepts. Philosophers generally believe that any phenomenon that reveals complex facts about the world can be analyzed into a simpler phenomenon, and that this recursive process can be carried out until an atomic form of the original proposition is reached (Wittgenstein, 1974; Staab et al., 2002). Eventually through this process the real world can be represented using a group of propositions and a set of factual data. Following this methodology, information inside Web content that is relevant to further processes of reasoning and response generation would be possible to be presented in forms of data with predefined data schema and factual propositions.

However, data schema and the implicit knowledge of concepts that is contained in propositions cannot make themselves known to software agents, and therefore an auxiliary artifact is needed to make the implicit information explicit. The artifact that is used is similar to that which is implemented by HTML. Analogous to the same method that is used to annotate the configuration to present effects by the HTML label, the implicit semantics of the elemental components of Web content is marked up by the annotation of an explicit terminological system, which will be related to an explicit declared knowledge base. By the supply of the relevant information in the knowledge base, the software agent would be able to acquire enough auxiliary clues to the interpretation of the discourse in Web.

A knowledge organization should be provided for semantic interpretation. As has been stated, the attempt to explicitly declare semantics presumes the existence of a relevant knowledge base that helps software agents to recognize the required knowledge. Therefore, the establishment of a useful knowledge base to the interpretation of the annotation becomes one of the important subjects under discussion. The approach of deploying a knowledge base as the solution to the provision of implicit information has been studied by artificial intelligence experts for a long time. The foundation of the knowledge base approach is the dismantling of the bundle of procedural knowledge and declarative knowledge. This intention is similar to the same practice in the implementation of database management systems, which involves the efforts to separate the data schema from the future processes that will deploy it. By the same token, philosophers and cognitive psychologists believe that the knowledge that we have about the world, or declarative knowledge, and the knowledge that we use to implement processes, or procedural knowledge, are separable according to the structure and functions of knowledge. Yet, in classical programming practice, while an application is tailored to a specific problem domain, the knowledge that is used to describe the problem, which relates to declarative knowledge, and the knowledge that is used to describe the application domain, which relates to procedural knowledge, are implicitly intertwined in the coding of the application. Moreover, the knowledge to develop the applications is only contained by experts in such knowledge domain. A knowledge base is the aggregation of explicit descriptions that is extracted from the experts of specific problem domains. A suitable knowledge base in Semantic Web should be represented in a form that is neutral to the applications that will operate using the knowledge, which means that the reusability of the declarative knowledge will be extended and will not be constrained by the future procedural knowledge.

To assure the relevant and efficient retrieval of declarative knowledge, the propositions and concepts should be correlated in a well-constructed knowledge organization. There are several possible models to provide such well-constructed knowledge organizations. Among those proposed solution, two models are most representative and widely adopted: the categorical concepts model and the semantic network model. The categorical concepts model mainly provides a taxonomical architecture for the maintenance of implicit relationships among concepts and categories. The concepts in this model are described by a set of feature components that singly perform unique elemental concepts and jointly define the distinctive existence of the mother concepts in the organization. According to the similarity of the shared defining features, several concepts can be grouped into a less detailed category. This consolidation process can be iterated from the bottom to the upper level until ultimately general categories are reached. Knowledge Organization constituted with this model provides two kinds of crucial information, which can be directly revealed in its structure. It tells us the elemental features that used to define and identify the concepts. And, it tells us the inheritance relationship as well as the differences among affiliated concepts. The semantic network model use a propositional network to relates propositions. The first model of a propositional network, the semantic network, was presented in 1969 by Allan Collins and Ross Quillian (Collins & Quillian, 1969). In this framework, the concepts are also represented by elemental nodes in the network, yet the connections between nodes are determined by the relationships asserted by propositions, and it is labeled with different lexicon. The connections utilized in propositional network then can represent more than one kind of relationships. The information that can be provided by the propositional network is also revealed in its structure. The semantics of the specific labeled relationships correlates individual concepts to factual propositions. And the related propositions are maintained and organized in the network adjacent to each others. Using chaining operations both forward and backward, the most relevant factual propositions could be discovered from the semantic networks. Additionally, in a semantic network, the theory of conceptual categories can also be built as one kind of labeled relationship. In consequence, the information can be revealed by concepts categorization is usually contained in a knowledge organization constructed with semantic network model.

Semantics will be inferred by agents with automated reasoning ability. In the articulation of the processes of human understanding in the previous section, it was stated that humans usually use reasoning to gain a deeper understanding of the discourse of others. By the same token, as the agents in the Semantic Web are required to perform as human proxies, it is necessary for them to maintain a similar level of understanding of Web content as a human might attain. Therefore, several automated reasoning abilities have been proposed by artificial intelligence experts to simulate similar reasoning principles to those that are normally practiced in the interpretation process. Generally, automated reasoning ability is provided by special modules of applications that are called inference engines. Inference engines use formal logic to support concluding inferences and induce new knowledge. To verify different reasoning processes with their different goals and contexts, logicians have developed many distinctive forms of logic. Illustrated in the following elaboration, three examples among others are picked to demonstrate the role of formal logics implemented in inference engine. First order propositional logic, for instance, deals with the most general requirements for the implementation of a rule-based inference engine. If a subtle prediction that should made base on several alternative possible results, then modal logic can be used to enact a computational reasoning process in the inference engine. Moreover, humans often make conclusions based on a locally available knowledge base. Sometime, as updated information results in a conclusion that conflicts with previous predictions, a human must judge between the conflicting predictions and revise the conclusion. This reasoning process could be simulated by the adoption of a non-monotonic logic in inference engines. More details on these different kinds of logic can be found in Baader (1999), Brewka (1991), Chellas (1980), and Ginsberg (1987).

Procedural semantics should be developed in the community for collaboration. The ultimate goal of the Semantic Web is to facilitate collaboration among humans and software agents. Speaking more specifically, the realization of the vision of the Semantic Web depends on the pragmatic materialization of automatic collaboration of an agent society. This means that an agent that is commissioned can autonomously search for help on the Web to gain resources, normally from its agent colleagues, to achieve its goal of solving certain problems. In this sense, the Semantic Web infrastructure provides a preliminary but fundamental infrastructure to identify the necessary resources. Unfortunately, standing in the way of this ultimate goal of automatic collaboration in an agent society is a problem that has puzzled artificial intelligence experts scientists for a long time—that of how to give software agents problem solving abilities. Problem solving ability has been modeled in the field of artificial intelligence as a series of processes that includes recognizing problem types, formulating a goal as a testable criterion, formulating the problem of what action to take and what states to consider in the description of the phenomenon, and then finding the path to guide the transition from the initial states to the final goal state (Russell & Norvig, 2003). Artificial intelligence scientists have proposed two approaches in finding an appropriate path to reach the goal: problem-solving agents and planning agents. Both agents may function well in a well-formulated problem in specific domains, but real-world problems are usually ill defined, and the analysis that is required to map potential problems into solvable models is usually lacking, which hinders these two solutions from being pragmatic proposals in the beginning stages.

However, the pressures from business demands often result in the speedy resolution of problems, and in this case instead of providing agents with the ability to compute a solution to a problem, some practitioners have suggested simply articulating all possible paths to the goal and maintaining them as templates. Once the problem types have been identified and matched with the premise of the template, then the template can be adopted. A typical example is the adoption of the workflow templates as a solution to generate collaboration process among participating parties for the enterprise application integration. The RossetaNet (www.rossetanet.org) , a nonprofit consortium being consisted of more than 500 organizations mainly in computer and consumer electronic industry, provides a directory of "Partner Interface Processes" as the instant access procedural knowledge for business collaboration. This comprehensive framework categorizes all possible business processes into seven clusters according to different roles of business operations of the supply chain. Obviously, these kinds of solutions must acquire consensus in a community before they are put to use. Within the community, procedural knowledge is then agreed upon in the form of standards or specifications that are publicly accessible by community members.

Semantic Web Technology

It should be evident from the previous sections that the development of Semantic Web technology has employed a lot of research results from cognitive psychology and artificial intelligence (Schwartz, 2003). In this emergent stage of Semantic Web technology, scientists in the artificial intelligence community seem to be the most engaged in the problem, and many research results on the implementation of the Semantic Web have been adapted from artificial intelligence techniques, such as knowledge representation and organization, planning and rule-based systems, machine learning in dealing with large scale ontology extraction, and ontology management for developmental evolution and comparison processes (Goble, 2003).

However simply perceiving the Semantic Web to be an extended application of artificial intelligence theory and technology is a misconception (Goble, 2003). First of all, research on Semantic Web development and artificial intelligence development differ in the goals that are to be achieved. Artificial intelligence research aims to help systems to think like humans and act like humans, or at least to think rationally and to act rationally (Russell & Norvig, 2003). In fact, this goal has been considerably reduced from the original goal, which was to create a machine with complete humanlike intelligence (Searle, 1980). However, this goal of creating a machine that could compete with the human brain was found to require not only an algorithm for the ability to reason, but also a huge amount of memory space. A successful example of the application of artificial intelligence was the defeat of the human world chess champion Gary Karsparov by the famous IBM project "Deep Blue" in May 1997 (www.research.ibm.com/deepblue/), but the achievement in this specific task took a enormous investment on the establishment of super computing ability. The investment in hardware is a 30-node RS/6000 SP-based computer system that was enhanced with 480 ASIC chips that specialized in playing chess. And the super computing ability can perform 100 million position evaluations per second. As a comparison, the milestones for the Semantic Web are not founded on the breakthrough of reasoning using a huge information space. Instead, the aim is to provide the efficient and effective automation of the comprehension of information and the provision of procedural integration among networked resources. From this perspective, machines in the future may well be able to defeat humans in the performance of iterative operations in terms of reliability and efficiency.

Secondly, the basic distinction of the Semantic Web is the Web itself. The Web has several distinct characteristics (Goble, 2003; Mendelson, 1997; Risvik & Michelsen, 2002) that serve to differentiate Web-oriented technology from other technology. As an

Table 1. Basic characteristics of the Web and its challenge to Semantic Web technology (Summarized from Goble, 2003)

Basic characteristics	Challenge to the researcher
The Web is vast	Solutions should be able to scale the large Web resource universe.
The Web already exists	Solutions should consider migrating the existing non-semantic Web to the envisioned semantic Web.
The Web is democratic	Solutions should cater to the demands of the full range of information users and creators.
The Web grows from the bottom up	Solutions should consider the nature of the Web architecture, which is better suited to bottom-up development and peer-to-peer structure than top-down development and a centralized structure.
The Web is volatile and changeable	The availability of online resources is uncertain, and the resource content will change frequently.
The Web is dirty	It is difficult to ensure the consistency, trustworthiness, and provenance of the information on the Web.
The Web is heterogeneous	There will be multiple solutions, ontologies, and conceptual models to agree on before translation to a key practice.

elaboration of the distinctive features of the Web environment, Goble provided a framework (please refer to Table 1) to categorize the challenges to researchers who are interested in deploying Semantic Web technology (Goble, 2003).

The Development of the Semantic Web

Initial attention to the concept of a Semantic Web can be dated to 2000 (Fensel, Lassila, et al., 2000). In February 2004, the first Semantic Web language specification, RDF schema 1.0 (www.w3.org/TR/rdf-schema/), was accepted as a stable version of the World Wide Web Consortium's (W3C) recommendations (www.w3.org/2004/02/Process-20040205/) for industrial usage. Judging from this, Semantic Web technology can be considered to be at the emergent stage.

In the following discussion, I introduce the development of Semantic Web technology, in which the technology is separated into three main functions: language, infrastructure, and application. Semantic Web language provides a group of Web-specific languages for the presentation of knowledge and the building of a knowledge organization. Semantic Web infrastructure aids the acquisition, development, and management of the knowledge organization, and Semantic Web applications reflect efforts to leverage the infrastructure for better collaboration in future society, which involves contributions from both humans and software agents.

The development of a formal logic is also of importance to Semantic Web technology, as it will provide the formalism for knowledge representation and the rational reasoning for the inference machine. However, the development of formal logic is more related to the research of logicians and therefore in the following sections this topic is not covered.

Semantic Web Language

Semantic Web language provides two basic utilities for the representation and organization of knowledge. First, it provides a neutral language for knowledge representation that enables the construction of a portable knowledge organization, and second, it provides an annotation system to denote the relation of an expression in Web content to a pre-specified knowledge organization to enrich the semantic capacity of the expression. A new knowledge representation language has had to be developed for the Semantic Web because of the distinct nature of the Web. The Web is heterogeneous and democratic, and therefore we need a neutral language system to enhance its compatibility. Knowledge organizations that are built using Semantic Web language can be published over the World Wide Web, easily transported to the Internet, and recognized and reused by interested parties, which is why they are known as portable.

As Semantic Web language is a fresh descriptive foundation for existing Web expression, it basically makes use of extensible markup language (XML) to specify a new

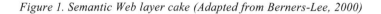

Figure 1. Semantic Web layer cake (Adapted from Berners-Lee, 2000)

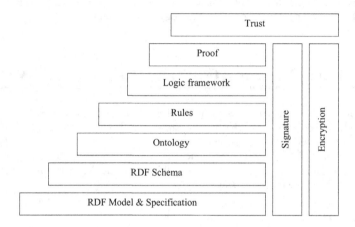

labeling schema. The annotation of discourse by the labeling system serves as the bridge between the discourse and the referring meaning in the knowledge organization. In this way, the meanings of the key words used in the documents are enriched by the recognition of the referring meaning in the knowledge organization.

Using XML as the specification language provides another benefit to the development of Semantic Web language. As the World Wide Web evolves with the advancement of the Web technology, the legacy Web must be migrated to the new infrastructure. It is also expected in the way we represent semantics of the Web content. As new technologies or new conceptual constructs are introduced to provide new capability for semantic interpretation, the new Semantic Web language will be established by the provision of new XML schemas. And the newly established XML schema is able to contain existing schemas as its foundation. In this way, the evolution of the Semantic Web language extends the semantic capacity by adding a new layer to the existing foundation stacks. Thus, the original layer of Semantic Web language will not become obsolete as concepts evolve.

In explaining the language advantage and developing the roadmap for Semantic Web languages, Tim Berners-Lee has proposed a "Semantic Web layer cake" of the expected standards and technologies. In the lower half of the cake, the resource definition framework (RDF) model and specification (www.w3.org/TR/rdf-concepts/) and RDF schema (RDFS) (www.w3.org/TR/rdf-schema/) represent two specifications that collaboratively work together to express propositions. Above this layer is an ontology layer, the corresponding language of which, ontology Web language (OWL) (www.w3.org/TR/owl-features/), enables the construction of a kind of categorical organization of concepts, or ontology. W3C has already proposed recommendation standards for these

Figure 2. An RDF graph describing the relationship "On (Apple, Table)"

three layers. Base on these layers, academia and industry are still working on proposing clear-cut executive implications and corresponding language standards.

In the following sections, I elaborate some of the basic concepts that are related to Semantic Web language.

Resource description framework (RDF). The RDF is a data model for the presentation of propositional relationships in a graph-like illustration. The most atomic relationship is a *Triple*, which relates a *Subject* to an *Object* through a directed relationship, which is described by a *Predicate*. The symbolic representation of the *Triple* relationship can simply be *Predicate (Subject, Object)* (please refer to Figure 2 for an example of an RDF graph).

This simple *Triple* representation can be used to describe any proposition that involves tangible or intangible entities in the real world as a kind of resource that is described on the World Wide Web. For example, the preposition "*the Apple is ON a Table*" can be represented as *ON(Apple, Table)*. To maintain relationships among more than three elements, the presentation allows a null resource assignment (expressed as _), and therefore the *Triple* can be extended by chaining elements via null elements. For example, *Predicate1(Subject, _), Predicate2(_, Object1), …, Predicate2(_, ObjectN)*. In this way, a set of propositions that is composed of a long chain can be employed to represent a complicated expression.

Ontology. An ontology is the one of the most widely used way of representing knowledge organizations. An ontology provides shared and common domain propositions and axioms to rule out ambiguity, while conducting communication and reasoning processes (Ding, 2001). As the Web is heterogeneous, democratic, vast, volatile, and changeable, an ontology is one of the most important components for the integration and reconciliation of ambiguity, and research on the applications of ontology engineering has become a core academic interest of the Semantic Web technology (Geller, Perl, & Lee, 2004; Ouksel & Sheth, 1999; Staab, Gomez-Perez, Daelemana, Reinberger, & Noy, 2004).

Ontology is an ancient theory that dates back to ancient Greek philosophy, but the term was later adopted by computer scientists in 1991 by Neches et al. (Corcho, Fernandez-Lopez, & Gomez-Perez, 2003; Neches et al., 1991). The knowledge representation community that deals with ontology includes various disciplines, such as knowledge engineering, knowledge representation, qualitative modeling, language engineering, database design, information retrieval and extraction, and knowledge management and organization (Guarino, 1998). Since ontology caught the attention of computer scientists, its conceptualization and definition have gone through many iterations as scholars from different disciplines have used different approaches. The history and research of the various approaches can be found in the literature (Crow & Shadbolt, 2001; Ding, 2001; Gomez-Perez, Fernandez-Lopez, & Corcho, 2004; Guarino, 1997). Here, I use the most commonly cited studies in the knowledge representation community and focus on the

Semantic Web in looking at ontology. The following definition of ontology combines the ideas of Gruber (1993), Borst (1997), Corcho et al. (2003) and Studer, Benjamins, and Fensel (1998): "Ontology is a formal, explicit specification of a shared conceptualization." "Conceptualization" refers to the abstract model by which the phenomena in the real world are represented (Studer et al., 1998). *Explicit* here means an explicit definition of the types of concepts, and constraints on the usage of these types should be provided. *Formal* refers to the features of the specification that serve to exclude ambiguity in communication between machines. *Shared* refers to the fact that once parties adopt a specific ontology, they all agree to conceptualize phenomena in the same way.

In terms of Semantic Web technology, an ontology can be considered as a typical form of implementation of a knowledge organization. It is a taxonomy for a set of concepts that includes concepts, categories, and the relationships between them, as well as a set of inference rules for the engagement of useful reasoning functions (Berners-Lee et al., 2001; Ding, 2001). Ontology developers use their own views to develop their own ontologies according their preferred goals and favored development methodologies, and this wide variety of perceptions and methodologies leads to a rather volatile research environment. General examples of ontology include the Yahoo directory classification, or enterprise ontology (Uschold et al., 1998), in which the taxonomy consists only of a lexicon and the semantics of the taxonomy depends on human interpretation. More complex taxonomies involve concept tokens that have a higher semantic capacity, which can be created by assigning concept tokens with described or defined features and then relating the separate concepts to propositional relationships. The cost of improving the usage of semantics in an ontology is paid off by the fact that other parties with similar interests can share and reuse the ontology (Gomez-Perez et al., 2004). Moreover, the domains and functions of ontological taxonomies also differ. A discussion of the different kinds of classifications for various kinds of ontologies can be found in Ding (2001), Fensel, Hendler, Lieberman and Wahlster (2003), Gomez-Perez et al. (2004), and Jurisica, Mylopoulos, and Yu (2004).

W3C provides an ontological description language, OWL, to cater to the demands for managing ontologies over the World Wide Web. The goal of the OWL specification is to facilitate better ontology management for the reuse, change, integration, and detection of inconsistency in ontologies (Heflin, 2004). The taxonomy that is offered in OWL provides the ability to assert basic logical descriptions by sanctioning reasoning against description logic that refers to the concept that describes a domain. Description logic is developed to represent terminological knowledge and concept classification (Baader, 1999). The utility of description logic seems to properly match the need for ontological development in the Semantic Web paradigm. Therefore, it is natural to leverage software agents that can infer additional assertions on the back of stated assertions and ontologies. The basic concept in the utilization of description logic is to develop subsumption relationships in a list of terms. Therefore, inference engines that reason using description logic provide efficient computing power to assert additional propositions from a repository of facts and an ontology. In addition to the efforts of W3C, other ontology languages have also been proposed and used in different contexts, tools, and applications for various purposes. Nevertheless, they have not been proposed for use in a Web context. Details can be found in Corcho et al. (2003) and Ding, Fensel, Klein, and Omelayenko (2002).

The Semantic Web Infrastructure

The Semantic Web infrastructure refers to the facilities, services and installation for transferring current Web content into the forms that the software agents are able to understand. It is done by adding formal explicit semantic, which is in terms of metadata and knowledge organization, to the Web contents. In this perspective, the services or facilities to provide Semantic Web infrastructure can be divided in three major clusters: (1) the services to transfer the discourse formatted in natural language into data and proposition forms, complying to Semantic Web languages specification, (2) the services to provide large scale availability of annotation within Web contents to correlate the metadata of the knowledge organization to the occurrence of the key words in Web content, (3) and the services to establish the metadata and knowledge organization to a scale of critical mass so that it can support enough information for semantic interpretation. The study of the first clusters is crucial to the enablers of the ability for software agent to understand meaning of Web content commonly formatted in natural language today, yet the research efforts are mainly related to the works done by those researchers who are dedicated in natural language processing. Therefore, the elaboration of this subject is considered as irrelevant to the scope of my discussion. In stead, the elaboration on major academic efforts on providing Semantic Web infrastructure focus on the following two clusters of infrastructure.

The efforts done to provide services of second cluster can be generally referred to "semantic annotation", which is assisted by tools to annotate Web pages or RDF documents with semantic tags that reference to ontology or other forms of knowledge organization. Typically three approaches can be found in literature to provide cluster two services. The first approach provides tools to link ontology with structural data. It is done by the mapping between ontology and the data schema of the structural data. The second approach uses an existing ontology to describe semi-structured Web content, and a corresponding XML DTD, XML Schema, or RDFS document is then generated as a reference for the validation of the Web content and to provide hints as to the links between the ontology and the Web content. The third approach converts totally unstructured content into a format that conforms to RDF/XML specifications and generated XML schema referencing to existing ontology (Dill et al., 2003; Kiryakov, Popov, Terziev, Manov, & Ognyanoff, 2004). There are several tools that can found in literature to semantic annotation services, such as Protégé-2000 (Noy et al., 2001), OntoAnnotate (Hartmann, Staab, & Ciravegna, 2002), Annotea (Kahan & Koivunen, 2001), SHOE (Heflin & Hendler, 2000), and SemTag (Dill et al., 2003) among others. However, the task assisted by the state of the art still takes much human effort, and the annotation results are prone to containing errors (Erdmann, Maedche, Schnurr, & Staab, 2000).

Current research efforts on the cluster three services focus on the development and management of large scale ontologies. It is elaborated here in two sub-subjects: one is Ontology editing and generation, and the other is Ontology engineering.

Ontology editing and generation. An ontology is either generated by human experts with the assistance of ontology editors, or is automatically established by an ontology learning mechanism. An ontology editor such as Protégé 2000, which was developed by

Stanford Medical Informatics (SMI), assists experts to build ontologies manually (Noy et al., 2001). Ontology learning is the ability to automatically learn and validate the ontology of a domain from groups of Web pages (Maedche & Staab, 2001; Missikoff, Navigli, & Velardi, 2002), and generated ontologies are managed and queried in an ontology repository. Further details of this function are available in the study of Ding (2002).

Ontology engineering. As the knowledge in an ontology is generated by various parties, it is not unified. Moreover, the perception of an ontology will change frequently to conform to the dynamic features of the World Wide Web. Therefore, ontology management, which is also called ontology engineering, is faced with the problem of how to align, merge and coordinate the differences among ontologies and how to manage the evolution issue in ontologies.

Research on ontology engineering predates the emergence of the Semantic Web (Ding, 2001; Ding & Foo, 2002), and actual Semantic Web ontology research was essentially launched after the proposed ontology languages for the Semantic Web became widely accepted and applied to research (Broekstra et al., 2002; Fensel, van Harmelen, Horrocks, McGuinness, & Patel-Schneider, 2001; Gomez-Perez & Corcho, 2002). In the Semantic Web scenario, ontology engineering must confront new challenges that result from the natural features of the Web, in which task-relative ontologies are established by different autonomous organizations. Therefore, ontology engineers need to tackle the problems that arise from the operation of ontologies when they merge (Cruz & Rajendran, 2003; Michalowski et al., 2004), translation and mapping between ontologies (Martin & Azvine, 2003), the evaluation and selection of an appropriate ontology (Lozano-Tello & Gomez-Perez, 2004; Staab et al., 2004), the evolution of ontologies that adapt to changes of environment, and the management of different versions of the same ontology that are created over time (Noy & Musen, 2004).

Applications of the Semantic Web

Since the emergence of Semantic Web research, scholars from various disciplines have tried to apply Semantic Web technologies to many areas. These applications can be classed into two categories. The first category simply uses portions of Semantic Web technology to provide new services over the World Wide Web, some typical examples being calendar agents (Payne, Singh, & Sycara, 2002), which surf several Web pages to negotiate and schedule a satisfactory meeting; agenda; shopping agents (Guarino, 1997), which shop online for goods by the semantic meanings of product information, rather than by keywords; and ontology-based searches on a digital map (Hubner, Spittel, Visser, & Vogele, 2004).

The applications in the second category adopt Semantic Web technology as an enabler to extend the new vision of the Semantic Web to old application areas, some typical examples of which are knowledge management and Web services. In the following section, I illustrate more specifically how Semantic Web technology is applied in these two areas in this category.

Knowledge management. Knowledge management involves the acquisition, extraction, management, and dissemination of human knowledge in explicit forms. Recent research and practice on knowledge management has focused on the extraction of knowledge from Web pages (Ding et al., 2002; Fensel et al., 2000). As all of the content on the World Wide Web can be transformed into machine-readable propositions and knowledge organizations, the Semantic Web itself will be the biggest repository of knowledge in the world. Researchers who are interested in making this vision feasible have identified three major achievable components: a query interface to assist humans to formulate their expectations of the knowledge that they want to extract from the World Wide Web as a proper query, a Webcrawler to navigate the World Wide Web to collect the required information, and an inference engine to extract the relevant knowledge from the collected information (Ding et al., 2002; Fensel et al., 2000).

Web services. A Web service in its broadest sense is an e-Service synonym that refers to concepts that use an information system as the service performer or mediating channel to reach the consumers of the service (Hultgren & Eriksson, 2005). According to this loose definition, an online banking service or gateway for providing online news can be considered to be a Web service. However, there is now a consensus in the computer industry that a Web service should refer to a narrower view of service than e-Service. The narrower view describes a new operation paradigm in which the coarse granular functionality is performed by an encapsulated software component that can be accessed and invoked over the Internet by others. In the invocation process, service consumers need not know the details of the implementation procedures within the Web service, but must learn in advance the effect of the execution of the service (Chung, Lin, & Mathieu, 2003). Several recent articles (Curbera et al., 2002; Tsalgatidou & Pilioura, 2002; Wang, Huang, Qu, & Xie, 2004; Zhao & Cheng, 2005) and industry standards (W3C, 2004) have concurred that the Web service paradigm should comprise two features. First, the Web service should adopt the two standards that have been proposed by W3C, the Web services description language (WSDL) and simple object access protocol (SOAP). These two standards serve collaboratively to provide separate functions that are required to invoke a Web service. WSDL provides a formal, machine-readable description for service providers of the information that is necessary to invoke a service over the Internet. This includes the specification for accessing interface, accessing protocol, and endpoint. SOAP serves as a message exchange protocol through which collaborating parties convey messages over the Internet. Second, the Web service architecture should have an active strategy to aid service discovery in the World Wide Web universe. A registry service provider will stand between services seekers and providers to broker search enquiries. In actual practice, universal description, discovery, and integration (UDDI) servers will be the mediating performers. To make their services known to others, service providers will register related information on the UDDI servers, and all of the registration records will be maintained by the UDDI as in a Yellow Pages directory. Service requesters will go to the directory to find useful services, and once a service has been identified, the service requester will download specific WSDL documents for further usage.

Traditionally, computing resources are kept inside a boundary and cannot be reused easily by outsiders. Creating a messaging channel for resource exchange between application islands and providing remote access to computing resources consumes a great deal of human effort, and is deemed to be impractical. The Web service paradigm is therefore a promising foundation for process integration (Staab et al., 2003; Tsalgatidou & Pilioura, 2002), because of its higher interoperability, better protection of sensitive data, lower implementation cost, easier and faster deployment, and lower complexity in delivering the encapsulation of internal processes (Staab et al., 2003; Zhang, Chung, & Chang, 2004). Thus, the development of the Web services paradigm is a vital component in the realization of the Semantic Web vision of better collaboration between human and software agents. The implementation of Semantic Web applications should benefit from the breakthrough in the Web services paradigm to automatically integrate software agents as typical processes in collaborations. The development of a Web services paradigm also takes advantage of Semantic Web technology. In a practical implementation scenario, Web services must collaborate with each other to deliver complicated tasks. Given the nature of Web-oriented resources and the human limitations on the size of datasets, there is a tendency to rely on intelligent software agents as performers in many aspects of the deployment lifecycle, some typical examples being service discovery, invocation, composition, analysis, cancellation, and monitoring processes. To ensure the successful operation of software agents, Web services, which are important resources in the Semantic Web, must be represented by machine-readable semantics that are relevant to the whole deployment cycle. Research in this area is deemed to be the foundation of Semantic Web services (Paolucci & Sycara, 2003; Sycara, Paolucci, Ankolekar, & Srinivasan, 2003).

Currently, research on Semantic Web services is still in its emergent stage, as with Semantic Web technologies. A major research focus is the Web service language with more semantic descriptive capacity, such as WS-CDL (W3C, 2004), and OWL-S (www.daml.org/services/owl-s/1.1/overview/), and workflow language specific catering to the description of the Web services composition in the workflow, such as WS-BPEL (www.oasis.org). Other major areas of research are the discovery of sophisticated Web services in the resources universe (Klein & Visser, 2004; Paolucci & Sycara, 2003; Sreenath & Singh, 2004), and the development of a framework for Web service composition to establish and implement complicated service organizations (Benatallah, Dumas, & Sheng, 2005; Benatallah, Sheng, & Dumas, 2003; Medjahed & Bouguettaya, 2005; Sivashanmugam, Miller, Sheth, & Verma, 2003).

As both the Semantic Web and Web services are part of the same vision, they will evolve together to create a society that is composed of two equally contributing groups of citizens: humans and software agents.

Conclusion

This chapter describes the semantics for the Semantic Web as a type of explicitly declared machine-understandable semantics. The processes for the implementation of this type of semantics involve four steps. The semantics should be explicitly declared in a form that can be operated by a machine, knowledge organizations should be provided to support semantic interpretation, software agents must use automatic reasoning to obtain implicit knowledge, and procedural knowledge should be accessed in a community to generate response behavior. An inspection of the current progress of the development of the Semantic Web reveals that many enablers that are necessary to make the Semantic Web work are still missing. The Semantic Web languages that have been developed thus far only cater to the demand in describing instances and classes in a common knowledge organization. Researchers and practitioners are still debating the proper form that the language for higher level semantics should take, such as rules, proofs, and security. Most of the existing enablers for the establishment of a comprehensive Semantic Web infrastructure are lacking, and there is no consensus on a proper mechanism for large scale semantic annotation. The heterogeneity that commonly exists in the development methodology, schema, and conceptual models for the establishment of distributed ontologies also requires further development. The nascent status of Semantic Web technology has made it difficult to develop software agents that will enable automatic collaboration. Indeed, it is hard to predict at this point whether the Semantic Web will be successfully achieved in the future. However, once the limitations of the current World Wide Web become clear and the utility of the World Wide Web extends as it moves from cable connection to wireless connection, increasing investment will be made to forge the Semantic Web.

References

Baader, F. (1999). Logic-based knowledge representation. In M. J. Wooldridge & M. Veloso (Eds.), *Artificial intelligence today* (Vol. LNAI 1600, pp. 13-41). Berlin Heidelberg: Springer-Verlag.

Benatallah, B., Dumas, M., & Sheng, Q. Z. (2005). Facilitating the rapid development and scalable orchestration of composite Web services. *Distributed and Parallel Databases, 17*, 5-37.

Benatallah, B., Sheng, Q. Z., & Dumas, M. (2003). The self-serve environment for Web services composition. *IEEE Internet Computing, 7*(1), 40-48.

Berners-Lee, T. (2000). *RDF and the semantic Web.* Paper presented at the Presentation at XML2000 Conference. Retrieved June 27, 2005, from http://www.w3.org/2002/talks/04-sWeb/slide12-0.html

Berners-Lee, T., Hendler, J., & Lassila, O. (2001). The Semantic Web. *Scientific American, 284*(5), 34-43.

Borst, W. N. (1997). *Construction of engineering ontologies.* Unpublished PhD thesis, University of Tweenty, Enschede, NL.

Brewka, G. (1991). *Nonmonotonic reasoning.* Cambridge, UK: Cambridge University Press.

Broekstra, J., Klein, M., Decker, S., Fensel, D., van Harmelen, F., & Horrocks, I. (2002). Enabling knowledge representation on the Web by extending RDF schema. *Computer Networks, 39*(5), 609-634.

Chellas, B. F. (1980). *Modal logic: An introduction*. Cambridge, UK: Cambridge University Press.

Chung, J.-Y., Lin, K.-J., & Mathieu, R. G. (2003). Web services computing: advancing software interoperability. *Computer, 36*(10), 35-37.

Collins, A. M., & Quillian, R. M. (1969). Retrieval time from semantic memory. *Journal of Verbal Learning and Verbal Behavior, 8*, 240-248.

Corcho, O., Fernandez-Lopez, M., & Gomez-Perez, A. (2003). Methodologies, tools and languages for building ontologies. Where is their meeting point? *Data & Knowledge Engineering, 46*, 41-64.

Croft, D. W. (1997). *Intelligent software agents: Definitions and applications*. Retrieved from http://alumus.caltech.edu/~croft/research/agent/definition/

Crow, L., & Shadbolt, N. (2001). Extracting focused knowledge from the Semantic Web. *International Journal of Human-Computer Studies, 54*(1), 155-184.

Cruz, I. F., & Rajendran, A. (2003). Semantic data integration in hierarchical domains. *IEEE Intelligent Systems, 18*(2), 66.

Curbera, F., Duftler, M., Khalaf, R., Nagy, W., Mukhi, N., & Weerawarana, S. (2002). Unraveling the Web services Web: an introduction to SOAP, WSDL, and UDDI. *Internet Computing, IEEE, 6*(2), 86-93.

Dill, S., Eiron, N., Gibson, D., Gruhl, D., Guha, R., & Jhingran, A., et al. (2003). A case for automated large-scale semantic annotation. *Web Semantics: Science, Services and Agents on the World Wide Web, 1*(1), 115-132.

Ding, Y. (2001). A review of ontologies with the Semantic Web in view. *Journal of Information Science, 27*(6), 377.

Ding, Y., Fensel, D., Klein, M., & Omelayenko, B. (2002). The Semantic Web: Yet another hip? *Data & Knowledge Engineering, 41*(2-3), 205-227.

Ding, Y., & Foo, S. (2002). Ontology research and development. Part I—A review of ontology generation. *Journal of Information Science, 28*(2), 123.

Du, T. C., Li, E. Y., & Wei, E. (2005). Mobile agents for brokering services in the electronic marketplace. *Decision Support Systems, 39*(3), 371-383.

Erdmann, M., Maedche, A., Schnurr, H.-P., & Staab, S. (2000, August). *From manual to semi-automatic semantic annotation: About ontology-based text annotation tools*. Paper presented at the COLING 2000 Workshop on Semantic Annotation and Intelligent Content, Saarbruecken, Germany.

Fensel, D., Decker, S., Erdmann, M., Schnurr, H.-P., Studer, R., & Witt, A. (2000). Lessons learned from applying AI to the Web. *Journal of Cooperative Information Systems, 9*(4).

Fensel, D., Hendler, J., Lieberman, H., & Wahlster, W. (Eds). (2003). *Spinning the semantic Web: bringing the World Wide Web to its full potential*. Cambridge, MA: MIT Press.

Fensel, D., van Harmelen, F., Horrocks, I., McGuinness, D. L., & Patel-Schneider, P. F. (2001). OIL: An ontology infrastructure for the semantic Web. *IEEE Intelligent Systems, 16*(2), 38.

Fensel, D., Lassila, O., van Harmelen, F., & Horrocks, I., et al., (2000). The semantic Web and its languages. *IEEE Intelligent Systems & their Applications, 15*(6), 67.

Fuggetta, A., Picco, G. P., & Vigna, G. (1998). Understanding code mobility. *IEEE Transactions on Software Engineering, 24*, 342-361.

Geller, J., Perl, Y., & Lee, J. (2004). Editorial: Ontology challenges: A thumbnail historical perspective. *Knowledge and Information Systems, 6*(4), 375-379.

Ginsberg, M. L. (Ed.). (1987). *Reading in nonmonotonic reading.* San Francisco: Morgan Kaufmann.

Goble, C. (2003). The semantic Web: An evolution for a revolution. *Computer Networks, 42*(5), 551.

Gomez-Perez, A., & Corcho, O. (2002). Ontology languages for the Semantic Web. *IEEE Intelligent Systems, 17*(1), 54.

Gomez-Perez, A., Fernandez-Lopez, M., & Corcho, O. (2004). *Ontological engineering: With examples from the areas of knowledge management, e-commerce and the semantic Web.* London; New York: Springer-Verlag.

Grosof, B. N., & Poon, T. C. (2004). SweetDeal: Representing agent contracts with exceptions using semantic Web rules, ontologies, and process descriptions. *International Journal of Electronic Commerce, 8*(4), 61.

Gruber, T. R. (1993). A translation approach to portable ontology specifications. *Knowledge Acquisition, 5*, 199-220.

Guarino, N. (1997). Understanding, building and using ontologies. *International Journal of Human-Computer Studies, 46*(2/3), 293-310.

Guarino, N. (1998, June). *Formal ontology and information systems.* Paper presented at the Formal Ontology in Information Systems, Trento, Italy.

Guarino, N., Carrara, M., & Giaretta, P. (1994). *An ontology of meta-level categories.* Paper presented at the Principles of Knowledge Representation and Reasoning: Proceeding of the 4th International Conference (KR94). San Francisco: Morgan Kaufmann.

Handschuh, S., Staab, S., & Ciravegna, F. (2002). *S-CREAM—Semi-automatic creation of metadata.* Paper presented at the 13th International Conference on Knowledge Engineering and Management (EKAW 2002), Siguenza, Spain.

Hartmann, J., & Sure, Y. (2004). An infrastructure for scalable, reliable semantic portals. *IEEE Intelligent Systems, 19*(3), 58.

Heflin, J. (2004). *Web ontology language (OWL) use cases and requirements.* Retrieved from http://www.w3.org/TR/Webont-req/: W3C

Heflin, J., & Hendler, J. (2000). *Searching the Web with shoe.* Paper presented at the AAAI-2000 Workshop on AI for Web search, Austin, Texas.

Hendler, J. (2001). Special issue on agents and the Semantic Web. *IEEE Intelligent Systems, 16*(2), 30-37.

Hendler, J. (2003). Science and the Semantic Web. *Science, 299*(5606), 520.

Hubner, S., Spittel, R., Visser, U., & Vogele, T. J. (2004). Ontology-based search for interactive digital maps. *IEEE Intelligent Systems, 19*(3), 80.

Hultgren, G., & Eriksson, O. (2005, March 15-16). *The concept of e-Service from a social interaction perspective*. Paper presented at the ALOIS 2005, Limerick, Ireland.

Johnson-Laird, P. N. (2000). Thinking: Reading. In A. E. Kazdin (Ed.), *Encyclopedia of psychology* (Vol. 8, pp. 75-79). Washington, DC: American Psychological Association.

Jurisica, I., Mylopoulos, J., & Yu, E. (2004). Ontologies for knowledge management: An information systems perspective. *Knowledge and Information Systems, 6*, 380-401.

Kahan, J., & Koivunen, M.-R. (2001). A*nnotea: An open RDF infrastructure for shared Web annotations*. Paper presented at the World Wide Web.

Kiryakov, A., Popov, B., Terziev, I., Manov, D., & Ognyanoff, D. (2004). Semantic annotation, indexing, and retrieval. *Web Semantics: Science, Services and Agents on the World Wide Web, 2*(1), 49-79.

Klein, M., & Visser, U. (2004). Semantic Web challenge 2003. *IEEE Intelligent Systems, 19*(3), 31-33.

Lozano-Tello, A., & Gomez-Perez, A. (2004). ONTOMETRIC: A method to choose the appropriate ontology. *Journal of Database Management, 15*(2), 1.

Maedche, A., & Staab, S. (2001). Ontology learning for the Semantic Web. *IEEE Intelligent Systems, 16*(2), 72.

Martin, T. P., & Azvine, B. (2003). Acquisition of soft taxonomies for intelligent personal hierarchies and the soft Semantic Web. *BT Technology Journal, 21*(4), 113.

McDowell, L., Etzioni, O., & Halevy, A. (2004). Semantic email: theory and applications. *Web Semantics: Science, Services and Agents on the World Wide Web, 2*(2), 153-183.

Medjahed, B., & Bouguettaya, A. (2005). A dynamic foundation architecture for Semantic Web services. *Distributed and Parallel Databases, 17*, 179-206.

Mendelson, E. (1997). *Introduction to mathematical logic* (4th ed.). London: Chapman.

Michalowski, M., Ambite, J. L., Thakkar, S., Tuchinda, R., Knoblock, C. A., & Minton, S. (2004). Retrieving and semantically integrating heterogeneous data from the Web. *Intelligent Systems, IEEE* (see also IEEE Expert), *19*(3), 72-79.

Missikoff, M., Navigli, R., & Velardi, P. (2002). Integrated approach to Web ontology learning and engineering. *Computer, 35*(11), 60-63.

Neches, R., Fikes, R. E., Finin, T., Gruber, T. R., Senator, T., & Swartout, W. R. (1991). Enabling technology for knowledge sharing. *AI Magazine, 12*(3), 36-56.

Noy, N. F., & Musen, M. A. (2004). Ontology versioning in an ontology management framework. *Intelligent Systems, IEEE* (see also IEEE Expert), *19*(4), 6-13.

Noy, N. F., Sintek, M., Decker, S., & Crubezy, M., et al. (2001). Creating Semantic Web content with Protege-2000. *IEEE Intelligent Systems, 16*(2), 60.

Ouksel, A. M., & Sheth, A. (1999). A brief introduction to the research area and the special section. *SIGMOD Record* (Special Section on Semantic Interoperability in Global Information Systems), *28*(1), 5-12.

Paolucci, M., & Sycara, K. (2003). Autonomous Semantic Web services. *IEEE Internet Computing, 7*(5), 34-41.

Payne, T. R., Singh, R., & Sycara, K. (2002). Calendar agents on the Semantic Web. *IEEE Intelligent Systems, 17*(3), 84.

Risvik, K. M., & Michelsen, R. (2002). Search engines and Web dynamics. *Computer Networks, 39*(3), 289-302.

Russell, S., & Norvig, P. (2003). *Artificial intelligence: A modern approach* (2nd ed.). Upper Saddle River, NJ: Prentice Hall.

Schwartz, D. G. (2003). From open IS semantics to the Semantic Web: The road ahead. *IEEE Intelligent Systems, 18*(3), 52.

Searle, J. R. (1980). Minds, brains, and programs. *Behavioral and Brain Sciences, 3*(3), 417-457.

Sheth, A. (2005). Semantics for the Semantic Web: The implicit, the formal, and the powerful. *International Journal on Semantic Web & Information Systems, 1*(1), 1-18.

Sivashanmugam, K., Miller, J. A., Sheth, A. P., & Verma, K. (2003). *Framework for Semantic Web process composition* (No. Technical Report 03-008): Large Scale Distributed Information System Lab, Dept of Computer Science, UGA.

Smith, I. A., Cohen, P. R., Bradshaw, J. M., Greaves, M., & Holmback, H. (1998, July 3-7). *Designing conversation policies using joint intention theory.* Paper presented at the 3rd International Conference on Multiagent Systems (ICMAS-98), Paris.

Sreenath, R. M., & Singh, M. P. (2004). Agent-based service selection. *Web Semantics: Science, Services and Agents on the World Wide Web, 1*(3), 261-279.

Staab, S., Aalst, W. V. D., Benjamins, V. R., Sheth, A., Miller, J. A., & Bussler, C., et al. (2003). Web services: been there, done that? *IEEE Intelligent Systems, 18*(1), 72-85.

Staab, S., Gomez-Perez, A., Daelemana, W., Reinberger, M.-L., & Noy, N.F. (2004). Why evaluate ontology technologies? Because it works! *Intelligent Systems, IEEE* (see also IEEE Expert), *19*(4), 74-81.

Staab, S., Santini, S., Nack, F., Steels, L., & Maedche, A. (2002). Emergent semantics. *Intelligent Systems, IEEE* (see also IEEE Expert), *17*(1), 78-86.

Sternberg, R. J. (2003). *Cognitive psychology* (3rd ed.). Thomson Wadsworth.

Stork, D. G. *The end of an era, the beginning of another? HAL, Deep Blue and Kasparov.* Retrieved June 25, 2005, from http://www.research.ibm.com/deepblue/learn/html/e.8.1.shtml

Studer, R., Benjamins, V. R., & Fensel, D. (1998). Knowledge engineering: principles and methods. *Data & Knowledge Engineering, 25*, 161-197.

Su, Z., Jiang, J., Liu, T., Xie, G. T., & Pan, Y. (2004). Market intelligence portal: An entity-based system for managing market intelligence. *IBM Systems Journal, 43*(3), 534.

Sycara, K., Paolucci, M., Ankolekar, A., & Srinivasan, N. (2003). Automated discovery, interaction and composition of Semantic Web services. *Web Semantics: Science, Services and Agents on the World Wide Web, 1*(1), 27-46.

Trastour, D., Bartolini, C., & Preist, C. (2003). Semantic Web support for the business-to-business e-commerce pre-contractual lifecycle. *Computer Networks, 42*(5), 661.

Tsalgatidou, A., & Pilioura, T. (2002). An overview of standards and related technology in Web services. *Distributed and Parallel Databases, 12*, 135-162.

Uschold, M. (2003). Where are the semantics in the Semantic Web? *AI Magazine, 24*(3), 25-36.

Uschold, M., King, M., Moralee, S., & Zorgios, Y. (1998). The enterprise ontology. *The Knowledge Engineering Review, 13*, 31-89.

Varile, G. B., & Zampolli, A. (Eds.). (1997). *Survey of the state of the art in human language technology*. Pisa: Giardini.

W3C. (2004). *Web services architecture requirements*. W3C Working Group Notes.

Wang, H., Huang, J. Z., Qu, Y., & Xie, J. (2004). Web services: Problems and future directions. *Web Semantics: Science, Services and Agents on the World Wide Web, 1*(3), 309-320.

Wason, P. C., & Johnson-Laird, P. N. (1972). *Psychology of reasoning: Structure and content*. Cambridge, MA: Harvard University Press.

Williams, R. N. (2000). Epistemology. In A. E. Kazdin (Ed.), *Encyclopedia of psychology* (Vol. 3, pp. 225-232). Washington, DC: American Psychological Association.

Wittgenstein, L. (1974). *Tractatus logico-philosophicus* (Revised ed., D. F. Pears & B. F. McGuinness, Trans.). London: Routledge and Kegan Paul.

Zhang, J., Chung, J.-Y., & Chang, C. K. (2004). *Migration to Web services oriented architecture: A case study*. Paper presented at the ACM Symposium on Applied Computing.

Zhao, J. L., & Cheng, H. K. (2005). Web services and process management: A union of convenience or a new area of research? *Decision Support System, 40*(1), 1-8.

Chapter II

Semantic Descriptions of Web Services

Farshad Hakimpour, UK

Suo Cong, University of Zurich, Switzerland

Daniela E. Damm, Zuhlke Engineering Ltd., UK

Abstract

This chapter introduces the emerging technology of Semantic Web services. It concentrates on two dominant specifications in this domain, namely OWL-S (Web ontology language for services) and WSMO (Web services modeling ontology). We briefly introduce Web services and Semantic Web, two main technologies underlying the Semantic Web services technology and then explain most of the key features of this technology together with simplified examples. We discuss three aspects of Semantic Web services: specifications for semantic descriptions of services, intelligent discovery and selection of services using semantic descriptions, and finally, building more complex services by composing existing ones. Our main goal in this chapter is not only to present an abstract view of this technology but also the introduction of the technical details of the two existing specifications.

Introduction

Semantic Web services technology lays its foundation on both Web services (W3C, 2004a) and Semantic Web (Berners-Lee, Hendler, & Lassila, 2001; Decker et al., 2000). Web services offer a promising approach to accomplish a loose coupling of processes across organizational boundaries. Web services technologies present specifications that cover the details required for an automated interoperation among client agents and services on the Web, with a minimum interference of human agents. A Web service may provide any of the following or their combinations:

- **static information**, e.g., retrieving geographic or statistical data;
- **digital processes**, e.g., unit conversion or currency exchange; or
- **actual services with concrete effects**, e.g., booking a flight or selling a book and shipping it to an address.

On the other hand, Semantic Web offers computer interpretable semantic knowledge to facilitate a smarter selection of services and assists combining them to build composite services or applications. Such objectives can be achieved by describing the capabilities of a service using semantic descriptions. Programs on the Web will be able to find each other (other Web services) by matching their requirements with the capabilities of available services. Semantic Web technologies can be applied to describe provided capabilities and/or desired requirements of a service.

We believe Semantic Web services technology will improve and facilitate discovery, composition, and interaction with Web services. Semantic Web services facilitates the process of composing several Web services to build a more complex service, while it exposes and behaves as one single service to a client agent. That includes both aspects of facilitating automatic service composition as well as providing specification to describe a composition. The interaction with Web services not only considers invocation and brokering, but would often follow a specific message interchange protocol. Semantic Web services technology provides specifications for Web services to describe their interaction pattern. Description of interaction patterns can be used by client agents during the discovery as well as the execution time.

The main objective of this chapter is to introduce the emerging technology of Semantic Web services. As we introduce this technology, we also discuss the two dominant specifications in this domain, namely OWL-S (Web ontology language for services; Martin et al., 2004a) and WSMO (Web services modeling ontology; WSMO, 2004a). We present all essential features of these specifications and provide simplified examples.

The chapter is organized as follows:

- We start by giving an overview of Web services technologies and Semantic Web. In two sections, we provide the background knowledge for Web services and then briefly introduce Semantic Web, the notion of ontology and the Web ontology language (OWL) specification. These two sections give the necessary basic understanding of these technologies that is required for the remainder of the chapter.

- The next section motives the augmentation of Web services by adding semantics. In addition, it briefly introduces the two major specifications in this domain, OWL-S and WSMO. We use these specifications to present our example descriptions through the chapter.

- Subsequently, we explain how the semantics of Web services are described by their functional and nonfunctional properties; also how semantic descriptions are bound to the service descriptions.

- We discuss intelligent service discovery as one of the motivations of Semantic Web service technology in the next section.

- The next section introduces topics relevant to service composition modeling. We explain the OWL-S composition model and briefly introduce WSMO orchestration and choreography.

- Finally, we present a summary of the chapter and discuss the types of the tools needed for applying Semantic Web services technology.

In this chapter, concepts or relations specific to OWL-S are denoted by Arial and those of WSMO are capitalized. In figures, rounded corner boxes illustrate concepts in OWL-S and boxes show concepts in WSMO. The arrows in the diagrams ($\rightarrow$) show relations between concepts with the arrows pointing to the range of the relation. The name of the relation and the cardinality (if relevant) appear next to the arrow head. The solid triangular ($\twoheadrightarrow$) arrows show the specialization relation with the arrow pointing to the superclass.

Table 1. Elements and tasks in a typical Web services architecture

	Service Description	Service Discovery	Service Use
Service Provider	Define a complete description of the service interface: - Basic description - Semantic description - Business description	Publish the service description to enable any interested requester can find the service.	Support the provision of a specific service via its published interface for: - Service implementation - Service deployment - Service management
Discovery Agent	Collect and organize the descriptions of services: - Search-oriented (crawler engine) - Storage-oriented (service registry)	Perform matches between requests and service descriptions: - Keyword-based - Semantics-based	Facilitate the automatic provision, discovery, and use of services.
Service Consumer	Acquire and understand the description of the required service, either by human assistance or by an intelligent system.	Define a request for a service discovery either at the design time or at the run time.	Make use of the required service: - Binding (Invoking) - Coordination/ Composition - Service management

Web Services

A Web service is a software program that exposes a coherent functionality via an interface described in a machine-processable format (e.g., WSDL) and supports interoperable machine-to-machine interactions with other programs via XML-based messages (e.g. SOAP) conveyed using Web-related standards (W3C, 2004a). The basic elements of a typical Web services architecture are summarized in Table 1.

A primary contribution of Web services toward conquering the limitations of conventional middleware and proprietary EAI/EDI infrastructures is to enforce standardization in defining, describing, and discovering services. Such standardization should support interactions with other programs in a peer-to-peer fashion based on middleware protocols within the service-oriented paradigm leading to a design strategy that everything could be exposed and used as a service (Alonso, Casati, Kuno, & Machiraju, 2004). The most distinct feature of using Web services is the designed machine-interpretability supporting a Web service discovery and invocation by other software systems, and consequently interaction with the service. The foundation of the machine-interpretable Web services is to express the knowledge required for properly interacting with a Web service in a format that can be processed automatically by any service requester. A requester analyzes a service description to determine whether a Web service is qualified for fulfilling a given request and to acquire the details of how to use a Web service. The rest of this section contains a brief background to Web services and their three main pillars, namely SOAP, WSDL, and UDDI technologies.

SOAP

The simple object access protocol (SOAP) is a specification for interactions among Web services across the Internet. SOAP uses XML to exchange structured and typed information. It defines bindings to actual transport protocols such as HTTP or SMTP (W3C, 2003). Most software vendors support SOAP as the common specification for interacting with a Web service.

What makes SOAP different from prior technologies, such as CORBA/ORBs or Java RMI, are few following characteristics (W3C, 2003):

- SOAP is an XML-based protocol. Instead of passing objects of complicated structure, which may vary in different implementations, SOAP employs a simple messaging approach. Packaged XML messages are passed between the interacting applications. This makes it easier to achieve common standards among different vendors. Furthermore, SOAP message processors can easily use an underlying XML processor.

- SOAP extensively leverages the HTTP protocol. SOAP can use the HTTP protocol (the protocol underlying the World Wide Web) as its transport protocol. In other words, an HTTP server (i.e. Web server) can recognize a request containing a SOAP message and pass it to a SOAP processor or take the necessary action. However,

SOAP is a neutral messaging protocol and does not rely on any underlying protocol, including HTTP, and it can use any other transport protocol.

- SOAP is about messaging. SOAP messages can carry the application semantics. It is neutral towards representation of application semantics. Therefore, it leads to an infrastructure of interoperability and extensibility.

- SOAP is a W3C recommendation and not a vendor dependent messaging protocol, unlike messaging underlying different CORBA/ORB vendor implementations or Java RMI.

SOAP defines a simple messaging framework to transfer XML messages between an initial sender and an ultimate receiver. For a successful interaction between the sender and the receiver, the receiver must understand how the sender encodes the message. A particular encoding form is proposed in the SOAP protocol. However, SOAP is not limited to use any specific encoding mechanism.

A SOAP message is composed of two parts: an optional SOAP header element and a mandatory SOAP body element. The SOAP header is used to carry "control" information to indicate how to handle the message such as routing, authentication, and transactions which are not included in the application payload. The SOAP body element carries the actual message to be delivered to the ultimate receiver via any number of intermediaries. Only the ultimate receiver is expected to understand the semantics of the application payload.

SOAP provides two kinds of interactions between the sender and the receiver: RPC-based and Document-based. In RPC-based paradigm, the messages are translated into corresponding RPC method signatures and the result/output parameters. In Document-based paradigm, the interactions are realized by exchanging the documents from one application to another.

WSDL

In principle, a service description is defined to express the information required to invoke a service properly. A service invoker needs to understand the complete description of a Web service to determine whether it is qualified to fulfill a specific purpose or task and how to use it. A complete description of a Web service normally involves multiple layers (e.g., in Alonso et al., 2004). In order to distinguish the concept of complete description with the concept of basic description typically at communication level, we consider a complete service description as a service comprehension that consists of three levels of information of using a service properly: communication level, semantic level, and business level.

At the communication level, each Web service must have a machine-processable description to specify the necessary information, including schematic information (i.e., message formats and data types) and transport protocols, to enable a client agent to invoke and interact with a service. The dominant specification at this level is the Web services description language (WSDL; W3C, 2005). WSDL documents offer service

Listing 1. Example source code for a service calculating a freight service cost

```
1   package swsExamples.services;
2   public class Freight {
3           public int cost (String destination,
4                   swsExamples.physicalMeasures.Volume size) {
5   . . .
6     }
7   }
8
9   package swsExamples.physicalMeasures;
10  public class Volume {
11          public int value;
12          public String unit;
13 }
```

requesters the potential to discover Web services autonomously and automatically with reduced human intervention.

The information in WSDL model can be divided in two parts: an abstract part which describes a Web service in terms of the messages it sends and receives, and a concrete part which specifies the details of how to access a Web service. In the reminder of this chapter we focus on the abstract part and describe how it can be augmented by semantic descriptions.

An example of a WSDL description is shown in Listing 2. The WSDL description is automatically generated for the service in Listing 1 and consists of the following elements:

- **Messages:** Client agents communicate to the service through two messages: costRequest and costResponse (lines 26 to 32).

- **Types:** Complex data types can be also described in the WSDL description. In this example Volume is describe in lines 12 to 25.

- **Port Types:** Port types are analogous to the interface definitions. Our Port Type between lines 33 to 40 describes the interface for the Freight class.

- **Operations:** A Port Type contains a set of operations. In our example, Freight contains only the cost operation. Operations are described in terms of the messages that can be used to invoke them.

- **Bindings:** Several bindings can be defined for a Port Type. Bindings define encoding and transport protocol for messages used in the operations of a Port Type. In our example, one binding is defined for cost operation, using SOAP.

- **Services:** A service consists of one or more Port Types and at least one binding for each Port Type (lines 62 to 68). Service also specifies an end point or the location where the operations reside on the Web (lines 66 and 66).

Listing 2. The WSDL definition for the service in Listing 1

```
1   <?xml version="1.0" encoding="UTF-8"?>
2   <wsdl:definitions
3   targetNamespace="http://www.example.com/axis/WSDL/freight.wsdl"
4   xmlns:apachesoap="http://xml.apache.org/xml-soap"
5   xmlns:impl="http://www.example.com/axis/WSDL/freight.wsdl"
6   xmlns:intf="http://www.example.com/axis/WSDL/freight.wsdl"
7   xmlns:soapenc="http://schemas.xmlsoap.org/soap/encoding/"
8   xmlns:wsdl="http://schemas.xmlsoap.org/wsdl/"
9   xmlns:wsdlsoap="http://schemas.xmlsoap.org/wsdl/soap/"
10  xmlns:xsd="http://www.w3.org/2001/XMLSchema">
11  <!--WSDL created by Apache Axis version: 1.2-->
12  <wsdl:types>
13  <schema targetNamespace=
14       "http://www.example.com/axis/WSDL/freight.wsdl"
15       xmlns="http://www.w3.org/2001/XMLSchema">
16  <import
17     namespace="http://schemas.xmlsoap.org/soap/encoding/"/>
18  <complexType name="Volume">
19   <sequence>
20    <element name="value" type="xsd:int"/>
21    <element name="unit" nillable="true" type="xsd:string"/>
22   </sequence>
23  </complexType>
24  </schema>
25  </wsdl:types>
26  <wsdl:message name="costRequest">
27   <wsdl:part name="destination" type="xsd:string"/>
28   <wsdl:part name="size" type="impl:Volume"/>
29  </wsdl:message>
30  <wsdl:message name="costResponse">
31   <wsdl:part name="costReturn" type="xsd:int"/>
32  </wsdl:message>
33  <wsdl:portType name="Freight">
34   <wsdl:operation name="cost"
35           parameterOrder="destination size">
36    <wsdl:input message="impl:costRequest" name="costRequest"/>
37    <wsdl:output message="impl:costResponse"
38          name="costResponse"/>
39   </wsdl:operation>
40  </wsdl:portType>
41  <wsdl:binding name="FreightPortSoapBinding"
42          type="impl:Freight">
43   <wsdlsoap:binding
44       style="rpc"
45       transport="http://schemas.xmlsoap.org/soap/http"/>
46   <wsdl:operation name="cost">
47    <wsdlsoap:operation soapAction=""/>
48    <wsdl:input name="costRequest">
49     <wsdlsoap:body
50      encodingStyle="http://schemas.xmlsoap.org/soap/encoding/"
51      namespace="http://www.example.com/axis/WSDL/freight.wsdl"
52      use="encoded"/>
53    </wsdl:input>
54    <wsdl:output name="costResponse">
55     <wsdlsoap:body
```

Listing 2. continued

```
56    encodingStyle="http://schemas.xmlsoap.org/soap/encoding/"
57    namespace="http://www.example.com/axis/WSDL/freight.wsdl"
58    use="encoded"/>
59  </wsdl:output>
60  </wsdl:operation>
61 </wsdl:binding>
62 <wsdl:service name="FreightService">
63 <wsdl:port binding="impl:FreightPortSoapBinding"
64        name="FreightPort">
65   <wsdlsoap:address
66    location="http://www.example.com/axis/services/freight"/>
67  </wsdl:port>
68 </wsdl:service>
69</wsdl:definitions>
```

One of the topics covered in the rest of this chapter is how the WSDL descriptions are enhanced by semantics. In other words, we show how Semantic Web service technology can help us to describe semantics of data types and operations for Web services. We enhance Messages, Types, PortType and Operation elements of the WSDL description in Listing 2 as we progress in this chapter.

UDDI

At present, there are two major types of approaches to find service descriptions: search-oriented and storage-oriented. The search-oriented approach employs a crawler to collect description on the Web (Dong, Halevy, Madhavan, Nemes, & Zhang, 2004; see also http://www.webservicelist.com). The storage-oriented approach uses storages to store and organize the service descriptions submitted by service providers actively. The storage of service descriptions can be constructed as a registry, an index, or a peer-to-peer system (W3C, 2004a). To use a service properly, especially in mission-critical business applications, a trusted business service registry is preferred as it can improve the protection of both the service requesters against malicious providers, and the service providers against malicious requesters. One of the most eminent business service registries is the Universal Description, Discovery, and Integration specification (UDDI; OASIS, 2004).

A UDDI registry allows registering of Web service descriptions for businesses and facilitates their discovery (Figure 1). The core of the UDDI specification consists of a data model defined to represent Web services as UDDI data, and a collection of *API sets* for

Figure 1. Role of UDDI registries and other Web services technologies

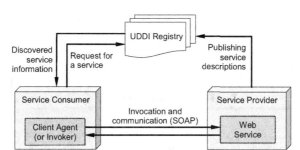

manipulating the stored UDDI data. We briefly introduce the UDDI data model as its understanding is necessary in the rest of this chapter.

UDDI Data Model

The canonical UDDI data model defines six major categories of information to represent Web services. The data model enables the registry to find a qualified Web service according to a specific request. Each category is defined as an entity expressed in XML.

- **businessEntity:** the description of a business or service provider and the services it provides. It specifies the name of a provider, contact and classification information. businessEntity includes service descriptions and technical information, using businessService and bindingTemplate.

- **businessService:** a logical group of Web services belonging to a service provider represented by a businessEntity. It contains general information of Web services included in a logical group, such as, names, descriptions and classification information. This structure stands between the level of businessEntity and the level of bindingTemplate for the sake of assembling a number of services in a logical relationship, for example, services related to travel planning.

- **bindingTemplate:** the necessary technical information to invoke a specified Web service. Each bindingTemplate represents either the access point or a pointer to the access point of an individual Web service.

- **tModel:** a technical model which can be reused to represent any kind of specification. tModels can be used to describe a Web service classification scheme, a protocol used by a Web service, or a namespace in a standard way. A tModel is a 'technical fingerprint' used to describe some common characteristics of Web services.

- **publisherAssertion:** a relationship between two service providers each represented by a businessEntity.

- **subscription:** Standing request to receive the notifications of changes of specified
  UDDI entities.

Semantic Web

The universal Web provides an immense platform for exchanging and sharing huge amount of data world wide. In order to enable the machines to process the data over the Web automatically and intelligently, a number of relevant metadata should be provided alongside the data. Such metadata can contain *schematic* knowledge, for example in form of XML Schemas (W3C, 2004c) and WSDL (W3C, 2005), or *semantic* knowledge to represent the intended meaning of data.

Inspired by the desire of exchanging machine-processable information, the idea of Semantic Web has been proposed to extend the current Web infrastructure to represent data of well-defined meaning (Berners-Lee, et al. 2001). The Semantic Web initiative is to study the feasible approaches of introducing metadata to describe meanings of Web resources residing at the decentralized Internet. The semantic descriptions are aimed to be interpreted by programs that eventually help users to avoid misinterpretation of available data. Semantic Web technologies assists us in describing terms such as "destination" (in Listing 2) to avoid possible misinterpretation by different people (see Figure 2).

Figure 2. Various interpretation of a term in a service description.

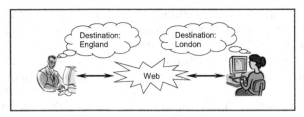

Listing 3. Part of a simplified OWL ontology for quantities describing "volume" (used in our example)

```
1   <?xml version="1.0" encoding="ISO-8859-1" ?>
2   <rdf:RDF xmlns:rdf="http://www.w3.org/1999/02/22-rdf-syntax-ns#"
3     xmlns:rdfs="http://www.w3.org/2000/01/rdf-schema#"
4     xmlns:owl="http://www.w3.org/2002/07/owl#"
5     xmlns:xsd="http://www.w3.org/2001/XMLSchema">
6     xmlns="http://www.example.com/owl/Hi-Onto/Quantities.owl#"
7   <owl:Ontology about="">
8     <rdfs:comment>
9         An Ontology defining quantities.
10    </rdfs:comment>
11    <owl:imports rdf:resource=
12        "http://www.w3.org/1999/02/22-rdf-syntax-ns" />
13    <owl:imports rdf:resource=
14        "http://www.w3.org/2000/01/rdf-schema" />
15    <owl:imports rdf:resource=
16        "http://www.w3.org/2002/07/owl" />
17  </owl:Ontology>
18  <!-- Definition forVolume -->
19  <owl:Class rdf:ID="Volume">
20    <owl:subClassOf rdf:resource=
21        "http://www.w3.org/2002/07/owl#Thing"/>
22  </owl:Class>
23  <owl:Property rdf:ID="magnitude">
24    <rdfs:range rdf:resource=
25        "http://www.w3.org/2001/XMLSchema#int"/>
26    <rdfs:domain rdf:resource="#Volume"/>
27  </owl:Property>
28  <owl:Property rdf:ID="unit">
29    <rdfs:range rdf:resource="#VolumeUnit"/>
30    <rdfs:domain rdf:resource="#Volume"/>
31  </owl:Property>
32  <owl:Class rdf:ID="VolumeUnit">
33    <owl:oneOf rdf:parseType="Collection">
34    <DeliveryType rdf:ID="Liter"/>
35    <DeliveryType rdf:ID="QubicMeter"/>
36    <DeliveryType rdf:ID="Pint"/>
37    </owl:oneOf>
38  </owl:Class>
39  . . .
40  </rdf:RDF>
```

Ontologies

Interpretation of terms in data or schematic definitions is usually taken for granted. Ontologies are the means to avoid the misinterpretation of terms by formally describing a conceptualization (Guarino, 1998). They are used to describe the semantics of terms in different domains. As we show in the rest of this chapter, ontologies play an important role in semantic descriptions of Web services. Ontologies explicitly describe terms often using logical expressions. Using a formal and logical language, enables computers to process the knowledge encoded in an ontology. Ontologies guarantee that the information in any instance of communication is consistently interpreted by both involved parties. Using ontologies, communities are able to reduce the risk of misinterpretation while keeping their diversity.

Ontologies may appear in various forms. They can have a simple form of a taxonomy tree that relates terms by specialization and generalization relations; or in a more complicated form, they may use complex logical expressions to describe terms in relation to each other. Formalized definitions of terms in ontologies can be processed by computer programs and help us to improve the reliability of data interpretation.

Listing 4. Ontology describing the concepts particularly used in the semantic description of freight service

```
1   <?xml version="1.0" encoding="ISO-8859-1" ?>
2   <rdf:RDF
3   xmlns:rdf="http://www.w3.org/1999/02/22-rdf-syntax-ns#"
4   xmlns:rdfs="http://www.w3.org/2000/01/rdf-schema#"
5   xmlns:xsd="http://www.w3.org/2001/XMLSchema#"
6   xmlns:owl="http://www.w3.org/2002/07/owl#"
7   xmlns:geo="http://www.example.com/owl/Hi-Onto/geospatial.owl#"
8   xmlns="http://www.example.com/owl-s/freight/Concepts.owl#">
9   <owl:Ontology rdf:about="">
10   <owl:imports rdf:resource=
11       "http://www.example.com/owl/Hi-Onto/geospatial.owl"/>
12   </owl:Ontology>
13   <owl:Class rdf:ID="Dest_City">
14   <rdfs:label>destination</rdfs:label>
15   <rdfs:subClassOf rdf:resource=
16       "http://www.example.com/owl/Hi-Onto/geospatial.owl#city"/>
17   <rdfs:subClassOf>
18     <owl:Restriction>
19      <owl:onProperty rdf:resource=
20      "http://www.example.com/owl/Hi-Onto/geospatial.owl#inside"/>
21      <owl:hasValues rdf:resource=
22      "http://www.example.com/owl/Hi-Onto/geospatial.owl#Europe"/>
23     </owl:Restriction>
24   </rdfs:subClassOf>
25   </owl:Class>
26   . . .
27   </rdf:RDF>
```

Web Ontology Language (OWL)

OWL (McGuinness & Harmelen, 2004) defines a formal language for defining ontologies. It is a W3C recommendation for describing ontologies based on other W3C recommendation, RDF and XML. OWL recommendation consists of three sublanguages: OWL-Lite, OWL-DL, and OWL-Full. The underlying reason for having different sublanguages is the different levels of details needed in different application (as mentioned in earlier section).

OWL-Lite is a simple subset of OWL that can be used to describe taxonomy trees. OWL-DL is a more complex language and its expressions can be processed by most Description Logic reasoning systems. OWL-Full is the complete expressive language that offers maximum expressivity but might not be fully processed by the existing systems, due to the complexity of the language.

Listing 3 and Listing 4 show two examples of ontologies defined in OWL. Both are used in our later examples for describing semantics of the service introduced in an earlier section. Listing 3 illustrate a generic ontology defining terms related to physical quantities. We show how Volume is defined in this ontology as a combination of a magnitude and a unit. Listing 4 shows another ontology specific to our service. Note that this ontology is importing another generic ontology, named geo-spatial, which defines the destination city as a subclass of European cities.

It is good practice to separate ontologies specific to the application from more generic ontologies. It is also a common convention in the OWL-S community to name application specific ontology as Concepts (in our example, Concepts.owl is an ontology specific to our Web service). It is also a common practice to separate ontologies specific to a domain (also called domain ontology), for example a Transport ontology, from more generic ontologies (also called higher-level ontologies), such as the Quantity ontology.

Semantic Web Services

Web services technology offers the ability for programs to find, invoke and interact with each other in a dynamic fashion and on the fly. However, there are still limitations on the Web service technology that Semantic Web services aims to overcome. In the following subsections, first we show the limitations of Web services technology that motivated the initiatives such as OWL-S and WSMO. Then we show overviews of both OWL-S and WSMO.

Challenges to Web Services

From the perspective of service requesters, a conventional process of using Web services includes three steps: define the request for a Web service, discover and locate the interface of a qualified service, and invoke the corresponding service implementation via the binding of the published service interface. A typical scenario of developing a client application which makes use of Web services is as follows. First, the programmer defines what functionality is required to fulfill the application requirements. Then she searches for Web services qualified for that purpose. The programmer can search manually or use appropriate tools to assist the query processing. The result of the search normally contains a number of candidate Web services satisfying the search parameters. Then, the programmer has to decide which Web service is the best candidate. If none of them is qualified, a new query has to be issued. After a qualified service is found, the programmer retrieves the information of the service interface and writes the code to call it in the client application. In this "traditional" way of using Web services, only the binding between the service implementation and the service interface is dynamic and could be decided at the run time. The search for services is conducted at the design time and the decision whether a service is qualified or not is made by human agents. In most cases, the call of a service is hard-coded as a call to a service interface. Although the service implementation is decoupled from the client applications, the service interface is still tightly coupled with client applications.

An ideal automated process of using Web services should enable client applications to handle the three steps automatically by machines instead of a programmer and the switch from one step to another should be seamless without human intervention. However, current Web services technologies are not capable of supporting such an ideal auto-mated invocation of Web services. The intervention of human is still inevitable for the grand scenario in which a requester can find and invoke a qualified service on the fly.

In the past, different service providers have developed their unique style and manner of doing various businesses, and the corresponding enterprise information systems as well as business applications have been developed independently by developers who might think differently. As a result, the prevalence of semantic heterogeneity in Web services published by different providers is inevitable and thus it leaves some obvious gaps in the steps of using Web services which needs human intervention to assist the process manually.

The first gap is between step of defining a service request and step of discovering services that is caused by the lack of complete specification for description of Web services. For the purpose of automated service discovery, the requests for Web services must be composed in machine-processable format. On one side, it is the request of a Web service from a service requester. And on the other side, it is the service description published by a service provider. The discovery process is defined to match the service request against a number of service descriptions.

A comprehensive description of a Web service consists of three levels of knowledge how to use this Web service: communication, capability and functionality, and business description. The lowest level is the communication level service description, e.g., provided by WSDL description. The middle level of a service comprehension defines the service semantics by expressing the functionality and the capability of a Web service. In general, the functionality of a Web service prescribes its intended purpose. The quantitative and qualitative constraints on the functionality of a service are expressed by a capability specification. Business descriptions facilitate the communication and negotiation to set up commercial relationships in order to use services commercially and legally.

The second gap lies between the step of service discovery and the step of service invocation because of the degree of precision of service discovery. Within the process of service discovery, the matching process lacks an accurate measure of how well a service is qualified to fulfill a service request. The result of a discovery is to return all services that are "sufficiently similar" to the request. This implies that human assistance is still required to determine whether a 'sufficiently similar' service is the desired one. Therefore, the support of automatic service discovery, invocation, and composition is rather limited. Furthermore, a considerable amount of customer code has to be implemented in the client applications.

Beyond WSDL Descriptions and UDDI Discovery

Using the Web services technology, we can describe the data types used in communicating with a Web service (e.g., through input and output description in WSDL). The UDDI discovery is a keyword based search on service description stored in the registry. Two major types of solutions can improve the discovery of Web services are emerging.

The first type is to apply mathematical models and methods to analyze the WSDL documents attached with Web services to infer the underlying semantics. Dong et al. (2004) proposes an effective approach of searching Web services by clustering parameter names of operations on a set of Web services into semantically meaningful concepts.

These clustering can be used to determine similarity of Web services, based on statistics computed over a large number of WSDL documents. This trend of research work focus on input/output matching to find a list of operations with similar inputs (outputs) with a given inputs (outputs) of an operation, and operation matching to find a list of operations similar with a given operation.

The second type is to define standard description languages at a higher level of abstraction on top of WSDL and matching algorithms to compare the capabilities provided in such description languages. Semantic Web services provide the capability that input and outputs can be described by ontologies. Further than describing services by inputs and outputs, Semantic Web describes services by a set of conditions that must hold before the service execution and will hold after the service execution. These features provide more expressiveness and precision to describe a service as compared to that of WSDL and potentially improve the discovery process. A number of matching algorithms have been proposed for semantic description models by Paolucci, Kawamura, Payne, and Sycara (2002b) and Sycara, Paulocci, Ankolekar, and Srinivasan (2003) The matchmaker proposed by Paolucci et al. (2002b) integrates semantic matching into UDDI. For a request, the proposed algorithm performs a match between all the outputs of the request against outputs of a service advertisement (a service description published in a registry) and a match between all the inputs of a service advertisement against the inputs of the request to determine the degree of match such as exact, plug in, subsumes, and fail.

Beyond Stateless Services

Web services technology, particularly WSDL, is based on the assumption that a service is stateless. In other words, a service receives a set of data as an input (input messages) before it starts execution and produces output data (output messages) after its execution. However, in general, a service can be more complicated with a more complex pattern of message exchange. A challenge to Web services technology is to provide the possibility of defining complex patterns of interactions as compared to one step execution in stateless services.

Describing patterns of message exchange is essential when we require building more complex services by combining a set of existing services. The improvement of the discovery process (as described in the last section) allows dynamic composition of the services that can have two different aspects. One is building composed services that its components are dynamically found and invoked on the fly. Second, the descriptions can be used in more intelligent tools to compose Web services automatically or semiautomatically.

OWL-S

OWL-S is a specification for describing semantics of Web services (Martin et al., 2004a). It is a subsequent development of the DAML-S specifications and developed as part of the DAML program (DARPA Agent Markup Language, see http://www.daml.org). While

Figure 3. Overview of main concepts in OWL-S ontology for Web service description

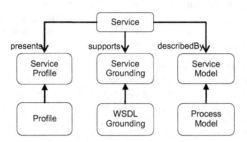

DAML-S was built upon the DAML+OIL, since version 1.0 OWL-S is based on OWL (McGuinness, 2004).

OWL-S lays its basis on a process ontology and benefits from developments in workflow modeling as well as the agent technology (McIlraith, Son, & Zeng, 2001). OWL-S describes services by three components namely, `ServiceModel`, `ServiceProfile` and `ServiceGrounding`. The diagram in Figure 3 illustrates the three components and their relations, and their description is as follows:

- The significant part of the three is the `ServiceModel` that includes descriptions such as, definition of functional parameters, the interaction pattern of a service with the invoker, and its execution mechanism in case of a composite service. To that end, OWL-S presents (but is not limited to) `ProcessModel`. The `ProcessModel` describes a service as a Process (see Figure 3) by its functional parameters: `Inputs`, `Outputs`, `Preconditions` and `Effects` (IOPEs). It also specifies the component processes of a composite service and their execution order and binding of the inputs and outputs of component processes.

- The `ServiceProfile` foresees information that can be required to search for a service in a service registry. An OWL-S `Profile` consists of information such as, `ContactInformation` of the service providers, `ServiceCategory` and other nonfunctional service parameters. Furthermore, a `Profile` contains a replication of the functional parameters (IOPEs) presented in its `ProcessModel`.

- The `ServiceGrounding` binds the semantic description to the details of accessing and executing a service, such as communication protocol and message format. At present, OWL-S offers specifications for grounding to WSDL descriptions.

Many tools are developed and available based on OWL-S specifications and we briefly introduce them at the end of this chapter. At the time of writing, OWL-S 1.1 is also proposed to W3C as a recommendation.

Figure 4. Main classes used in the description of WSMO Web services

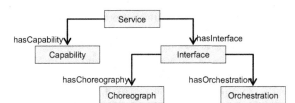

WSMO

The Web service modeling ontology (WSMO) is a specification to describe the various aspects related to Semantic Web services (WSMO, 2004a; see also http://www.wsmo.org). The WSMO specification is mainly developing in relation to SDK project cluster (see www.sdkcluster.org). It is presented in WSML that is a language for formalizing Web service descriptions (WSML, 2005). The role of WSML for WSMO is comparable to that of OWL for OWL-S. However, WSML has been particularly developed for WSMO.

WSMO lays its foundation on knowledge representation and logical reasoning and benefits from experiences gained in developing UPML (Omelayenko et al., 2000) and several case studies (e.g., WSMO, 2004b) in different application domains. The main components of WSMO specifications are Goals, Web services, Ontologies and Mediators, described in the following:

- WSMO describes Web services by their Capabilities and Interfaces (see Figure 4). The Interface description contains two closely related notions of Choreography and Orchestration. Choreography defines the information required to interact with the Web service and Orchestration contains information describing a composite Web service.

- Goals represent the types of objectives that users would like to achieve via Web services. The WSMO definition of goal describes a request for a service by means of defining the state of the desired information space and the desired state of the world after the execution of the intended service.

- Ontologies provide the definition of the concepts and relations used in the other three component descriptions. For example, a goal can import existing concepts and relations defined in an ontology by either extending or simply reusing them as appropriate.

- Finally, Mediators specify interoperability mechanisms. All component descriptions use mediators to define a valid interaction with any other component.

WSMO is a recent initiative in comparison to the OWL-S specification, consequently, still under development and subject to modification. As a result, this chapter tends to present more detailed discussions along with examples based on OWL-S, since it is a solid specification. Alternatively, our discussion around WSMO is based on the available documents at the time of writing this chapter.

It is worth mentioning that WSMO and OWL-S have different technical coverage. For example, the WSMO initiative presents specifications for architecture and execution environment as well as a language for ontology definitions, while these lay outside the scope of the OWL-S initiative. In fact, DAML recently started initiatives on these topics (see http://www.daml.org/services/swsa/). Our focus here is limited to the specifications for describing semantics of services.

Semantic Service Descriptions

The first step in the development of Semantic Web services is to define the semantics of services. Later steps are concerned with the usage of the semantic descriptions. The next section shows how semantics are being used for intelligent discovery while this section is dedicated to the aspects of the former step.

We divide this section to three parts: first describing the properties defining the functionality of a service; then, describing properties that do not affect the functionality but contributing to the service descriptions; finally, describing the association of the semantic descriptions to schematic definitions. We discuss how these descriptions are presented in OWL-S and WSMO, along with examples from OWL-S that are related to our examples of WSDL descriptions and OWL ontologies in last sections.

Functional Properties

Describing semantics of a service in terms of its input and output parameters is an intuitive approach. WSDL descriptions provide a schematic description of these parameters. For example, in a service for selling books, credit card information and book information are inputs and purchase acknowledgement is the output. Furthermore, services can be described by (1) the conditions required for a service to perform successfully -such as the validity of the credit card; and (2) the conditions that would hold after the successful execution of a service -in other words, the charged credit card and the shipped book. Both these types of conditions can be expressed in a logical language. The former conditions are called `Precondition`s and the later are named `Effect`s, in OWL_S. The collection of the above descriptions (Input, Output, Precondition and Effect) is generally referred to as functional properties or *capabilities*.

OWL-S describes a service by a process model (see Figure 3). A `Process` is described in terms of its `Input` and `Output` types as well as `Precondition` and `Effect` expressions (IOPEs). We show a simple example of the semantic description of a process

Listing 5. OWL-S process definition for the example in Listing 2

```
1   <rdf:RDF
2   xmlns:rdf="http://www.w3.org/1999/02/22-rdf-syntax-ns#"
3   xmlns:rdfs="http://www.w3.org/2000/01/rdf-schema#"
4   xmlns:xsd="http://www.w3.org/2001/XMLSchema#"
5   xmlns:owl="http://www.w3.org/2002/07/owl#"
6   xmlns:expr=
7   "http://www.daml.org/services/owl-s/1.1/generic/Expression.owl#"
8   xmlns:swrl="http://www.w3.org/2003/11/swrl#"
9   xmlns:process="http://www.daml.org/services/owl-s/1.1/Process.owl#"
10  xmlns:geo="http://www.example.com/owl/Hi-Onto/geospatial.owl#"
11  xmlns="http://www.example.com/owl-s/freight/Process.owl#"
12  xml:base="http://www.example.com/owl-s/freight/Process.owl">
13  <!-- Atomic Process : Freight_cost -->
14  <!--Inputs-->
15  <process:Input rdf:ID="Freight_destination">
16   <process:parameterType
17   rdf:datatype="http://www.w3.org/2001/XMLSchema#anyURI">
18   http://www.example.com/owl-s/freight/Concepts.owl#Dest_City
19   </process:parameterType>
20  </process:Input>
21  <process:Input rdf:ID="Freight_size">
22   <process:parameterType
23   rdf:datatype="http://www.w3.org/2001/XMLSchema#anyURI">
24   http://www.example.com/owl/Hi-Onto/Quantities.owl#Volume
25   </process:parameterType>
26  </process:Input>
27  <!--Outputs-->
28  <process:Output rdf:ID="Freight_costReturn">
29   <process:parameterType
30   rdf:datatype="http://www.w3.org/2001/XMLSchema#anyURI">
31   http://www.example.com/owl/Hi-Onto/Quantities.owl#Charge
32   </process:parameterType>
33  </process:Output>
34  <!--Locals-->
35  <process:Local rdf:ID="Freight_origin">
36   <process:parameterType
37   rdf:datatype="http://www.w3.org/2001/XMLSchema#anyURI">
38   http://www.example.com/owl/Hi-Onto/geospatial.owl#City
39   </process:parameterType>
40  </process:Local>
41  <!--Process-->
42  <process:AtomicProcess rdf:ID="Freight_cost">
43   <process:hasInput
44   rdf:resource="#Freight_destination"/>
45   <process:hasInput
46   rdf:resource="#Freight_size"/>
47   <process:hasOutput
48   rdf:resource="#Freight_costReturn"/>
49  <!--Preconditions-->
50   <hasPrecondition>
51   <expr:SWRL-Condition rdf:ID="OriginIsLondon">
52    <rdfs:label>
53     SameAs(Freight_Origin, London)
54    </rdfs:label>
55    <expr:expressionLanguage rdf:resource=
```

Listing 5. continued

```
56    "http://www.daml.org/services/owl-
s/1.1/generic/Expression.owl#SWRL" />
57    <expr:expressionBody rdf:parseType="Literal">
58    <swrl:AtomList>
59    <rdf:first>
60     <swrl:IndividualPropertyAtom>
61      <swrl:propertyPredicate
62        rdf:resource="#SameIndividualAtom" />
63      <swrl:argument1
64        rdf:resource="#Freight_origin" />
65      <swrl:argument2 rdf:resource=
66    "http://www.example.com/owl/Hi-Onto/geospacial.owl#London"/>
67     </swrl:IndividualPropertyAtom>
68    </rdf:first>
69    <rdf:rest rdf:resource=
70       "http://www.w3.org/1999/02/22-rdf-syntax-ns#nil"/>
71    </swrl:AtomList>
72    </expr:expressionBody>
73   </expr:SWRL-Condition>
74  </hasPrecondition>
75  <hasPrecondition>
76   <expr:SWRL-Condition rdf:ID="DestinationLimitation">>
77    <rdfs:label>
78      One_of(Freight_Destination, (Rome, Berlin, Madrid))
79    </rdfs:label>
80    [Expression body in SWRL.]
81   </expr:SWRL-Condition>
82  </hasPrecondition>
83 </process:AtomicProcess>
84</rdf:RDF>
```

in Listing 5. This process description defines the semantics for the WSDL description in Listing 2. The input and output types in Process descriptions are defined by ontologies unlike WSDL, where input and output types are defined by their structure and representation (schemata). In a later section, we explain how the semantic descriptions (in Listing 5) are bound to the WSDL descriptions (in Listing 2).

Listing 5 shows the input parameters defined in OWL-S (lines 15 to 26). The input type "Destination" is defined as a city that is in turn defined in the OWL ontology in Listing 4 and the size is of type Volume defined in Listing 3. The output parameter costReturn is also defined as charge that is also defined in Quantity ontology (see Listing 3). Using such description, a client agent can find out that the destination is the name of a city and not a country.

We can also see the third type of parameters in OWL-S Process descriptions called Locals. Their only use is to describe semantics of the services. Local parameters are neither provided by the invoker as input to a service, nor are they being returned to the invokers as output. They may be evaluated by any other means or they may only being used in logical expressions without any value being assigned to them at run time (as in our example). Local parameters appeared in OWL-S since version 1.1.

The Local parameter in our example is defined as the city of origin (lines 35 to 40). Our example shows how the semantic service description assumes the origin of the Freight-Cost operation. This is the answer to a question that possibly appears to anyone who reads the code in Listing 1. In fact, our service provider offers the service only from London. Precondition in lines 50 to 74 shows the assumption about the origin of the Freight service taken into account when it calculates the cost. A second precondition (lines 75 to 82) states that the submitted destination must be one of the cities of Rome, Berlin or Madrid.

WSMO takes a different approach to describe functional properties. It describes Web services by two components: Interface and Capability (see Figure 4). The Web Service Interface determines the information needed for executing and interacting with the Web service. We discuss the Interface later on in subsequent sections. Here we continue with Capability; which describes the functional properties of a service by means of a set of conditions to hold before its invocation and a set of conditions that would hold after its execution.

WSMO Capability describes service functionality in terms of the following parameters:

- **Preconditions:** conditions that should hold for the information space before the Web service is performed;

- **Post-conditions:** conditions that will hold for the information space after a successful completion of the Web service;

- **Assumptions:** conditions that should hold for the state of the world before the Web service is performed; and

- **Effects:** set of conditions that will hold in the state of the world after a successful completion of the Web service.

A distinction between the information space and real world state is made by WSMO. An example of a WSMO Precondition for a service is validity of the credit card of a customer. This condition can be evaluated in the information space available to the service, for example, by checking the credit card number with another service.

An Assumption is a condition on the state of the world that would not be evaluated in the information space available to the service. An example of an Assumption is the condition on the origin of the Cost service, in our earlier example. This Assumption is not to be evaluated in the available information space. Note that, if origin was part of the service interface and could be evaluated in the information space, then it should appear as a Precondition. An Assumption can be evaluated against a request for a service. Furthermore, an intelligent invoker of a service can be informed that the service provider is assuming a condition before invoking the service. In our example, the invoker would be informed that the origin of the service is London. One can see the difference with the Precondition here. In the second OWL-S Precondition, a condition on the destination is defined. In this case the condition is defined on a value that is provided in the information space and provided by the invoker. OWL-S treats both these types of

Listing 6. WSMO capability description for the same service described in Listing 5

```
1  Namespace
2  geo: <<http://www.example.com/owl/Hi-Onto/geospatial.wsml#>>
3  quantity:
4      <<http://www.example.com/owl/Hi-Onto/Quantities.wsml#>>
5  concept:
6      <<http://www.example.com/owl-s/freight/Concepts.wsml#>>
7  dc: <<http://purl.org/dc/elements/1.1#>>
8  targetnamespace:
9      <<http://www.example.com/wsmo/freight/FreightWS#>>
10 Webservice
11     <<http://www.example.com/wsmo/freight/FreightWS.wsml>>
12 nonFunctionalProperties
13 ... [for non-functional properties see section Error! Reference source not found.]
14 endNonFunctionalProperties
15 importedOntologies {
16 <<http://www.example.com/owl/Hi-Onto/geospacial.wsml>>,
17 <<http://www.example.com/owl/Hi-Onto/Quantities.wsml>>,
18 <<http://www.example.com/owl-s/freight/Concepts.wsml>>}
19 capability freightCapability
20 precondition
21  axiom freight_precondition
22   definedBy
23    forAll ?Freight_size, ?Freight_Destination
24    (
25     ?Freight_Destination memberOf concept:Dest_city and
26     ?Freight_size memberOf quantity:volume and
27     (?Freight_Destination = berlin or
28      ?Freight_Destination = rome or
29      ?Freight_Destination = madrid
30     )
31    ).
32 postcondition
33  axiom freight_postcondition
34   definedBy
35    forAll ?Freight_costReturn
36    (
37     ?Freight_costReturn memberOf quantity:charge and
38    ).
39 assumption
40  axiom freight_assumption
41   definedBy
42    forAll ?Freight_Origin
43    (
44     ?Freight_Origin = london
45    ).
46 interface freight_Interface
47  choreography ...
48  orchestration ...
```

conditions as precondition. As we can see in Listing 5, both above conditions appear as OWL-S `Precondition`.

WSMO treats input and output type description implicitly as part of its Preconditions and Post-conditions. One can specify input or output types of a service as a constraint in WSMO Preconditions or Post-conditions, respectively. WSMO treats Local parameters also implicitly in its Capability descriptions, just as input and output type descriptions.

An example of the WSMO service description for the service description of Listing 2 is shown in Listing 6. The underlying language for WSMO is Web Service Modeling Language (WSML, 2005). At the first glance, one can see that WSML is not an XML-based language.

The Capability description for the service starts from line 19. The input and output type definitions appear in the Precondition (lines 25 and 26) and Post-condition (line 37), respectively. One can also observe how the two OWL-S `Preconditions` appear in WSMO Precondition (line 27 to 30) and Assumption (line 44).

Since OWL-S version 1.1, the collection of `Outputs` and `Effects` along with a condition is called `Result`. The `Result` binds service `Outputs` and/or `Effects` to a condition. Conditions assigned to these elements add further dynamism to the OWL-S descriptions. These conditions are introduced to describe a service that may have alternative outcomes (i.e. `Outputs` and/or `Effects`) depending on the circumstances. That is, if a service produces different output message under special conditions, a `Result` in form of combination of a condition and an output is used to describe it.

In a more complex example here, we show the difference between Effects and Post-conditions in WSMO and further clarify the conditional `Results` in OWL-S. In the following we describe a book-selling service that can have two possible alternative outcomes.

- First, a successful purchase in case the book is in stock that results in:
  - charging the credit card, i.e., WSMO Post-condition and OWL-S `Effect`; and
  - shipping the book to the customer's address, i.e., WSMO Effect and OWL-S `Effect`; and
  - sending a purchase acknowledgement to the client agent, i.e., WSMO Post-condition and OWL-S `Output`.
- Second, a successful reservation for the book when book is not in stock that results in:
  - reserving a book on the next delivery, i.e., WSMO Post-condition and OWL-S `Effect`; and
  - sending a reservation acknowledgment, i.e., WSMO Post-condition and OWL-S `Output`.

The above OWL-S `Results` will take place depending on the condition: "if the book title is in stock". OWL-S allows us to define two different sets of results under different conditions. Such conditions appear explicitly in OWL-S as a discrete part of description of Results—see Martin et al. (2004a) for example code of conditional Result. We refer to the description of the conditional Results in the later section on choreography, because in fact, it is a way of describing the massage exchange pattern in OWL-S.

Listing 7. OWL-S profile

```
1   <rdf:RDF xmlns:rdf="http://www.w3.org/1999/02/22-rdf-syntax-ns#"
2   xmlns:rdfs="http://www.w3.org/2000/01/rdf-schema#"
3   xmlns:owl="http://www.w3.org/2002/07/owl#"
4   xmlns:xsd="http://www.w3.org/2001/XMLSchema"
5   xmlns:process="http://www.daml.org/services/owl-s/1.1/Process.owl#"
6   xmlns:profile="http://www.daml.org/services/owl-s/1.1/Profile.owl#"
7   xmlns:actor=
8       "http://www.daml.org/services/owl-s/1.1/ActorDefault.owl#"
9   xml:base="http://www.example.com/owl-s/freight/Profile.owl">
10  <profile:Profile rdf:ID="Freight_Cost">
11   <profile:serviceName>
12   Freight_Cost_Calculator
13   </profile:serviceName>
14   <profile:textDescription>
15   This service claculates the cost of transporting goods
16   from London to some cities in Europe.
17   </profile:textDescription>
18   <profile:contactInformation>
19   <actor:Actor rdf:ID="customer-relation">
20    <actor:name>John Doe</actor:name>
21    <actor:title>Sales Manager</actor:title>
22    <actor:email>john.d@freight.com</actor:email>
23   </actor:Actor>
24   </profile:contactInformation>
25   <profile:serviceParameter>
26   <profile:ServiceParameter>
27   <profile:serviceParameterName
28    rdf:datatype="http://www.w3.org/2001/XMLSchema#string">
29     SomeQualityRating
30   </profile:serviceParameterName>
31   <profile:sParameter rdf:resource=
32  "http://www.example.com/owl/Hi-Onto/ServiceQuality.owl#qualityRating_Good" />
33   </profile:ServiceParameter>
34   </profile:serviceParameter>
35   <profile:hasInput>
36   <process:Input rdf:ID="Freight_destination">
37    <process:parameterType rdf:datatype=
38     "http://www.w3.org/2001/XMLSchema#anyURI">
39  http://www.example.com/owl-s/freight/Process.owl#Freight_destination
40   </process:parameterType>
41   </process:Input>
42   </profile:hasInput>
43   <profile:hasInput>
44   <process:Input rdf:ID="Freight_size">
```

Listing 7. continued

```
45   <process:parameterType rdf:datatype=
46     "http://www.w3.org/2001/XMLSchema#anyURI">
47       http://www.example.com/owl-s/freight/Concept.owl#Volume
48   </process:parameterType>
49   </process:Input>
50  </profile:hasInput>
51  <profile:hasOutput>
52   <process:Output rdf:ID="Freight_costReturn">
53    <process:parameterType rdf:datatype=
54      "http://www.w3.org/2001/XMLSchema#anyURI">
55 http://www.example.com/owl-s/freight/Process.owl#Freight_costReturn
56    </process:parameterType>
57   </process:Output>
58  </profile:hasOutput>
59 </profile:Profile>
60</rdf:RDF>
```

Listing 8. An example definition of a non-functional properties for the WSMO Web service in Listing 6

```
1   Webservice
2   <<http://www.example.com/wsmo/freight/FreightWS.wsml>>
3   nonFunctionalProperties
4     dc:title hasValue "Freight cost calculator"
5     dc:creator hasValue "Our Imaginary Freight Ltd."
6     dc:description hasValue
7       "A Web Service for calculating the freight cost from
8        London to some European cities."
9     dc:publisher hasValue
10      "DERI International"
11    dc:type hasValue <<http://www.wsmo.org/2004/d2/#webservice>>
12    dc:format hasValue "text/html"
13    dc:language hasValue "en-us"
14    dc:relation hasValues
15      {<<http://www.example.com/wsml/Hi-Onto/Quantities.wsml>>,
16       <<http://www.example.com/wsml/Hi-Onto/geospatial.wsml>>,
17       <<http://www.example.com/wsmo/freight/Concepts.wsml>>}
18    dc:coverage hasValues {tc:austria, tc:germany}
19 endNonFunctionalProperties
```

Non-Functional Properties

Apart from the properties discussed previously that directly influence the functionality of services, there are other properties that are important to describe a service. A good example is the information about the service provider, while they may be important for the service consumer, they do not affect the service functionality. Both OWL-S and WSMO provide specifications to define nonfunctional properties.

Nonfunctional properties appear in the service Profile for OWL-S (see Figure 3). There are three properties presenting the nonfunctional properties in `Profile`, namely:

- `contactInformation` provides the information for contacting individuals in charge of the service. Early versions of OWL-S provided a specific OWL class called Actor to define this information. Using Actor specification is now optional and any other specification can be used to provide the contact information—e.g., VCard. We use `Actor` in out example in Listing 7 (lines 19 to 23).

- `serviceCategory` offers the possibility of defining a service category. Here, we can define the service type in different national or international categorization scheme. Note that there is another way of defining ontological service type by building a taxonomy tree for service `Profiles`—see Martin et al. (2004a) for `ProfileHierarchy`.

- `serviceParameter` allows defining a name-value pair for extending nonfunctional parameters, that is to say adding optional parameters. We defined an imaginary quality rating parameter in our example (lines 25 to 34).

The main purpose of OWL-S `Profile` is to present information needed for registries such as UDDI and formulating service requests. As a result, `Profile` contains more than, merely, nonfunctional properties. OWL-S functional properties appear in the `Profile` as well as in the `Process` description, but only as a replication of IOPEs in the `Process`. OWL-S does not impose any constraint on the consistency of IOPEs in the `Profile` with those in the `Process` (Martin et al., 2004a). The IOPEs presented in the `Process` description is a more reliable source of knowledge, although, either one could be taken into account. In our example of a `Profile`, the first input parameter appears as a pointer to the input definition in the `Process` description (see lines 35 to 41); while the second input parameter definition points directly to the ontology file (see lines 42 to 49). We believe the former approach is good practice as it prevents inconsistencies between `Profile` and `Process` descriptions. The later practice may cause inconsistencies in case the Process description is modified without affecting the `Profile`.

The notion of nonfunctional properties has a much wider interpretation in WSMO. Nonfunctional properties are bound to most concepts in WSMO. They may be assigned not only to services but also to other component definitions such as Ontologies, Goals, etc. WSMO defines a very detailed set of nonfunctional properties that are suitable to be used by service registries (WSMO, 2004a). We show an example of such description in Listing 8 including a few of the properties.

Binding Semantics to Services

Grounding is a mechanism to assign the semantic descriptions of a service to its schematic description. We discuss only the OWL-S grounding in the following as WSMO grounding is still under development at the time of writing.

OWL-S presents two approaches for binding the `Process` description to the WSDL description. In the first approach, grounding defines the bindings between an `AtomicProcess` to an operation in a WSDL description (see Figure 5), without the need to modify the WSDL description. In the second approach, OWL-S offers an extension to the WSDL description. This extension provides the possibility of defining the bindings to the OWL-S semantic description inside the WSDL description. One may

Listing 9. Grounding descriptions for binding the semantics in Listing 5 to WSDL description in Listing 2

```
1   <rdf:RDF
2   xmlns:rdf="http://www.w3.org/1999/02/22-rdf-syntax-ns#"
3   xmlns:service="http://www.daml.org/services/owl-s/1.1/Service.owl#"
4   xmlns:grounding=
5     "http://www.daml.org/services/owl-s/1.1/Grounding.owl#"
6   xml:base="http://www.example.com/owl-s/freight/Grounding.owl">
7   <grounding:WsdlGrounding rdf:ID="WsdlGrounding">
8    <service:supportedBy rdf:resource="FreightService"/>
9    <grounding:hasAtomicProcessGrounding
10      rdf:resource="#Freight_cost_Grounding"/>
11  </grounding:WsdlGrounding>
12  <grounding:WsdlAtomicProcessGrounding
13      rdf:ID="Freight_cost_Grounding">
14    <grounding:owlsProcess rdf:resource=
15  "http://www.example.com/owl-s/freight/Process.owl#Freight_cost"/>
16    <grounding:wsdlOperation>
17     <grounding:WsdlOperationRef>
18      <grounding:portType rdf:datatype=
19        "http://www.w3.org/2001/XMLSchema#anyURI">
20        http://www.example.com/axis/WSDL/freight.wsdl#Freight
21      </grounding:portType>
22      <grounding:operation rdf:datatype=
23        "http://www.w3.org/2001/XMLSchema#anyURI">
24           cost
25      </grounding:operation>
26     </grounding:WsdlOperationRef>
27    </grounding:wsdlOperation>
28    <grounding:wsdlInputMessage rdf:datatype=
29      "http://www.w3.org/2001/XMLSchema#anyURI">
30      http://www.example.com/axis/WSDL/freight.wsdl#costRequest
31    </grounding:wsdlInputMessage>
32    <grounding:wsdlInput>
33     <grounding:WsdlInputMessageMap>
34      <grounding:owlsParameter rdf:resource=
35        "http://www.example.com/owl-s/freight/Process.owl#Freight_destination"/>
36      <grounding:wsdlMessagePart rdf:datatype=
37        "http://www.w3.org/2001/XMLSchema#anyURI">
38       http://www.example.com/axis/WSDL/freight.wsdl#destination
39      </grounding:wsdlMessagePart>
40     </grounding:WsdlInputMessageMap>
41    </grounding:wsdlInput>
42  . . .
43  </grounding:WsdlAtomicProcessGrounding>
44  </rdf:RDF>
```

Listing 10. Grounding by extension to WSDL description

```
1    <wsdl:operation name="cost"
2        owl-s-process=
3    "http://www.example.com/owl-s/freight/Process.owl#Freight_cost"
4        parameterOrder="destination size">
```

Figure 5. OWL-S Grounding relates Atomic processes to WSDL descriptions

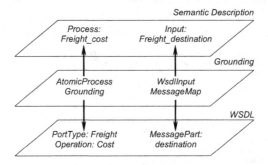

use any of the two approaches depending on the possibility of modifying the WSDL description and suitability of hard coding the bindings to the WSDL description.

Listing 9 shows the grounding for binding the semantic description of the OWL-S Process in Listing 5 to the WSDL description in Listing 2, using the first approach. Our WSDL Grounding (line 12) binds the OWL-S process "Freight_cost" (lines 14 and 15 in Listing 5) to an operation in the WSDL description (lines 16 to 25 in Listing 2). The WSDL operation is uniquely defined by its PortType (Freight) and its Operation name (cost).

The rest of the example (lines 28 to 41) shows how the destination parameter from the WSDL description is bound to the Input parameter Freight_destination in the OWL-S description.

To follow the second approach for grounding we should alter the WSDL description. For example, the operation definition in Listing 2 (lines 34 to 35) should be modified as in Listing 10—see Martin et al. (2004b) for details. Using this approach the binding to the semantic descriptions is hard-coded into the WSDL description.

Intelligent Service Discovery

In this section we describe how semantics adds value to the Web services discovery. One of the motivations of research on Semantic Web services is to improve the functionality of service registries. The goal of discovery is to find an appropriate Web service that meets certain functional and nonfunctional criteria stated by a service consumer. The most crucial issue in service discovery is to match service requests with service descriptions to find the most appropriate service or a list of services.

The discovery process can be performed either at design time or run time by a requester human using software tools (discovery service) or by a client agent (a program). The key to facilitate smarter and more flexible automation of service provision (from the perspective of providers) and use (from the perspective of requesters) is the ability to discover, select and invoke the appropriate services dynamically according to the requirements of requesters and the constraints of providers at run time.

Listing 11. Example of how an OWL-S profile may appear in UDDI data model Paolucci et al. (2002a)

```
1   <businessEntity businessKey="">
2   <name>V-Transport</name>
3   <contacts>
4    <contact useType="Sales Manager">
5     <personName>John Doe</personName>
6     <email>john.d@freight.com</email>
7    </contact>
8   </contacts>
9   <businessServices>
10  <businessService serviceKey="">
11   <name>Freight_Cost_Calculator</name>
12   <description>
13      This service claculates the cost of transporting goods
14      from London to some cities in Europe.
15   </description>
16   <categoryBag>
17    <keyedReference
18     keyValue="http://www.example.com/owl-s/freight"
19     tModelKey="[the key for OWL-S service description]"/>
20    <keyedReference keyName="Freight_size"
21     keyValue=
22      "http://www.example.com/owl-s/freight/Concept.owl#Volume"
23     tModelKey="[the key for OWL-S Profile input]"/>
24    <keyedReference
25     keyName="Freight_destination"
26     keyValue="http://www.example.com/owl-s/freight/Process.owl#Freight_destination"
27     tModelKey="[the key for OWL-S Profile input]"/>
28    <keyedReference
29     keyName="Freight_costReturn"
30     keyValue=
31      "http://www.example.com/owl/Hi-Onto/Quantities.owl#Charge"
32     tModelKey="[the key for OWL-S Profile output]"/>
33   </categoryBag>
34  </businessService>
35  </businessServices>
36 </businessEntity>
```

Discovery approaches based on WSDL/UDDI are based on keyword matching of WSDL descriptions, and businesses, services, and tModels in UDDI repository. Current UDDI specification allows publishing and discovery of service descriptions. One way of improving the functionality is to augment the service descriptions in the registry. Adding information about the semantics to the UDDI can provide richer result. For example, the UDDI registry can provide information about the input and output data types defined in an ontology. A way of augmenting service descriptions in UDDI is presented in (Paolucci, Kawamura, Payne, & Sycara, 2002a), where the OWL-S profile information is stored in UDDI registries using tModels (see section 2.3). Following our OWL-S example, we show how our `Profile` (in Listing 7) can appear in a UDDI information model in Listing 11. Using this approach a service consumer can access the OWL ontological description of the input and output types through the information stored in the UDDI. Consequently, an intelligent invoker can match the desired input and output with those of services.

Another way of improving the functionality of the registry is to enhance its discovery, rather than only augmenting the stored information and the outcome of a service. In other words, UDDI service discovery is mainly keyword-based and bringing semantics to Web services is to push the service discovery one step ahead. To that end, we need inference engines capable of interpreting semantic description of services. An intelligent matching is based on matching the input and output types as well as the preconditions and effects. Therefore, inference engines are required for interpreting logical expressions describing the service capabilities and matching them with the service requests. This issue is indeed the most important step at present and attracts much research.

There are two main approaches to make use of inference engines; first by adding intelligent matching functionalities to the existing registries. The OWL-S community made an effort to bring such intelligent matching functionalities to UDDI (Paolucci et al., 2002a, 2002b). The second approach is to implement a registry on top of an inference engine. A good example of this approach is the Internet Reasoning System (IRS-III; Domingue, Cabral, Hakimpour, Sell, & Motta, 2004). IRS-III is built on top of an inference engine and implemented intelligent service matching capabilities for WSMO specifications.

As the service matching becomes more complex the service request itself becomes a discrete topic. A specification for service request is to enable a client agent to express its need without the need to determine the implementation details. That is, it should allow us to define a set of requirements free from details present in description of services. Again, OWL-S and WSMO have different approaches to perceive a service request. In OWL-S, `Profile` is seen not only as a collection of information for the registries but also as a template for expressing a service request. A request for a transport consulting service that produces charges by receiving a city origin, a city of destination and the size is presented in Listing 12.

Paolucci et al. (2002a, 2002b) show how matching for services are performed for OWL-S service descriptions. The service request in Listing 12 can be performed by existing OWL-S tools. In Listing 13, we show how the request in Listing 12 can be coded in Java using the OWL-S Matchmaker tool (Paolucci et al., 2002a; details of the API at http://www.daml.ri.cmu.edu/ matchmaker/). Note that the existing tools offer only partial support for matching the OWL-S service descriptions.

Listing 12. Simplified example of a service request Profile

```
1   <profile:Profile rdf:ID="Transport_Consulting_Service_Request">
2   <profile:hasInput>
3    <process:Input rdf:ID="Origin">
4     <process:parameterType>
5     http://www.example.com/owl/Hi-Onto/geospatial.owl#City
6     </process:parameterType>
7    </process:Input>
8   </profile:hasInput>
9   <profile:hasInput>
10   <process:Input rdf:ID="Destination">
11    <process:parameterType>
12     http://www.example.com/owl/Hi-Onto/geospatial.owl#City
13    </process:parameterType>
14   </process:Input>
15  </profile:hasInput>
16  <profile:hasInput>
17   <process:Input rdf:ID="size">
18    <process:parameterType>
19     http://www.example.com/owl/Hi-Onto/Quantities.owl#Volume
20    </process:parameterType>
21   </process:Input>
22  </profile:hasInput>
23  <profile:hasInput>
24   <process:Input rdf:ID="Cost">
25    <process:parameterType>
26     http://www.example.com/owl/Hi-Onto/Quantities.owl#Charge
27    </process:parameterType>
28   </process:Input>
29  </profile:hasInput>
30  <profile:serviceCategory>
31   <addParam:NAICS rdf:ID="NAICS-category">
32    <profile:value>Freight Consulting Services</profile:value>
33    <profile:code>541614</profile:code>
34   </addParam:NAICS>
35  </profile:serviceCategory>
36 </profile:Profile>
```

Requests for services in WSMO appear in form of Goals. Notion of Goal has a root in knowledge representation domain—see *Task* (Omelayenko et al., 2000). Capability descriptions appear in both WSMO Goal and WSMO Web service (WSMO, 2004a). In the WSMO service description, Capability determines the provided service and in a Goal it specifies the desired service. WSMO perceives a Goal as a generic problem definition that many different Web services can offer solutions for. A notable difference between the Goals and profiles is that Goals are by definition invocable unlike profiles that can only be used to formulate requests. When a WSMO Goal is invoked, the discovery process finds suitable Web service descriptions and may execute the corresponding service. To see the difference we show an example Java code from IRS-III (Domingue et al., 2004) in Listing 14.

Listing 13. Simplified example of an intelligent discovery based on OWL-S Matchmaker

```
1  //Defining the inputs and outputs types.
2  CapabilitySearch srch = new CapabilitySearch();
3  srch.addInput(
4     "http://www.example.com/owl/Hi-Onto/geospatial.owl#City");
5  srch.addInput(
6     "http://www.example.com/owl/Hi-Onto/geospatial.owl#City");
7  srch.addInput(
8     "http://www.example.com/owl/Hi-Onto/Quantities.owl#Volume");
9  srch.addOutput(
10    "http://www.example.com/owl/Hi-Onto/Quantities.owl#Charge");
11 //Seaching for the service.
12 OWLSMatchmakerClient mc;
13 mc = new OWLSMatchmakerClient();
14 MatchmakerResultList mrl = mc.query(srch);
15 If (mrl.size > 1) {
16   MatchmakerResult mr = mrl.get(int i);
17   String uddiKey = mr.getUddiKey();
18 //uddiKey can be used for invokation by the Web Services technology.
19 } //else: no suitable service found;
```

Listing 14. Simplified example of an intelligent discovery and invocation based on WSMO by IRS-III

```
1  // Defining Inputs and the output types.
2  goalInputTypes.add(new GoalRole("origin", "City"));
3  goalInputTypes.add(new GoalRole("destination", "City"));
4  goalInputTypes.add(new GoalRole("size", "Volume"));
5  GoalRole goalOutputType = new GoalRole("cost","Charge");
6  // Creating the Goal
7  Goal goal = new Goal(
8          nonFunctionalProperties,
9          goalInputTypes,
10         goalOutputType,
11         goalUsedMediators,
12         goalPostcondition,
13         goalEffect);
14 . . .
15 Colume vol = new Volume (3, "QubicMeter")
16 // Defining the actual input values for invocation.
17 achieveGoalInputValues.add( new
18              AchieveGoalInput("origin", "London"));
19 achieveGoalInputValues.add( new
20              AchieveGoalInput("destination", "Paris"));
21 achieveGoalInputValues.add( new
22              AchieveGoalInput("size", vol);
23 // invoking the service.
24 String response6 = irsServer.achieveGoal(goal, achieveGoalInputs);
```

An example of a service request can illustrate the dynamism required in a complex case of an intelligent discovery and show where the Semantic Web services technology is heading. In the following we present two Goals:

- **Goal1:** buying a computer printer.
- **Goal2:** buying a HP Color LaserJet printer model: 2550 for a price less than £450.

In the description of the Goal1, the information: "buying a printer" is typically used by discovery mechanism to find a service. Such constraint is evaluated to find a service and satisfied before the service is invoked. However, constraints such as price and printer model, in Goal2, are typically inputs to perform an instance of a service. That is, in response to Goal2 the discovery mechanism finds services selling computer peripherals as well as those selling HP products; and execution mechanism finds the desired printer by executing the service. WSMO Goal descriptions allow a user to describe her desire freely with no consideration of what information is used by discovery and what is used by the execution mechanism. It is the discovery and execution mechanisms that extract the relevant information from a Goal.

Furthermore, WSMO offers the specification to describe the reduction of a generic goal (e.g., Goal1) to a more specific Goal or a sub-Goal (e.g. Goal2) by means of ggMediators. WSMO (2004b) presents a set of detailed thorough examples.

Mediators

The notion of Mediator is specific to WSMO and it is one of its fundamental components. Mediator descriptions may be seen as a wrapper for a Web service or a Goal that its objective is mediation. This wrapper keeps particular descriptions specific to a Mediator. All Mediators in WSMO are in fact Web services; however, WSMO allows further semantics assigned to such mediation services. OWL-S services may describe mediators but no specific semantics is assigned to such services. That is, one can define a Web

Figure 6. Different types of mediators in WSMO

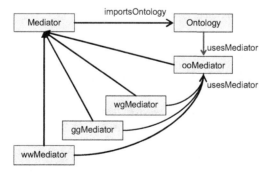

service to perform mediation without explicitly describing it as a mediator and vise versa; we cannot simply distinguish mediators from services by their OWL-S descriptions.

WSMO Mediators keep the following information:

- **Mediation Service:** a Goal or a Web service to perform the mediation,
- **Source:** the entity providing inputs to the mediator,
- **Target:** where the result of the mediation will be provided to.

Different types of mediators are seen to mediate data or ontology in interaction between different components. Four types of Mediators (WSMO, 2004a) are introduced by WSMO as following (see Figure 6):

- wgMediator mediates Web services to Goals. This mediator represents mediation between a Web service and a Goal type that it fulfills. For example, different Web services fulfilling Goal1 in the last section can have different mediators to mediate between the Web service and the Goal1. As a result all Goals specializing Goal1 can use the same dediators.
- ggMediator mediates between two Goals. This mediator represents the reduction of the source Goal description into the target Goal.
- wwMediator mediates the information between two Web services.
- ooMediator imports ontologies, resolve possible terminology mismatches and find mappings between ontologies—ooMediators are not meant to resolve syntactic mismatches (WSMO, 2004b). This mediator type can be used by the other three types of mediators to resolve ontological mismatches in the description of their source and target entities.

Another important use of WSMO mediators are in service compositions where we can use mediators to mediate between the component services of a composition. OWL-S only allows direct data bindings between component services and any mediator would appear as a distinct service component in the composition. As OWL-S does not distinguish between Web services and mediators, it is not a straight forward process to correspond an OWL-S service description to a WSMO Mediator.

Service Composition

Reusability is a characteristic of Web services that makes them suitable for building composite Web services. A composed service is a more complex service that is built by combining existing services. Web service composition attracted much attention in domain of Semantic Web services and artificial intelligence (Sirin, Hendler, & Parsia, 2003; Sirin, Parsia, & Hendler, 2004; Ponnekanti & Fox, 2002), particularly research on automatic service composition. For example, service composition has also been addressed in domain of Web services—e.g., BPEL4WS (IBM, 2003). Nevertheless, this section focuses mainly on issues related to OWL-S composition models as well as existing WSMO Orchestration model (WSMO, 2005).

Automatic service composition can be considered from two different points of view. The first perspective concentrates on developing the design time tools. The objective is to build intelligent tools to help composition designer. Sirin et al. (2004) and Sell, Hakimpour, Domingue, Motta, and Pacheco (2004) show examples of such tools. These tools help the designer by matching input or output types of services in the composition with those in a repository and suggest suitable services to the composition designer. The second pint of view is to build a composition automatically on the fly. In an extremely ideal perspective a request for a service can result in building a new composition of the existing services that satisfies the request. The current technology allows us to build template composition that their components can be decided and invoked at the execution time. Both OWL-S and WSMO present the necessary features in their specification to define such templates. These templates consist of components that can result in a discovery process. As we show in our example in the next section, OWL-S `SimpleProcess` (as well as WSMO Goals) can play the role of such components.

Composition Modeling

To build a service composition, we need (1) a mechanism to describe the order of execution, which is known as *control flow*; (2) a mechanism to describe exchange of data, which is known as *data flow*. The control flow mechanism offers the possibility of performing alternative services based on conditions, repetition and so on. The data flow mechanism should be expressive enough to describe exchange of data among the component services in the composite service, as well as between the component services and the invoker. In the following we describe the composition model in OWL-S with a brief look into the WSMO composition model.

OWL-S `Process` is classified in three subclasses: `AtomicProcess`, `CompositeProcess` and `SimpleProcess` (see Figure 7). An `AtomicProcess`

Figure 7. Types of OWL-S process

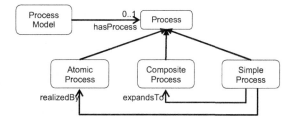

Listing 15. A simplified example of a composed service for ordering a freight service

```
1   <process:CompositeProcess rdf:ID="Freight_Process">
2   <!—IOPE definitions-->
3   . . .
4   <process:composedOf>
5    <process:Sequence>
6     <process:Components>
7      <process:Perform>
8       <process:AtomicProcess rdf:resource="#Freight_Cost"/>
9      </process:Perform>
10     <process:Perform>
11      <process:AtomicProcess rdf:resource="#Credit_Card_Input"/>
12     </process:Perform>
13     <process:Perform>
14      <process:SimpleProcess rdf:resource="#Validate_Card"/>
15     </process:Perform>
16     <process:If-Then-Else>
17      <process:ifCondition>
18       <expr:SWRL-Condition>
19        [SWRL condition: If the credt information is valid?]
20       </expr:SWRL-Condition>
21      </process:ifCondition>
22      <process:then>
23       <process:Perform>
24        <process:AtomicProcess rdf:resource="#Accept_Order"/>
25       </process:Perform>
26      </process:then>
27     </process:If-Then-Else>
28    </process:Components>
29   </process:Sequence>
30  </process:composedOf>
31 </process:CompositeProcess>
```

is, in fact, a stateless service that receives a set of inputs to start the process and produces a set of outputs after it is executed. A `CompositeProcess` is composed of component `Processes`. As a result, a `CompositeProcess` can be stateful (Foster et al., 2004). In other words, it may accept inputs and produce output messages at different stages during its execution. The `SimpleProcess` is not directly executable. It is an abstract description of a process that can be realized and performed by any of the other two types of processes.

OWL-S description of the control flow is based on a set of `ControlConstructs`, such as a `Sequence`, `IfThenElse`, `Concurrent`, etc., to describe the control flow. It follows the structured design paradigm—similar to that of BPEL4WS (IBM, 2003). Every `ControlConstruct` is composed of a set of other constructs or processes. A simplified example of OWL-S service composition is presented in Listing 15. The Process is composed of four components, as follows. First service estimates the cost of transport. Then another service receives the credit card information. Third service validates the credit information. Finally, *if* the credit information is valid according to the third service the order is placed. The third process in the example is a `SimpleProcess` that would

Listing 16. An example of data binding in OWL-S CompositProcess

```
1      <process:Perform>
2       <process:AtomicProcess rdf:resource="#Accept_Order"/>
3       <process:hasDataFrom>
4        <process:InputBinding>
5         <process:toParam rdf:resource="#estimated_charge" />
6         <process:valueSource>
7          <process:ValueOf>
8           <process:theVar rdf:resource="#Freight_costReturn"/>
9           <process:fromProcess rdf:resource=
10     "http://www.example.com/owl-s/freight/Process.owl#Freight_cost"/>
11          </process:ValueOf>
12         </process:valueSource>
13        </process:InputBinding>
14       </process:hasDataFrom>
15      <process:Perform>
```

be assigned to a concrete (executable) processes at run time. Finding a concrete process by the execution mechanism is, in fact, a services discovery process. This discovery process can be guided by exploring the realizedBy and expandsTo links (in Figure 7) to find the concrete processes.

OWL-S defines the SimpleProcess as a process with a higher level of abstraction (Martin et al., 2004a). This is, indeed, a similar characteristic of Goals and SimpleProcesses. In practice, using a Goal or a SimpleProcess can trigger a discovery mechanism. As shown in Listing 15, this is the main role of the Validate_Card in our example. The use of a SimpleProcess as a component in the composition provides a useful level of dynamism. In such cases, a desired service is to be discovered at the execution time.

Furthermore, OWL-S provides the means to define data bindings between the component processes. For example, would like to bind the Freight_costReturn output from the Freight_cost service (see Listing 5), to an input of the Accept_Order service called estimated_charge. To define this binding, the code between lines 23 and 25 (in Listing 15) is rewritten in Listing 16.

In WSMO, description of service compositions appears in the Interface. The Web Service Interface determines the information needed for executing and interacting with the Web Service. Interface descriptions in WSMO have two major parts namely Choreography and Orchestration. Choreography describes the pattern of interaction with the Web service. We introduce the Choreography in the next section. For a composite service, Orchestration presents a description of composition of Goals or Web services. It is to provide the necessary details for the execution of all the component services in a composition.

WSMO model for describing composition is still under development (WSMO, 2005). However, one can immediately notice a difference between the two specifications; WSMO has only one type of service descriptions as compared to three different types of processes in OWL-S. The general idea of distinction between data flow and control flow is already described in the available documents.

WSMO Mediators also play an important role in WSMO data flow. The data flow in WSMO composition can be defined by Mediators (Hakimpour, Sell, Cabral, Domingue, & Motta, 2005). Unlike the static binding shown in Listing 16, WSMO allows using a Mediator in bindings, in other words, for changing the currency of the Freight_costReturn. Furthermore, one can use WSMO Goals similar to OWL-S SimpleProcess for building dynamic composition. Using Goals in the compositions triggers the discovery process and invocation of the result at the execution time (Hakimpour et al., 2005).

A difference between the two descriptions is that WSMO has only one type of Web service and it does not distinguish a composite service from an atomic one, as opposed to OWL-S Process model. WSMO keeps the composition description as part of its Interface description (see Figure 4). It is one of the basic ideas in WSMO descriptions to hide execution complications from the service consumer. In fact in extreme cases, the Orchestration can be a proprietary piece of knowledge for the provider, and therefore, not accessible to others including the client agent. Yet, it is important for a client to know if the service is stateful or stateless; or how to interact with a service. That piece of knowledge is provided in the WSMO Choreography. The service consumer can obtain the information needed to interact with the service by accessing the Choreography, with no need for the details of the composition.

Choreography in Interaction with Web Services

Interaction with stateless Web services requires the information that can be found in an interface description such as WSDL. However, the interaction with stateful (Foster et. al., 2004) services, such as most composite services, requires more information than that can be provided by WSDL. A stateful service may receive input messages after it is started and produces output messages before it is finished. An intelligent invoker or a programmer should be ultimately able to gain the knowledge of how to interact with a stateful Web service.

Choreography determines the pattern of messages exchanged between services (also called business protocol). Two major parts of choreography are the specification of the message types and their order. World Wide Web Consortium (W3C) recommends a model for choreography (W3C, 2004c) that defines three levels for choreography descriptions. The most abstract level contains the same two parts, message types and the message order. Other parts of the choreography descriptions defined by W3C (2004c), such as messages structures, endpoints, used technologies appear only in other levels, neither are they the concern of Semantic Web services technologies. In fact, such information can be obtained through the grounding mechanisms in both WSMO and OWL-S.

WSMO describes the information required to interact with a Web service in a discrete part. Choreography appears as part of the Web Service Interface definition in WSMO (2005). That is, one would not need to access information in the Web service composition to extract the information about exchange of the messages with the service. Since a composition may include far more information needed for the service consumer or composition description may be a private property of the service provider.

Whilst Choreography has been addressed by WSMO, OWL-S does not represent such notion in its specification, yet. However, the information about Web service choreography is embedded in the OWL-S descriptions. Service consumer may extract the information about the pattern of message exchange with a service by referring to the `Result` and the composition descriptions of an OWL-S `Process`.

Finally, it is important to note that in spite of the similarity in description of the Choreography in WSMO (2005) and W3C (2004b); there is major difference in their perspective. WSMO (2005) presents the Choreography for a type of Web services, that is, a specification for defining the interaction for Web services. Alternatively, W3C (2004b) presents a language to describe protocols for interaction between businesses and are not meant to present a Web Service Interface. Several business partners may take part in a W3C choreography by assuming the *role*s in the description and perform the relevant activities.

Summary and Future Work

Semantic Web offers a promising approach to overcome some of the shortages or loopholes of today's Web services technologies. Particularly the service description and subsequently the discovery of Web services can be improved by using Semantic Web services technologies. Furthermore, Semantic Web services present specifications for semantic description of composed services as well as facilitating automatic composition of services. Semantic Web services enhances Web service by semantic descriptions that can be related to the existing schematic specifications offered by today's Web service standards (i.e., WSDL, UDDI).

Semantic Web services provide following enhancements of Web services descriptions:

- Information that contribute to the semantic description of Web services:
  - **Input and output parameters:** definition of the semantics of data in input and output messages using ontologies.
  - **Capability conditions:** describing services by defining conditions before and after service execution.
  - **Service type:** definition of the type of service type either using existing standards for service categorization or using existing potentials in ontologies.
  - **Nonfunctional properties:** definition of other relevant information such as service provider and quality of services.
- Grounding of semantic descriptions relates the semantic descriptions to schematic description of services such as WSDL descriptions.
- Intelligent registries are an ultimate goal of Semantic Web services technology. Intelligent registries provide the possibility:
  - To store the semantic information for service consumers. This information then helps the client agent to have an error free interaction with the Web service.

- ○ To improve their service matching functionalities from a keyword-based search to semantic based search.
- Semantic Web services present ontological description of a composed service as well as facilitating automatic composition of services.

The last two topics, namely intelligent registries and automatic composition, although explored to an extent, still demand much further research.

These improvements result not only in an enhanced description of Web services but also in enrichment of formulating service requests. Eventually, the improvements lead to more intelligent Web service registries that are the ultimate goal of Semantic Web service technologies. Intelligent registries will allow:

- The storage of the semantic information for service consumers which can help a client agent to have an error free interaction with the Web service.
- An improvement of the Web service matching functionalities from a keyword-based search to semantic based search.

We explore the two major Semantic Web service specifications, OWL-S and WSMO, in this chapter. We show the similarities and the differences of the two standards as wells as their contribution to facilitate Web service discovery and invocation.

Whether Semantic Web services technologies and the above specifications will be accepted in the industry or not depends on the usability and the availability of the appropriate tools. Here we identify the tools needed for applying this technology.

- **Semantic description generator:** The first step is to automatically generate semantic descriptions from available documents. There are a few tools at the moment to generate a skeleton for OWL-S descriptions. Such tools can generate a template OWL-S service description (i.e. `Profile`, `Process` and `Grounding`) from WSDL files or JAVA classes. The descriptions should be modified and further information added to them to present the semantics of services.
- **Editing tools:** Tools to generate, modify and validate semantic descriptions are needed. These tools are used to add further semantics to the template descriptions generated by tools explained above. There are several tools available for both OWL-S and WSMO.
- **Registration and browsing:** After building complete and valid semantic descriptions for services we can store the semantic descriptions in existing registries and then retrieve the semantic information. OWL-S presents such tool for UDDI registries. At the moment WSMO descriptions can be stored and browsed in specific WSMO registries.
- **Discovery:** Both OWL-S and WSMO present repositories with enhanced match making functionality. OWL-S community developed tools integrated with UDDI

and WSMO present such functionalities on top of inference engines (at the time of writing).

- **Composition tools:** Composition tools that can help composers in a semiautomatic way have also been available. These tools can help composers to build the composition by matching the capabilities of the services.

Information about OWL-S tools can be found on: www.daml.ri.cmu.edu/tools/details.html, www.daml.org/services/ owl-s/tools.html or www.mindswap.org/2004/owl-s. Information about WSMO tools can be found at www.wsmo.org/ wsmo_tools.html.

In this chapter, we introduce most of the existing features in the specifications, while the above tools neither exploit all the features nor offer all the corresponding functionalities, at the moment. One important example of such lack of support is in discovery tools. The existing discovery tools match inputs and outputs types, but they do not offer a complete support for matching of preconditions and effects. There is still much work required for development of suitable tools in order to make use of all the aspects of existing specifications, which may in turn result in further enrichment of the specifications.

While a large amount of research work focuses on defining, exchanging, and processing standard descriptions of Web services at communication and semantic levels, there is still need for more research work on the specifications for the description of the business policies and regulations. It is very important for both the service requesters and providers to communicate and negotiate to set up commercial relationships in order to use services commercially and legally in business applications. For example, a provider may stipulate different payment models for different service usages.

One of the ultimate goals of Semantic Web services technology is to improve the business negotiation that precedes the actual invocation of Web services. Semantic Web services can potentially facilitate (1) informed decisions during the business negotiation and (2) automatic (or semiautomatic) binding of suitable Web services based on business negotiations. Use of Semantic Web service descriptions in business negotiations is a major future challenge.

Note

At the time of writing, the chapter authors were unaware of the work on WSDL-S. Please consult http://www.w3.org/Submission/WSDL-S/ for information regarding this work.

References

Alonso, G., Casati, F., Kuno, H., & Machiraju, V. (2004). *Web services: Concepts, architectures and applications.* Springer-Verlag.

Berners-Lee, T. (2002). *Web services*. Retrieved from http://www.w3.org/ DesignIssues/ WebServices.html

Berners-Lee, T., Hendler, J., & Lassila, O. (2001, May). The Semantic Web. *Scientific American*.

Decker, S., Melnik, S., Harmelen, F. V., Fensel, D., Klein, M., & Broekstra, J., et al. (2000). The semantic web: The roles of XML and RDF. *IEEE Internet computing, 4*(5), 63-74.

Domingue, J., Cabral, L., Hakimpour, F., Sell, D., & Motta, E. (2004). IRS-III: A platform and infrastructure for creating WSMO-based semantic web services. In *Proceedings of the Workshop on WSMO Implementations*, Open University, UK. Retrieved from http://www.iswc2004.semanticweb.org/demos/45/paper.pdf

Dong, X., Halevy, A., Madhavan, J., Nemes, E., & Zhang, J. (2004, August 31-September 3). Similarity search for web services. In *Proceedings of 30th International Conference on Very Large Databases* (VLDB Conference), Toronto, Canada. St. Louis, MO: Morgan Kaufmann Publishers.

Foster, I., Frey, J., Graham, S., Tuecke, S., Czajkowski, K., & Ferguson, D., et al. (2004). *Modeling stateful resources with web services*. Retrieved from http://www-106.ibm.com/developerworks/library/ws-resource/ws-modelingresources.pdf

Guarino, N. (Ed.). (1998). *Formal ontology in information systems*. IOS Press.

Hakimpour, F., Sell, D., Cabrall, L., Domingue, J., & Motta, E. (2005). Semantic Web service composition in IRS-III: The structured approach. In *Proceedings of the 7th International IEEE Conference on E-Commerce Technology (IEEE CEC '05)* (pp. 484-487).

IBM Corporation (2003). *Business process execution language for web services*. Retrieved from http://www-128.ibm.com/developerworks/library/specifications/ws-bpel/

Martin, D., Burstein, M., Hobbs, J., Lassila, O., McDermott, D., & McIlraith, S., et al. (2004a). *OWL-S: Semantic markup for web services*. Retrieved from http:// www.daml.org/ services/owl-s/1.1/overview/

Martin, D., Burstein, M., Lassila, O., Paolucci, M., Payne, T., & McIlraith, S. (2004b). *Describing Web Services using OWL-S and WSDL*. Retrieved from http:// www.daml.org/services/owl-s/1.1/owl-s-wsdl.html

McGuinness, D. L., & Harmelen, F. V. (Eds.). (2004). *OWL web ontology language overview*. Retrieved from http://www.w3.org/ TR/owl-features/

McIlraith, S. A., Son, T. C., & Zeng, H. (2001). Semantic web services. *IEEE Intelligent Systems, 16*(2), 46-63.

OASIS (2004). UDDI specifications, Version 3. Retrieved from http://uddi.org/pubs/ uddi_v3.htm

Omelayenko, B., Crubézy, M., Fensel, D., Ding, Y., Motta, E., & Musen, M. (2000). *Meta data and UPML*. UPML Version 2.0. Retrieved from http://www.cs.vu.nl/~upml/ upml2.0.pdf

Paolucci, M., Kawamura, T., Payne T. R., & Sycara, K. (2002a). Importing the semantic web in UDDI, WES 2002, Springer-Verlag, LNCS 2512, 225–236.

Paolucci, M., Kawamura, T., Payne T. R., & Sycara, K. (2002b). Semantic matching of web services capabilities. In *Proceedings of the 1st International Semantic Web Conference (ISWC'02)* (pp. 333-347).

Ponnekanti, S. R., & Fox, A. (2002). SWORD: A developer toolkit for web service composition. In *Proceedings of the 11th International World Wide Web Conference* (WWW2002). USA.

Sell, D., Hakimpour, F., Domingue, J., Motta E., & Pacheco, R. C. S. (2004). Interactive composition of WSMO-based semantic web services in IRS-III. *AKT Workshop on Semantic Web Services.*

Sirin, E., Hendler, J., & Parsia, B. (2003). Semi-automatic composition of web services using semantic descriptions. In *Proceedings of the Workshop on Web Services: Modeling, Architecture and Infrastructure, in the 5th International Conference on Enterprise Information Systems* (ICEIS-2003), France.

Sirin, E., Parsia, B., & Hendler, J. (2004). Filtering and selecting Semantic Web Services with interactive composition techniques. *IEEE Intelligent Systems, 19*(4), 42-49.

Sycara, K., Paolucci, M., Ankolekar, A., & Srinivasan, N. (2003). Automated discovery, interaction and composition of semantic web services. *Journal of Web Semantics, 1*(1).

W3C (2003). *SOAP Version 1.2 Part 1: Messaging framework.* Retrieved from http://www.w3.org/TR/soap12/

W3C (2004a). *Web services architecture.* Retrieved from http://www.w3.org/TR/ws-arch/

W3C (2004b). *Web services choreography description language.* Retrieved from http://www.w3c.org/TR/ws-cdl-10/

W3C (2004c). *Web services choreography model overview.* Retrieved from http://www.w3.org/TR/ws-chor-model/

W3C (2004c). *XML Schema Part 0: Primer second edition.* Retrieved from http://www.w3.org/TR/xmlschema-0/

W3C (2005). *Web services description language (WSDL) Version 2.0 Part 1: Core Language.* Retrieved from http://www.w3.org/TR/wsdl20/

WSML (2005). *Web service modeling language.* Retrieved from http://www.wsmo.org/TR/d16/

WSMO (2004a). *Web Service Modeling Ontology–Standard. Deliverable 2, version 1.0.* Retrieved from http://www.wsmo.org/ 2004/d2/

WSMO (2004b). *WSMO Use Case: Virtual Travel Agency. Deliverable 3, version 0.1.* Retrieved from http://www.wsmo.org/ 2004/d3/d3.3/

WSMO (2005). *Ontology-based Choreography and Orchestration of WSMO Services.* Deliverable 14, Version 0.2. Retrieved from http://www.wsmo.org/2004/d14/

Chapter III

Developing Intelligent Semantic Web Services

Sam Lee, Texas State University - San Marcos, USA

Abstract

This chapter introduces an approach to the development of intelligent Semantic Web services, which are envisioned as system cells that actively discover, learn, and communicate knowledge on the Web. The development of these systems often involves not only standardized Web technology, but also the integration of heterogeneous information. The approach in this chapter adopts the Semantic Web services specifications that are given by the DARPA agent markup language (DAML) program, utilizes a system behavior model to represent an intelligent agent, and proposes a high degree of automatic synthesis using code generation and program templates. The author reviews the various techniques that are available to aid the development process, and provides an example to illustrate the stages of software synthesis in the development of such systems.

Introduction

Intelligent Semantic Web services are envisioned as system cells that actively discover, learn, and communicate knowledge on the Web. Semantic Web services are intelligent in the sense that they are agents that act in the Web environment. An agent is anything that can perceive its environment through sensors and act upon its environment through effectors (Russell & Norvig, 1995; Nilsson, 1995). With the well-established artificial intelligence theories and techniques for the development of intelligent content, the emergent Semantic Web service specifications provide opportunities for the large-scale and reliable collaboration of Web agents in intelligent information systems.

A coalition of researchers is currently developing standardized Semantic Web services. Spearheading these efforts is the DARPA agent markup language DAML program (www.daml.org), which has released several versions of a semantic markup language for Web services (DAML-S) since 2001. Researchers in the artificial intelligence community have proposed DAML-S extensions that turn Web services into agents with behavioral intelligence (Bryson, Martin, McIlraith, & Stein, 2002). After version 1.0, DAML-S was renamed OWL-S, as it is built on the ontology Web language (OWL) that was produced by the Web-Ontology Working Group at the World Wide Web Consortium (DAML, 2003; W3C, 2004).

Modeling is useful for building and maintaining intelligent Semantic Web services for business information systems. The author believes that the development approach to these systems should be based on the use of agent-oriented models that describe the behavior of Web services at a high level of abstraction. The final implementation should be made using code generation and code templates that enable the automation of software synthesis from this high level of abstraction as far as is possible. The implementation of these systems should utilize the Semantic Web as the universal platform to aid the integration of Web services and intelligent agents.

This chapter investigates the specifications for Semantic Web services, which are the foundations for building intelligent Web applications. A significant part of the design of such applications is focused on the interconnection of the services, and inside these services agents often determine reactions to incoming knowledge. In this chapter, an approach is suggested for weaving agents into the Semantic Web. An example will be demonstrated that uses parts of the event-driven customer relationship management system that was devised by Chiu et al. (2003).

The remainder of this chapter is organized as follows: the next section gives an introduction to Semantic Web service specifications. The following section discusses intelligent agent modeling. An approach to agent software synthesis on the Web is presented next. Then, an example of an intelligent Semantic Web service is given, and finally the conclusion of the chapter.

Semantic Web Service Specification

Efforts toward the creation of a Semantic Web are gaining momentum (W3C, 2004). W3C states on its Web site that "in February 2004, the World Wide Web Consortium released the resource description framework (RDF) and the Web ontology language (OWL) as W3C Recommendations. RDF is used to represent information and to exchange knowledge in the Web. OWL is used to publish and share sets of terms called ontologies, supporting advanced Web search, software agents and knowledge management." The Semantic Web is an answer to the increasing complexity of systems development in Web computing environments. More and more Web sites not only provide static information, but also services that are capable of performing tasks, and therefore applications can be integrated using the services in a distributed network. OWL is a fundamental tool that is designed to define an unambiguous, machine-comprehensible form for the interpretation of Web services on the Semantic Web.

A Semantic Web service operates as a process (DAML, 2003). The process can be triggered from an event input by outside users, and a response with a set of outputs is then delivered. The states of the process are maintained to determine the effects that generate the responses. For a complex service, the process can be composed of many subprocesses that are executed serially or simultaneously.

Process

In general, a process produces a set of inputs from a set of inputs to a set of outputs and a transition from one state to another, where the transition is defined by the preconditions and effects of the process. A process has several properties. Inputs specify the data that is used to activate the process operations, and the process receives inputs through its networked information environments. Output is the data that is generated by the operations, which is sent to other processes or other Web services. Precondition defines the conditions that must be checked before the operations are performed. Effect is the result of the operations. Performing an operation may result in different effects, the outputs of which are specified accordingly. For example, the results of a book ordering process vary, in that the success and failure effects may cause the outputs of order confirmation and out-of-stock notification, respectively.

The OWL-S 1.0 process model identifies atomic and composite processes. The basic elements of the processes are atomic processes that directly connect to Web services. An atomic process must be executed in a single step and be associated with a grounding definition that enables the service requester to construct input or output messages. The composite processes are decomposable into subprocesses (atomic processes or other composite processes), which must include a control construct. The decomposition is defined by flow control components, such as sequences, if/else selection, and repeat/until. The current process model provides a limited mechanism for relating the inputs and outputs of the control components to the parameters of other process components.

Grounding

A grounding can be considered to be the mapping from conceptual process models to physical Web service definition elements. In particular, it specifies how to communicate with Web services by messages, transport protocols, and addressing. OWL-S makes uses of the Web services description language (WSDL) to define the message format that is required to transmit messages.

WSDL documents contain a Header section for namespaces, a Service Schema section that defines the element types, a Message section for element Request and Response mapping, a Port Type section that defines end points for services, a Binding definition for input and output parameters, and a Security declaration (Venkatraman, *2004*).

The binding determines the transport protocol in the communication network. Simple object access protocol (SOAP) has been with hypertext transfer protocol (HTTP), because it provides a high degree of interoperability. On today's Web, information is transmitted based on HTTP requests and responses, and browsers are built to display HTTP-formatted data. SOAP is designed for the sending or receiving of messages between software objects that reside in heterogeneous information systems. SOAP defines the messages in extended markup language (XML) format, which is easily embedded into the requests or responses in the HTTP communication channels.

Advanced object-oriented applications are often developed using events to trigger system functions, for which the synchronous request/response model is inadequate. Web service standards are still evolving in the area of asynchronous transport, and currently SOAP over Java message service (JMS) binding can be used to implement asynchronous event-based communication. However, the bindings that are used by all implementations, including WebSphere, are currently proprietary (Endrei et al., 2004).

Intelligent Agent Modeling

The agent-oriented approach to building the Semantic Web views a system as a collection of agents, and emphasizes that the Web is about services (Bryson et al., 2002). Services are a form of behavior. According to the Turing Test, behavior is the fundamental attribute of intelligence.

Agent Services

The OWL-S specifications draw upon emerging standards in process and workflow technology, such as the workflow management coalition effort (www.aiim.org/wfmc). However, the focus of the OWL-S process is on agent services, rather than business workflows. Agent services and business workflows can both be modeled as processes, but there are essential differences between them, and researchers that are involved in agent research have offered a variety of definitions (Franklin & Graesser, 1996). The following discussion focuses on the differences between the models of agent services and workflows that are the automation of business processes.

A major difference between agents and workflows is their autonomy. An agent should be able to act without the direct intervention of humans (or others agents), and should have control over its own actions and internal state (Jennings, Sycara, & Wooldridge, 1998). A workflow typically requires human participants to play business roles.

Reactivity is another major difference between the two process models. Pattie Maes (Maes, 1995), who is one of the pioneers of agent research, states that "autonomous agents are computational systems that inhabit some complex dynamic environment, sense and act autonomously in this environment and by doing so realize a set of goals or tasks for which they are designed." The computational environments of agents are dynamic, and their models need to have well-defined input/output parameters so that they can act reactively and continuously according to their programmed logics. In contrast, workflow modeling can be viewed as the realization of paths for networking activities to achieve business goals. Therefore, appropriate methods can be developed to effectively evaluate network performance and verify the correctness of models (Son, Kim, & Kim, 2005).

The final difference between agents and workflows is that agent services put more emphasis on reasoning. Intelligent agents continuously perform three functions: the perception of dynamic conditions in the environment; the undertaking of action to affect conditions in the environment; and reasoning to interpret perceptions, solve problems, draw inferences, and determine actions (Hayes-Roth, 1995). Techniques such as rule-based and simulation-based decision making are employed to enable agents to take measures proactively (Kuehne, Wille, & Dumke, 2005). In contrast, decision making in workflow management systems is usually not automatic, and relies on the inputs of the workflow participants.

The model choices for designing intelligent Semantic Web services depend on the characteristics of the agent service. Several modeling approaches are discussed in the following sections to illustrate the choices that are available.

Activity Diagram

Unified modeling language (UML) is useful for modeling information systems (Booch, 1999). UML provides an activity diagram that shows the activities within a system (Booch, Rumbaugh, & Jacobson, 1999), and is ideally suited to modeling simple anonymous agents that react to a single event. An initial activity is triggered when an event occurs and input data is passed from the event to an agent. Activities are then performed sequentially or alternatively based on flow controls, such as branching, forking, and joining, until the agent finishes the final activity. The activities are essentially defined by operations that send out messages or evaluate an expression internally.

Statechart Diagram

A statechart diagram that is also provided by UML shows a state machine that consists of states, transactions, events, and activities (or actions). This diagram is especially useful for the modeling of reactive systems (Booch et al., 1999). The state machine describes an agent as an interactive software object, the behavior of which is specified by sequences of state transitions. The agent's state transaction is defined by a group of data members (or local variables) and messages about events and actions.

The initial state is given by the default values of the data members. A state transaction consists of events, actions, and conditions. The state transaction responds to events that are triggered by internal actions or messages that are detected by external systems. When an event occurs, actions are performed to manipulate the data member values that effectively capture the agent's state. Certain conditions may be defined to guard the transaction, which must be satisfied to activate its associated actions. The conditions are often expressed as a set of value ranges of the data members.

An action may be executed in several situations of state transaction, and cannot be interrupted by events. First, entry/exit actions are executed on entering and exiting the state. Second, an action is defined to run during the course of the state transaction. Finally, the "do" actions are performed in the state. "Do" actions are used to define triggerless transactions that are represented by a transaction with no event triggers. A triggerless transaction is triggered implicitly when the state has completed its "do" action.

Basic Reactive Plan

In statechart models, the number of state transitions grows quadratically if all of the nodes have transitions in them. The basic reactive plan has been proposed to cope with the complexity of modeling agent behavior in a large state space in very dynamic and unpredictable environments (Bryson, 2003). The basic reactive plan is defined as the elaboration of a simple sequence that allows reactive responses to dynamic environments (Bryson et al., 2002), and consists of a series of steps, each of which is associated with a priority in which the final step has the highest priority. The steps use a Boolean expression releaser to guard the execution of the action in the step. The basic reactive plan reacts to an event by first looking for all operable actions. If there is more than one operable action, then the priorities of the steps determine which action will be executed.

Synthesis

By "synthesis," we mean stages in the building up of separate components into a whole connected system. For intelligent Semantic Web services systems, this can be divided into three stages: mapping to architecture; componentizing, in which the parts of a specification are bound to architectural units; and software synthesis, in which details of the units are filled out by the OWL-S grounding definitions.

Mapping to Architecture

Intelligent Semantic Web services are composed of services, such as order placement and catalog requests; agent processes, such as monitoring product returns or insurance claims; and events, such as receiving returned products or payment. Figure 1 shows the

Figure 1. J2EE architecture for implementing intelligent Semantic Web services

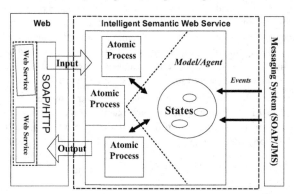

implementation architectures of intelligent Semantic Web services using the Java 2 Platform, Enterprise Edition (J2EE).

The service oriented architecture (SOA) in J2EE has been developed to support the implementation of information systems in enterprise environments. A service is viewed as a course-grained, discoverable software entity that exists as a single instance and interacts with a loosely coupled, message-based communication model (Endrei et al., 2004). Based on the SOA that supports SOAP, an application or another service can request the service irrespective of its specific implementation technologies, such as J2EE or Microsoft.Net. In the OWL-S model, services are defined as atomic processes and are then used to compose the agent process.

A model defines the agent process, which is transformed into a software component, and therefore the implementation infrastructure and programming languages need to be considered. In J2EE only the Java language is supported, but Enterprise JavaBeans technologies are provided for building secure and robust objects.

The event mechanism is currently restricted by the infrastructure selection. In J2EE, the JMS standard allows Java programs to create, send, receive, and read messages in enterprise systems (Sun Micro Systems, 1998). A JMS system that can be utilized as an event engine supports the Publish/Subscribe model. The agent process contains JMS clients that subscribe to messages from a node in a content-based hierarchy, which JMS calls node topics. It is worth noting that some event engines, such as IBM Websphere MQ, allow a Java object to listen to events that are triggered by .Net Web Services (Davies et al., 2004).

Service Oriented Analysis and Design

Most input and output messages, except for some events that are defined in the agent process models, are sent to or received from Web services. Componentization means acquiring Web service components to implement the requirements of the input and output message specifications. The componentization concepts are essentially covered by the service oriented analysis and design (SOAD) approach. In practice, the SOAD approach requires a "meet in the middle" model, rather than a pure top-down or bottom-up method (Zimmerman, Korgdahl, & Gee, 2004). Web services may be purchased from software venders, but it is often necessary to build software components that connect to organizational legacy systems and expose them as Web services. The scope of SOAD has not yet been formally defined, and there are some overlaps with the traditional object oriented analysis and design methods. In the design of intelligent Semantic Web services, SOAD must consider the spilt between the agent process and Web services, the maintenance of a Web service catalog for looking up reusable services, and the construction of cross-enterprise semantics.

Software Synthesis

Although the process components that we use to present the development approach are Java based, they are designed to interface with heterogeneous information implementation. The Java process components access Web services can be implemented in .Net or J2EE servers, and in addition the rules that are constructed to represent the knowledge of the agent process are modularized and executed in a rules engine that may be proprietary.

The synthesis procedure starts with an agent process model, which transforms the model to an OWL-S process specification for the development of programming codes. The Semantic Web service specifications do not support the expression of the agent models directly, but processes can be constructed from composite processes that are composed of several atomic processes. Composite processes define the input/output messages of the agent model, local variables for the parameters of the agent's action conditions, and the rule representations of the conditions. An example of deriving the OWL-S process definition from a statechart diagram is discussed later in this chapter.

The code development can be presented as four steps. First, the grounding of the atomic processes is provided by identified Web services using WSDL files. With the WSDL files, Java proxies of the Web services are generated using a Java programming tool, such as WebSphere Studio Application Developer. The Java proxies provide methods for connecting to the Web services, sending output messages to invoke the services, and receiving the responses of the services as input messages.

Second, an agent class is written to interface a rules engine that hosts the action conditions. For example, the local process variables for a state machine and the current state are passed to the rules engine to determine the state transactions and their associated actions. The class also provides methods for creating, updating, and destroying agent objects with some parameters that are defined in the OWL-S process. In particular, the update method executes the rule engine, changes the agent's state if necessary, and executes the appropriate actions. An agent can be destroyed when it reaches its final state.

Third, a message listener object is needed to handle each event. A simple listener template is demonstrated in Figure 2 that requires an agent object that observes the event to

Figure 2. A Java listener template created from a JMS interface

```
import javax.jms.*;

public class ListenerTemplate implements javax.jms.MessageListener{

    /* JMS topics for event messages */
    public static final String EVENT_TOPIC_NAME = "";


    /* Parameters for creating and updating an agent */
    //TODO: defining parameters

    /* Constructor. Establish JMS subscriber */
    public  ListenerTemplate (Agent anAgent){
       //the details are omitted here:
       //1. Connect to a JMS server.
       //2. Subscribe the specified JMS topic.
    }

    /* Receive message from topic subscriber */
    public void onMessage(Message message) {
       try {
          TextMessage textMessage = (TextMessage) message;
          String text = textMessage.getText( );
          //TODO:
          //1. Determine if the message is for this agent object.
          //2. Update the agent object using the above message.
       } catch (JMSException jmse){ jmse.printStackTrace( ); }
    }
}
```

construct a listener object that connects to a JMS server to subscribe to the JMS topic of the event. The "onMessage" method that is defined by the JMS interface is called up automatically when a message is published on the topic, and thus the event occurs. The method translates the message to a group of data values, decides whether the message is meant for this agent, and if necessary the agent's update method is invoked by passing the data as the method parameters.

Finally, a main program is developed to start the agents, which may be scheduled to run periodically. The start program is responsible for creating agents and registering them with all of the event listeners by calling on event listener constructors. The listener that is shown in the Figure 2 listens to a single event.

Example

The development of an intelligent Semantic Web service can be illustrated by the building of a customer relations management (CRM) service in the e-brokerage industry.

Chui et al. (2003) presented an e-brokerage CRM solution that provides a broker center and a client portal. The broker center is designed to satisfy a broker's needs, and delivers instant client information and alerts to brokers. The solution is based on a framework for the effective detection of business events that trigger the execution of customer-related activities that are associated with predefined conditions. This example implements the event-condition-action model through the design of a statechart diagram.

Web Services

Several Web services must be made available to the CRM service, including stock quote queries, client account management, and message delivery to clients and brokers. A few companies (such as Xignite Inc.) have developed priced Web services that provide quote information for equities and major indices. In general, the operation of obtaining a quote is supported by the messages in Table 1. Account management typically involves searching for or updating the information in a company's customer database. The service of searching for a customer profile can be built up using the message types in Table 2.

The message delivery service receives names, email addresses, and alert messages for the clients or brokers, and then sends the messages via an email system. There is no output from this service, as the client is designed to respond to messages from brokers by email or telephone.

Table 1. Messages of a stock quote Web service

Msg. Type	Message	Parameters	Type
Input	GetQuoteRequest	Symbol	String
Output	GetQuoteResponse	Response	QuoteType*

* QuoteType *is a sequence of items consisting of* Symbol, Date, Time, Previous_Day_Close_Price, Bid_Price, Ask_Price, *and* Percent_Change, *etc.*

Table 2. Messages of a customer profile Web service

Msg. Type	Message	Parameters	Type
Input	SearchCustomerRequest	Account_ID	String
Output	SearchCustomerResponse	Response	CustomerProfile*

* CustomerProfile *is a sequence of items consisting of* AccountID, Name, Account_Type, *(such as* Margin *or* Cash*), a list of* Holding_Stock_Symbol's, Total_Holding_Values, *and* Payment_Due

Figure 3. Statechart diagram of a CRM agent process

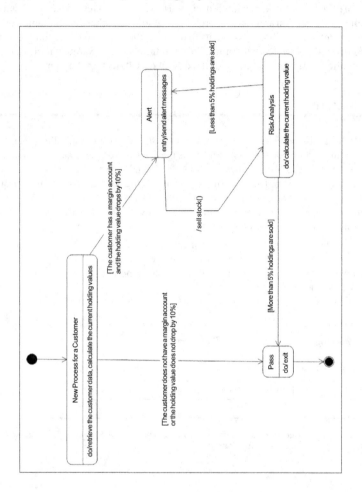

Statechart Diagram

Using a statechart diagram, the agent that provides the CRM service can be modeled as a composite process of atomic processes that include searching a customer profile, finding stock prices, and delivering messages. The input and output of the atomic processes are messages that are described in their corresponding Web services, and therefore the grounding of the atomic processes can be easily specified by WSDL.

Periodically, the CRM program runs a list of account IDs that are given as input data. An agent object is then instantiated for each ID, and registers the agent object to the event listener for the "Sell Stock" message. The state machine is implemented inside the agent, as is described earlier. The state machine is started by searching a customer object that includes the customer's stock portfolio by an account ID. It then retrieves all of the stock prices of the symbols in the portfolio and calculates the current total holding value. The first state is triggerless, and its state transition occurs after the calculation has been finished.

A rules engine is involved in the state transition that determines the next state and the execution of guarded activities. The agent stays in the "Alert" state, and an alert message is sent if the customer uses a "margin" account and the holding value drops by more than 10 percent; otherwise, it moves to the "Pass" state and exits. The agent is idle in the "Alert" state until it detects a "sell stock" message that is published for the customer. The event message triggers another state transaction, and the state machine conducts another stock holding calculation. To pass the examination, the customer is required to sell five percent of the holding to increase the cash amount in their account. The statechart diagram that represents the agent process is illustrated in Figure 3.

Model Transformation

The statechart diagram is designed as the transformation for an OWL-S process model. The input/output parameters and local variables can be captured and maintained by investigating the data elements that are required for the state machine. For example, the inputs of the CRM service include account ID, a list of stock symbols, and the total holding value of the previous day. The key to the transformation of the state machine is the use of rules. For example, the following rule can be used to represent the state transition of the CRM agent process.

Rule Name: Rule-New-to-Alert

If (state is "new process") **and** (account type is "margin") **and** (the difference between the current holding value and the previous day's holding value is greater than 10 percent of the previous day's holding value) **then** (the next state is "alert").

Currently, the OWL-S specification does not provide a standard to express such rules. However, the Semantic Web Rules Language is under development at W3C (see the appendix) and tools such as SweetJess are available for the implementation of XML rules in Java-based rules engines (Grosof, Mahesh, Gandhe, & Finin, 2002).

Conclusion

Semantic Web services standards provide tools to aid the development of intelligent agents on the Web. This chapter presents an approach that adheres to good software development practices, such as standardization, system modeling, and code generation. Using the J2EE standards as a computing infrastructure, agents learn events inside a company through a JMS messaging server, and utilize specified Web services to discover and communicate knowledge on the Web. The agents implement human knowledge by designing a behavior model in which an autonomous process senses messages and acts accordingly to reach a set of goals. Eventually, the model is efficiently transformed into a software agent by the code generation of Web services proxies, program templates, and rule modules in a rules engine.

This chapter shows the use of state of the art technologies for the development of intelligent Semantic Web services. This technology will open up many opportunities for the building of intelligent agent applications that enhance cross-organizational collaboration. Development is being pursued in a few business areas, including business negotiation and active decision support. Negotiation agents in e-business have been introduced to negotiate with e-shops simultaneously and to propose counter offers based on responses and customer preferences (Wang, Tan, & Ren, 2004). In addition, active decision support systems that use agents in a problem-solving sense offer the high-level integration of decision support components (Vahidov, 2002).

References

Booch, G. (1999). UML in action. *Communications of the ACM, 42*(10), 26-28.

Booch, G., Rumbaugh, J., & Jacobson, I. (1999). *The unified modeling language user guide.* Reading, MA: Addison-Wesley.

Bryson, J. J. (2003). Action selection and individuation in agent based modelling. *The Proceedings of Agent 2003: Challenges of Social Simulation.*

Bryson, J. J., Martin, D. L., McIlraith, S. A., & Stein, L. A. (2002). Toward behavioral intelligence in the semantic web. *IEEE Computer, 35*(11), 48-54.

Chiu, D. K., Chan, W. W., Lam, G. W., Cheung, S. C., & Luk, F. T. (2003). An event-driven approach to customer relationship management in brokerage industry. *Proceedings of the 36th Hawaii International Conference on System Sciences.*

Davies, S., Hamann, M., Kulkarni, S., Shan, T., Shppard, A., Soyannwo, O. O., et al. (2004). *WebSphere MQ Solutions in a Microsoft .Net Environment.* IBM Redbook, ISBN 00738498521.

DAML (2003). *OWL-S: Semantic markup for Web services.* Retrieved from http://www.daml.org/services/owl-s/1.0/owl-s.html

Endrei, M., Ang, J., Arsanjani, A., Chua, S., Comte, P., Krogdahl, P., et al. (2004). *Patterns: Service-oriented Architecture and Web Services.* IBM Redbook, ISBN 073845317X.

Franklin, S., & Graesser, A. (1996). Is it an agent, or just a program? A taxonomy for autonomous agents. In *Proceedings of the 3rd International Workshop on Agent Theories, Architectures, and Languages.* Springer-Verlag, New York.

Grosof, B. N., Mahesh, D., Gandhe, M. D., & Finin, T. W. (2002). SweetJess: Translating DamlRuleML to Jess. In *Proceedings of International Workshop on Rule Markup Languages for Business Rules on the Semantic Web,* Sardinia, Italy.

Hayes-Roth, B. (1995). An architecture for adaptive intelligent systems. *Artificial Intelligence: Special Issue on Agents and Interactivity, 72,* 329-365.

Jennings, N. R., Sycara, K., & Wooldridge, M. (1998). A roadmap of agent research and development. *International Journal of Autonomous Agents and Multi-Agent Systems, 1*(1), 7-38.

Kuehne, R., Wille, C., & Dumke, R. (2005). Software agents using simulation for decision-making. *ACM SIGSOFT Software Engineering Notes, 30*(1).

Maes, P. (1995). Artificial life meets entertainment: life like autonomous agents. *Communications of the ACM, 38*(11), 108-114.

Nilsson, N. (1995). Eye on the prize. *AI Magazine, 16*(2), 9-16.

Russell, S., & Norvig, P. (1995). *Artificial intelligence: A modern approach.* Englewood Cliffs, NJ: Prentice Hall.

Son, J. H., Kim, J. S., & Kim, M. H. (2005). Extracting the workflow critical path from the extended well-formed workflow schema. *Journal of Computer and System Sciences, 70*(1), 86-106.

Sun Micro Systems (1998). Java messaging service. Retrieved from http://java.sun.com/products/jms/jms-101-spec.pdf

Vahidov, R. (2002). Decision station: A notion for a situated DSS. In *Proceedings of the 35th Hawaii International Conference on System Sciences.*

Venkatraman, S. S. (2004). Web services – The next evolutionary stage of e-business. *Journal of International Technology and Information Management, 13*(2), 111-122.

Wang, Y., Tan, K. L., & Ren, J. (2004). PumaMart: A parallel and autonomous agents based Internet marketplace. *Electronic Commerce Research and Applications, 3*(3), 294-310.

World Wide Web Consortium (W3C) (2004, February). OWL Web ontology language reference. Retrieved from http://www.w3.org/TR/2004/REC-owl-ref-20040210/

Zimmerman, O., Korgdahl, P., & Gee, C. (2004, June 4). Elements of service-oriented analysis and design. *IBM developerWorks.*

Appendix:
Semantic Web Rule Language

The Semantic Web rule language (SWRL) is based on a combination of OWL and rule markup language (RuleML.org). Briefly speaking, an SWRL rule formally expresses an if-then rule using the OWL syntax. A rule expresses the implication relationship between the classes of body (the "if" clause) and head (the "then" clause), both of which consist of kinds of atoms. Figure 4 shows a simple rule that defines that parent and brother properties imply an uncle property. More complete syntax information can be found in the SWRL specification (http://www.daml.org/rules/).

For the sake of readability, a rule is often written in the following form:

antecedent ⇒ consequent,

where both *antecedent* and *consequent* are conjunctions of the atoms that are written as $a_1 \wedge ... \wedge a_n$. Variables are indicated using the standard convention of prefixing them with a question mark (e.g., ?x). Using this syntax, the sample rule in Figure 4 would be written as follows:

hasParent(?personA, ?personB) ∧ hasBrother(?personB, ?personC) ⇒
hasUncle(?personA, ?personC).

Next, some rules that specify state transitions of the CRM agent process in Figure 3 are given in Figure 5.

Figure 4. A simple Semantic Web rule

```
<ruleml:imp>
  <ruleml:_rlab ruleml:href="#example1"/>
  <ruleml:_body>
    <swrlx:individualPropertyAtom  swrlx:property="hasParent">
      <ruleml:var>personA</ruleml:var>
      <ruleml:var>personB</ruleml:var>
    </swrlx:individualPropertyAtom>
    <swrlx:individualPropertyAtom  swrlx:property="hasBrother">
      <ruleml:var>personB</ruleml:var>
      <ruleml:var>personC</ruleml:var>
    </swrlx:individualPropertyAtom>
  </ruleml:_body>
  <ruleml:_head>
    <swrlx:individualPropertyAtom  swrlx:property="hasUncle">
      <ruleml:var>personA</ruleml:var>
      <ruleml:var>personC</ruleml:var>
    </swrlx:individualPropertyAtom>
  </ruleml:_head>
</ruleml:imp>
```

Figure 5.

```
<?xml version='1.0' encoding='ISO-8859-1' ?>
<!DOCTYPE swrlx:Ontology [
        <!ENTITY swrlb 'http://www.w3.org/2003/11/swrlb'>
        <!ENTITY xsd 'http://www.w3.org/2001/XMLSchema'>
        <!ENTITY ex 'http://www.txstate.edu/example-ont'>
]>

<swrlx:Ontology
 xmlns:owlx="http://www.w3.org/2003/05/owl-xml"
 xmlns:swrlx="http://www.w3.org/2003/11/swrlx"
 xmlns:ruleml="http://www.w3.org/2003/11/ruleml">

<ruleml:var>customer</ruleml:var>
<ruleml:var>percentage</ruleml:var>
<ruleml:var>valueOpen</ruleml:var>
<ruleml:var>valueClose</ruleml:var>
<ruleml:var>valueSold</ruleml:var>
<ruleml:var>valueDifference</ruleml:var>
<ruleml:var>changeOpen</ruleml:var>
<ruleml:var>changeSold</ruleml:var>

<ruleml:imp>
 <ruleml:_rlab ruleml:href="#ruleNewToAlert"/>
 <ruleml:_body>
  <swrlx:individualPropertyAtom
swrlx:property="&ex;#hasAccountType">
   <ruleml:var>customer</ruleml:var>
   <owlx:Individual owlx:name="&ex;#margin"/>
  </swrlx:individualPropertyAtom>
  <swrlx:datavaluedPropertyAtom
swrlx:property="&ex;#percentageChangeTodayOpen">
   <ruleml:var>customer</ruleml:var>
   <ruleml:var>percentage</ruleml:var>
  </swrlx:datavaluedPropertyAtom>
  <swrlx:builtinAtom swrlx:builtin="&swrlb;#greaterThanOrEqual">
   <ruleml:var>percentage</ruleml:var>
   <owlx:DataValue owlx:datatype="&xsd;#double">10.0</owlx:DataValue>
  </swrlx:builtinAtom>
  <swrlx:individualPropertyAtom swrlx:property="&ex;#hasCurrentState">
   <ruleml:var>customer</ruleml:var>
   <owlx:Individual owlx:name="&ex;#newState"/>
  </swrlx:individualPropertyAtom>
 </ruleml:_body>                      •
 <ruleml:_head>
  <swrlx:individualPropertyAtom swrlx:property="&ex;#hasNextState">
   <ruleml:var>customer</ruleml:var>
   <owlx:Individual owlx:name="&ex;#alertState"/>
  </swrlx:individualPropertyAtom>
 </ruleml:_head>
</ruleml:imp>

<ruleml:imp>
 <ruleml:_rlab ruleml:href="#ruleNewToPass"/>
 <ruleml:_body>
  <swrlx:datavaluedPropertyAtom
swrlx:property="&ex;#percentageChangeTodayOpen">
   <ruleml:var>customer</ruleml:var>
   <ruleml:var>percentage</ruleml:var>
```

Figure 5. continued

```
</swrlx:datavaluedPropertyAtom>
  <swrlx:builtinAtom swrlx:builtin="&swrlb;#lessThan">
   <ruleml:var>percentage</ruleml:var>
   <owlx:DataValue
owlx:datatype="&xsd;#double">10.0</owlx:DataValue>
  </swrlx:builtinAtom>
  <swrlx:individualPropertyAtom
swrlx:property="&ex;#hasCurrentState">
   <ruleml:var>customer</ruleml:var>
   <owlx:Individual owlx:name="&ex;#newState"/>
  </swrlx:individualPropertyAtom>
 </ruleml:_body>
 <ruleml:_head>
  <swrlx:individualPropertyAtom swrlx:property="&ex;#hasNextState">
   <ruleml:var>customer</ruleml:var>
   <owlx:Individual owlx:name="&ex;#passState"/>
  </swrlx:individualPropertyAtom>
 </ruleml:_head>
</ruleml:imp>

<ruleml:imp>
 <ruleml:_rlab ruleml:href="#ruleAnalysisToAlert"/>
 <ruleml:_body>
  <swrlx:datavaluedPropertyAtom
swrlx:property="&ex;#percentageChangeTodaySold">
   <ruleml:var>customer</ruleml:var>
   <ruleml:var>percentage</ruleml:var>
  </swrlx:datavaluedPropertyAtom>
  <swrlx:builtinAtom swrlx:builtin="&swrlb;#lessThan">
   <ruleml:var>percentage</ruleml:var>
   <owlx:DataValue owlx:datatype="&xsd;#double">5.0</owlx:DataValue>
  </swrlx:builtinAtom>
  <swrlx:individualPropertyAtom
swrlx:property="&ex;#hasCurrentState">
   <ruleml:var>customer</ruleml:var>
   <owlx:Individual owlx:name="&ex;#analysisState"/>
  </swrlx:individualPropertyAtom>
 </ruleml:_body>
 <ruleml:_head>
  <swrlx:individualPropertyAtom swrlx:property="&ex;#hasNextState">
   <ruleml:var>customer</ruleml:var>
   <owlx:Individual owlx:name="&ex;#alertState"/>
  </swrlx:individualPropertyAtom>
 </ruleml:_head>
</ruleml:imp>

<ruleml:imp>
 <ruleml:_rlab ruleml:href="#ruleAnalysisToPass"/>
 <ruleml:_body>
  <swrlx:datavaluedPropertyAtom
swrlx:property="&ex;#percentageChangeTodaySold">
   <ruleml:var>customer</ruleml:var>
   <ruleml:var>percentage</ruleml:var>
  </swrlx:datavaluedPropertyAtom>
  <swrlx:builtinAtom swrlx:builtin="&swrlb;#greaterThanOrEqual">
   <ruleml:var>percentage</ruleml:var>
   <owlx:DataValue owlx:datatype="&xsd;#double">5.0</owlx:DataValue>
  </swrlx:builtinAtom>
  <swrlx:individualPropertyAtom
swrlx:property="&ex;#hasCurrentState">
   <ruleml:var>customer</ruleml:var>
   <owlx:Individual owlx:name="&ex;#analysisState"/>
  </swrlx:individualPropertyAtom>
```

Figure 5. continued

```
    </ruleml:_body>
    <ruleml:_head>
     <swrlx:individualPropertyAtom  swrlx:property="&ex;#hasNextState">
      <ruleml:var>customer</ruleml:var>
      <owlx:Individual owlx:name="&ex;#passState"/>
     </swrlx:individualPropertyAtom>
    </ruleml:_head>
   </ruleml:imp>

   <ruleml:imp>
     <ruleml:_rlab ruleml:href="#percentageChangeTodayOpen"/>
     <owlx:Annotation>
      <owlx:Documentation>ex:percentageChangeTodayOpen
                   = (ex:holdingValueYesterdayClose –
   ex:holdingValueTodayOpen)/
              ex:holdingValueYesterdayClose
     </owlx:Documentation>
     </owlx:Annotation>
     <ruleml:_body>
      <swrlx:datavaluedPropertyAtom
   swrlx:property="&ex;#holdingValueTodayOpen">
       <ruleml:var>customer</ruleml:var>
       <ruleml:var>valueOpen</ruleml:var>
      </swrlx:datavaluedPropertyAtom>
      <swrlx:datavaluedPropertyAtom
   swrlx:property="&ex;#holdingValueYesterdayClose">
       <ruleml:var>customer</ruleml:var>
       <ruleml:var>valueClose</ruleml:var>
      </swrlx:datavaluedPropertyAtom>
     </ruleml:_body>
     <ruleml:_head>
      <swrlx:builtinAtom swrlx:builtin="&swrlb;#substract">
       <ruleml:var>valueDifference</ruleml:var>
       <ruleml:var>valueClose</ruleml:var>
          <ruleml:var>valueOpen</ruleml:var>
      </swrlx:builtinAtom>
      <swrlx:builtinAtom swrlx:builtin="&swrlb;#divide">
       <ruleml:var>changeOpen</ruleml:var>
       <ruleml:var>valueDifference</ruleml:var>
          <ruleml:var>valueClose</ruleml:var>
      </swrlx:builtinAtom>
      <swrlx:datavaluedPropertyAtom
   swrlx:property="&ex;#percentageChangeTodayOpen">
       <ruleml:var>customer</ruleml:var>
       <ruleml:var>changeOpen</ruleml:var>
      </swrlx:datavaluedPropertyAtom>
     </ruleml:_head>
   </ruleml:imp>

   <ruleml:imp>
     <ruleml:_rlab ruleml:href="#percentageChangeTodaySold"/>
     <owlx:Annotation>
      <owlx:Documentation>ex:percentageChangeTodaySold
                   = ex:hholdingValueTodaySold/ex:holdingValueTodayOpen
     </owlx:Documentation>
     </owlx:Annotation>
     <ruleml:_body>
```

Figure 5. continued

```
        <swrlx:datavaluedPropertyAtom
swrlx:property="&ex;#holdingValueTodayOpen">
        <ruleml:var>customer</ruleml:var>
        <ruleml:var>valueOpen</ruleml:var>
      </swrlx:datavaluedPropertyAtom>
      <swrlx:datavaluedPropertyAtom
swrlx:property="&ex;#holdingValueTodaySold">
        <ruleml:var>customer</ruleml:var>
        <ruleml:var>valueSold</ruleml:var>
      </swrlx:datavaluedPropertyAtom>
    </ruleml:_body>
    <ruleml:_head>
      <swrlx:builtinAtom swrlx:builtin="&swrlb;#divide">
        <ruleml:var>changeSold</ruleml:var>
        <ruleml:var>valueSold</ruleml:var>
            <ruleml:var>valueOpen</ruleml:var>
      </swrlx:builtinAtom>
      <swrlx:datavaluedPropertyAtom
swrlx:property="&ex;#percentageChangeTodaySold">
        <ruleml:var>customer</ruleml:var>
        <ruleml:var>changeSold</ruleml:var>
      </swrlx:datavaluedPropertyAtom>
    </ruleml:_head>
  </ruleml:imp>

</swrlx:Ontology>
```

Chapter IV

Semantic Web Support for Customer Services

Quan Thanh Tho, Nanyang Technological University, Singapore

Hui Siu Cheung, Nanyang Technological University, Singapore

A. C. M. Fong, Nanyang Technological University, Singapore

Abstract

This chapter discusses Semantic Web support for customer services. Customer service support is an important operation for most multinational manufacturing companies. It provides installation, inspection, and maintenance support for their worldwide customers. However, knowledge integrated in customer service support systems is typically closed in terms of exchanging information. Therefore, the systems do not easily share, reuse, or exchange knowledge. It causes difficulty when customers seek service support for products produced by various companies. In this chapter, we propose to incorporate Semantic Web services into customer service systems to solve such problems. In our system, KSOM neural network is first used to mine knowledge from reported cases. Then, ontology is used as a semantic representation for knowledge discovered and Semantic Web services are used to make constructed ontology accessible from different systems. As a result, users can use semantic knowledge distributed across various sources on the Internet to solve their problems. Performance evaluation on the system is also present in the chapter.

Introduction

Customer service support has become an integral part of many multinational manufacturing companies that manufacture and market machines and electronic equipment. A customer service department is usually set up to provide installation, inspection, and maintenance support for their customers, which may be located worldwide. Insertion and surface mount machines are expensive and require efficient maintenance during machine down time. Although most customers have some engineers to handle day-to-day maintenance and small-scale troubleshooting, expert advice is often required for more complex maintenance and repair jobs. Prompt response to request from customers is needed to maintain customer satisfaction. Therefore, the multinational corporation has set up a hotline service center (or help desk) to answer frequently encountered problems.

Customer service on faulty machines or customer enquiries is traditionally supported by the service center or help-desk of the customer service department via telephone calls. When a problem is reported, a service engineer will suggest a series of checkpoints to the customers to implement or check as a means to rectify the reported problem. Such suggestions are based on past experience or extracted through a customer service database that contains previous service records that are identical or similar to the current one.

With these checkpoints, the customer attempts problem solving and subsequently confirms with the service center if the problem is resolved. If the problem still persists after all the suggested checkpoints are exhausted, the center will dispatch the service engineers to the customer's premise for an onsite repair. During such trips, the service engineers will carry along with them past records of the customer's machine, related manuals, and spare parts that may be required to carry out the repair. Such a process is inconvenient and often involves bringing redundant materials.

At the end of each service cycle, a customer service report is used to record the reported problem and proposed remedies or suggestions taken to rectify the problem. This is for billing purposes, as well as maintaining a corporate knowledge base. The service centre then updates the customer service report in the customer service database.

This traditional customer support process suffers from a number of disadvantages:

- The process is time-consuming and expensive. More often than not, service engineers are required to travel to a customer's site for an onsite service even for a small problem. As a result, the problem cannot be resolved efficiently and the machine downtime can be significant. In addition, as the customers communicate with the help desk centre via telephone calls, they incur long distance telephone charges as most of them are located overseas.

- A certain number of service engineers are maintained in order to provide the service support. It needs to keep on training new service engineers, and at the same time, come up with new incentive scheme to retain experienced service engineers.

- Expert advice to the problem is given either through the experience of the service engineers or the available past service information in the service database. No automatic provision of expert advice is available.

As can be seen from this mode of operation, the identification of machine faults relies heavily on the service support engineers' past experience or the information drawn from the service database. This method has a problem of training and maintaining a pool of expert service engineers. Thus, instead of relying on the knowledge of service engineers, an intelligent fault diagnosis system that captures the expert knowledge of machine diagnosis to assist customers identify machine faults becomes extremely useful. This system should be able to generate suggested remedial actions automatically or through user-interaction based on the observed fault-conditions.

With the advancement of the Internet, companies start supporting customer service online over the Web with Web-based applications (Muller,1996). Instead of relying on the knowledge of service engineers, Web-based service support systems improve the traditional approach by applying intelligent or data mining techniques (Balakrishnan & Honavar, 1998; Watson, 1997) to mine the customer service database to capture the expert knowledge of machine diagnosis to assist customers identify machine faults. Suggested remedial actions can then be generated automatically or through user-interaction based on the observed fault-conditions over the Web.

Recently, Semantic Web (Berners-Lee, Hendler, & Lassila, 2001) has been introduced as a common framework that allows data to be shared and reused across application, enterprise, and community boundaries. Ontology is used to represent knowledge on the Semantic Web. Basically, ontology is a conceptualization of a domain into a human understandable, but machine-readable format consisting of entities, attributes, relationships, and axioms (Guarino & Giaretta, 1995). As such, programs can use the knowledge from the Semantic Web for processing information in a semantic manner.

This chapter describes the Semantic Web support for customer services on machine faults. As compared with Web-based systems, the Semantic Web support approach enables individual machine service knowledge to be shared over the Semantic Web. As such, machine service knowledge from different machines or models provided by different manufacturers can be shared and integrated. This is important as many customers may have different types of machines and models from different manufacturers. As such, users can retrieve the required Semantic Web services for a machine problem of a specific model of a machine manufactured by a particular manufacturer. This approach can improve considerably performance in terms of reducing machine down time and increasing productivity for the customer. In this chapter, we first review the existing intelligent fault diagnosis systems. Then, we describe the current development of Semantic Web and Semantic Web services. The proposed architecture of the Semantic Web support system for customer services is presented. We then discuss our proposed approach for automatic generation of service ontology, which can be shared and used by Semantic Web services on machine fault diagnosis.

Intelligent Fault Diagnosis

For the past few decades, there have been a proliferation of intelligent systems for fault diagnosis and related applications (Balakrishnan & Honavar, 1998). Traditionally, case-based reasoning (CBR) has been successfully applied to fault diagnosis for customer service support or help desk (House, 1994; Law, Foong, & Kwan, 1997; Liu & Yan, 1997; Patterson & Hughes, 1997; Shimazu, Shibata, & Nihei, 1994). CBR systems rely on building a large repository of diagnostic cases (or past service reports) in order to circumvent the difficult task of extracting and encoding expert domain knowledge (Riesbeck & Schank, 1989). It is one of the most appropriate techniques for customer service support as it learns with experience in solving problems and hence emulates humanlike intelligence. However, the performance of CBR systems depends critically on the adequacy as well as the organization of cases and the algorithms used for retrieval from a large case database. Most CBR systems (Watson, 1997) use the nearest neighbor algorithm for retrieval from the flat-indexed case database, which are inefficient, especially for a large case database. Other CBR systems use hierarchical indexing such as CART (Breiman, Friedman, Olshen, & Stone, 1984), decision trees (Quinlan, 1986) and C4.5 (Quinlan, 1993). Although this performs efficient retrieval, building a hierarchical index needs the supervision of an expert during the case-authoring phase.

The artificial neural network (ANN) approach provides an efficient learning capability from detailed examples. Supervised neural networks such as learning vector quantization (LVQ3) (Kohonen, 1990) are used when the training data consists of examples with known classes. LVQ3 performs retrieval based on nearest neighbor matching, since it stores the weight vectors as the code-book or exemplar vector for the input patterns. The matching is based on a competitive process that determines the output unit that is the best match for the input vector, similar to the nearest neighbor rule. However, in LVQ3, the search space is greatly reduced because of the generalization of knowledge through training. In contrast, the CBR systems need to store all the cases in the case database in order to perform accurate retrieval that greatly increases the search space. The CBR systems that store only relevant cases for an efficient retrieval lack the accuracy as well as the learning feature of the neural networks. Hence, supervised neural networks become a very suitable complement for case retrieval.

Therefore, a hybrid CBR and ANN system (Lees & Corchado, 1997; Papagni, Cirillo, & Micarelli, 1997; Richter, 2000) that operates under the framework of CBR cycle (Aamodt & Plaza, 1994) is deemed to be one of the most effective and intelligent techniques for fault diagnosis. Such a system behaves most similar to the human beings in problem solving through recalling prior experience or cases and subsequently learning through experience in solving the problems.

Semantic Web Services

Currently, information available on the Web has been designed for human to understand. Programs can be written to process, analyze, and index Web pages to help us to process the information. However, due to the lack of machine-readable structure and knowledge representation in Web documents, programs are unable to comprehend Web page contents precisely, and hence semantic information from Web documents cannot be extracted. The Semantic Web is therefore proposed as an extension to the current Web, in which information is given well-defined meaning, better enabling computers and people to work in cooperation (Berners-Lee et al., 2001). The basis for the Semantic Web is on its ability to represent real-life domains accurately, so that it enables programs to completely understand the environment in which they operate.

Web services (Austin, Barbin, Ferris, & Garg, 2002) have recently become an important feature in the Web community since they provide a new level of interoperability between applications. Web services are based on agent technology (Franklin & Graesser 1996). Agents are encapsulated computer programs that are capable of autonomous behavior and processing. Similar to agents, Web services are self-describing and self-contained modules that can be accessed from other programs. Web services differs from agents in that Web services use XML-based languages to describe their functions. A Web service is identified by a URI (Universal Resource Identifier) (Berners-Lee, 2000), whose public interfaces and bindings are defined and described using XML-based service description languages. This enables its definition to be discovered by other agent systems. These agent systems can then interact with the Web services in a manner prescribed by its definition using XML based messages conveyed by the Internet protocols (Austin et al., 2002).

Typical Web service techniques such as Web services description services (WSDS) (Christensen, Curbera, Meredith, & Weerawarana, 2001) or universal description, discovery and integration (UDDI) (UDDI, 2000) provide technical information on service accessibility (including the service address and the service port), but it lacks the description on service capability. In addition, functions offered by typical Web services are accessible, but not fully understandable by other programs. This problem can be tackled by the Semantic Web. The Semantic Web uses ontology as a standard for knowledge presentation. Therefore, knowledge can be shared, reused, and exchanged on the Semantic Web. Based on DAML+OIL (van Harmelen, Patel-Schneider, & Horrocks, 2001), an ontology language description language, DAML-S (Ankolekar et al., 2001) was introduced to describe Web services in a semantic manner. Thus, DAML-S can be used to describe a Web service as an ontology instance, and its intensional information (e.g., its input and output parameters) can be understood by other applications. DAML-S is recently considered as a standard for presenting Web services containing semantic information or Semantic Web services.

Machine Service Ontology

In traditional customer service support, a customer service report is used to record the reported machine problem and the proposed remedies or suggestions taken to rectify the problem. This is generally for billing purposes, as well as maintaining a corporate knowledge base. The service center then stores the customer service report in the

Figure 1. Machine service ontology generation

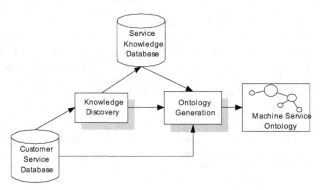

customer service database. As such, the customer service database serves as a reposi-tory of invaluable information and knowledge that can be utilized to assist the customer service department to support customer service activities. In fact, the service engineers from the service center have made use of such database to help them to recommend suggestions to customers. Further, Web-based customer service support systems have also made use of the database for extracting the knowledge to provide online sugges-tions.

To generate machine service ontology for the Semantic Web, we extract machine service knowledge from the customer service database. This is shown in Figure 1. The machine service ontology generation process consists of two major processes: Knowledge Discovery and Ontology Generation. The Knowledge Discovery process uses an intelligent clustering technique to mine machine service knowledge from the Customer Service Database to form the Service Knowledge Database. Then, the Ontology Genera-tion process constructs the Machine Service Ontology from the Service Knowledge Database and the Customer Service Database.

The proposed ontology generation technique has been incorporated into a Customer Service Database of a multinational corporation in Singapore that manufactures insertion and surface mount machines in the electronics industry.

Customer Service Database

Service records (or reports) are currently defined and stored in the customer service database to keep track of all reported machine problems and remedial actions. Each service record consists of customer account information and service details. Customer service details contain two types of information: *fault-condition* and *checkpoint information*. Fault-condition contains the service engineer's description of the machine fault. Checkpoint information indicates the suggested actions or services to be carried

Figure 2. Customer service database

Fault-condition	3008 PCB CARRY MISS ERROR. PCB WAS NOT TRANSFERRED BY THE CARRIER DURING LOADING BUT STAYED AT THE DETECTION POSITION OF PCB DETECTION SENSOR 2.	
Checkpoint group: AVF_CHK007		
Priority	Checkpoint description	Help file
1	CONFIRM WHETHER THE CARRY GUIDE PINS ARE IN LINE WITH PCB.	AVF_CHK007-1.GIF
2	CONFIRM WHETHER THE PCB IS IN CORRECT DIRECTION.	AVF_CHK007-2.GIF
3	CONFIRM THE POSITION OF THE GUIDE LOWER LIMIT SENSOR. (I/O 0165)	AVF_CHK007-3.GIF
4	CONFIRM THE TIMING FOR PCB 2 DETECT SENSOR.	AVF_CHK007-4.GIF
5	CONFIRM THE TIMING FOR THE CARRIER START TIMING.	AVF_CHK007-5.GIF

out to repair the machine into normal condition based on the occurred fault-condition given by the customer. Checkpoint information contains checkpoint group name and checkpoint description with priority and an optional help file. The checkpoint group name is used to specify a list of checkpoints defined under the group. Each checkpoint is associated with a priority, which determines the sequence in which it can be exercised, and a help file that gives visual details on how to carry out the checkpoint. An example of fault-condition and its checkpoint information for a service record is given in Figure 2.

In addition, the customer service database also stores data related to sales, customers, and employees. Currently, six major tables are defined in the customer service database to store this information. Two tables, namely, MACHINE_FAULT and CHECKPOINT, are used to store the knowledge base on common machine fault-conditions and the checkpoints of the fault-conditions. These are unstructured textual data. The remaining four tables are used to store information on customers, employees, sales, and mainte-nance. These four tables store only the structured data.

There are over 70,000 service records in the customer service database. Since each of the fault-conditions has several checkpoints, there are over 50,000 checkpoints. In addition, information on over 4,000 employees, 500 customers, 300 different machine models and 10,000 sales transactions are also stored.

Knowledge Discovery

The knowledge discovery process discovers hidden knowledge from the customer service database for machine fault services. The reported machine problems stored in the service database are assumed to be technically related to each others in terms of machine fault conditions. These similar machine fault conditions can be clustered together for knowledge discovery. Therefore, we discover the hidden knowledge from the database based on the relatedness of machine fault conditions. Clustering techniques (Berkhin, 2002) that can be used to cluster machine fault conditions into groups based on their similarities are traditionally used for this purpose. In this research, we have applied one

Figure 3. Knowledge discovery process

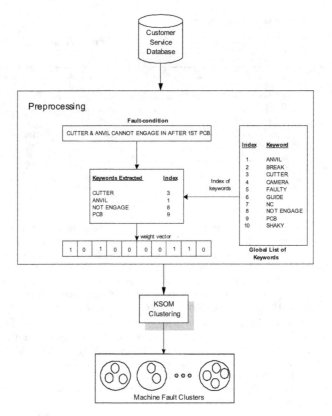

of the most effective clustering techniques known as Kohonen self-organizing map (KSOM) neural network (Kohonen, 2001) for knowledge discovery. Figure 3 shows the knowledge discovery process that comprises the following two steps: preprocessing and KSOM clustering.

As discussed earlier, each service record in the customer service database refers to a technical machine fault condition. The machine fault condition is described in textual format in the fault-condition attribute of the database. Therefore, the fault-condition attribute can be used for clustering similar faults. However, as fault conditions are stored in textual format, text processing techniques are required to preprocess the fault conditions before it can be fed into the KSOM neural network for clustering.

In preprocessing, the textual descriptions of the fault conditions of the service records from the customer service database are preprocessed to extract the keywords or key phrases. Preprocessing is carried out using word-list, stop-list, and algorithms from Wordnet (2004). To generate the weight vectors, we first extract all the significant keywords of fault-conditions from the database. The extracted keywords are then used to form a list of keywords for the database. Then, we parse each fault-condition and identify the indices of the keywords using the keyword list. The extracted keywords are then used to form the *weight vectors* for clustering using the KSOM neural network.

The KSOM neural network is one of the most suitable unsupervised techniques for clustering and visualizing multidimensional weight vectors. To cluster the multidimensional weight vectors, the KSOM neural network is first organized as an array of neurons. The number of neurons is equal the number of desired clusters. Therefore, each neuron refers to a distinct cluster. Each neuron is also associated with a *neural vector*, which has the same dimensions as the weight vectors. Initially, neural vectors are assigned with random values. Then, the keyword weight vectors are used to train the KSOM neural network. The training algorithm is given in Kohonen (2001). After the KSOM neural network is trained, the neural vectors are updated with appropriate values. After training, a set of clusters for fault conditions (or associated keyword weigh vectors) are generated, and they are referred to as *machine fault clusters*.

When clustering a new input fault condition for machine services, the trained KSOM neural network can be used to determine the winning neuron whose neural vector has the closest Euclidean distance to the weight vector of the new fault condition. In this way, the new fault condition can be classified into the most appropriate machine fault cluster according to the wining neuron. The checkpoints of the corresponding fault conditions from the machine fault cluster can then be inspected to solve the machine problem.

Service Knowledge Database

The service knowledge database stores the machine fault cluster knowledge discovered by the knowledge discovery process. Each machine fault cluster groups similar fault conditions together, and each fault condition refers to a reported machine problem. To represent such knowledge, each record stored in the service knowledge database has two attributes *machine fault cluster* and the corresponding *machine fault* contained in it.

Ontology Generation

The ontology generation process creates the machine service ontology to represent the knowledge on machine fault services. The machine fault cluster knowledge can be obtained from the customer service database and service knowledge database. It can be used to create classes, relations and instances for the service ontology. The machine fault service knowledge stored in the customer service database is known as *schematic knowledge*, while the fault condition clustering knowledge from the service knowledge database is called *discovered knowledge*. The schematic knowledge and discovered knowledge are combined together to construct the machine service ontology. The ontology generation process is shown in Figure 4, which comprises the following steps:

Figure 4. The machine service ontology generation process

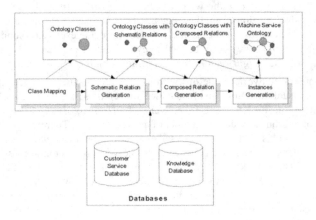

Figure 5. Machine service ontology

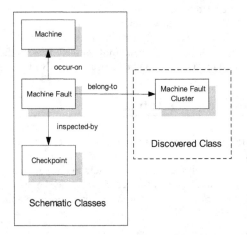

class mapping, schematic relation generation, composed relation generation, and instances generation. Figure 5 shows the generated machine service ontology.

Class mapping maps the schematic and discovered knowledge into ontology's *schematic* and *discovered classes*. Generally, information is stored in tables of the databases. The tables are mapped into the corresponding ontology classes. The names of the ontology classes can be generated automatically using the names of the tables. Attributes in tables are mapped into the appropriate properties of the corresponding classes. For example, information of the reported problems is stored in a table named *machine fault*, and the relevant information of its machine model and checkpoints are stored in tables named *machine* and *checkpoint* respectively as shown in Figure 5. These three tables are mapped into three schematic ontology classes named *machine, machine fault,* and *checkpoint*. Similarly, the discovered class which can be mapped from the service knowledge database is named as *machine fault cluster* class.

Schematic relation generation generates relations between schematic classes. Such relations can be identified automatically using the relations between tables defined in the customer service database. However, human interpretation is still needed to label the relations. For example, the relations between tables *machine, machine fault,* and

Figure 6. The machine service ontology represented by DAML+OIL

```
<rdf:RDF>
    xmlns:rdf ="http://www.w3.org/1999/02/22-rdf-syntax-ns#"
    xmlns:rdfs="http://www.w3.org/2000/01/rdf-schema#"
    xmlns:xsd ="http://www.w3.org/2000/10/XMLSchema#"
    xmlns:daml="http://www.w3.org/2001/10/daml+oil#"
    <daml:Ontology rdf:about="Machine Service Ontology">
        <daml:versionInfo>
            $Id: daml+oil-ex.daml,v 1.8 2001/03/27 21:24:04 horrocks Exp $
        </daml:versionInfo>
    <rdfs:comment>
        An ontology of Customer Service
    </rdfs:comment>
    <daml:imports rdf:resource="http://www.w3.org/2001/10/daml+oil"/>
    <daml:Class rdf:ID="Faulty_Theme ">
        <dmal:label> "Faulty Theme"</daml:label>
        <daml:ObjectProperty rdf:ID="ThemeNo">
            <rdf:type rdf:resource="http://www.daml.org/2001/03/daml+oil#UniqueProperty"/>
            <rdfs:range rdf:resource="http://www.w3.org/2000/10/XMLSchema#nonNegativeInteger "/>
        </daml:DatatypeProperty>
    </daml:Class>
    <daml:Class rdf:ID="Checkpoint ">
        <dmal:label> Checkpoint</daml:label>
    </daml:Class>
    <daml:Class rdf:ID="Machine_Fault">
        <dmal:label> "FaultCondtion"</daml:label>
        <daml:ObjectProperty rdf:ID="BelongTo">
            <rdf:type rdf:resource="Faulty_Theme"/>
            <rdfs:range rdf:resource=" Faulty_Theme "/>
        </daml:DatatypeProperty>
        <daml:ObjectProperty rdf:ID="contains_of">
            <rdf:type rdf:resource="Checkpoint"/>
            <rdfs:range rdf:resource="Checkpoint "/>
        </daml:DatatypeProperty>
    </daml:Class>
    <daml:Class rdf:ID="Machine">
        <dmal:label> Machine Model </daml:label>
        <daml:ObjectProperty rdf:ID="damaged_by ">
            <rdf:type rdf:resource="Machine_Fault"/>
            <rdfs:range rdf:resource="Machine_Fault "/>
        </daml:DatatypeProperty>
    </daml:Class>
    </daml:Ontology>
</rdf:RDF>
```

checkpoint in the customer service database are mapped into relations between the corresponding schematic classes that are labeled as *occur-on* and *inspected-by* as shown Figure 5.

Composed relation generation it generates the relation between the schematic class and discovered class. Since the service knowledge database stores fault clustering knowledge mined from the customer services database, it should contain information on relations between the mined knowledge and the schematic knowledge. Such relations are mapped to the corresponding relations between the schematic and discovered ontology classes. Human interpretation is also needed to label such relations. For example, the relation between the table *machine fault cluster* in the service knowledge database and the table *machine fault* in the customer service database is mapped to the composed relation labeled manually as *belong-to* in the corresponding ontology classes.

Instances generation generates instances for the schematic and discovered classes based on the data available on the customer service database and service knowledge database. Each instance corresponds to a record in the database. The attributes of an instance will automatically be supplied with appropriate values from the corresponding records in the database. For example, since the table *machine fault* has a relation to the table *checkpoint*, each record in the table *machine fault* will have an attribute that contains the relation to a record in the table *checkpoint*. Such relation has been converted into ontology relation *inspected-by* as discussed earlier. The records will be mapped respectively to the instances of machine fault and checkpoint classes, in which the machine fault instance contains the *inspected-by* attribute that relates to the checkpoint instance.

Figure 5 shows the generated classes and their relations of the machine service ontology. The generated ontology can be represented using an ontology description language that enables it to be shared over the Semantic Web by Web-based applications. For illustration, Figure 6 represents the machine service ontology using DAML+OIL, a typical ontology description language.

System Architecture

Currently, there are many multinational manufacturing corporations which produce insertion and surface mount machines in the electronics industry. For each type of machine, there are also many models to satisfy different manufacturing requirements. Their customers usually will have different types of models and machines for fulfilling different segments of the markets. It is also quite possible for a customer to use multiple machines (possibly from different manufacturers) for manufacturing a particular product. When a machine problem occurs, the customer is then required to obtain customer service support from different manufacturers. With conventional Web-based service support systems, the customer has to access different Web sites, and retrieve different service support suggestions in order to rectify the machine fault problem. This is troublesome and cumbersome, and there is also the integration problem to tackle by the customer. To rectify this problem, we propose to use the Semantic Web for integrated customer service support.

Figure 7. The Semantic Web customer services

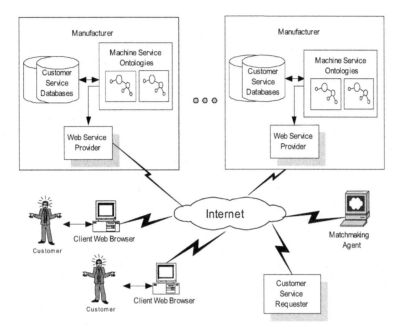

Figure 7 shows the system architecture for the Semantic Web support for customer services. One of the major components is the machine service ontology. Semantic Web enables the knowledge or service ontology to be made available and sharable. As such, manufacturers can produce and generate the service ontology for their machines and models. These service ontologies can then be accessed by Semantic Web services for the support of machine problems. However, the ontology generation process must be simple, and preferably automatic. One possible way to build machine service ontology is to mine the customer service database that maintains the knowledge of past machine service records using an intelligent data mining algorithm such as KSOM. The automatic machine service ontology generation process has been discussed in Section 3.

Once the machine service ontology is made available for different machines and models from different manufacturers, customer service can be supported over the Semantic Web using the *Web service requester*, *matchmaking agent* and *Web service provider* as shown in Figure 2.

Web Service Provider

The Web service provider, which is a kind of Web services, provides machine service support. There are probably many *instances* of a Web service provider existing concurrently on the Internet. An instance of the Web service Provider can be considered as a program that can access the machine service ontology to retrieve machine service knowledge for a given reported problem. Moreover, an instance of the Web service provider can interact with other programs. That is, it can be called by other programs and return the outputs to the calling programs. In order to be known to other programs, instances of the Web service provider must be registered with a specific agent known as the matchmaking agent that serves as a registry and lookup service. Moreover, each instance of the Web service provider also provides a *profile file* that describes its parameters and capabilities. XML (extensible markup language) is used in most Web services to represent the information contained in the profiles. However, traditional XML lacks of the capabilities of representing semantic information. To overcome this problem, the Web service provider uses ontology-based service description language DAML-S to describe information in its profile. Hence, we describe the service as DAML+OIL ontology and its intentional information can be fully understood by other programs.

Figure 8 shows an example of the profile file of the Web service provider. Using DAML-S language, it provides the name of the service as "SearchFaultCase_ProviderService". The profile given in the figure is considered as a *template profile* that provides necessary

Figure 8. Template profile of Web service requester represented by DAML-S

```
<rdf:RDF>
    <daml:Class rdf:ID="SearchFaultCase_ProviderService">
            <rdfs: subClassOf rdf:resource="&process;#AtomicProcess"/>
    </daml:Class>
    <rdf:Property rdf:ID="FaultDescription">
            <rdfs:subPropertyOf rdf:resource="&process;#input">
            <rdfs:domain rdf:resource="#SearchFaultCase">
            <rdfs:range rdf:resource="&xsd;#string">
    </rdf:Property>
    <rdf:Property rdf:ID="FoundCase">
            <rdfs:subPropertyOf rdf:resource="&process;#output">
            <rdfs:domain rdf:resource="#SearchFaultCase">
            <rdfs:range rdf:resource=" Machine_Fault">
    </rdf:Property>
    <daml:Class rdf:ID="SearchFaultCase_ProviderService">
            <daml: sameClassAs>
                    <daml: Restriction daml: cardinality="1">
                        <daml: onProperty rdf: resource="#occur-on">
                            <daml onProperty rdf; resource="ModelName">
                                <hasValue rdf:resource="#NameList">
                    </daml:Restriction>
            </daml: sameClassAs>
    </daml:Class>
</rdf:RDF>
```

information for other programs to use the service. When an instance of the service is actually called, a similar profile with actual data filled will be correspondingly created. In the template profile, input and output parameters are also given using the ontology formalism. The type of input parameter is declared as the standard string type of DAML+OIL, which should be the string that describes the problem. The type of output parameter is the ontology class *Machine Fault* that has been defined in the machine service ontology. It implies that the output values are instances of the *Machine Fault* ontology class. As such, other programs can determine the necessary inputs that need to be passed to a service instance as well as understanding the returned outputs. Moreover, since each service instance only supports certain kinds of machine models, the list of supported models is also provided in the profile file as a restriction declaration. When an instance of the Web service Provider registers its service with the Matchmaking Agent, its profile is sent to the agent. Such information will be used for web service matching purpose as discussed later.

Web Service Requester

The Web service requester, which enables access to customer support for machine services, is also a kind of Web services. Instances of the Web service requester can be created from a Web rquester server where its address is accessible for all users through the Web. When encountering a problem, a user can use the Web to connect the Web requester server in order to create an instance of the Web service requester. The created instance runs as a Web-based program. That is, its can use the Web to interact with the user and other programs. Through the Web, the Web service requester instance provides an interface for the user to enter their reported problem as shown in Figure 9. Through

Figure 9. Input interface for requester Web service

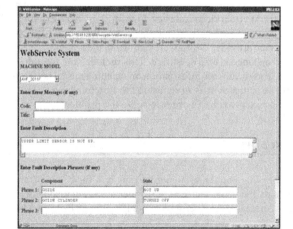

Figure 10. A profile of the Web service requester

```
<rdf:RDF>
        <daml:Class rdf:ID="SearchFaultCase_RequesterService">
                <rdfs: subClassOf rdf:resource="&process;#AtomicProcess"/>
        </daml:Class>
        <rdf:Property rdf:ID="FaultDescription">
                <rdfs:subPropertyOf rdf:resource="&process;#input">
                <rdfs:domain rdf:resource="#SearchFaultCase_RequesterService">
                <rdfs:range rdf:resource="&xsd;#string">
        </rdf:Property>
        <rdf:Property rdf:ID="FoundCase">
                <rdfs:subPropertyOf rdf:resource="&process;#output">
                <rdfs:domain rdf:resource="#SearchFaultCase_RequesterService">
                <rdfs:range rdf:resource=" Machine_Fault">
        </rdf:Property>
        <rdf:Property rdf:ID="Machine_Model">
                <rdfs:domain rdf:resource="#SearchFaultCase_RequesterService">
                <rdfs:range rdf:resource="&xsd;#string">
        </rdf:Property>

        <Request rdf:ID = "Request_00001">
                <instanceOf>
                        <resourceRef xlink:href="#SearchFaultCase_RequesterService "/>
                </instanceOf>
                <FaultDescription>
                        <ResourceData>"Upper limit sensor is not up"</ResourceData>
                </ FaultDescription >
                <MachineModel>
                        <ResourceData>"AVF_2011F"</ResourceData>
                </MachineModel>
        </Request>
</rdf:RDF>
```

the interface, the user can specify the encountered fault as a textual string. The user is also required to enter the code of the machine model. The given information is used to form a profile for the Web service requester. Figure 10 gives an example of a profile of a Web service requester. The description of the Web service provider is quite similar to that of the Web service provider. Moreover, apart from the service description, information of the created instance is also specified. This includes the fault description that is inputted as string. In addition, the information on machine model is also specified in the instance. The profile is then sent as a request to the matchmaking agent in order to seek a potential Web service provider in order to solve the problem.

Matchmaking Agent

As discussed earlier, the matchmaking agent registers functions offered by the Web service provider and other Web services. It is a specific agent responsible for finding an appropriate Web service that matches with a specific request from a user or another Web service.

When the matchmaking agent receives machine service requests from the Web service requester, it locates the appropriate Web services that can fulfill the request. At that moment, instances of the Web service provider should have completely registered to the matchmaking agent. Since the input and output parameters of the Web service provider and Web service requester are described in the format as shown in Figure 8 and Figure 10, the agent will then be able to determine the appropriate Web service provider to answer the request. In addition, using the information on the machine model provided in the profile files of Web service provider instances, the matchmaking agent can determine the instance that supports the machine model specified in the request. Finally, the matchmaking agent can make a connection between the Web service requester instance and the selected Web service provider instance.

Online Machine Service Support

When the Web service provider and Web service requester instances have been connected through the matchmaking agent, the input string on problem description specified in the Web service requester instance is transferred as the input for the Web service provider instance. Then, the Web service provider instance preprocesses the input string (i.e., the machine fault problem description) and clusters it using the KSOM neural network. After clustering, the machine fault cluster that is potentially related to the machine problem request is retrieved. Hence, instances of the machine fault ontology class that belong to the retrieved cluster are retrieved accordingly and are returned as outputs of the Web service provider instance.

When the Web services requester receives the machine fault instances from the Web service provider instance, it extracts the information of the fault-conditions and the associated checkpoints that can be used to solve the machine problem. Then, it ranks

Figure 11. Information of fault-condition retrieved

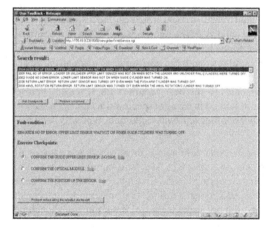

the fault-conditions based on their Euclidean distances to the input string and displays them accordingly to the user as shown Figure 11. Based on the information displayed, the user can try to solve the problem.

Service Reporting and Ontology Update

The user uses the retrieved list of fault conditions to help diagnose and solve the problem by inspecting each fault condition on the list and testing whether the corresponding checkpoints can be used to solve the problem. If the problem can completely be solved, a service report on the machine problem and its associated service information will be sent from the Web service requester instance to the Web service provider instance. The service report is then stored in the corresponding customer service database. However, in the case that if the knowledge from the machine service ontology is insufficient to solve the problem, the user can also report the problem on the service report. The respective manufacturing corporation will then contact the customer, and a service engineer will then be dispatched to the customer site for onsite machine service. After the service has been performed, the service report will be updated. The service reports will subsequently be used to train the KSOM neural network again to update the corresponding machine service ontology.

Performance Evaluation

To evaluate the performance of the proposed approach, an experiment has been conducted. In the experiment, a customer service database, which contains 70,137 fault-conditions, was used as a training dataset. The number of extracted keyword from those fault-conditions was 2,173. The maximum number of keywords allowed in a fault-condition or in the input was 20.

The service machine ontology was then generated as described previously. Knowledge stored in the generated ontology was retrieved to support potential solutions for reported problems. The quality of the ontology was evaluated based on the accuracy of information retrieved. Since KSOM neural network was used as the key technique for knowledge discovery and retrieval, the performance evaluation was carried out on the retrieval accuracy of KSOM. To measure that performance, we first investigated the distance metric that achieved the best accuracy for KSOM. Then, we evaluated the retrieval performance of KSOM in terms of speed and accuracy. We also compared KSOM performance with other popular retrieval techniques typically used in customer support services.

There are two testing datasets conducted for retrieval accuracy evaluation. The first dataset, denoted as *DS1*, is a set of 15,850 fault-conditions, used as input strings for retrieval. As the fault descriptions in the first set were manually created by experts, the second set, denoted as *DS2*, consists of 50 fault descriptions formed from nonexpert users. It is used to test the performance when the input is less technically precise.

Table 1. Retrieval accuracy of distance metrics

Distance Metric	Retrieval Accuracy
Euclidean	78.9%
Inner-product	84.5%
Normalized Euclidean	90.3%

Distance Metric Selection

As discussed earlier, KSOM neural network is adopted for the proposed system. The advantage of KSOM is that it is capable of adapting itself to improve the accuracy when users input contains new keywords that did not appear on the list of extracted keywords. In KSOM, the retrieval accuracy is based on the correctness of the fault-condition in the retrieved cluster that is closet to the input string. The "closeness" is measured using the corresponding weight vectors' distance of the fault-condition and the input string. As such, the method for calculating distances between weight vectors crucially affects the retrieval accuracy of KSOM.

In the experiment, three methods were used for calculating distances between weight vectors in KSOM. The first method computed traditional *Euclidean distance* between vectors. In the second method, *inner-product* was used to calculate the distance between vectors. Finally, the vectors had been normalized as unit vectors before their *normalized Euclidean distances* were calculated. Table 1 gives the retrieval accuracy achieved when a testing set *DS1* was used. Since the normalized Euclidean distance gave the best retrieval accuracy, it was adopted for the KSOM neural network in the experiment.

Performance Evaluation Result

KSOM is an unsupervised learning technique, therefore it can automatically discover hidden knowledge in data without using prior knowledge given by human experts. For experimental comparison purpose, a supervised neural network, Learning Vector Quantization Version 3 (or LVQ3), is also adopted in the experiment. In addition, k-nearest neighbor (kNN) technique has been typically used for retrieval purpose in traditional customer service system. Therefore, apart of two mentioned neural networks, we also made use of kNN for retrieval evaluation. There are two popular variations of kNN techniques were adopted. The first variation, denoted as kNN1, bases on vector's normalized Euclidean distance to find the fault-conditions closest to the input string. The second, denoted as kNN2, makes use of fuzzy-trigram technique (Inference, 99) to do so. Then, we evaluate the performance of adopted techniques using two criteria: speed and accuracy.

Table 2. Retrieval speed evaluation

Description	Time			
	LVQ3	KSOM	kNN1	kNN2
Training	96 min 44 sec	264 min 35 sec	N/A	N/A
Average on-line retrieval	1.9 sec	0.8 sec	15.3 sec	16.7 sec

Table 3. Retrieval accuracy evaluation

Retrieval Technique	Retrieval Accuracy	
	Based on *DS1*	Based on *DS2*
kNN1	81.4%	72%
kNN2	77.6%	76%
LVQ3	93.2%	88%
KSOM	90.3%	86%

Retrieval Speed Evaluation

We evaluate the speed performance based on average online retrieval. For KSOM and LVQ3 neural networks, training time was also measured and compared. As a unsupervised learning technique, KSOM can automatically make use the data in the Customer Service Database for training. However, LVQ3 needs human interpretation to determine target fault-condition corresponding to each given training input.

The dataset *DS1* was used for speed evaluation. The statistics information of training and online-average retrieval time of four mentioned techniques is given in Table 1. It states that even though kNN techniques do not need to be trained before performing retrieval, their performance was outperformed by neural networks techniques in terms of speed. As compared to LVQ3, KSOM requires longer time for training, but it performs more efficiently in terms of online retrieval speed. Since the training process can be carried out in off-line mode, neural networks, particularly KSOM, are more suitable for an online retrieval system than the typical kNN technique.

Retrieval Accuracy Evaluation

Retrieval accuracy was evaluated based on the accuracy of fault-conditions retrieved. The way to evaluate retrieval result of KSOM has been discussed earlier. The retrieval accuracy of LVQ3 and kNN techniques could be determined directly through the correctness of fault-conditions retrieved. Table 3 gives the accuracy of retrieval measured on two datasets *DS1* and *DS2*. As can be seen in the table, the accuracies of two neural networks KSOM and LVQ3 were better than those of kNN technique variations. The retrieval accuracy on the dataset *DS2* set was lower than on *DS1*. It is expected due to the fact that technical terms might be not properly used by nonexpert users when conducting fault-conditions in *DS2*. In both data sets, LVQ3 achieved better performance than KSOM. It is also expected since a supervised learning technique often obtains better accuracy than an equivalent unsupervised one when applied in a same domain. However, since LVQ3 always needs human interpretation for training, it may encounter problem when dealing with large dataset.

Conclusion

In this chapter we propose a semantic-based customer support service system, in which the Semantic Web is used for knowledge sharing, reusing, and exchanging purpose. As such, the proposed system can integrate knowledge of customer support services offered by multiple multinational manufacturing corporations. Therefore, when a machine problem occurs, a customer can obtain customer service support from different manufacturers in automatical manner instead of manually searching as in conventional Web-based service support system. To support ontology, which is considered as a standard of knowledge representation in the Semantic Web, a framework is proposed to mine knowledge in the customer service database using KSOM neural network and convert it into machine service ontology. In the proposed system, *Web service requester*, *matchmaking agent* and *Web service provider* are constructed to allow customer support can be granted to users over the Semantic Web environment from multiple machine customer ontologies available. To evaluate the performance, an experiment has been conducted to perform retrieval from knowledge mined from an experimental customer service database. The experimental results showed that neural network techniques outperform typical kNN technique in both speed and accuracy criteria. As compared to KSOM, LVQ3 required less training time and gained more accurate retrieval. However, as KSOM gave faster average online retrieval speed and does not need human interpretation during training, it is more suitable for online customer support service system.

References

Aamodt, A., & Plaza, E. (1994). Case-based reasoning: Foundational issues, methodological variations, and system approaches. *Proceedings of Artificial Intelligence Communications (AICom)*, 7(1), 39-59.

Ankolekar, A., Burstein, M., Hobbs, J. R., Lassila, O., Martin, D. L., McIlraith, S. A., et al. (2001). DAML-S: Semantic markup for Web services. In *Proceedings of the International Semantic Web Working Symposium*, Stanford, CA.

Austin, D., Barbin, A., Ferris, C., & Garg, S. (2002). *Web Services Architecture Requirements*. Retrieved from http://www.w3c.org/TR/wsa-reqs

Balakrishnan, K., & Honavar, V. (1998). Intelligent diagnosis systems. *Journal of Intelligent Systems*, 8(3), 239-290.

Berkhin, P. (2002). *Survey of clustering data mining techniques.* Technical Report, Accrue Software Inc. Retrieved from http://citeseer.nj.nec.com/berkhin02surve y.html

Berners-Lee, T. (2000). *Weaving the web: The original design and ultimate destiny of the World Wide Web.* HarperBusiness Publishers.

Berners-Lee, T., Hendler, J., & Lassila, O. (2001). The semantic web. *Scientific American.* Retrieved from http://www.sciam.com/2001/0501issue/0501berners-lee.html

Breiman, L., Friedman, J., Olshen, R., & Stone, C. (1984). *Classification of regression trees.* Wadsworth.

Christensen, E., Curbera, F., Meredith, G., & Weerawarana, S. (2001). *Web services description language (WSDL) 1.1.* Retrieved from http://www.w3.org/TR/wsdl

Franklin, S., & Graesser, A. (1996). Is it an agent, or just a program?: A taxonomy for autonomous agents. In *Proceedings of the 3rd International Workshop on Agent Theories, Architectures, and Languages.* Springer-Verlag.

Guarino, N., & Giaretta, P. (1995). *Ontologies and knowledge bases: Towards a terminological clarification. Toward very large knowledge bases: Knowledge building and knowledge sharing.* Amsterdam: IOS Press.

House, W. C., (1994, October 6-8). Automating help desk operations using case-based reasoning: a practical application of expert systems technology. In *Proceedings of the Annual Conference of the International Association for Computer Information Systems* (pp. 100-106), Washington, DC, USA.

Inference Corporation. CBR Content Navigator. Retrieved from http://www.inference.com/ products/

Kohonen, T. (1990). The self-organising map. *Proceedings of the IEEE, 78*(9), part I, 464-480.

Kohonen, T. (2001) *Self-Organizing Maps.* Berlin: Springer.

Law, Y. F. D., Foong, S. W., & Kwan, S. E. J. (1997). An integrated case-based reasoning approach for intelligent help desk fault management. *Expert Systems with Applications, 13*(4), 265-274.

Lees, B., & Corchado, J. (1997). *Case based reasoning in a hybrid agent-oriented system.* In *Proceedings of the 5th German Workshop on Case-Based Reasoning* (pp. 139-144).

Liu, Z. Q., & Yan, F. (1997). Fuzzy neural network in case-based diagnostic system. *IEEE Transactions on Fuzzy Systems, 5*(2), 209-222.

Muller, N. J. (1996). Expanding the help desk through the World Wide Web. *Information Systems Management, 13*(3), 37-44.

Papagni, M., Cirillo, V., & Micarelli, A. (1997). *A hybrid architecture for a user-adapted training system.* In *Proceedings of the 5th German Workshop on Case-Based Reasoning* (pp. 181-188).

Patterson, D. W. R., & Hughes, J. G. (1997). Case-based reasoning for fault diagnosis. *The New Review of Applied Expert Systems, 3,* 15-26.

Quinlan, J. R. (1986). Induction of decision trees. *Machine Learning, 1*, 81-106.

Quinlan, J. R. (1993). *C4.5: Programs for machine learning*. San Mateo, CA: Morgan Kaufman Publishers.

Richter, A. G. (2000). *PATDEX: A case-based reasoning tool for diagnosis*. Online document available at <URL: http://www.agr.infomatik.uni-kl.de>

Riesbeck, C. K., & Schank, R. C. (1989). *Inside case based reasoning*. Lawrence Erlbaum Associates Inc.

Shimazu, H., Shibata, A., & Nihei, K., (1994). Case-based retrieval interface adapted to customer-initiated dialogues in help desk operations. In *Proceedings of the Twelfth National Conference on Artificial Intelligence* (Vol. 1, pp.513-518). Seattle, WA.

Van Harmelen, F., Patel-Schneider, P., & Horrocks, I. (2001). *DAML + OIL*. Retrieved from http://www.daml.org/2001/03/reference.html

Watson, I. D., (1997). *Applying case-based reasoning: Techniques for enterprise systems*. San Mateo, CA: Morgan Kaufman Publishers.

UDDI (2000). *The UDDI Technical White Paper*. Retrieved from http://www.uddi.org/

Wordnet (2004). *Wordnet: A lexicon database for the English language*. Retrieved from http://www.cogsci.princeton.edu/~wn/

Chapter V

A Tutorial on RDF with Jena

Wan-Yeung Wong, The Chinese University of Hong Kong, Hong Kong, China

Tak-Pang Lau, The Chinese University of Hong Kong, Hong Kong, China

Irwin King, The Chinese University of Hong Kong, Hong Kong, China

Michael R. Lyu, The Chinese University of Hong Kong, Hong Kong, China

Abstract

This chapter gives a tutorial on resource description framework (RDF), its XML representation, and Jena, a set of Java-based API designed and implemented to further simplify the manipulation of RDF documents. RDF is a W3C standard which provides a common framework for describing resources in the World Wide Web and other applications. Under this standard framework with the Jena, different resources can be manipulated and exchanged easily, which leads to cost reduction and better efficiency in business applications. In this tutorial, we present some basic concepts and applications of RDF and Jena. In particular, we use a television object to illustrate the usage of RDF in describing various resources being used, the XML syntax in representing the RDF, and the ways Jena manipulate various RDF documents. Furthermore, complete programming codes with detailed explanations are also presented to give readers a better understanding of Jena. References are given at the end for readers' further investigation.

Introduction

The resource description framework (RDF) (W3C, 2004a) is a W3C (W3C, 2005b) standard which is commonly used to describe resources for any application. For business applications, a resource may be a product, a service, or a person. Since having a standard framework to manipulate different resources often leads to cost reduction and better efficiency, RDF is widely used in business applications. In this chapter, we give a simple tutorial on RDF, the language (RDF/XML) used by RDF, and a Java API (Jena) for manipulating RDF/XML. We assume that readers should have some background knowledge on URI, XML, and Java. Readers may refer to Wu (2004) for more information about programming in Java.

We mention that RDF is used to describe resources such as products, services, or people. It provides the data model and XML (W3C, 2005a) syntax so that RDF documents can be easily exchanged by different applications. The XML language used by RDF is called RDF/XML. Moreover, the use of RDF/XML makes RDF documents to be both human readable and computer readable. There are some examples for using RDF such as RDF Site Summary (RSS) (RSS-DEV Working Group, 2000) and Friend of a Friend (FOAF) (Brickley, 2005). The former one is designed for the Web syndication, while the latter one is designed to describe people, interests, and interconnections.

The first work on RDF was started by R. V. Guha when he was with Apple Computer and later with Netscape. In 1999, the specification of RDF data model and XML syntax was published in W3C. The work continued and a new specification of RDF was published in 2004, completely replacing the old specification rather than being assigned a new version number.

In this tutorial, we first use a television product as a resource example. In RDF, we use a *URI* to uniquely identify a *resource* (The Internet Society, 2005). The URI of a television resource may consist of the company information (e.g., www.kingstv.com), category (e.g., plasma), and model number (e.g. PSM2000) like "http://www.kingstv.com/plasma/PSM2000". Unlike the URL of a Web site, the URI of a resource is not necessary to be Internet accessible. For example, the aforementioned URI that begins with "http" does not necessarily have to represent that the television resource is accessible via HTTP. Such URI only denotes the abstract notion of world peace.

After defining the television resource, we can describe the resource by its *properties* and *property values*. A property is a resource that has a name, while a property value is the value of the property. For a television resource, the properties may be its model number, detail description, and price. Similar to the resource identification, we use a URI to uniquely identify a property. For example, the URI of the model number property may be "http://www.kingstv.com/tv_property/model" and its property value may be "PSM2000". In addition, a property value can be another resource. We may have a user property which value is a resource for describing a person who uses that television.

The whole scenario can be represented by a labeled, directed graph called *RDF graph* (see Figure 1). Inside an RDF graph, we use an *ellipse* to represent a resource, an *arrow* to represent a property, and a *rectangle* to represent a non-resource property value (literal). For a literal (rectangle), further properties are not allowed. On the other hand,

Figure 1. An RDF graph representing a television resource

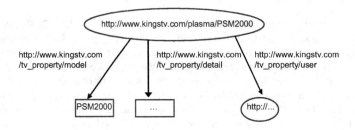

Table 1. RDF triples representing a television resource

Subject	Predicate	Object
http://www.kingstv.com/plasma /PSM2000	http://www.kingstv.com /tv_property/model	PSM2000
http://www.kingstv.com/plasma /PSM2000	http://www.kingstv.com /tv_property/detail	...
http://www.kingstv.com/plasma /PSM2000	http://www.kingstv.com /tv_property/user	http://...

Figure 2. An RDF graph containing an intermediate node and a loop

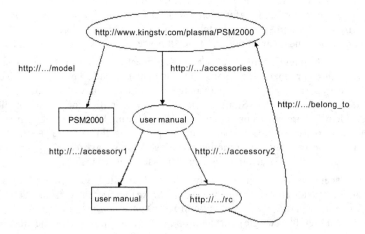

Table 2. The corresponding RDF triples

Subject	Predicate	Object
http://www.kingstv.com /plasma/PSM2000	http://.../model	PSM2000
http://www.kingstv.com /plasma/PSM2000	http://.../accessories	genid:A123
genid:A123	http://.../accessory1	user manual
genid:A123	http://.../accessory2	http://.../rc
http://.../rc	http://.../belong_to	http://www.kingstv.com /plasma/PSM2000

further properties are allowed for a resource (ellipse). In this example, the user resource has no further property although further properties are allowed. Besides the RDF graph, the whole scenario can be represented by a list of RDF statements. An RDF statement is a *triple* that contains a subject (resource), a predicate (property), and an object (property value). Table 1 shows a list of RDF triples, which is equivalent to the RDF graph in Figure 1.

Figure 2 shows a more complicated example of an RDF graph. The television resource contains two properties "model" and "accessories". The "model" property specifies the model number of the television which is similar to the previous example. The "accessories" property refers to an intermediate node without URI reference which contains two accessories user manual and remote controller (http://.../rc). Since the intermediate node does not represent an actual resource, it does not have a URI and we generate an arbitrary ID (A123) to represent it. Furthermore, the "accessory2" property refers to a remote controller resource of the television which has a "belong_to" property. This property refers back to the television resource that forms a loop in the graph. Table 2 shows the corresponding RDF triples.

Syntax of RDF/XML

So far, we explain how to use graphs and triples to describe resources in RDF. Besides graphs and triples, we can use XML to describe resources. The XML language used by RDF is called RDF/XML. By using RDF/XML, plain text RDF data can be easily stored in computers. We can also easily edit the data which is human readable. In this section, we give a simple tutorial on RDF/XML.

Listing 1.

```
1:   <?xml version="1.0"?>
2:   <rdf:RDF xmlns:rdf="http://www.w3.org/1999/02/22-rdf-syntax-ns#"
3:     xmlns:tv="http://www.kingstv.com/tv_property/">
4:     <rdf:Description rdf:about="http://www.kingstv.com/plasma/PSM2000">
5:        <tv:model>PSM2000</tv:model>
6:        <tv:detail>This is a plasma TV.</tv:detail>
7:        <tv:user rdf:resource="http://www.kingstv.com/user/1"/>
8:     </rdf:Description>
9:   </rdf:RDF>
```

Consider the example in Figure 1, Listing 1 shows the corresponding RDF/XML.

Line 1 is the XML declaration which specifies the XML version of the document. In line 2 and 3, we specify the root <rdf:RDF> element of the RDF document. The URI of the "rdf" namespace for all predefined RDF elements and attributes must be "http://www.w3.org/ 1999/02/22-rdf-syntax-ns#". In line 3, we defined our "tv" namespace which is the URI prefix of all television resource properties. Starting from line 4, we describe our resources. For each resource, we use the <rdf:Description> element to enclose the resource description. Inside the <rdf:Description> element, we use the "rdf:about" attribute to specify the resource URI. The "rdf:about" attribute can be omitted if the resource does not have a URI. In that case, the application should automatically generate an arbitrary ID to represent that resource. In line 5 and 6, we specify two properties "model" and "detail" by using our defined elements <tv:model> and <tv:detail> which values are literal. Since "tv" is our defined namespace which URI is "http://www.kingstv.com/tv_property/", the URI of "model" property is concatenated and becomes "http://www.kingstv.com/tv_property/ model". Similarly, the URI of "detail" property is concatenated and becomes "http:// www.kingstv.com/tv_property/detail". In line 7, we specify the "user" property by using our defined <tv:user> element. However, its property refers to another resource with URI "http://www.kingstv.com/user/1" which is specified by the "rdf:resource" attribute. Since the user resource has no further property, we need not further describe the user resource by using the <rdf:Description> element. Finally, line 8 and 9 are the closing tags for line 4 and 2 respectively.

Currently, W3C provides a useful online RDF validation service in W3C (2004b) (see Figure 3). After inputting the RDF document, the validation engine parses the RDF document and checks its validity. If it is valid, a list of RDF triples (see Figure 4) and the RDF graph (see Figure 5) will be displayed.

Figure 3. An online RDF validation service provided by W3C

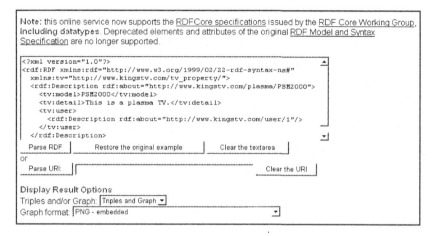

Figure 4. Results displayed by triples

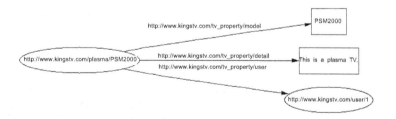

Figure 5. Results displayed by a graph

Consider the more complicated example in Figure 2, Listing 2 shows the corresponding RDF/XML.

There are two main resources which are described in line 4 and 14. The former one describes the television resource, while the latter one describes its remote controller resource. As shown in Figure 2, the "accessories" property refers to the intermediate node, which does not represent an actual resource. Therefore, under the <tv:accessories> element in line 6, we use the <rdf:Description> element in line 7 to represent the intermediate

Listing 2.

```
1:    <?xml version="1.0"?>
2:    <rdf:RDF xmlns:rdf="http://www.w3.org/1999/02/22-rdf-syntax-ns#"
3:      xmlns:tv="http://www.kingstv.com/tv_property/">
4:      <rdf:Description rdf:about="http://www.kingstv.com/plasma/PSM2000">
5:        <tv:model>PSM2000</tv:model>
6:        <tv:accessories>
7:          <rdf:Description>
8:            <tv:accessory1>user manual</tv:accessory1>
9:            <tv:accessory2
10:               rdf:resource="http://www.kingstv.com/plasma/PSM2000/rc"/>
11:          </rdf:Description>
12:        </tv:accessories>
13:      </rdf:Description>
14:      <rdf:Description
15:        rdf:about="http://www.kingstv.com/plasma/PSM2000/rc">
16:        <tv:belong_to
17:          rdf:resource="http://www.kingstv.com/plasma/PSM2000"/>
18:      </rdf:Description>
19:    </rdf:RDF>
```

node without URI which ID should be automatically generated by the application. Then we describe two accessories from line 8 to 10. The "accessory2" property in line 9 refers to the remote controller resource which is further described in line 14. Similarly, the "belong_to" property of the remote controller resource in line 16 refers to the television resource which is already described in line 4.

The use of intermediate nodes represented by <rdf:Description> elements makes the RDF document nested. Although the document in the previous example is still easy to read, it is hard to read if there are too many nested <rdf:Description> elements. A better solution is to take out the descriptions of all intermediate nodes to the same level as the actual resources. Listing 3 shows another RDF/XML, which is equivalent to the example in Figure 2.

Listing 3.

```
1:   <?xml version="1.0"?>
2:   <rdf:RDF xmlns:rdf="http://www.w3.org/1999/02/22-rdf-syntax-ns#"
3:     xmlns:tv="http://www.kingstv.com/tv_property/">
4:     <rdf:Description rdf:about="http://www.kingstv.com/plasma/PSM2000">
5:        <tv:model>PSM2000</tv:model>
6:        <tv:accessories rdf:nodeID="A123"/>
7:     </rdf:Description>
8:     <rdf:Description rdf:nodeID="A123">
9:        <tv:accessory1>user manual</tv:accessory1>
10:       <tv:accessory2
11:          rdf:resource="http://www.kingstv.com/plasma/PSM2000/rc"/>
12:    </rdf:Description>
13:    <rdf:Description
14:       rdf:about="http://www.kingstv.com/plasma/PSM2000/rc">
15:       <tv:belong_to
16:          rdf:resource="http://www.kingstv.com/plasma/PSM2000"/>
17:    </rdf:Description>
18:  </rdf:RDF>
```

The main difference between the current and previous examples is in line 6. As shown in Figure 2, the "accessories" property refers to the intermediate node which ID is "A123". Therefore, we use the "rdf:nodeID" attribute in line 6 to refer to the intermediate node which description is taken out to the same level as the actual resources (see line 8 to 12). The value of the "rdf:nodeID" attribute must be an alphanumeric string and begin with an alphabet. When we compare line 4 with line 8, we use the "rdf:about" attribute to indicate that the current resource is an actual resource, whereas we use the "rdf:nodeID" attribute to indicate that the current resource is an intermediate node. By taken out the descriptions of all intermediate nodes, the RDF document is less nested and easier to read.

In the previous example, the television resource contains multiple accessories. If we add more accessories, we may need to add more <tv:accessory*N*> elements where *N* is an

Listing 4.

```
1:    <?xml version="1.0"?>

2:    <rdf:RDF xmlns:rdf="http://www.w3.org/1999/02/22-rdf-syntax-ns#"

3:      xmlns:tv="http://www.kingstv.com/tv_property/">

4:      <rdf:Description rdf:about="http://www.kingstv.com/plasma/PSM2000">

5:        <tv:model>PSM2000</tv:model>

6:        <tv:accessories>

7:          <rdf:Bag>

8:            <rdf:li>user manual</rdf:li>

9:            <rdf:li

10:               rdf:resource="http://www.kingstv.com/plasma/PSM2000/rc"/>

11:          </rdf:Bag>

12:        </tv:accessories>

13:      </rdf:Description>

14:      <rdf:Description

15:        rdf:about="http://www.kingstv.com/plasma/PSM2000/rc">

16:        <tv:belong_to

17:          rdf:resource="http://www.kingstv.com/plasma/PSM2000"/>

18:      </rdf:Description>

19:    </rdf:RDF>
```

integer. However, using such method to represent multiple items of a property is inextensible because we need to increase N manually and modify our application to process those new <tv:accessory$N$> elements. In RDF/XML, we can use the container element to describe a list of items and Listing 4 shows an example which is functionally equivalent to the previous example.

In this example, we no longer use our defined intermediate node to represent the multiple items of the "accessories" property. Instead, we use the <rdf:Bag> element in line 7 to represent the unordered list of accessories. For each item in the list, we use the <rdf:li> element to describe its value (see line 8 to 10). Figure 6 shows the corresponding RDF graph. The "accessories" property refers to the intermediate node which is generated by the <rdf:Bag> element. The ID (A123) of the intermediate node is automatically generated

Figure 6. An RDF graph with a property containing multiple items

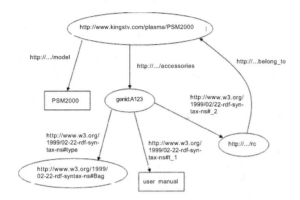

too. Unlike Figure 2, the intermediate node has an extra "type" property with URI "http:/ /www.w3.org/1999/02/22-rdf-syntax-ns#type" which refers to the "Bag" container resource with URI "http://www.w3.org/1999/02/22-rdf-syntax-ns#Bag". The "Bag" container resource specifies the property value of the "accessories" property to be an unordered list. Each item in the list is referred by the auto-numbered property with URI "http:// www.w3.org/1999/02/22-rdf-syntax-ns#_*N*" where *N* is an integer. Beside the <rdf:Bag> element, the <rdf:Seq> and <rdf:Alt> elements can also be used. The <rdf:Seq> element represents an ordered list of items, while the <rdf:Alt> element represents a list of alternative items. All <rdf:Bag>, <rdf:Seq>, and <rdf:Alt> elements may contain duplicate items. To use the <rdf:Seq> or <rdf:Alt> element in this example, we only need to replace "Bag" in both line 7 and 11 by "Seq" or "Alt". For the RDF graph, the URI of the "Seq" resource is "http://www.w3.org/1999/02/22-rdf-syntax-ns#Seq", while the URI of the "Alt" resource is "http://www.w3.org/1999/02/22-rdf-syntax-ns#Alt". Other values remain unchanged.

Syntax of Jena

In the previous section, we describe how to write the RDF/XML code manually. However, we may need to integrate RDF with our own applications. It is time consuming if we write our own code to compose and parse RDF documents even if we use some general purpose XML libraries. Therefore, using specific purpose libraries like Jena (Hewlett-Packard Development Company, 2005; McBride, 2001) helps us to process RDF documents more easily. Jena is a Java framework for building semantic Web applications which provides a programmatic environment for RDF and other related technologies. In addition, Jena is open source and grown out of work with the HP Labs Semantic Web Program. The official Web site of Jena is "http://jena.sourceforge.net". Currently, Jena 2.2 is the latest version. Hence, we give a simple tutorial on Jena 2.2 in this section.

Before using Jena, we need to download "Jena-2.2.zip" via the official Web site and extract the ZIP file. To install Jena, we need to copy all ".jar" files from "Jena-2.2/lib/" to "$JAVA_HOME/jre/lib/ext/" directory where "$JAVA_HOME" is the JDK (Sun Microsystems, Inc. 2005) home path. For a Linux platform, JDK is usually installed under the "/usr/java/" directory. For a Windows platform, JDK is usually installed under the "C:\" or "C:\Program Files\Java\" directory. To test Jena, we may create "Test.java" with the following code which composes an empty RDF document without any resource. Then we compile and run "Test.java" (Listing 5) so that the output should be the same as Figure 7.

We begin the Jena tutorial by showing how to compose a simple RDF document which is equivalent to the example in Figure 1. "Example1.java" (Listing 6) outputs the RDF file "example1.rdf" which can be viewed by any plain text editor.

In line 1 and 2, we import two packages "java.io" and "com.hp.hpl.jena.rdf.model". The former one contains classes for writing files, while the latter one contains classes for

Listing 5. Test.java

```
1:   import com.hp.hpl.jena.rdf.model.*;

2:

3:   public class Test

4:   {

5:     public static void main(String[] args)

6:     {

7:       Model model = ModelFactory.createDefaultModel();

8:       model.write(System.out);

9:     }

10:  }
```

Figure 7. Output of Test.java

```
<rdf:RDF

    xmlns:rdf="http://www.w3.org/1999/02/22-rdf-syntax-ns#" >

</rdf:RDF>
```

Listing 6. Example1.java

```
1:    import java.io.*;
2:    import com.hp.hpl.jena.rdf.model.*;
3:
4:    public class Example1
5:    {
6:      public static void main(String[] args) throws Exception
7:      {
8:        Model model = ModelFactory.createDefaultModel();
9:
10:       String tvNS = "http://www.kingstv.com/tv_property/";
11:       model.setNsPrefix("tv", tvNS);
12:
13:       Resource psm2000 = model.createResource(
14:         "http://www.kingstv.com/plasma/PSM2000");
15:       Resource user1 = model.createResource(
16:         "http://www.kingstv.com/user/1");
17:
18:       Property tvModel = model.createProperty(tvNS, "model");
19:       Property tvDetail = model.createProperty(tvNS, "detail");
20:       Property tvUser = model.createProperty(tvNS, "user");
21:
22:       model.add(psm2000, tvModel, "PSM2000");
23:       model.add(psm2000, tvDetail, "This is a plasma TV.");
24:       model.add(psm2000, tvUser, user1);
25:
26:       FileOutputStream fileOut = new FileOutputStream("example1.rdf");
27:       model.write(fileOut);
28:       fileOut.close();
29:      }
30:    }
```

composing RDF documents. Then we declare the public class called "Example1" in line 4 and declare the main method in line 6. There are six steps to compose the RDF document.

Step 1. First, we use the "createDefaultModel" method to create an empty RDF document which is represented by the "model" object in line 8.

Step 2. After creating the "model" object, we define the namespace in line 10 for the television properties and we use the "setNsPrefix" method to assign the namespace to the "model" object in line 11. The first parameter of the "setNsPrefix" method is the namespace and the second parameter is the corresponding URI.

Step 3. We use the "createResource" method to define two resources with their own URI from line 13 to 16. The television resource is represented by the "psm2000" object, while the user resource is represented by the "user1" object.

Step 4. We use the "createProperty" method to define all properties from line 18 to 20. The first parameter of the method is the namespace of the property and the second parameter is the name of the property.

Step 5. After defining the resources and properties, we use the "add" method to add the relationships between them to the "model" object in terms of RDF triples from line 22 to 24. The first parameter of the "add" method is the subject (resource), the second parameter is the predicate (property), and the third parameter is the object (literal or resource).

Step 6. Finally, the "model" object contains the composed RDF document and we use the "write" method to write the document to the "example1.rdf" file from line 26 to 28. The parameter of the "write" method can be any "OutputStream" object.

Consider the more complicated example in Figure 2, "Example2.java" (Listing 7) outputs the corresponding RDF file "example2.rdf".

Although Figure 2 is more complicated than Figure 1, their programs "Example2.java" and "Example1.java" are more or less the same. The extra feature of the current example is the presence of the intermediate node. To define the intermediate node, we do not pass the URI to the "createResource" method in line 14. The way for adding the relationships involved the intermediate node is the same as those actual resources (see line 22 to 26). In the previous section, we mention that the use of intermediate nodes represented by <rdf:Description> elements makes the RDF document nested and hard to read. Fortunately, Jena automatically takes out the descriptions of all intermediate nodes to the same level as the actual resources. We can see the effect by viewing the generated "example2.rdf" file.

Consider the example in Figure 6 which uses the "Bag" container, Listing 8, "Example3.java", outputs the corresponding RDF file "example3.rdf".

The main difference between the current and previous examples is that the current example creates a "Bag" container, which is represented by the "accessories" object in line 18, to replace the intermediate node in the previous example. Then we add the literal or resource to the container by using the "add" method in line 19 and 20. The way for adding the relationships involved the container is the same as those actual resources (see

Listing 7.

```
1:   import java.io.*;
2:   import com.hp.hpl.jena.rdf.model.*;
3:
4:   public class Example2
5:   {
6:     public static void main(String[] args) throws Exception
7:     {
8:        Model model = ModelFactory.createDefaultModel();
9:
10:       String tvNS = "http://www.kingstv.com/tv_property/";
11:       model.setNsPrefix("tv", tvNS);
12:
13:       Resource psm2000 = model.createResource(
14:          "http://www.kingstv.com/plasma/PSM2000");
15:       Resource rc = model.createResource(
16:          "http://www.kingstv.com/plasma/PSM2000/rc");
17:       Resource node = model.createResource();
18:
19:       Property tvModel = model.createProperty(tvNS, "model");
20:       Property tvAccessories = model.createProperty(tvNS, "accessories");
21:       Property tvAccessory1 = model.createProperty(tvNS, "accessory1");
22:       Property tvAccessory2 = model.createProperty(tvNS, "accessory2");
23:       Property tvBelongTo = model.createProperty(tvNS, "belong_to");
24:
25:       model.add(psm2000, tvModel, "PSM2000");
26:       model.add(psm2000, tvAccessories, node);
27:       model.add(node, tvAccessory1, "user manual");
28:       model.add(node, tvAccessory2, rc);
29:       model.add(rc, tvBelongTo, psm2000);
30:
```

Listing 7. continued

```
31:   FileOutputStream fileOut = new FileOutputStream("example2.rdf");
32:       model.write(fileOut);
33:       fileOut.close();
34:   }
35:  }
```

Listing 8.

```
1:   import java.io.*;
2:   import com.hp.hpl.jena.rdf.model.*;
3:
4:   public class Example3
5:   {
6:     public static void main(String[] args) throws Exception
7:     {
8:        Model model = ModelFactory.createDefaultModel();
9:
10:       String tvNS = "http://www.kingstv.com/tv_property/";
11:       model.setNsPrefix("tv", tvNS);
12:
13:       Resource psm2000 = model.createResource(
14:          "http://www.kingstv.com/plasma/PSM2000");
15:       Resource rc = model.createResource(
16:          "http://www.kingstv.com/plasma/PSM2000/rc");
17:
18:       Bag accessories = model.createBag();
19:       accessories.add("user manual");
20:       accessories.add(rc);
```

Listing 8. continued

```
21:
22:        Property tvModel = model.createProperty(tvNS, "model");
23:        Property tvAccessories = model.createProperty(tvNS, "accessories");
24:        Property tvBelongTo = model.createProperty(tvNS, "belong_to");
25:
26:        model.add(psm2000, tvModel, "PSM2000");
27:        model.add(psm2000, tvAccessories, accessories);
28:        model.add(rc, tvBelongTo, psm2000);
29:
30:        FileOutputStream fileOut = new FileOutputStream("example3.rdf");
31:        model.write(fileOut);
32:        fileOut.close();
33:    }
34: }
```

Listing 9. Example4.java

```
1: import java.io.*;
2: import com.hp.hpl.jena.rdf.model.*;
3:
4: public class Example4
5: {
6:    private static Model model = null;
7:
8:    public static void main(String[] args) throws Exception
9:    {
10:       model = ModelFactory.createDefaultModel();
11:
```

Listing 9. continued

```
12:     FileInputStream fileIn = new FileInputStream("example3.rdf");

13:     model.read(fileIn, "");

14:     fileIn.close();

15:

16:     System.out.println("Query 1:");

17:     NsIterator nsIterator = model.listNameSpaces();

18:     while (nsIterator.hasNext()){

19:         System.out.println(nsIterator.nextNs()+";");

20:     }

21:     System.out.println();

22:

23:     System.out.println("Query 2:");

24:     query(null, null, null);

25:

26:     System.out.println("Query 3:");

27:     query(model.createResource(

28:         "http://www.kingstv.com/plasma/PSM2000/rc"), null, null);

29:

30:     System.out.println("Query 4:");

31:     query(null,

32:         model.createProperty(model.getNsPrefixURI("tv"), "model"), null);

33:

34:     System.out.println("Query 5:");

35:     query(null, null, model.createLiteral("user manual"));

36:

37:     System.out.println("Query 6:");

38:     StmtIterator stmtIterator = model.listStatements(

39:         model.createResource("http://www.kingstv.com/plasma/PSM2000"),
```

Listing 9. continued

```
40:            model.createProperty(model.getNsPrefixURI("tv"), "accessories"),
41:            (RDFNode)null);
42:         Statement statement = stmtIterator.nextStatement();
43:         Bag bag = statement.getBag();
44:         NodeIterator nodeIterator = bag.iterator();
45:         while (nodeIterator.hasNext()){
46:            System.out.println(nodeIterator.next()+";");
47:         }
48:      }
49:
50:      private static void query(Resource s, Property p, RDFNode o)
51:      {
52:         StmtIterator stmtIterator = model.listStatements(s, p, o);
53:         while (stmtIterator.hasNext()){
54:            Statement statement = stmtIterator.nextStatement();
55:            System.out.println("("+statement.getSubject()+",");
56:            System.out.println(" "+statement.getPredicate()+",");
57:            System.out.println(" "+statement.getObject()+");");
58:         }
59:         System.out.println();
60:      }
61:   }
```

line 26 to 28). Besides the "Bag" container, we can use the "Seq" and "Alt" containers. To use them in this example, we only need to replace "Bag" in line 18 by "Seq" or "Alt", and replace "createBag" by "createSeq" or "createAlt".

So far, we describe how to use Jena to compose RDF documents. It is time to describe how to use Jena to read and query in RDF documents. We demonstrate this by using a long example "Example4.java" as shown in Listing 9.

In this example, we read the RDF file "example3.rdf" which is generated by the previous "Example3.java". The corresponding RDF graph is shown in Figure 6. In line 6, we declare the "model" object which represents the RDF document to be read. There are two methods "main" and "query" which are declared in line 8 and 50 respectively. The former one is the entry point of the program, while the latter one performs the query according to three input parameters and then prints the result on the screen. The program starts in line 10 which creates an empty RDF document by using the "createDefaultModel" method. Then we use the "read" method to read the RDF file "example3.rdf" and store it to the "model" object from line 12 to 14. The first parameter of the "read" method can be any "InputStream" object and the second parameter specifies the base to use when converting the relative URI to absolute URI. Starting from line 16, there are six queries.

Query 1. First, we want to query all namespaces which are used in this document. Therefore, we use the "listNameSpaces" method in line 17 to obtain a list of namespaces which are stored in the "nsIterator" object. Then in line 18, we use the "hasNext" method to check if the next namespace exists. Finally, we use the "nextNs" method in line 19 to get each namespace as a "String" object.

Query 2. In this query, we want to list out all RDF statements (triples) in this document. Therefore, we use our defined "query" method in line 24 which jumps to line 50. Inside the "query" method, we use the "listStatements" method in line 52 to obtain a list of statements which are stored in the "stmtIterator" object. The parameters "s", "p", and "o" of the "listStatements" method are null which means that we do not require matching the statement with the specific subject, predicate, and object respectively. Then we use the "hasNext" method in line 53 to check if the next statement exists and we use the "nextStatement" method in line 54 to get each "statement" object. Finally, we use the methods "getSubject", "getPredicate", and "getObject" to get the subject (resource), predicate (property), and object (literal or resource) respectively (see line 55 to 57). Please note that Jena automatically generates an ID (66c7f061:104e5c9bff0:-8000) for the node referred by the "accessories" property.

Query 3. In this query, we want to list out all RDF statements (triples) in this document which has the remote controller resource with URI "http://www.kingstv.com/plasma/PSM2000/rc". Therefore, we use our defined "query" method in line 27 and 28 which first parameter is our target resource. Before passing the first parameter to the "query" method, we need to use the "createResource" method to create the corresponding "Resource" object.

Query 1:

http://www.w3.org/1999/02/22-rdf-syntax-ns#;

http://www.kingstv.com/tv_property/;

Query 2:

(66c7f061:104e5c9bff0:-8000,

  http://www.w3.org/1999/02/22-rdf-syntax-ns#type,

  http://www.w3.org/1999/02/22-rdf-syntax-ns#Bag);

(66c7f061:104e5c9bff0:-8000,

  http://www.w3.org/1999/02/22-rdf-syntax-ns#_1,

  user manual);

(66c7f061:104e5c9bff0:-8000,

  http://www.w3.org/1999/02/22-rdf-syntax-ns#_2,

  http://www.kingstv.com/plasma/PSM2000/rc);

(http://www.kingstv.com/plasma/PSM2000,

  http://www.kingstv.com/tv_property/accessories,

  66c7f061:104e5c9bff0:-8000);

(http://www.kingstv.com/plasma/PSM2000,

  http://www.kingstv.com/tv_property/model,

  PSM2000);

(http://www.kingstv.com/plasma/PSM2000/rc,

  http://www.kingstv.com/tv_property/belong_to,

  http://www.kingstv.com/plasma/PSM2000);

Query 3:

(http://www.kingstv.com/plasma/PSM2000/rc,

  http://www.kingstv.com/tv_property/belong_to,

  http://www.kingstv.com/plasma/PSM2000);

Query 4:

(http://www.kingstv.com/plasma/PSM2000,

  http://www.kingstv.com/tv_property/model,

  PSM2000);

Query 5:

(66c7f061:104e5c9bff0:-8000,

http://www.w3.org/1999/02/22-rdf-syntax-ns#_1,

user manual);

Query 6:

user manual;

http://www.kingstv.com/plasma/PSM2000/rc;

Query 4. In this query, we want to list out all RDF statements (triples) in this document which has the "model" property. Therefore, we use our defined "query" method in line 31 and 32 which second parameter is our target property. Before passing the second parameter to the "query" method, we need to use the "createProperty" method to create the corresponding "Property" object. Moreover, the first parameter of the "createProperty" method is the namespace of the property which URI can be obtained by using the "getNsPrefixURI" method.

Query 5. In this query, we want to list out all RDF statements (triples) in this document which property value is "user manual". Therefore, we use our defined "query" method in line 35 which third parameter is our target property value. Before passing the third parameter to the "query" method, we need to use the "createLiteral" method to create the corresponding "Literal" object which is typecast to the "RDFNode" object when passing to the "query" method.

Query 6. In the last query, we want to list out all accessories of the television resource which URI is "http://www.kingstv.com/plasma/PSM2000". Therefore, we use the "listStatements" method from line 38 to 41 and we use the "nextStatement" method in line 42 to get the target statement. Then we use the "getBag" method in line 43 and the "iterator" method in line 44 to get the list of items which is represented by the "nodeIterator" object. Furthermore, we use the "hasNext" method in line 45 to check if the next item exists. Finally, we use the "next" method in line 46 to get each item.

In addition to the query operation, Jena provides three useful operations for manipulating RDF documents as a whole. These are the common set operations of *union*, *intersection*, and *difference*. The union operation creates a new RDF document containing all triples in this document together with all of those in another given document. Moreover, the intersection operation creates a new RDF document containing all triples which are in both this document and another. Since RDF documents are sets of triples, a triple contained in both documents only appears once in the resulting document. Finally, the difference operation creates a new RDF document containing all triples in this document which are not in another. We demonstrate the union of the examples in Figure 1 and Figure 2 in Listing 10, "Example5.java".

Listing 10. Example5.java

```
1:   import java.io.*;
2:   import com.hp.hpl.jena.rdf.model.*;
3:
4:   public class Example5
5:   {
6:     public static void main(String[] args) throws Exception
7:     {
8:       Model model1 = ModelFactory.createDefaultModel();
9:       Model model2 = ModelFactory.createDefaultModel();
10:
11:       FileInputStream fileIn = new FileInputStream("example1.rdf");
12:       model1.read(fileIn, "");
13:       fileIn.close();
14:
15:       fileIn = new FileInputStream("example2.rdf");
16:       model2.read(fileIn, "");
17:       fileIn.close();
18:
19:       Model model = model1.union(model2);
20:
21:       FileOutputStream fileOut = new FileOutputStream("example5.rdf");
22:       model.write(fileOut);
23:       fileOut.close();
24:     }
25:   }
```

Figure 8. An RDF graph after the union

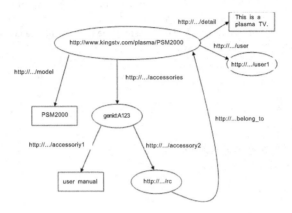

Using the union operation in Jena is simple as shown in this example. First, we use the "createDefaultModel" in line 8 and 9 to create two RDF documents. Second, we use the "read" method to read the RDF documents so that the "model1" object represents the "example1.rdf" file and the "model2" object represents the "example2.rdf" file (see line 11 to 17). Third, we use the "union" method in line 19 to perform the union operation and the "model" object represents the resulting RDF document. Finally, we use the "write" method to write the resulting document to the "example5.rdf" file from line 21 to 23. To use the intersection or difference operation in this example, we only need to replace "union" in line 19 by "intersection" or "difference". Figure 8 shows the corresponding RDF graph after the union.

Conclusion

In this chapter, we give a simple tutorial on RDF, RDF/XML, and Jena. The tutorial is summarized as follows.

For RDF, it is a W3C standard which is commonly used to describe resources for any application. We use RDF graphs to describe resources. An RDF graph contains resources, properties, and property values which are connected together. Resources are represented by ellipses, properties are represented by arrows, and literals are represented by rectangles. In addition, a list of RDF triples can also be used to describe resources. An RDF triple contains a subject, a predicate, and an object. The subject is the resource, the predicate is the property, and the object is the property value.

For RDF/XML, it is the XML language used by RDF. A resource is described by the <rdf:Description> element and its URI is specified by the "rdf:about" attribute. A property is described by our defined element under the <rdf:Description> element of a resource. A property value is enclosed by a property element. A list of items can be contained by using the "Bag", "Seq", or "Alt" container. The "Bag" container contains an unordered list of items, the "Seq" container contains an ordered list of items, and the "Alt" container contains a list of alternative items.

For Jena, it is a Java framework for building semantic Web applications which provides a programmatic environment for RDF and other related technologies. To compose an RDF document, there are six steps, which are (1) empty RDF document creation, (2) property namespace assignment, (3) resource creation, (4) property creation, (5) RDF triple creation, and (6) RDF file composition. Besides RDF document composition, Jena also provides API for reading and querying in RDF documents. Finally, Jena provides three useful operations for manipulating RDF documents as a whole. These are the common set operations of union, intersection, and difference.

Readers may refer to the resources listed in References section for further investigation. W3Schools (n.d.a), and W3Schools (n.d.b) provide good online tutorials on XML and RDF respectively. Antoniou and Harmelen (2004), Hjelm (2001), Klein (2001), Oberle (2005), Passin (2004), and Powers (2003) provide complete discussions on developing applications using RDF and the related Internet technologies.

References

Antoniou, G., & Harmelen, F. V. (2004). *A semantic web primer*. Cambridge, UK: The MIT Press.

Brickley, D. (2005). The Friend of a Friend (FOAF) Project Web site. Retrieved from http://www.foaf-project.org/

Hewlett-Packard Development Company (2005). Jena Semantic Web Framework Web site. Retrieve from http://jena.sourceforge.net/

Hjelm, J. (2001). *Creating the semantic web with RDF: Professional developer's guide*. New York: Wiley.

The Internet Society (2005). Uniform Resource Identifier (URI) Generic Syntax. Retrieved from http://www.gbiv.com/protocols/uri/rfc/rfc3986.html

Klein, M. (2001). XML, RDF, and relatives. *IEEE Intelligent Systems, 16*(2), 26-28.

McBride, B. (2001). Jena: Implementing the RDF Model and Syntax Specification. In *Proceedings of the 2nd International Workshop on the Semantic Web*, Hong Kong, China.

Oberle, D., Staab, S., Studer, R., & Volz, R. (2005). Supporting application development in the semantic web. *ACM Transactions on Internet Technology, 5*(2), 328-358.

Passin, T. B. (2004). *Explorer's guide to the semantic web*. Greenwich, CT: Manning Publications.

Powers, S. (2003). *Practical RDF*. Sebastopol, CA: O'Reilly.

RSS-DEV Working Group (2000). Resource Description Framework Site Summary (RSS) 1.0 Web site. Retrieved from http://web.resource.org/rss/1.0/

Sun Microsystems, Inc. (2005). Java 2 Platform, Standard Edition (J2SE) Web site. Retrieved from URL http://java.sun.com/j2se/

W3Schools (n.d.a). Extensible Markup Language (XML) Tutorial Web site. Retrieved from http://www.w3schools.com/xml/

W3Schools (n.d.b). Resource Description Framework (RDF) Tutorial Web site. Retrieved from http://www.w3schools.com/rdf/

World Wide Web Consortium (W3C) (2004a). Resource Description Framework (RDF) Official Web site. Retrieved from URL http://www.w3.org/RDF/

World Wide Web Consortium (W3C) (2004b). Resource Description Framework (RDF) Validation Service. Retrieved from http://www.w3.org/RDF/Validator/

World Wide Web Consortium (W3C) (2005a). Extensible Markup Language (XML) Official Web site. Retrieved from http://www.w3.org/XML/

World Wide Web Consortium (W3C) (2005b). World Wide Web Consortium (W3C). Retrieved from http://www.w3.org/

Wu, C. T. (2004). *An introduction to object-oriented programming with Java* (3rd ed.). New York: McGraw-Hill.

Chapter VI

A Semantic Web Service Architecture for Learning Object Repositories

José-Manuel López-Cobo, Atos Origin SAE, Spain

Sinuhé Arroyo, Digital Enterprise Research Institute, Austria

Miguel-Angel Sicilia, University of Alcalá, Spain

Salvador Sánchez-Alonso, University of Alcalá, Spain

Abstract

The evolution of learning technology standards has resulted in a degree of interoperability across systems that enable the interchange of learning contents and activities. Nonetheless, learning resource metadata does not provide formal computational semantics, which hampers the possibilities to develop technology that automates tasks like learning object selection and negotiation. In this paper, the provision of computational semantics to metadata is addressed from the perspective of the concept of Semantic Web service. An architecture based on the specifications of the WSMO project is described, including the definition of an ontology for learning object metadata, and issues of mediation, all under the perspective of the learning object repository as the central entity in learning object reuse scenarios. The resulting framework serves as a foundation for advanced implementations that consider formal metadata semantics as a mechanism for the automation of tasks related to the interchange of learning objects.

Introduction

Current standardized *e-learning* systems are centered on the concept of *learning object* (Wiley, 2001), which can be defined as "a self-standing and reusable unit predisposed to be used in learning activities" (Polsani, 2002). Several interrelated standardization efforts—including the IEEE LTSC, ADL SCORM and the IMS Consortium (Anido et al., 2002)—are devoted to produce and refine specifications oriented to fostering consistency in learning contents and related elements. These specifications currently cover learning object packaging and metadata, sequencing and composition of activities, and the definition of specialized types of learning objects like questionnaires, among other aspects. Nonetheless, these specifications do not provide details about the use of well-known knowledge representations for the sake of automating some processes like selection and composition of learning objects, or adaptation to the user or platform. In addition, the information schemas provided in such specifications are not free of controversial interpretations (Farance, 2003), which seriously hamper the possibility of implementing standardized "intelligent" behaviors. Such situation has lead to consider Semantic Web technology as a promising enhancement for learning object-based technology.

Ontologies are shared knowledge representations that form the basis of the current Semantic Web vision (Berners-Lee, Hendler, & Lassila, 2001) and that are becoming widespread due to the availability of common languages like OWL and associated modeling and development tools (Fensel, 2002). Ontologies have been described elsewhere (Lytras, Tsilira, & Themistocleous, 2003; Stojanovic, Staab, & Studer, 2001; Qin, & Finneran, 2002) as enablers of more flexible and advanced learning systems, but the mere use of Ontologies does not guarantee that consistent functionality will become available in the future, since it is also required an effort of specification about the *uses* of Ontologies *for each* particular learning technology scenario. Precise and unambiguous usage specifications for Ontologies in *e-learning* would eventually result in a higher level of automation in learning systems. But preciseness requires a clear separation of responsibilities for the participants in each scenario, along with concrete, machine-oriented interpretations for metadata elements, that is not the focus of current specification efforts.

Previous work (Sánchez-Alonso, Sicilia, & López-Cobo, 2004) has addressed how Web Service architectures combined with precise metadata descriptions can be used as a framework to specify learning object selection and composition processes, which are an essential part of any approach to automation in this area, pointing out to the appropriateness of using richer frameworks of Web Service description as the Web Service Modeling Ontology (Roman, Lausen, & Keller, 2004). Recent work has begun to explore the mapping of existing learning technology standards to the WSMO framework (López-Cobo, Sicilia, & Arroyo, 2004) in the area of metadata-based selection.

In this chapter, the architecture of a Semantic Web service based learning object repository is described, targeting selection and composition processes as basic scenarios for automation in the field of e-Learning. An ontology based on the LOM specification is used to specify both client goals and diverse offerings, and the surrounding issues of mediation are also explored.

The design described in the chapter is based on WSMO technology, and it provides an underlying substrate to machine-understandable semantics for learning object metadata which delivers benefits both to individuals and organizations engaged in e-Learning. In practice, such enhanced support for automation in repositories represents an important step in mass customization and electronic interchange as envisioned by the paradigm of learning objects (Martínez, 2001). The chapter focuses on ontologies as shared knowledge representations that can be used to obtain enhanced learning object metadata records—according to existing criteria (Duval, Hodgins, Sutton, & Weibel, 2002), and also to enable automated or semi-automated consistent processes inside *learning management systems* (LMS).

The rest of this paper is structured as follows. The second section provides background information and states the problem addressed in the rest of the chapter. The third section describes the role of Ontologies in describing learning object metadata. Then, the fourth section introduces how WSMO goals and capabilities can be used to semantically describe learning-object providing Web Services. The fifth section provides the overall architectural framework for selection and composition as based on those semantic descriptions. Finally, the last section is devoted to conclusions.

Background

In this section, background information on learning object technology and Semantic Web services is provided. Concretely, the state of relevant standards and specifications on learning technology is briefly summarized, and the main efforts related to Semantic Web service technology are sketched. The section also provides a definition of the problems of selection and composition of learning objects that are dealt with in the rest of the chapter, and the rationale for using Semantic Web services as the architecture for these processes.

Standards Related to Learning Objects

A number of specifications and standards that describe or make use of the learning object concept have evolved in the last years. The basic metadata elements associated to learning objects have been described in the IEEE LOM standard (IEEE, 2002), which organizes its conceptual metadata schema in nine categories: General, Lifecycle, Meta-Metadata, Technical, Educational, Rights, Relation, Annotation, and Classification. These cover basic description—title, coverage, and so forth—and general purpose annotations (General and Annotation), contributors, change control, and property matters (Lifecycle and Rights), technical characteristics of the Web contents (Technical), and the metadata record itself can also be described (Meta-metadata). The Educational category describes the envisioned educational characteristics of the object, including type of interactivity, typical educational context, typical age of intended learners, and the like. The Relation category describes relations between learning objects, which could be viewed as a form of "linking" able of specifying also character-istics related to the educational, in other words, related learning objects that constitute prerequisites or that cover semantically related elements (Sicilia, García, Aedo, & Diaz, 2004). Finally, the Classification element serves several different purposes, including stating the objectives of the learning object, the prerequisites of the learner and the overall classification of the contents inside taxonomical schemes or Ontologies.

Another important specification is ADL SCORM, which adopts IEEE LOM as the metadata language for learning resources, and provides specifications oriented towards achieving a degree of interoperability in the functioning of learning management systems (LMS). Concretely, the SCORM content packaging specification determines an interoperable format for the interchange of learning contents structured as hierarchical units, and the SCORM run-time specification specifies a common protocol and language for the Web browser-LMS communication, including the delivery of some kind of learning objects (called sharable content objects in SCORM) and the recording and tracking of the activities of each user. The recent sequencing and navigation specifica-tions go a step beyond and provide a language in which complex navigational patterns can be devised, including learning paths that adapt to the accomplishment of some objectives by the learner. The SCORM specifications together provide

The recent IMS learning design (LD) specification addresses the description of activity-based designs of learning activities, in which several different roles are joined together in each activity, and interact with learning objects and services (like chat services) to accomplish some goals. IMS LD implementations like the CopperCore engine provide a coordination support that is able to deliver the activities to the specified learners in the order and under the conditions specified in the learning design.

IEEE LTSC, IMS, and ADL, among other organizations, are currently active in the evolution and extension of the body of learning technology standards. Other areas currently covered and not discussed here for brevity include educational portfolios, learner descriptions, tests, digital repositories, and competency specification. An important specification for the objectives of this chapter is the IMS digital repositories interoperability (DRI) specification (IMS, 2003). The purpose of this specification is to provide recommendations for the interoperation of the most common repository func-tions, described in terms of XQuery and SOAP recommendations.

Semantic Web Services

The combination of machine-processable semantics facilitated by the Semantic Web with current Web Service technologies has coined the term Semantic Web Services. Semantic Web Services offer the means to achieve a higher level of value-added services by adding dynamism to the task driven assembly of inter-organization business logics. They count with the potential to make the Internet a global, common platform where agents (organizations, individuals, and software) communicate with each other to carry out various activities.

Semantic Web services represent an extension to current Web services technology. They broaden the Web from a distributed source of information to a distributed source of services (Lara, Lausen, Arroyo, De Bruijn, & Fensel, 2003), where software resources can be assembled on the fly to accomplish user's goals. They are defined as "*Decoupled, semantically marked-up Web Services (Tidwell, 2000), with concrete execution semantics, that can be published, discovered, selected, composed, mediated and executed across the Web, in a task driven way, carrying its interaction by means of document exchange (Arroyo, Lara, et al., 2004) following a choreographed or orchestrated approach.*"

In order to fully allow the usage and integration of Web Services their capabilities need to be semantically marked up, and their interfaces need to provide the means to understand how to consume their functionality. Further, the exchange of documents requires describing the meaning of the content in a way that can be understood and communicated independently of some particular domain knowledge.

WSMO (Roman et al., 2004) tries to alleviate these problems by defining the modeling elements for describing several aspects of Semantic Web services. WSMO is a formal ontology and language for describing the various aspects related to Semantic Web Services. It represents the backbone for the development of Web service modeling language (WSML) and Web Service Modeling Execution Environment (WSMX). The conceptual grounding of WSMO is based on the Web service modeling framework (WSMF) (Fensel & Bussler, 2002), wherein four main components are defined:

- **Ontologies** provide the formal semantics to the information used by all other components. Ontologies are used to: (1) express goals in a machine processable and understandable language; (2) they permit to enhance Web Services so they can be matched against goals; and (3) interconnect the different elements with each other by means of mediators. Ontologies are described by means of nonfunctional properties, used mediators, axioms, concepts, relations, and instances.

- **Goals** specify objectives that a client may have when consulting a Web Service. They provide the means to express high level description of a concrete task. The WSMO definition of goal is restricted to post-condition, effects, nonfunctional properties, and used mediators.

- **Web Services** represent the functional part which must be semantically described in order to allow their semi-automated use. Web Services are described, by means of a capability, interface, used mediators, and nonfunctional properties.

- **Mediators** used as connectors provide interoperability facilities among the rest of components. Currently the specification defines four different types of mediators, which are classified in two main classes: refiners (ggMediators and ooMediators) and bridges (wgMediators and wwMediators). While refiners are used to define new components as a specialization of an existing one, bridges help to overcome interoperability problems by enabling components to interact with each other. In the general case WSMO defines mediators by means of nonfunctional properties, source component, target component and mediation service, where source and target component can be a mediator, a Web service, and ontology or a goal.

WSMO facilitate the means to publish, discover, select, mediate, compose, execute, monitor, replace, compensate, and audit services, for the benefit of some agent who seeks to fulfill some user-defined task conceptualized as a goal, minimizing human intervention and realizing the process in a more dynamic way.

The set of all these steps has been termed Semantic Webservice usage process (Arroyo, Toma, et al., 2004). It allows to publish the description of the capability and interface of a service, discover different services suitable for a given goal, selecting the most appropriate services among the available ones, compose services to achieve the goal, mediate (data, protocol, process) mismatches among the combined services, execute services following programmatic conventions, monitor the execution process, replace services by equivalent ones, compensate and mitigate unwanted effects and audit service execution.

The Problems of Selection and Composition of Learning Objects

The problems of selection and composition addressed in this chapter are two aspects of the same process. The overall process of learning object seeking can be abstractly characterized as follows. The process starts with the raise of some kind of *learning need*. Such needs may be expressed in simple terms as plain *goals* like "learner L requires learning about topic T", but they could also be expressed in a complex form. Such complex descriptions may include requirements on the profile, learning style and previous knowledge of the learner, constraints of the technical platform in which the learning objects will be delivered, and even limitations on cost, duration, or calendar of the resulting online learning design. Even the theoretical positions on learning should be accounted for in learning object selection (Sicilia & Lytras, 2005). In addition, learning goals are intrinsically decomposable, in the sense that an overall goal can be broken up into simpler sub-goals that may be subject to independent inquiry.

In that concept, the process of learning selection can be defined as "the process of decision in which one or several learning objects are selected to fulfill a specific learning goal under concrete contextual circumstances." Then, selection must first search for a set of candidate learning objects on which the decision takes place. Candidate learning objects are to be found on local or public systems often called "learning object repositories", which should expose some kind of search services to resource seekers.

Learning object composition can be defined as the "process of combining several learning objects into a higher level instructional unit in order to fulfill some learning goals under concrete contextual circumstances". In consequence, composition actually requires selection as a constituent process. Nonetheless, composition imposes additional constraints on the process, since it may be possible that the selection processes generated by the breakdown of a goal into sub-goals results in selected learning objects that can not be joined together, for example, due to incompatible style designs or even to inconsistency in the pedagogical approach or level of description.

Selection and composition would therefore in many cases be intertwined in a sequence of steps as part of the overall process of assembling an online learning design. If no single learning object is available to selection for a particular goal or sub-goal, a process of composition may be started in an attempt to craft a new one from lower-level pieces. In turn, this composition process will trigger other selection activities. It should be noted also that the term learning object as used in this chapter not only includes pieces of static contents, but it may also encompass designs of activities involving multiple roles. For example, a LD method may be considered a composite learning object that has an internal activity-based structure.

The Role of Ontologies in Learning Object Descriptions

The benefits of using ontology description languages to express learning object metadata are of two fundamental kinds (Sicilia & García, 2005). On the one hand, those languages provide richer knowledge representation formalisms (Davis, Shrobe, & Szolovits, 1993) for metadata descriptions than using plain text, XML bindings, or even RDF. Here the benefits are the result of using description logics, instead of simply using structured data in XML format or using RDF, which is a less expressive language than DAML+OIL or OWL. On the other hand, the use of Ontologies may eventually produce synergies with the technological advances that are taking place under the overall label of "Semantic Web". The most prominent of such synergies may come from the availability of shared, consensual Ontologies on many domains along with tools to develop systems that exploit them for diverse "intelligent" behaviors.

In addition, Ontologies can be used to provide an explicit integration with broader organizational models. For example, a recent integration of learning activity-specific concepts provided elsewhere (Sicilia, Lytras, Rodríguez, & García, 2006) has integrated learning object concepts with the ontology of knowledge management (KM) described by Holsapple and Joshi (Holsapple & Joshi, 2004).

Describing Goals and Capabilities in Terms of Learning Objects

A basic ontology describing some essential metadata items in LOM could be described through the following definitions in WSML, which correspond to the main elements depicted in Figure 1. It basically addresses the central concept of the learning object and some related concepts as languages, life cycle, technical requirements, educational purposes, classification in different taxonomies, right management of the LO and complex treatment of the LO identifier. Some instances are defined for illustration purposes.

One of the most important concepts of the ontology is the "Relation" concept. With it, we can connect one learning object with other in terms of versioning, belonging, requirements and other useful relationships. These relationships could allow a reasoner to find and retrieve related learning objects with the selected by the customer.

Goals in these conceptual models are defined by the postconditions and the effects required on the learning objects selected. We have to consider here that the discovery and select of a learning object can be considered as the purchase of an item in a "Purchase

Figure 1. Excerpt form the ontology diagram for learning object description

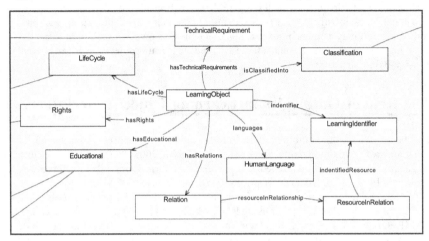

Listing 1. LOM4WSMO Ontology and some instances

```
namespace
_http://www.uah.es/ontologies/lom4WSM
O#

dc: _http://purl.org/dc/elements/1.1#
vcard: _http://www.w3.org/2001/vcard-
rdf/3.0#
xsd:
_http://www.w3.org/2001/XMLSchema#

ontology
_http://www.uah.es/ontologies/lom4WSM
O

nonFunctionalProperties
  dc:title hasValue "LOM Specification
for WSMO"
  dc:creator hasValues {vcard:UaH}
  dc:subject hasValues {"Learning
Object", "LOM", "Metadata"}
  dc:description hasValue {"LOM
Specification written in WSML for
WSMO"}
  dc:publisher hasValue {vcard:UaH}
  dc:contributor hasValues
{vCard:Ozelin, vcard:Sicilia,
vcard:Sinuhe}
  dc:date hasValue "2005-02-28"
  dc:type hasValue
_http://www.wsmo.org/2004/d2#ontologi
es
  dc:format hasValue "text/html"
  dc:identifier hasValue
_http://www.uah.es/ontologies/lom4WSM
O
  dc:language hasValue "en-UK"
  dc:relation hasValues
{_http://www.w3.org/2001/vcard-rdf/3.0}
  dc:rights hasValue
```

```
_http://www.uah.es/privacy.html
  version hasValue "$Revision: 0.2 $"
endNonFunctionalProperties

/**
Highlighted Concepts of the Ontology
**/

concept cost
nonFunctionalProperties
  dc:description hasValue "Cost of the
Learning Object, if it exists"
endNonFunctionalProperties
  amount ofType amount
  currency ofType currency

concept rights
nonFunctionalProperties
  dc:description hasValue "Right
Properties of the Learning Object"
endNonFunctionalProperties
  descriptionOfRights ofType xsd:string
  hasCopyright ofType xsd:boolean
  hasCost ofType xsd:boolean
  price ofType cost

concept humanLanguage
nonFunctionalProperties
  dc:description hasValue "a
humanLanguage is a language in which
can be expressed a Learning Object"
endNonFunctionalProperties
  name ofType xsd:string
  ISOCode ofType xsd:string
```

Listing 1. continued

```
concept taxon
nonFunctionalProperties
  dc:description hasValue "A pair {id, value}
which represents some node in a taxonomy. A
Taxon may have a father and may have
multiple sons"
endNonFunctionalProperties
  idTaxon ofType xsd:string
  valueTaxon ofType xsd:string
  sonOfTaxon ofType taxon
  fatherOfTaxons ofType set taxon

concept taxonPath
nonFunctionalProperties
  dc:description hasValue "one possible path
in a taxonomy classification for a Learning
Object"
endNonFunctionalProperties
  hasSourceTaxonPath ofType sourceTaxon
  hasTaxon ofType set taxon

concept classification
nonFunctionalProperties
  dc:description hasValue "Each LO can be
classified into many ways. A classification will
gather this information"
endNonFunctionalProperties
  purpose ofType purpose
  taxonPath ofType set taxonPath

concept educational
nonFunctionalProperties
  dc:description hasValue "The Educational
aspects of the Learning Object"
endNonFunctionalProperties
  descriptionOfEducational ofType xsd:string
  interactivityType ofType interactivityType
  learningResourceType ofType
learningResourceType
  hasInteractivityLevel ofType interactivityLevel
  hasDifficulty ofType difficulty
  contextEducational ofType
contextEducational
  intendedEndUserRole ofType
intendedEndUserRole

concept orCompositeTechnicalRequirement
nonFunctionalProperties
  dc:description hasValue "Define the
possibilities of a choice for a Technical
Requirement of a LO"
endNonFunctionalProperties
  minimumVersionOfTR ofType xsd:string
  maximumVersionOfTR ofType xsd:string
  typeOfRequirement ofType xsd:string
  nameOfRequirement ofType xsd:string

concept technicalRequirement
nonFunctionalProperties
  dc:description hasValue "A Technical
Requirement that a LO has to comply"
endNonFunctionalProperties
  installationRemarksOfTR ofType xsd:string
  formatOfTR ofType set xsd:string

sizeOfTR ofType xsd:string
locationOfTR ofType xsd:anyURI
durationOfTR ofType xsd:duration
hasOrCompositeRequirements ofType set
orCompositeTechnicalRequirement

concept learningIdentifier
nonFunctionalProperties
  dc:description hasValue "An unique and
unambiguous identifier for a LO"
endNonFunctionalProperties
  entryCatalog ofType xsd:string
  catalogIdentifier ofType xsd:string

concept resourceInRelation
nonFunctionalProperties
  dc:description hasValue "Describes the
Resource (LO) which is related with other LO"
endNonFunctionalProperties
  descriptionOfResource ofType xsd:string
  identifiedResource ofType learningIdentifier

concept relationship
nonFunctionalProperties
  dc:description hasValue "Describes one
relationship between the LO owner and other
LO"
endNonFunctionalProperties
  kindOfRelationship ofType kindOfRelation
  resourceInRelationship ofType
resourceInRelation

concept learningObject
nonFunctionalProperties
  dc:description hasValue "Any digital entity
that may be used for learning, education or
training"
endNonFunctionalProperties
  aggregationLevel ofType aggregationLevel
  languages ofType set humanLanguage
  isClassifiedInto ofType set classification
  hasRights ofType set rights
  hasTechnicalRequirements ofType set
technicalRequirement
  locationURI ofType xsd:anyURI
  hasEducational ofType educational
  identifier ofType learningIdentifier
  title ofType xsd:string
  structure ofType structure
  hasRelations ofType relationship

/**
Definition of the Relations of the Ontology
**/

relation hasAncestor
nonFunctionalProperties
  dc:description hasValue "(X,Y) is a tuple of
the binary relation iff X is ancestor of Y"
endNonFunctionalProperties
  ancestor ofType taxon
  descendant ofType taxon
```

Listing 1. continued

```
axiom relationOfBelonging
nonFunctionalProperties
   dc:description hasValue "One LO belongs to
other iff participates in a isPartOf relationship
and its aggregationLevel is greater than its
father"
endNonFunctionalProperties
definedBy
constraint
     ?A1 = ?A2 + 1
       equivalent
     ?A1 memberOf aggregationLevel and
     ?A2 memberOf aggregationLevel and
     ?LO1[aggregationLevel hasValue ?A1,
           hasRelations hasValue ?R1,
           identifier hasValue ?I1]
       memberOf learningObject and
     ?R1[ kindOfRelationship hasValue
     hasPart,
     resourceInRelation hasValue
     ?RiR1]  memberOf relationship and
     ?RiR1[identifiedResource hasValue
     ?I2]         memberOf
     resourceInRelation and
     ?LO2[ aggregationLevel hasValue
     ?A2,
           hasRelations hasValue ?R2,
           identifier hasValue ?I2]
       memberOf learningObject and
     ?R2[kindOfRelationship hasValue
     isPartOf,
     resourceInRelation hasValue
     RiR2]
       memberOf relationship and
     ?RiR2[identifiedResource hasValue
     ?I1] memberOf resourceInRelation.

axiom uniqueLearningIdentifier
nonFunctionalProperties
   dc:description hasValue "There can't be two
different Learning Objects with the same par
{catalog, entry}"
endNonFunctionalProperties
definedBy
constraint
     ?X = ?Y
       equivalent
     ?X memberOf learningIdentifier and
     ?Y memberOf learningIdentifier and
     ?X.entryCatalog = ?Y.entryCatalog and
     ?X.catalogIdentifier =
     ?Y.catalogIdentifier.

axiom minimumLevelOfAggregation
nonFunctionalProperties
   dc:description "A Learning Object that is not
composed by other learning objects has an
aggregation level of 1"
endNonFunctionalProperties
definedBy
?LO1 [aggregationLevel hasValue 1,
hasRelations hasValue ?R] memberOf
learningObject
```

```
impliedBy
not ?R[kindOfRelationship hasValue hasPart]
memberOf relationship.

axiom taxonLukeImYourFather
nonFunctionalProperties
   dc:description hasValue "If one taxon T1 has
a son T2, then the father of T2 is T1."
endNonFunctionalProperties
definedBy
constraint
?T2[sonOfTaxon hasValue ?T1]
memberOf taxon
   impliedBy
?T1[fatherOfTaxons hasValue ?T2]
memberOf taxon.

axiom taxonHolyGhost
nonFunctionalProperties
   dc:description hasValue "A taxon can not be
son of itself"
endNonFunctionalProperties
definedBy
constraint
   false
     impliedBy
   ?T1 memberOf taxon and ?T2 memberOf
taxon
     and ?T1 = ?T2 and ?T2[sonOfTaxon
hasValue ?T1].

axiom relationshipSelf
nonFunctionalProperties
   dc:description hasValue "A Learning Object
can not be related with itself"
endNonFunctionalProperties
definedBy
false
   impliedBy
?LO1[ hasRelations hasValue ?R, identifier
hasValue ?I] memberOf learningObject and
?R[ resourceInRelationship hasValue ?RiR]
memberOf relationship and
?RiR[ identifiedResource hasValue ?I]
memberOf resourceInRelation.

/**
Definition of the Knowledge Base of the
Ontology
**/

instance spanish memberOf
humanLanguages
name hasValue "spanish"^^xsd:string
ISOCode hasvalue "ES"^^xsd:string

instance englishUK memberOf
humanLanguages
name hasvalue "englishUK"^^xsd:string
ISOCode hasvalue "en-UK"^^xsd:string

instance euro memberOf currency
```

Listing 1. continued

```
currencyName hasvalue "Euro"^^xsd:string        instance lecture memberOf
currencyCode hasvalue "EUR"^^xsd:string         learningResourceType
                                                instance school memberOf
instance usDollar memberOf currency             contextEducational
currencyName hasValue "US                        instance higherEducation memberOf
Dollar"^^xsd:string                             contextEducational
currencyCode hasValue "USD"^^xsd:string          instance learner memberOf
                                                intendedEndUserRole
instance ARIADNE memberOf sourceTaxon           instance teacher memberOf
instance MESH memberOf sourceTaxon              intendedEndUserRole
                                                instance author memberOf
instance restrictions memberOf purpose          intendedEndUserRole
instance idea memberOf purpose                  instance isVersionOf memberOf
instance discipline memberOf purpose            kindOfRelation
instance active memberOf interactivityType      instance requires memberOf kindOfRelation
instance expositive memberOf                    instance hasPart memberOf kindOfRelation
interactivityType                               instance references memberOf
instance mixed memberOf interactivityType       kindOfRelation
                                                instance hasFormat memberOf
instance graph memberOf                         kindOfRelation
learningResourceType                            instance linear memberOf structure
instance exam memberOf                          instance atomic memberOf structure
learningResourceType
instance selfAssesment memberOf
learningResourceType
```

Order" paradigm. Acting this way we can reuse the purchase order ontology developed by the WSMO team. The cost of the Learning Object, if free, is irrelevant for the model of the goal and the ontology.

The overall goal *find learning objects in English that tell something about Internet Algorithms"* can be expressed as demonstrated in Listing 2.

The outcomes of the goal (once linked to a service execution) are instances of learning Object with a number of constraints. This goal has only constrained that the desired learning objects have to be complaint to the ARIADNE taxonomy and versed in "Internet algorithms". The rest of the constraints for a learning object are free to be matched against the repository of learning objects.

Capabilities offered by Web services can be described within the same ontological framework. The simple definition in Listing 3 specifies a capability that could eventually fulfill the need expressed in the previous goal. It has to be noticed that the capability of a Web service is more detailed than a goal, because it serves not only for matching purposes but for advertising in a repository where other goals from other requesters can be matched.

Learning object types could be integrated in goal and capability definitions directly, simply putting restrictions on type where necessary for filtering out some kinds of objects, since subsumption guarantees that specialized learning objects are directly considered.

Listing 2. Requester goal

```
goal
_http://www.uah.es/ontologies/goals/goalLO.w
sml
nonFunctionalProperties
  dc:title hasValue "Searching for a Learning
Object about Internet Algorithms"
  dc:creator hasValue vcard:UaH
  dc:description hasValue "Express the goal of
buying a Learning Object for learn Internet
Algorithms"
  dc:publisher hasValue vcard:UaH
  dc:contributor hasValues {vCard:Ozelin,
vcard:Sicilia, vcard:Sinuhe}
  dc:date hasValue "2005-02-07"
  dc:type hasValue
_http://www.wsmo.org/2004/d2#goals
  dc:format hasValue "text/html"
  dc:language hasValue "en-uk"
  dc:rights hasValue
_http://www.uah.es/privacy.html
  version hasValue "$Version: 0.1 $"
endNonFunctionalProperties

importedOntologies
{_http://www.uah.es/ontologies/lom4WSMO,
_http://www.wsmo.org/ontologies/purchase}

postcondition
axiom
purchasingLearningObject4InternetAlgorithms
nonFunctionalProperties
  dc:description hasValue "This goal
expresses the general desire of purchasing a
Learning Object in order to learn Internet
Algorithms"
endNonFunctionalProperties
definedBy
exists ?Purchase, ?Purchaseorder, ?Buyer,
?Product, ?PaymentMethod, ?LearningObject,
?Classification, ?Paths
(?Purchase memberOf po:purchase[
  po:purchaseorder hasValue
?Purchaseorder,

  po:buyer hasValue ?Buyer ] and
?Buyer memberOf po:buyer and
?Purchaseorder memberOf
po:purchaseOrder[
  po:product hasValues {?Product},
  po:payment hasValue ?PaymentMethod ]
and
?PaymentMethod memberOf
po:paymentMethod and
?Product memberOf po:product[
  po:item hasValues {?LearningObject} ] and
?LearningObject memberOf
lom4WSMO:learningObject[
  lom4WSMO:isClasssifiedInto hasValue
Classification? ] and
?Classifications memberOf
lom4WSMO:classification[
  taxonPath hasValues {?Paths} ] and
?Paths memberOf lom4WSMO:taxonPath[
  hasSourceTaxonPath hasValue
lom4WSMO:ARIADNE,
  hasTaxon? hasValues {valueTaxon
hasValue "Internet Algorithms"^^xsd:string} ]
).

effect
axiom havingTradeForLO
nonFunctionalProperties
  dc:description hasValue "The goal effect is
to get the purchased Learning Object
delivered to the buyer."
endNonFunctionalProperties
definedBy
exists ?Delivery, ?Product, ?Buyer,
?LearningObject
(?Delivery memberOf po:delivery[
  po:deliveryItem hasValues {?Product},
  po:receiver hasValue ?Buyer ] and
?Product memberOf po:product[
  po:item hasValues {?LearningObject} ] and
?Buyer memberOf po:buyer and

?LearningObject                      memberOf
lom4WSMO:learningObject ).
```

Listing 3. Web Service from a learning object provider

```
webservice
_http://www.uah.es/ontologies/ws.wsml
nonFunctionalProperties
  dc:title hasValue "Algorithm for Internet
Applications Learning Object Web Service"
  dc:creator hasValue vcard:UaH
  dc:description hasValue "Web service for
access the content of a Learning Object on
Algorithms and purchase it"
  dc:publisher hasValue vcard:UaH
  dc:contributor hasValues {vCard:Ozelin,
vcard:Sicilia,
vcard:Sinuhe}

  dc:date hasValue "2005-02-07"
  dc:type hasValue
_http://www.wsmo.org/2004/d2/#webservice
  dc:format hasValue
"text/html"
  dc:language hasValue "en-uk"
  dc:rights hasValue
_http://www.uah.es/privacy.html
  version hasValue "$Version: 0.1 $"
endNonFunctionalProperties

importedOntologies
_http://www.wsmo.org/ontologies/purchase
capability _#
```

Listing 3. continued

```
precondition
axiom _#
nonFunctionalProperties
  dc:description hasValue "The input to the
Web Service has to be a user with an intention
to select a Learning Object for learn
Algorithms for Internet applications"
endNonFunctionalProperties
definedBy
?Buyer memberOf po:buyer and
?LO memberOf lom4WSMO:learningObject[
  isClassifiedInto hasValues
{?Classifications},
  hasRights hasValue ?Rights,
  hasTechnicalRequirements hasValues
{?TRs},
  hasEducational hasValue ?Educational,
  languages hasValues
{lom4WSMO:englishUK},
  aggregationLevel hasValue "3"^^xsd:integer
  identifier hasValue ?Identifier,
  title hasValue "Algorithms for Internet
Applications (WS2001/02, lecture
14)"^^xsd:string ] and
?Identifier memberOf learningIdentifier[
  entryCatalog hasValue
lom4WSMO:ARIDANE,
  catalogIdentifier hasValue
"V3VIROR_v_3.1_nr_22"^^xsd:string ] and
?Classifications memberOf
lom4WSMO:classification[
  purpose hasValue lom4WSMO:discipline,
  taxonPath hasValues {?Paths} ] and
?Paths memberOf lom4WSMO:taxonPath[
  hasSourceTaxonPath hasValue
lom4WSMO:ARIADNE,
  hasTaxon? hasValues {
  idTaxon hasValue
"000000001"^^xsd:string,
  valueTaxon hasValue "Exact, Natural and
Engineering Sciences"^^xsd:string,
    fatherOfTaxons hasValues {
    idTaxon hasValue
"000000002"^^xsd:string,
    valueTaxon hasValue "Informatics &
Information Processing"^^xsd:string,
    fatherOfTaxons hasValues {
    idTaxon hasValue
"000000003"^^xsd:string,
    valueTaxon hasValue
"General"^^xsd:string}
    },
    idTaxon hasValue
"000000004"^^xsd:string,
    valueTaxon hasValue "Internet
Algorithms"^^xsd:string }] and
?Rights memberOf lom4WSMO:rights[
  descriptionOfRights hasValue "The cost of
this LO is 5 Euros",
  hasCopyright hasValue
"true"^^xsd:boolean,
```

```
  hasCost hasValue "true"^^xsd:boolean,
  price memberOf lom4WSMO:cost[
  amount hasValue "5.0"^^xsd:float,
  currency hasValue lom4WSMO:euro]]
and
?TR memberOf
lom4WSMO:technicalRequirements[
  installationRemarksOfTR hasValue "unzip
archive and read further instructions in
README"^^xsd:string,
  formatOfTR hasValues {"application/x-aof",
"audio/x-aiff", "image/gif", "text/html"},
  sizeOfTR hasValue
"162099200"^^xsd:string,
  hasOrCompositeRequirements hasValues {
  typeOfRequirement hasValue "operating
system"^^xsd:string,
  nameOfRequirement hasValue "Multi-
OS"}] and
?Educational memberOf
lom4WSMO:educational[
  interactivityType hasValue
lom4WSMO:expositive,
  learningResourceType hasValue
lom4WSMO:video,
  hasInteractivitLevel hasValue
lom4WSMO:mediumInteractive,
  hasDifficulty hasValue
lom4WSMO:mediumDifficulty,
  intendedEndUserRol hasValue
lom4WSMO:learner ].

postcondition
axiom _#
nonFunctionalProperties
  dc:description hasValue "the output of the
service is a Learning Object about Internet
Algorithms."
endNonFunctionalProperties
definedBy
?LO memberOf lom4WSMO:learningObject[
  identifier hasValue ?Identifier] and
?Identifier memberOf learningIdentifier[
  entryCatalog hasValue
lom4WSMO:ARIDANE,
  catalogIdentifier hasValue
"V3VIROR_v_3.1_nr_22"^^xsd:string ].

effect
axiom _#
nonFunctionalProperties
  dc:description hasValue "there shall be a
trade for the Learning Object of the
postcondition"
endNonFunctionalProperties
definedBy
?someTrade memberOf po:trade[
  po:items hasValues {?LO},
  po:payment hasValue ?acceptedPayment ]
and ?acceptedPayment memberOf
po:creditCard.
```

Figure 2. Functional architecture of the semantic learning object repository

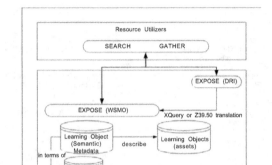

Mediators and the Overall Architecture

The overall architecture for learning object repositories based on Semantic Web Services is depicted in Figure 2 as an extension to the functional architecture of the IMS DRI 1.0 specification (IMS, 2003) in what concerns to resource search. Concretely, only the core function EXPOSE is depicted, since it is the base function required by selection and composition. In these processes, the results of the search process would eventually result in REQUESTS and subsequent DELIVER of the assets required, but this is out of the scope of the problems addressed in this chapter. The STORE core function is also omitted, since it does not have direct impact in the process of Semantic Web service-based selection and composition processes.

The DRI specification addresses the selection and composition problems as complex problems in which different and heterogeneous repositories may play a role. In order to address such heterogeneity, the model introduces an optional intermediary component that may accomplish one or several of the following functions:

1.   A *Translator* function translates formats of descriptions.

2.   An *Aggregator* function gathers data from multiple repositories and makes these metadata available for search.

3.   A *Federator* function passes a search query to multiple repositories and manages the responses.

The concept of mediator in WSMO is aimed at addressing interoperability problems of a diverse kind, and is thus candidate components for the semantic implementation of the just described DRI functions.

In the case of the *Translator* function the application of ooMediators is straight forward. ooMediators allow to link two Ontologies, resolving the possible mismatches that might occur among them. Thus, a translator function is assimilated with an ooMediator in which the translation logic is defined. Listing 4 shows an example of the WSMO specification of the ooMediator required in to translate Ontologies A and B into C.

For the *Aggregator* function, ooMediators can also solve the problem, as far as the data gathered from the different sources has some ontological meaning. In the event of requiring translation to the translator functions would help to present a consistent view of all the data gathered.

And finally for the *Federator* function the pattern follows is quite similar to the one used in the previous functions. Eventually, each one of these repositories will use its one vocabulary thus requiring data and meaning conversion, as provided by translators by means of ooMediators. Once the responses are submitted, the process will be inverse, requiring that the Federator functions convert the different vocabularies to an unified one. Also in this case ooMediators will help to solve the problem.

In order to be completely compliant with the WSMO specification, more mediators are required. Each one of the three functions will be initially specified as goal. In case no existing goal fully achieves the individual functions, ggMediators will be used to link and refine existing ones, until the exact behavior is achieved. Of course, new goals can be defined. By means of wgMediators goals are linked to Web services who will, in the latest state, be responsible for carrying the execution of the individual functionalities. Figure

Listing 4. OOmediator that imports and translates ontology A and B into C

```
namespace{
  dc    _"http://purl.org/dc/elements/1.1",
  wsml _"http://www.LOM.com"
}
ooMediator <"Learning Object Ontology Mediator">
nonFunctionalProperties
    dc#title hasValue "OO Mediator import and translate ontology A and B into C"
    dc#creator hasValue <"Sicilia, Lopez y Arroyo">
    dc#description hasValue "Mediator to import and translate ontology A and B into C"
    dc#publisher hasValue _"http://www.SiLoArorg/"
    dc#contributor hasValue _"http://www.uah.es/#Pepe"
    dc#date hasValue "2005-02-03"
    dc#type hasValue _"http://www.wsmo.org/2004/d2/#ooMediator"
    dc#identifier hasValue _"http://example.org/AandBtoC-Mediator.wsml"
    dc#language hasValue "en-us"
    dc#relation hasValue {_"http://daml.umbc.edu/ontologies/ittalks/person/",
                           _"http://example.org/tripReservationOntology"}
    dc#rights hasValue _"http://www.deri.org/privacy.html"
    version hasValue "$Revision: 0.1 $"
endNonFunctionalProperties
  source {_"http://www.deri.org/ontologyA/", _"http://www.deri.org/ontologyB/"}
  target _"http://www.uah.es/OntologyC"
  useService _"http://www.uah.es:8080/TranslatorService/AandB2C"
```

Figure 3. WSMO elements required in the Translation function

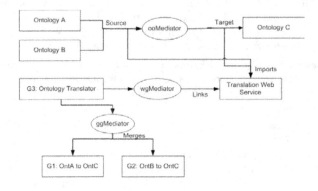

3, shows an example of how all the different WSMO elements are used in the case of the translator function.

Conclusion

Semantic Web service architectures provide a framework for the implementation of distributed learning object repositories that enable semantic matching. This chapter has described the motivation for such approach, and the main elements of the solution architecture, based on the WSMO framework. These elements include the ontology of learning object description, the overall architecture and the consideration of mediation as a technique for solving semantic integration and distribution issues.

References

Anido, L. E., Fernández, M. J., Caeiro, M., Santos, J. M., Rodríguez, J. S., & Llamas, M. (2002). Educational metadata and brokerage for learning resources. *Computers & Education, 38*(4), 351-374.

Arroyo, S., Lara, R., Gómez, J. M., Berka, D., Ding, Y., & Fensel, D. (2004). Semantic aspects of Web Services. In M. P. Singh (Ed.) *Practical Handbook of Internet Computing.* Baton Rouge, LA:Chapman Hall, &, CRC Press.

Arroyo, S., Toma, I., Roman, D., Drumm, C., Dimitrov, M., Spork, M., et al. (2004). *D3.1 Report on State of the Art and Requirements analysis.* DIP project deliverable FP6 −507483.

Berners-Lee, T., Hendler, J., & Lassila, O. (2001). The Semantic Web. *Scientific American, 284*(5), 34-43.

Davis, R., Shrobe, H., & Szolovits, P. (1993) What is a knowledge representation? *AI Magazine, 14*(1), 17-33.

Duval, E., Hodgins, W., Sutton, S. A., & Weibel, S. (2002, April). Metadata principles and practicalities. *D-Lib Magazine, 8*(4). Retrieved May 31, 2006, from http://www.dlib.org/dlib/april02/weibel/04weibel.html

Farance, F. (2003, January). IEEE LOM Standard Not Yet Ready For "Prime Time". *IEEE LTTF Learning Technology Newsletter, 5*(1). Retrieved May 31, 2006, from http://lttf.ieee.org/learn_tech/issues/january2003/index.html#8

Fensel, D. (2002). Language standardization for the Semantic Web: The long way from OIL to OWL. In *Proceedings of the 4th International Workshop on Distributed Communities on the Web*, Lecture Notes in Computer Science, 2468 (pp. 215-227).

Fensel, D., & Bussler, C. (2002, Summer), The Web service modeling framework WSMF. *Electronic Commerce Research and Applications, 1*(2), 113-137.

Holsapple, C. W., & Joshi, K. D. (2004). A formal knowledge management ontology: Conduct, activities, resources, and influences. *Journal of the American Society for Information Science and Technology, 55*(7), 593-612.

IEEE Learning Technology Standards Committee (2002). *Learning Object Metadata (LOM), Final Draft Standard, IEEE 1484.12.1-2002.*

IMS (2003). *IMS Digital Repositories Interoperability—Core Functions Information Model,* Version 1.0 Final Specification

Lara, R., Lausen, H., Arroyo, S., de Bruijn, J., & Fensel, D. (2003). Semantic Web Services: Description requirements and current technologies. In *International Workshop on Electronic Commerce, Agents, and Semantic Web Services, In conjunction with the 5th International Conference on Electronic Commerce* (ICEC 2003), Pittsburgh, PA.

López-Cobo, J. M., Sicilia, M. A., & Arroyo, S. (2004, November 7-11). Specifying Learning Object-Based Goals and Capabilities with WSMO. In: *Proceedings of the Workshop on Applications of Semantic Web Technologies for E-Learning in conjunction with ISWC'04* (SW-EL'04 @ ISWC'04), in conjunction with ISWC 2004: International Semantic Web Conference, Hiroshima, Japan.

Lytras, M., Tsilira, A., & Themistocleous, M. G. (2003). Towards the semantic e-Learning: an Ontological Oriented Discussion of the new research agenda in e-Learning. In *Proceedings of the 9th Americas Conference on Information Systems.*

Martinez, M. (2001). Successful learning—Using learning orientations to mass sustomize learning. *International Journal of Educational Technology, 2*(2). Retrieved June 17, 2003, from http://www.outreach.uiuc.edu/ijet/v2n2/martinez

Polsani, P. R. (2002). The use and abuse of reusable learning objects. *Journal of Digital Information, 3*(4).

Qin, J., & Finneran, C. (2002, July 18). Ontological representation of learning objects. In *Proceedings of the Workshop on Document Search Interface Design and Intelligent Access in Large-Scale Collections (JCDL'02),* Portland.

Roman, D., Lausen, H. & Keller, U. (2004). Web Service modeling ontology. WSMO Working Draft v0.3. Retrieved from http://www.wsmo.org/2004/d2/v1.0/

Sánchez-Alonso, S., Sicilia, M. A., & López-Cobo, J. M. (2004). Design contract-based selection and composition of learning objects. In *Proceedings of the 6th International Symposium on Computers in Education*—SIIE 2004, Caceres, Spain.

Sicilia, M.A., & García, E. (2005). On the Convergence of Formal Ontologies and Standardized e-Learning. *Journal of Distance Education Technologies, 3*(2), 12-28.

Sicilia, M. A., García, E., Aedo, I., & Díaz, P. (2004). Using links to describe imprecise relationships in educational contents. *International Journal for Continuing Engineering Education and Lifelong Learning, 14*(3), 260-275.

Sicilia, M. A., & Lytras, M. (2005). On the representation of change according to different Ontologies of learning. *International Journal of Learning and Change, 1*(1).

Sicilia, M. A., Lytras, M., Rodríguez, E., & García, E. (2006, May). Integrating descriptions of knowledge management learning activities into large ontological structures: A case study. *Data and Knowledge Engineering, 57*(2), 111-121.

Stojanovic, L., Staab, S., & Studer, R. (2001, October 23-27) E-learning based on the Semantic Web. In *Proceedings of the World Conference on the WWW and Internet* (WebNet 2001), Orlando, FL.

Tidwell, D. (2000). *Web services: The Web's next revolution.* Retrieved from http://www.ibm.com/developerWorks

Web Services Architecture Requirements (2002). Retrieved October 2002, from http://www.w3.org/TR/wsa-reqs/

Wiley, D. A. (Ed.). (2001). *The Instructional Use of Learning Objects* [online version]. Association for Educational Communications and Technology, Bloomington. Retrieved May 31, 2006, from http://www.reusability.org/read/

Chapter VII

Using Semantic Web to Facilitate Agent-to-Agent Argumentation for E-Commerce

Shiu-li Huang, Ming Chuan University, Taiwan

Fu-ren Lin, National Tsing Hua University, Taiwan

Abstract

This chapter designs a multi-agent argumentation system for e-commerce. This system applies Semantic Web technology to facilitate agents to share ontologies and describe their own mental states and arguments. All arguments are connected by attacking relations and can be proved or defeated via a dialectical game. In this system, buyer and seller agents can understand arguments and argue over product attributes. This system can help buyers to delegate their buyer agents to search products that exactly match their needs, and help sellers to delegate seller agents to present products and persuade buyer agents into believing that the products can satisfy the buyers' needs.

Introduction

Many efforts have been spent on supporting automated commerce activities on the Internet, such as selling, searching, auction, and payment. Agent technologies have been used for reaching a certain level of autonomy to release human's cognition and manual loads. For example, many e-marketplaces provide search agents to help buyers to search products that match their preferences and provide comparison agents to help buyers to compare products and make purchasing decisions, for example, mysimon.com and bizrate.com. Additionally, many intelligent bargaining agents for e-marketplace have been researched (Matwin, Szapiro, & Haigh, 1991; Oliver, 1997; Wasfy & Hosni, 1998; Zeng & Sycara, 1998; Lin & Chang, 2001; Dumas, Governatori, Hofstede, & Oaks, 2002; Huang & Lin, 2005). However, to enable agents with the semantic argumentation ability is still a trial due to many obstacles.

The first obstacle is how to enable a buyer agent to understand product descriptions presented by a seller agent. Semantic Web enables Web information to be machine-understandable and facilitates agents to understand information. It seems that Semantic Web can transcend this obstacle. Although current Semantic Web can tolerate information contradiction, it only supports monotonic reasoning that new information cannot retract previous information, and facts and entailments can only be added but never defeated. In a used-car e-marketplace, for example, a buyer delegates a buyer agent to find out good-condition cars. In this case, the buyer and sellers may have different definitions of the concept of "good-condition car." Therefore, the second obstacle is how to issue arguments between agents to prove or disprove the counterpart's proposition.

Argumentation in a multi-agent context is a process by which one agent attempts to convince another agent of the truth (or falsity) of state of affairs. This process involves agents putting forward arguments for and against propositions, together with justifications for the acceptability of these arguments (Wooldridge, 2002). In an argumentation process, a truth can be defeated when new information appears. Through argumentation, following the above example, a seller agent can persuade a buyer agent to believe its car is in a good condition even both have different definitions for a good-condition car. To facilitate multi-agent argumentation, a defeasible reasoning approach can be developed upon the Semantic Web.

This study aims to design a multi-agent e-marketplace, in which buyer and seller agents can argue over product attributes via argumentation. This study adopts OWL, a Web ontology language, to clearly express arguments and uses a dialectical game approach to support defeasible reasoning. Using this system, a buyer can delegate a buyer agent to search products that exactly match his/her need, and a seller can delegate a seller agent to present products and persuade buyer agents into believing that the products can satisfy their masters' needs.

The rest of this chapter is structured as follows. The next section describes the related works about Semantic Web, existing matchmaking platforms that use Semantic Web technology, and defeasible reasoning for argumentation. Then, we design the multi-agent argumentation system using Semantic Web and defeasible reasoning, and illustrate the architecture of this system. Finally, we conclude this study and indicate future directions.

Background

This section firstly introduces Semantic Web. Several matchmaking systems using Semantic Web technology addressed how to rank the matching results rather than how to filter the results. This study introduces argumentation to the matchmaking process that a buyer agent may be persuaded by a seller agent into believing that the product can satisfy the buyer's need. To grant agents the ability to handle argumentation, this study adopts abstract argumentation framework to perform defeasible reasoning and presents it in this section.

Semantic Web

The World Wide Web nowadays is a large information space; however, the information encoded as HTML on the Web is mainly designed for human to read. Machine-understandable information encoded as XML-based Semantic Web facilitates the information exchange between systems (Berners-Lee, Hendler, & Lassila, 2001).

The Semantic Web provides a common framework that allows Web information to express meanings and knowledge for various application domains. Meaning is expressed not only by terms but also by the relations among terms. Knowledge is represented by inference rules that software agents can use to conduct automated reasoning. To represent various concepts, different applications can develop their own ontologies in which inconsistent definitions of common concepts are allowed. Ontology, in the philosophical view, is a discipline that deals with the nature and the organization of being (Maedche, 2002). In the field of Semantic Web, an ontology is a document or a file that contains a taxonomy and inference rules to formally define the relations among terms (Berners-Lee et al., 2001). The ontology of a concept is identified by a universal resource identifier (URI) and a software agent refers to different concepts defined by ontology using distinct URIs to avoid confusion.

The basic languages for developing the Semantic Web are ectensible markup language (XML) and the resource description framework (RDF). Developers can use XML to create their own concept terms but cannot define their relations. RDF can describe relationships using RDF triples, subject, verb and object, which assert that particular things have properties with certain values. To support more plentiful meaning and knowledge, the U.S. Defense Advanced Research Projects Agency (DARPA) developed the DARPA agent markup language (DAML) as an extension to XML and RDF. DAML+OIL adds Ontology Inference Layer (OIL) into DAML to enhance the reasoning power for description logic. After that, the World Wide Web Consortium (W3C) slightly revised DAML+OIL to evolve ontology Web language (OWL), and nowadays, OWL becomes a main Web ontology language to develop the Semantic Web.

Existing Matchmaking Systems Based on Semantic Web

Li and Horrocks (2004) designed a service matchmaking prototype that used DAML-S to provide the vocabulary for service descriptions. DAML-S is written in DAML+OIL and designed for describing Web services. The matchmaking prototype is a repository where agents can advertise and search for services that match a semantic description. Matchmaking here is defined as a process that requires a repository host to take a query or an advertisement as input, and then to return information that satisfies the requirement specified in the input query or advertisement. Five matching degrees are defined and listed as follows:

- **Exact:** If advertisement A and request R are equivalent concepts, it is an Exact match, denoted as $A \equiv R$.

- **PlugIn:** If request R is a subconcept of advertisement A, it is a PlugIn match, denoted as $R \sqsubseteq A$.

- **Subsume:** If request R is a super-concept of advertisement A, it is a Subsume match, denoted as $A \sqsubseteq R$.

- **Intersection:** If the intersection of advertisement A and request R is satisfiable, it is an Intersection match.

- **Disjoint:** Otherwise, it is a Disjoint match.

The matches from the most to the least desirable are listed as Exact, PlugIn, Subsume, intersection, and disjoint, accordingly.

Tomaz, Labidi, and Wanghon (2003) designed a matchmaker agent to compute the degree of similarity among customers' requests and suppliers' advertisements in a B2B system. Customers and suppliers use DAML-S to express requests and advertisements, respectively. DAML-S provides standardization on how to describe the Web services functionalities (Service Profile), how it performs the task (Service Model) and how we can access it (Service Grounding). The Service Profile class specifies a service in terms of input (what the Web service requires to produce the expected output), output (what the Web service supplies as answer to a request), preconditions (the conditions must be true so that the service may be performed), and effects (changes or actions in the world). The matchmaker agent first compares the requirement's output with the outputs of each advertisement stored in the advertisement's database, and then compares the advertisements' inputs with the requirements' inputs. The agent distinguishes the four degrees of combinations among two inputs or two outputs; they are exact (the advertisement's output/input is equal or it is a subclass of the request's output/input), plugin (the advertisement's output/input is a group that includes the request's output/input), subsumes (the request's output/input is a group that contains the advertisement's output/input), and fail (there isn't any connection among advertisement and request). The criterion for the classification of the matching is firstly based on the outputs. The inputs are just considered as tie breaking criteria. A matching on the preconditions similar to the one accomplished with the inputs where outputs are treated as a second criterion of breaking tie.

Noia, Sciascio, Donini, and Mongiello (2003) presented a matchmaking facilitator that allows one to categorize and rank matches according to their logical relation. The authors distinguished between Exact match (all requests in demand are available in supply or vice versa), potential match (some requests in demand are not specified in supply), and partial match (some requests in demand are in conflict with supply). Regarding potential match, the ranking of potential matches is monotonic over subsumption that the more specific the better. Regarding partial match, a ranking of partial matches is antimonotonic over subsumption that the more specific the worse. Two algorithms *rankPotential* and *rankPartial* were proposed based on these ranking principles. If there are a demand *apartment with bedroom wanted, no pets*, and the following advertisements, supply1: *single room in an apartment of smoking persons*, supply2: *two double rooms in an apartment, no pets allowed*, supply3: *apartment to let, with a pet*, supply4: *lodging with bathroom, two pets2*, and supply5: *apartment*. The *rankPartial* algorithm will point out that demand cannot be satisfied by supplies 3 and 4. The *rankPotential* algorithm will show that supply2 is an exact match w.r.t. the given demand and supplies 1 and 5 are potential matches, that is, there is no characteristic conflict, but some of the requests in demand are not explicitly available.

Abstract Argumentation Framework

Monotonic logic is mainly concerned with the formalization of universal truths, which hold without exception and for all time. Non-monotonicity or defeasibility arises from the fact that arguments can be defeated by stronger counterarguments. Logics for defeasible argumentation, such as Pollock (1992), Prakken and Sartor (1997), and Vreeswijk (1997), is an approach to formalize defeasible reasoning that reasons with incomplete information. Conclusions may be withdrawn if more information becomes available. Another abstract approach specializes in the relations among arguments rather than the logic structures in arguments. Dung (1995) developed an argumentation framework (AF), a form of defeasible reasoning denoted as AF = <*AR*, attacks>, where *AR* is a set of arguments, and an attack is a binary relation on *AR*. Here, an argument is an abstract entity whose role is solely determined by its relations to other arguments. The advantage of this framework is that it pays no special attention on the internal structure of the arguments.

An argument $a \in AR$ is *acceptable* with respect to a set S of arguments if and only if b attacks a, b is attacked by S for each argument $b \in AR$. The relation that an argument b is attacked by a set of arguments S means that S contains an attacker of b. A set S of arguments is *conflict-free* if no arguments in S attack an argument in S. Dung also proposed argument-theoretic semantics, such as admissibility, preferential, and stable semantics, to capture the notion of acceptability of arguments (Dung, 1995; Bondarenko, Dung, Kowalski, & Toni, 1997). A set of conflict-free arguments S is *admissible* if and only if each argument in S is acceptable with respect to S. A set of arguments is a *preferred extension* of an argumentation framework if it is a maximal admissible set of the argumentation framework. A set of arguments is a *stable extension* if and only if it is conflict-free and attacks every argument outside of it.

Dung (1995) and Bondarenko et al. (1997) also proved some theorems and lemmas. Each admissible set is contained in a ⊆-maximally admissible set. Every stable extension is a preferred extension, but not vice versa. Stable extensions do not always exist; preferred extensions always exist. Therefore, the input of this non-monotonic reasoning approach is a set of arguments ordered by a binary relation of "attack", and it outputs one or more argument extensions, which are maximal sets of arguments that survive in the competition of all input arguments. The argument-theoretic semantics represent a status of a set of arguments on the basis of their mutual attack relations. An argumentation framework also needs a "proof-theory" to compute that a particular argument has a certain status.

Vreeswijk and Prakken (2000) proposed a dialectical form of an argument game between a proponent (defender or pro) and an opponent (challenger or con) of a proposition (main argument) as a natural form of such proof theory. In this game, an opponent starts with an argument, and the opponent attacks this argument with a counterargument with sufficient strength. The initial argument (main argument) is provable if its proponent has a winning strategy; that is, if s/he can make the opponent run out of moves against her/his any possible attacks. The procedure is mainly to construct an admissible set around the main argument. If it succeeds, the main argument is contained in an admissible set and it is acceptable. Suppose that a main argument belongs to A which is admissible, the proponent can win every dispute by starting with a, and replying with arguments from A only.

Figure 1 illustrates two argument games, where a node means a *move* that can be an initial move $M_1 = (Player, Arg)$ or a replying move $M_i = (Player, Arg, Move)$ ($i > 1$). *Player* is the one who moves, *Arg* is an argument, and *Move* is an indication of the move to which it replies. The argument proposed by a proponent is denoted as a black node and that by the opponent is a white node. For example, in both trees, M_1 is (proponent, P1) and M_2 is (opponent, O1, M_1). The notation "←" is an attack relation between two arguments. The relation P1 ← O1 denotes that P1 is attacked by O1, where O1 is an attacker of P1, or O1 is a counterargument of P1. According to the dialectical proof theory proposed by

Figure 1. Two trees of proof-theoretical dialogues

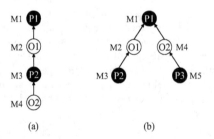

(a)   (b)

Figure 2. Disputation statuses of moves

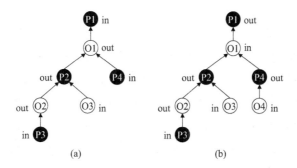

(a)　　　　　　　　　　　　(b)

Vreeswijk and Prakken (2000), in game (a), the proponent fails to construct an admissible set around P1 because s/he cannot find arguments to against O2 and cannot find another argument, which is different from P2, against O1. Therefore, P1 is unacceptable (not in an admissible set and not in a preferred extension). In game (b), P1 is acceptable since the opponent is unable to find other arguments against P1, P2, or P3 and therefore the set {P1, P2, P3} is an admissible set. Note that the arguments uttered by the proponent must be consistent with his/her previous arguments (conflict-free).

Prakken (2001) defined the disputation statuses of dispute moves in which a move *M* of a dispute *D* is *in* in *D* if and only if all moves in *D* that reply to it are *out* in D. Otherwise, *M* is *out* in *D*. The status of a move is *in* means that the argument of this move is acceptable. Figure 2 illustrates this concept and we can find that the leaf nodes must be *in* because they have no attackers. If M_1 is *in*, P1 is acceptable and it is included in an admissible set that contains all arguments belonging to the proponent's *in* moves. In game (a), for instance, P1 is acceptable and included in the admissible set {P1, P3, P4}. In game (b), however, P1 is unacceptable.

This research designs a multi-agent argumentation system based on Dung's argumentation framework and calculates the status of each move according to Vreeswijk and Prakken's (2000) dialectical game approach.

Agent-to-Agent Argumentation

This study aims to design seller and buyer agents which can automatically argue over product attributes. A seller agent tries to persuade a buyer agent to believe how nice a product is, and the buyer agent may attack the seller agent's claims. Therefore, the seller agent is a proponent of its claim and the buyer agent is an opponent. These two agents have their own mental states, but they share the same argumentation ontology and dialectical domain ontology.

Argumentation Ontology

The argumentation ontology describes the abstract argumentation framework proposed by Dung (1995). The basic classes to represent the framework include Move, Player, Argument, and MoveStatus. The properties hasPlyer, hasArgument, and hasMoveStatus form the relations between Move and Player, Argument, as well as MoveStatus, respectively. The properties hasDefenderMove and hasAttackerMove build the attacking and defending relations between two moves. These two properties are inverse properties of each other. A move is a thing that has at least one player and one argument. The InitialMove is a subclass of Move, and it is the move that has only a proponent player. The ReplyingMove is also a subclass of Move, and a replying move attacks at least one move. In OWL, all classes are subclasses of owl:Thing. Figure 3 illustrates the taxonomy in this ontology.

Although Dung's abstract argumentation framework can work without considering argument structure, this study adopts Toulmin model to enrich argument structure in the

Figure 3. Class hierarchy in the argumentation ontology

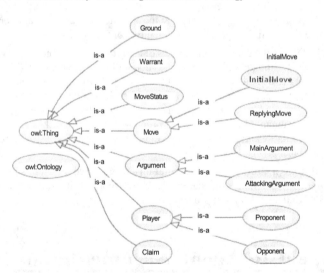

Figure 4. Toulmin model of argument structure

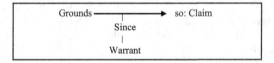

system. Toulmin model (Toulmin, 1958) can simply describe an argument structure using the basic triad: *claim*, *ground*, and *warrant* (see Figure 4). A claim is a stand on an issue, the position taking, and the purpose for arguing. The ground is the evidence, fact, data, or information that provides the reasons and verification for the claim. A warrant forms the link between grounds and claim, and justifies the mental leap from grounds to claim.

According to Toulmin model, an argument in the argumentation ontology can have claim, ground, or warrant. In this ontology, MainArgument and AttackingArgument are subclasses of the class Argument. A main argument is the argument of an initial move which is a claim that the proponent wants to prove. An attacking argument is the argument of a replying move which is a claim, ground, or warrant.

Dialectical Domain Ontology

The dialectical domain ontology defines the dialectical scope of topics and terms. Both seller and buyer agents share this ontology to know what topics they can interact. For example, in a used-car trading marketplace, a car seller may claim his/her car is a safety car because it has some safety features. A car seller may claim that this car is in a good condition because it has no damage and has conducted periodical maintenance. In this domain, whether the car is a safety car or a good-condition car are topics that both seller and buyer can argue over, and things such as safety features, damage, and periodical maintenance should be described in the dialectical domain ontology. Figure 5 depicts a simple ontology of a used-car trading example. Notably, the class UnSafetyCar is a complement class of SafetyCar, which means that a car which is not a safety car must be an unsafety car, and vice versa. The class BadConditionCar is a complement class of GoodConditionCar, which means that a car which does not belong to a good-condition car must belong to a bad-condition car, and vice versa. This study demonstrates a dialectical game example based on the used-car trading domain ontology in the next section.

Figure 5. Dialectical domain ontology of used-car trading

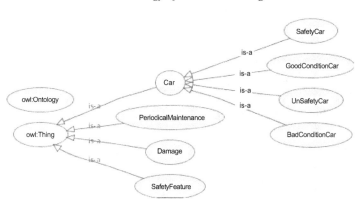

Agent Mental State Ontology

Seller and buyer agents maintain their own mental state ontologies. An agent's mental state represented by three mental attitudes: *believe*, *desire*, and *intention* (Rao & Georgeff, 1995). A belief is an agent's informative component that represents the information on its environmental states. A desire is an agent's motivational state that represents the objectives it expects to accomplish. An intention is an agent's deliberative component that represents the currently chosen course of action. Seller and buyer agents share the argumentation ontology and dialectical domain ontology to understand the argumentation rule and domain. Moreover, their owners (seller and buyer) build dialectical strategy trees that represent all possible moves and attacking relations in their mental state ontologies. The root of a strategy tree is an initial move that contains a main argument issued by a seller agent which represents its seller. A main argument contains a claim about a certain proposition supported by the seller agent and represents a topic to start with. The replying moves following an initial move are all possible counterarguments uttered by the buyer agent to attack the seller agent's main argument.

A strategy tree grows up by extending all possible arguments and counterarguments based on the attacking relations. On one hand, once the strategy trees are built, the seller agent desires to prove that the claims in the initial moves are true. On the other hand, the buyer agent desires to attack the seller agent's claims. When a dialectical game starts, both agents intend to choose actions (the arguments to utter) based on their own strategy trees and only the moves with *in* status will be selected. Arguments uttered interactively and are connected by attacking relations to form an instance tree. In an instance tree, if the seller agent can make the buyer agent run out of moves, the seller agent's claim is proved true.

The argument contents described in ontology language express clear meanings. The claims, grounds, or warrants in arguments represent what facts and rules an agent believes in. This study uses the example of the used-car trading domain, and proposes a dialogue instance to elaborate the sequence of agent argumentation. Suppose that a seller agent presents a used car to a buyer agent, and the seller agent's main argument is "This car has antilock brakes, and a car with antilock brakes is a safety car, so that this car is a safety car." The seller agent claims that the used car is a safety car, and in its mental state ontology, this claim can be expressed by OWL.

```
<SafetyCar rdf:ID="ThisCar"/>
```

This expression represents that "ThisCar" as an individual belongs to the SafetyCar class.

This claim supported by the fact that this car has the safety feature, that is, antilock brakes. Therefore, the ground in this argument can be expressed as:

```
<Car rdf:ID="ThisCar">
    <hasSafetyFeature rdf:resource="#AntilockBrakes"/>
</Car>.
```

The seller agent believes that a car with antilock brakes is a safety car, and lay out the ground. Therefore, the warrant of this argument can be represented as follows:

```
<owl:Class rdf:ID="SafetyCar">
  <owl:equivalentClass>
    <owl:Class>
      <owl:intersectionOf rdf:parse Type="Collection">
       <owl:Class rdf:about="#Car"/>
        <owl:Restriction>
         <owl:onProperty>
           <owl:ObjectProperty rdf:ID="hasSafetyFeature"/>
         <owl:onProperty>
         <owl:hasValue>
           <SafteyFeature rdf:ID="AntilockBrakes"/>
         <owl:hasValue>
        <owl:Restriction>
      <owl:intersectionOf>
    <owl:Class>
  </owl:equivalentClass>
</owl:Class>
```

After the seller agent uttered the main argument, the buyer agent checks whether the claim consists with its own mental state ontology. If this claim is provable in buyer agent's mental state, the buyer agent utters a speech act to agree to this claim; otherwise, it utters an attacking argument based on its strategy trees. In this example, we assume that the buyer agent believes that a safety car must have antilock brakes and airbags, and then utters the attacking argument, "This car only has antilock brakes; however, a safety car must have both antilock brakes and airbag, this car is not a safety car." In this argument, the claim "this car is not a safety car" can be omitted because the attacking argument has to disagree on the claim of the attacked argument. The ground and warrant in this argument using OWL can be described as follows.

Ground:

```
<Car rdf:ID="ThisCar">
  <hasSafetyFeatre rdf:resource="#AntilockBrakes"/>
</Car>
```

Warrant:

```
<owl:Class  rdf:ID="SafetyCar">
  <owl:equivalentClass>
    <owl:Class>
      <owl:intersectionOf rdf:parse Type="Collection">
       <owl:Class rdf:about="#Car"/>
        <owl:Restriction>
         <owl:onProperty>
          <owl:ObjectProperty rdf:ID="hasSafetyFeature"/>
         <owl:onProperty>
          <owl:hasValue rdf:resource="#AntilockBrakes"/>
        <owl:Restriction>
        <owl:Restriction>
         <owl:onProperty>
            <owl:ObjectProperty rdf:ID="hasSafetyFeature"/>
         <owl:onProperty>
          <owl:hasValue rdf:resource="#AirBag"/>
       <owl:Restriction>
      <owl:intersectionOf>
    <owl:Class>
  </owl:equivalentClass>
</owl:Class>
```

Notably, if the seller agent also states that this car has no airbags in the main argument, this attacking argument can also be spoken like "This car has no airbags; since an unsafe car is a car that has no airbags, this car is an unsafe car." The claim expresses that this car belongs to unsafe car, and is described as:

```
<UnSafetyCar rdf:ID="ThisCar"/>
```

The fact the buyer agent believes is that "this car has no airbags," so that the ground can be expressed as:

```
<Car rdf:ID="ThisCar">
  <hasNoSafetyFeature rdf:resource="#AirBag"/>
</Car>
```

Since the buyer agent believes that lack of either antilock brakes or airbags makes a car unsafe, and an unsafe car is not a safety car. The warrant is represented as follows:

```
<owl:Class rdf:ID="UnSafetycar">
  <owl:equivalentClass>
    <owl:Class>
      <owl:intersectionOf rdf:parseType="Collection">
        <owl:Restriction>
         <owl:onProperty>
           <owl:ObjectProperty rdf:ID="hasNoSafetyFeature"/>
         <owl:onProperty>
         <owl:hasValue rdf:resource="#AirBag"/>
        <owl:Restriction>
        <owl:Class rdf:about="#Car"/>
      <owl:intersectionOf>
    <owl:Class>
  <owl:equivalentClass>
  <owl:equivalentClass>
    <owl:Class>
      <owl:intersectionOf rdf:parseType="Collection">
        <owl:Restriction>
         <owl:onProperty>
           <owl:ObjectProperty rdf:ID="hasNoSafetyFeature"/>
         <owl:onProperty>
         <owl:hasValue rdf:resource="#AntilockBrakes"/>
        <owl:Restriction>
        <owl:Class rdf:about="#Car"/>
      <owl:intersectionOf>
    <owl:Class>
  <owl:equivalentClass>
  <rdfs:subClassOf>
    <owl:Class>
      <owl:complementOf>
      <owl:Class rdf:ID="SafetyCar"/>
      <owl:complementOf>
    <owl:Class>
  <rdfs:subClassOf>
<owl:Class>
```

After this, if the seller agent cannot find another argument to attack the buyer agent's argument, the claim "This car is a safe car." cannot be proved. At this moment, the seller agent can start another topic to utter if another strategy tree exists. We assume that the seller agent utters another main argument, "This car has no frame damage and water damage, and a car that has no frame damage and water damage is a good-condition car, so that this car is a good-condition car." The claim, ground, and warrant are described in OWL as follows:

Claim:

```
<GoodConditionCar rdf:ID="ThisCar"/>
```

Ground:

```
<Car rdf:ID="ThisCar">
 <hasNoDamage rdf:resource="#FrameDamage"/>
 <hasNoDamage rdf:resource="#WaterDamage"/>
</Car>
```

Warrant:

```
<owl:Class rdf:about="#GoodConditionCar">
 <owl:equivalentClass>
  <owl:Class>
    <owl:intersectionOf rdf:parseType="Collection">
       <owl:Class rdf:about="#Car"/>
       <owl:Restriction>
         <owl:onProperty>
          <owl:ObjectProperty rdf:ID="hasNoDamage"/>
         <owl:onProperty>
         <owl:hasValue>
          <Damage rdf:ID="FrameDamage"/>
         </owl:hasValue>
       </owl:Restriction>
       <owl:Restriction>
         <owl:onProperty>
          <owl:ObjectProperty rdf:ID="hasNoDamage"/>
         </owl:onProperty>
         <owl:hasValue>
          <Damage rdf:ID="WaterDamage"/>
         </owl:hasValue>
       </owl:Restriction>
       </owl:intersectionOf>
   </owl:Class>
  </owl:equivalentClass>
 </owl:Class>
```

However, the buyer agent thinks that the condition that a car without frame damage and water damage is insufficient to support the claim, and then utters another attacking argument, "A car that does not only have no fame and water damages, but also has periodical maintenance is called a good condition car." This argument represented in OWL is listed as follows:

```
<owl:Class  rdf:about="#GoodConditionCar">
  <owl:equivalentClass>
    <owl:Class>
      <owl:intersectionOf rdf:parseType="Collection">
        <owl:Class rdf:about="#Car"/>
        <owl:Restriction>
          <owl:onProperty>
            <owl:ObjectProperty rdf:ID="hasNoDamage"/>
          <owl:onProperty>
          <owl:hasValue>
            <Damage rdf:ID="FrameDamage"/>
          </owl:hasValue>
        </owl:Restriction>
        <owl:Restriction>
          <owl:onProperty>
            <owl:ObjectProperty rdf:ID="hasNoDamage"/>
          </owl:onProperty>
          <owl:hasValue>
            <Damage rdf:ID="WaterDamage"/>
          <owl:hasValue>
        </owl:Restriction>
        <owl:Restriction>
          <owl:onProperty>
            <owl:ObjectProperty rdf:ID="hasPeriodicalMaintenance"/>
          <owl:onProperty>
           <owl:someValuesFrom rdf:resource="#PeriodicalMaintenance"/>
        </owl:Restriction>
        </owl:intersectionOf>
    </owl:Class>
  </owl:equivalentClass>
</owl:Class>
```

After receiving this argument, the seller agent replies with a new fact, "This car has the periodical maintenance every one year." expressed in OWL as follows:

```
<Car rdf:ID="ThisCar">
  <hasPeriodicalMaintenance>
    <PeriodicalMaintenance rdf:ID="EveryOneYear"/>
  </hasPeriodicalMaintenance>
</Car>
```

At this moment, the buyer agent cannot return an attacking argument and the main argument "This car is a good-condition car." is proved true.

System Architecture

This study designs a multi-agent argumentation system, in which a seller and a buyer agent can argue over product attributes in an e-marketplace. Figure 6 illustrates the system architecture. Each agent has its own mental state ontology that shares the same argumentation ontology and dialectical domain ontology via URIs. A user builds its agent's mental state ontology by argumentation mechanisms. Once a dialectical game starts, an agent's argumentation mechanism is responsible for choosing arguments to utter, and its reasoner helps to check the consistency between the other agent's arguments and its own mental state.

Figure 6. Architecture of multi-agent argumentation system

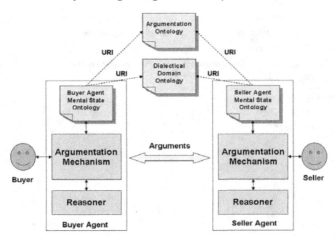

To handle dialogues between these agents, the argumentation mechanism deals with three subtasks: (1) selecting a main argument, (2) replying the other agent's counterarguments, and (3) determining when to change a dialectical topic.

Main Argument Selection

When a dialectical game starts, a seller agent tries to persuade the buyer agent to believe its claim about product features. Main arguments can be chosen from strategy trees which have been built. The first decision for a seller agent is to determine which topic (main argument) to start with. The seller agent selects a main argument from candidate arguments. Only an acceptable main argument can be a candidate, and main argument cannot be reused in a game. Since strategy trees are built according to the argumentation ontology, the seller agent can use a reasoner to identify the candidate main arguments. For example, by following query in Racer Query Language based on Racer reasoner (http://www.sts.tu-harburg.de/~r.f.moeller/racer/), an agent can look up which arguments belong to initial moves and the move statuses are *in*.

```
(retrieve (?y)(AND (?x |InitialMove|)(?x |In| |hasStatus|)(?x ?y |hasArgument|)))
```

However, there should be a selection function in the argumentation mechanism to determine the uttering sequence of the candidate main arguments. This selection function can be developed using machine learning techniques such as case-based reasoning or reinforcement learning, or just simply given a fixed uttering sequence by a seller.

Counterargument Reply

Both seller and buyer agents may receive the other agent's attacking arguments, and then reply these counterarguments according to their strategy trees. Figure 7 depicts two sample strategy trees built in the seller agent's mental state ontology.

In a seller agent's view, the following examples that refer to these strategy trees explain how an agent replies to the other agent's attacks.

Example 1: If the main argument b has been uttered, the buyer agent utters an argument that matches d to attack b. In this situation, the seller agent has two choices to reply this attack: arguments i or j. The seller agent follows a winning strategy that can make the opponent run out of moves to react to any attacks. For this purpose, it must reply with arguments only in an admissible set and argument i must be chosen.

Example 2: If the main argument b has been uttered, the buyer agent utters an argument that matches e to attack b. In this situation, the seller agent has two choices to reply this attack: argument k or l. Since both k and l are in an admissible set, the seller

Figure 7. Dialectical strategy trees

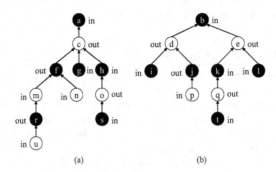

(a)　　　　　　(b)

agent will select an argument that can make the buyer agent not to move quickly. The argument *l* is better than *k* because *l* is already the end of branch.

Example 3: If main argument *a* has been uttered, the buyer agent issues an argument that matches *c* to attack *a* and then the seller agent uses *g* to react to it. After this, the buyer agent utters an argument that matches *o* to attack *a*. In the strategy tree (a), the argument *o* directly attack *h* and indirectly attack *a*, but in a real dialectical game, the buyer agent utters *o* to attack *a* directly. In this case, the seller agent also follows a winning strategy to select argument *s* to reply.

Example 4: If main argument *a* has been uttered, the buyer agent utters an argument that matches *c* to attack *a* and then the seller agent utters *g* to attack it. After this, the buyer agent utters an argument that matches *m* to attack *a*. In this case, the seller agent cannot select argument *r* to reply because *r* is unacceptable. An argument that is in an admissible set and near the argument *a* will be selected, hence *h* is chosen.

Example 5: If main argument *b* has been uttered, the buyer agent utters an argument that matches *e* to attack *b* and then the seller agent uses *l* to attack back. After this, the buyer agent utters argument *v* to attack *l*, which makes the initial move become *out* in the corresponding instance tree. In this case, *v* is not defined in the strategy tree (b) in advance and the seller agent cannot attack *v*. However, the seller agent can utter *k* to attack *e* and keep main argument *b* acceptable.

These examples represent the following heuristics for replying the other agent's counterarguments, respectively.

1. Replying with acceptable arguments.
2. Selecting an argument that can freeze the other agent's move as soon as possible.
3. Replying with an argument that directly attacks the other agent's counterargument.

4.   If no arguments in the strategy tree can directly attack the other agent's counterargument, an agent selects an argument from the admissible set which is close to the attacked argument.

5.   If no arguments in the strategy tree can match the other agent's counterargument, an agent selects an argument from the admissible set which changes the current status of the initial move in the current instance tree.

Decision Making to Change Dialectical Topic

A seller agent changes the topic when no acceptable arguments can be selected or when the buyer agent agrees to the seller agent's claim. In this situation, the seller agent will utter another new main argument if any unused arguments exist; otherwise, the dialectical game is terminated.

Future Trends

Agents equipped with the Semantic Web capability enable the automation of argument composition and issuing between agents. In agent-enabled e-commerce applications, agents are usually used to bargain prices based on users' risk aspects and learned price negotiation patterns. However, it is in an early stage for a seller agent to persuade a prospect buyer to raise its product valuation through automated argument formation and issuing. This study goes further to propose the use of Semantic Web to facilitate agent-to-agent argumentation. The agent-to-agent argumentation facilitated by the Semantic Web can be used by a seller agent to issue arguments to persuade a buyer agent to raise its product valuation. The buyer agent can attack arguments issued by the seller agent with commonly understandable semantics. The future research can spend efforts on effectively deriving agent-to-agent persuasion strategies to realize the agent-to-agent argumentation mechanisms. Then, the resulting agent-to-agent persuasion system can be applied to online selling activities.

Conclusion

Argumentation between agents has to express clear and machine-readable arguments, and an argument can be defeated when a stronger counterargument appears. This chapter designs a multi-agent argumentation system that allows seller and buyer agents to argue over product attributes. This system applies Semantic Web technology to facilitate agents to share ontology and describe their own mental states and arguments. All arguments are connected by attacking relations and can be proved or defeated via a dialectical game. This study used a used-car trading example to demonstrate agent-to-

agent argumentation. The system can be extended and applied to other product categories. In future research, the acquisition of knowledge from human to compose arguments
for agents can be further addressed. A prototyping system can be developed to evaluate
the proposed framework.

References

Berners-Lee, T., Hendler, J., & Lassila, O. (2001, May). The semantic web. *Scientific American*, 35-43. Retrieved from http://www.sciam.com/article.cfm?articleID=00048 144-10D2-1C70-84A9809EC588EF21

Bondarenko, A., Dung, P. M., Kowalski, R. A., & Toni, F. (1997). An abstract argumentation-theoretic approach to default reasoning. *Artificial Intelligence, 93*(1-2), 63-101.

Dumas, M., Governatori, G., Hofstede, A. H. M., & Oaks, P. (2002). A formal approach to negotiating agents development. *Electronic Commerce Research and Applications, 1*(2), 193-207.

Dung, P. M. (1995). On the acceptability of arguments and its fundamental role in nonmonotonic reasoning, logic programming and N-persons games. *Artificial Intelligence, 77*(2), 321-357.

Huang, S.-l., & Lin, F.-r. (2005). Designing intelligent sales-agent for online selling. In *Proceedings of the 7th International Conference on Electronic Commerce* (pp. 279-286). Xi'an, China.

Li, L., & Horrocks, I. (2004). A software framework for matchmaking based on semantic web technology. *International Journal of Electronic Commerce*, Special Issue on Semantic Web services and their Role in Enterprise Application Integration and E-Commerce, *8*(4), 39-60.

Lin, F.-r., & Chang, K.-y. (2001). Enhancing the on-line automated bargaining process using bargaining pattern and dynamic price issuing approaches. *IEEE Intelligent Systems*, Special Issue on Intelligent E-Business, *16*(4), 41-47.

Maedche, A. D. (2002). Ontology: Definition & overview. In A. Maedche (Ed.), *Ontology Learning for the Semantic Web* (pp. 11-28). Boston: Kluwer Academic Publishers.

Matwin, S., Szapiro, T., & Haigh, K. (1991). Genetic algorithm approach to a negotiation support system. *IEEE Transactions on Systems, Man, and Cybernetics, 21*(1), 102-114.

Noia, T. D., Sciascio, E. D., Donini, F. M., & Mongiello, M. (2003). A system for principled matchmaking in an electronic marketplace. In *Proceedings of the International WWW Conference* (pp. 321-330). Budapest, Hungary.

Oliver, J. R. (1997). A machine learning approach to automated negotiation and prospects for electronic commerce. *Journal of Management Information Systems, 13*(3), 83-112.

Pollock, J. (1992). How to reason defeasibly. *Artificial Intelligence, 57*(1), 1-42.

Prakken, H. (2001). Relating protocols for dynamic dispute with logics for defeasible argumentation. *Synthese, 127*(1-2), 187-219.

Prakken, H., & Sartor, G. (1997). Argument-based extended logic programming with defeasible priorities. *Journal of Applied Non-Classical Logics*, *7*(1), 25-75.

Rao, A, & Georgeff, M. (1995). BDI agent: From theory to practice. In *Proceedings of the 1st International Conference on Multi-Agent Systems* (pp. 312-319). San Francisco.

Tomaz, R. F., Labidi, S., & Wanghon, B. (2003) A semantic matching method for clustering traders in B2B systems. In *Proceedings of the IEEE/LA-Web First Latin American Web Congress*, Santiago, Chile.

Toulmin, S. E. (1958). *The uses of argument*. Cambridge, UK: Cambridge University Press.

Vreeswijk, G. (1997). Abstract argumentation systems. *Artificial Intelligence*, *90*(1-2), 225-279.

Vreeswijk, G., & Prakken, H. (2000). Credulous and sceptical argument games for preferred semantics. In *Proceedings of JELIA '2000, The 7th European Workshop on Logic for Artificial Intelligence* (pp. 239-253). Berlin: Springer Verlag.

Wasfy, A. M., & Hosni, Y. A. (1998). Two-party negotiation modeling: An integrated fuzzy logic approach. *Group Decision and Negotiation*, *7*(6), 491-518.

Wooldridge, M. (2002). Reaching agreements. In M. Wooldridge (Ed.), *An Introduction to Multi-agent Systems* (pp. 129-162). John Wiley & Sons.

Zeng, D., & Sycara, K. (1998). Bayesian learning in negotiation. *International Journal of Human-Computer Studies*, *48*(1), 125-141.

Chapter VIII

Building Dynamic Business Process in P2P Semantic Web

Timon C. Du,
The Chinese University of Hong Kong, Hong Kong, China

Eldon Y. Li,
National Chengchi University, Taiwan &
California Polytechnic State University, USA

Abstract

Business process management systems such as the workflow management system and the enterprise application integration system manage process flow on a minute-by-minute basis in various application domains. In the conventional approach, the business process must be predefined before it is implemented. However, involving business users in the early stage of the design phase is neither efficient nor realistic in the dynamic business world. This study proposes a framework to implement a dynamic business process in the P2P Semantic Web, which provides the flexibility to dynamically alter business process and to take semantic data into consideration. The system is demonstrated by a case of a manufacturer that is processing an order.

Introduction

In the past decade, the Internet technology boom has encouraged the development and sharing among people, organizations, and enterprises of vast ranges of information. However, most of that information is written in hypertext markup language (HTML), which mainly follows a predefined format to express the content, where well-formatted information is normally written for human comprehension rather than machine automation. This means that when the information volume grows, the time to locate and digest the information increases even more rapidly. In this way, users need to make a tremendous effort to locate information that fits their needs. There are many possible solutions to resolve the information overloaded problem, such as paying money to the search engine to improve visibility, which is called "paid placement" or "paid inclusion." Sophisticated solutions such as allowing users to write a query paragraph rather than simply inputting keywords are also possible. In the years to come, we will see many more innovative solutions to the problem.

The Web has also evolved to become a service-providing medium. Web services use software applications to provide interoperability, whereby they discover, describe, and access other services from the Internet, Intranets, and Extranets. This leads to the adoption of XML (extensible markup language) technology in which information is shared in text format. Note that XML provides independence of applications and data, which allows data to be shared among applications. However, the problem lies in determining what kinds of information can be shared and how it can be shared. As the Web is no longer a media for human-to-human communication because the information available is overwhelming, there is a need to seek help from machines in organizing and locating specific information. The evolution will take place in two dimensions: from syntactic to semantic and from static to dynamic. This will move the Web toward being a Semantic Web and Web service, and then advance the Web service into an intelligent Web service and the Semantic Web into Semantic Web services.

The Semantic Web structures Web content into semantic data for both humans and machines. The semantic data are the information and the meaning of the information. These are presented as structured collections of information and sets of rules. Although both the knowledge representation and rules have been studied for years in the area of artificial intelligence, the traditional approaches have rigid structures to ensure that new knowledge can be inferred from existing data and rules. In contrast, the decentralized nature of the Semantic Web allows individual Web sites to represent knowledge in their own ways. This provides an opportunity for Web sites to grow independently and diversely.

This study will use the properties provided in the Semantic Web to build dynamic business processes, where "a business process is a collection of related structure activities that produce a specific outcome for a particular customer" (http://en.wikipedia.org). The process can be defined by attributes such as name, description, date, version, component, operation, and so forth. It is worth noting here the difference between workflow and business process. A workflow is a complex business process that normally involves many *tasks*; it is static and has to be well defined before applying. This also means that the *roles* assigned to specific tasks are predefined even though the *users* that are assigned to roles can be dynamically identified. A workflow can be activated many times, and each implementation is called a *case*, which has a unique identity and a limited lifetime. In this case, the business process is a concept mingling the workflow and the case because it indicates which task must be carried out for a specific customer. As workflow schemas are static and predefined, they are difficult to adopt in the rapidly changing environment, particularly for collaboration among partners (Zeng et al., 2003).

Figure 1. An example of dynamically modifying a business process

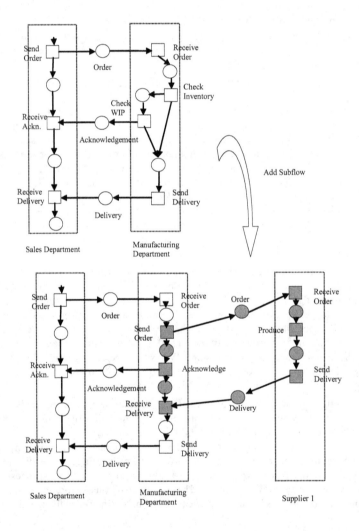

Moreover, problems of consistency after changing the workflow, resource optimization in the dynamic environment, the reuse of workflow, the workflow engine that is used to manage the changing workflow, and the flexibility to adapt workflow to new environments are all our concerns (Cichocki & Rusinkiewicz, 2004).

In this study, the business process is developed in the peer to peer (P2P) architecture of the Semantic Web. The P2P architecture is used as a communication platform in which each party (node) has a similar role and a similar ability to handle business processes with other parties directly or through a community service (http://searchnetworking. techtarget.com). Moreover, each node is built with Semantic Web technology that allows the semantics of Web content to be included in the handling of business processes. The advantages of this approach are: (1) Web sites that participate in the business process are dynamically selected (for example, the selection of suppliers); (2) information and support for implemented tasks are dynamically collected (for example, order processing); (3) the implementation of business processes can be automated (such as in outsourcing); and (4) the business process can be dynamically modified (such as in business process collaboration). Figure 1 exhibits an example of how a business process is dynamically modified. The remaining sections are organized as follows: A brief introduction to the links between business and the Semantic Web, an illustration of the architecture, a demonstration, and discussion.

Business Process and Semantic Web

A business process defines the activities, including input, output, and method, that are necessary to complete a specific assignment. A business process is created to deal with a specific *case* in an organization, such as applying for a mortgage, placing orders or proceeding with engineering tests. The structure of a business process can be very complex. It can be composed of many subprocesses (also called processes), such as a workflow. The work in a business process can be identified as a *task*, which represents the indivisible unit of work. The task is carried out by a *process*. When the processes are carried out in a business process they follow a specific sequence that determines which task needs to be performed next. A case should be completed within a certain time limit and should exit the system when the work is completed. This also means that attributes are needed to describe the state and content of the process.

There are four different types of sequences in a complex business process: *sequential*, *parallel*, *selective*, and *iterative* routings. Sequential routing confines one task to be executed before another task, whereas parallel routing allows two tasks to be performed without feedback from each other. Selective routing provides a choice between or among tasks, and iteration allows the same task to be performed more than once.

During implementation, the process must be enacted to perform a task. Tasks are assigned to designated *roles* following principles such as the separation of duties, least privilege assignment and data abstraction (Sandhu, Coyne, Feinstein, & Youman, 1996). These principles ensure the successful implementation of the business process. For example, the separation of duties assigns two sensitive tasks to two exclusive roles so that conspired perpetration can be avoided. This principle is easily adopted within an organization (by using an Intranet) and can be accepted in supply chain collaboration (by using an extranet), but it is difficult to use on the Internet, in which the new assignments can go to any participant. In a client-server type of community, the duty to maintain the principle is normally assigned to a community server, which becomes a bottleneck because it needs to trace every business process. This study uses P2P architecture to develop the business process. As stated earlier, P2P architecture offers the advantage of sharing workloads (King, Ng, & Sia, 2004). Hence, the duty to maintain the principle should fall on any node in the community that uses the business process. Similarly, the least privilege policy, also called the "need to know" policy (Castano, Fugini, Martella, & Samarati, 1995), provides only minimum information for completing the task. Information sharing between nodes is also based on this principle, whereby only the minimum information is carried via agents that roam between nodes. However, as information is limited, when one node receives separate information from two sources that belong to the same business process that information cannot be composed back to the original message, which means that sensitive data can be leaked.

A business process management system manages the process flow on a minute to minute basis in various application domains such as office automation, finance, healthcare, telecommunication, manufacturing and production (Bertino, Jajodia, & Smarati, 1999). As has been discussed, in conventional business process systems, such as the workflow management system (WFMS), the process is static and predefined. However, it is unrealistic to apply a static and predefined process in a dynamic business world. Much research has tried to resolve dynamic business process problems. Examples of these problems include (1) evolving the process when the system parameters, the relationships among parameters, or communication among different partners in the supply chain changes (Rouibah & Caskey, 2003); (2) differentiating a shared public workflow from a private workflow to alleviate the effect of a change in a public workflow on a private domain (van der Aalst, 2003); (3) using different agents to manage the variation of workflows, in which the interagent workflow concerns control flow, data flow, and material flow between agents, and the intra-agent workflow provides flexibility in performing the activities on the work-list (Zhuge, 2003); (4) applying knowledge-based techniques to make workflow systems more adaptive and to provide more flexible process management (Chung et al., 2003); and (5) not forming the business process until runtime to tolerate the dynamics (Zeng et al., 2003; Su, Meng, Krithivasan, Degwekar, & Helal, 2003)

The Semantic Web brings structure to the meaningful content of Web pages, whereby software agents roam from one page to another to carry out sophisticated tasks for users (Berners-Lee, Hendler, & Lassila, 2001). The implementation of the Semantic Web should be decentralized, with structured information and tasks carried out by the software agents, and with sets of inference rules helping the software agents to retrieve information. Most current studies on the Semantic Web focus mainly on the services carried out by software agents, such as ontology design, the visual environment for browsing, RDF (resource description framework) model and syntax specification, and Web services with ontologies, as opposed to individual servers (http://www.w3.org/). Less attention has been paid to the coordinated efforts of the servers to form a group ideology.

A Semantic Web is similar to a deductive database and a knowledge-based system, where new knowledge is deduced by applying rules to existing facts (Du, 2002). The differences between these systems are that the knowledge-based system does not use secondary storage to house data as do deductive databases and the Semantic Web, and both the knowledge-based system and deductive database apply rigid structures to the knowledge representation and deduction rules to ensure that new knowledge can be obtained from inference. In contrast, the Semantic Web allows Web sites to represent the knowledge and the relationships of the knowledge in their own ways. The information on Web sites can then be shared for use in different domains. For example, a query can be interpreted by the semantics interpreter through the query statement in such a way that the query results are more relevant (Jain, Aparicio, & Singh, 1999; Karvounarakis et al., 2003).

In the Semantic Web, the software agent is used to roam from page to page to carry out tasks that are assigned by users. However, it can do more than being a messenger because a mobile agent is an autonomous object that is created for dynamic and distributed applications that execute designated tasks. Referring to Wooldridge (Wooldridge & Jennings, 1995), agents can be identified as either *strong* or *weak*. Strong agents are capable of mentalist notions, rationality, veracity, adaptability, and learning. These capabilities come mainly from the technology of artificial intelligence. Weak agents, in contrast, can complete tasks autonomously, interact with external objects, and are reactive or proactive toward environmental change based on a pre-planned scheme. Software agents have been implemented in many distributed environments to share system loading and increase flexibility. Several applications have been successfully developed using mobile agents: for example, the supply chain SMART project (http://smart.npo.org), the virtual enterprise (Jain et al., 1999), information retrieval (Cabri, Leonardi, & Zambonelli, 2000), the Internet-based auction house (Sandholm & Huai, 2000), secured transactions (Castano et al., 1995), and distributed network management (Du, Li, & Chang, 2003). Some studies have further integrated mobile agents with CORBA, such as MESIS resource management (Bellavista, Corradi, & Stefanelli, 2000) and broadband intelligent networks (Chatzipapadopoulos, Perdikeas, & Venieris, 2000). In general, the software agent system can be applied to the areas of electronic commerce, personal assistance, secure brokering, distributed information retrieval, telecommunication network services, workflow applications and groupware, monitoring and notification, information dissemination, and parallel processing (Lange & Oshima, 1998).

The Architecture of Semantic Business Process

To implement a P2P framework, a node must first download a P2P networking program, such as IBM's advanced peer-to-peer networking (APPN), and a semantic business process program, such as semantics flow builder (SFB) and mobile agents. The SFB supports four functions—implementation manager, process planner, resource manager, and process monitor—and three mobile agents—a configure agent, a runtime agent, and a supervise agent—as shown in Figure 2. The three agents and four SFB functions interact as shown in Table 1.

Figure 2. The architecture of the semantics business process

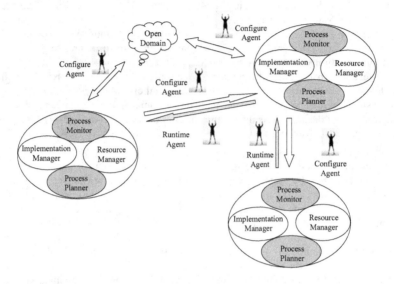

Table 1. The correlation of builder functions and mobile agents

	Process Planner	Resource Manager	Process Monitor	Implementation Manager
Configure Agent	✓	✓		✓
Runtime Agent	✓			✓
Supervise Agent			✓	

SFB Functions

Four SFB functions are responsible for different duties. The *Process Planner* is used to design business processes and assign the processes to roles (Web sites). The Planner sends the configure agent to search for another network member that can implement the next task through community directory services (similar to UDDI). Once the agent finds another qualified network member, it connects to that member and then carries the job assignment to the Web site (on a need-to-know basis). If none of members (Web sites) qualifies, then the Planner aborts the process. If more than one candidate Web site is found, then the configure agent activates the Resource Manager to determine which web site should be chosen (the separation of duty is sustained at this moment).

When a new task arrives at the next member, the Process Planner of the new Web site activates a runtime agent, which is dispatched to collect data, report to the initiated Web site whenever needed, and execute the task and work locally with the Implementation

Manager (which will be explained later). When the task is completed, the member either returns the work to the initiated web site or searches for a new member to continue the work, depending on the business process. In the latter case, a new configure agent is sent to the community directory service to search for another member that can be the candidate for the next task. This procedure repeats until it reaches to the end of the process blueprint designed by the initiated Web site. Meanwhile, a member may need to interact with previous members or the initiated Web site if it needs more information to execute its work. When a Web site encounters the completion of the process, it should report to the web site that activated it (stacking).

It should be noted that this design allows a member to dynamically modify the business process according to local needs. This is based on the understanding that the local member should have a better knowledge of how to implement a particular task than any other member. However, when authority is given to a Web site, the business process can grow unpredictably. Therefore, it is the duty of the local Process Planner to check the soundness if the Web site extends the business process (this will be discussed later.) Fortunately, based on the hierarchical conceptualization of workflow theory, a complex workflow can be divided into many sub-flows, and if the sub-flows are sound the parent flow is also sound (Aslst & Hee, 2002). Formally, business processes are modified as: Business process $BP(W, T, F)$ where W is the finite set of Web sites, w; T is a finite set of tasks, t, $(W \cap T = \varnothing)$; and $F \subseteq (W \times T) \cup (T \times W)$ is a set of flow relations.

If *inf(M)* is a strictly increasing function of the distance between current belief τ' and original belief τ; $inf(M) = | \tau' - \tau | = \sum_{i=1}^{m} (\tau_i - \tau_i')^2$ is the change of belief due to semantic information; and $t_i \notin t$ where t_i is the new task to implement τ'

then $BP \subset BP'$ where $F' \subseteq (W' \times T') \grave{E} (T' \times W')$ and $w \subseteq w'$

       dispatch Configure Agent

       activate Resource Manager

       call Reachability Graph checking

endif

The *Resource Manager* is responsible for assigning activities to resources. This manager should interact with the Implementation Manager to execute the task and the Process Monitor to ensure that constraints are upheld. Moreover, the Resource Manager has guidelines (such as separation of duty) to determine the allocation of sources when more than one Web site is found. This is where the Semantic Web can play a significant role. In general, the guidelines can be as simple as providing rules of thumb, such as the cheaper the better or the faster the better, or more advanced rules, such as providing resource clustering, preconditioning, exclusion, or case attributes. The selection should refer to the semantic data. Note that the semantics refers to the meanings and the logic of the requisition. It is important for the Resource Manager to make the right selection based on sufficient information.

The *Process Monitor* oversees the activities of the business process and uses the Supervise Agent to communicate with participating members. The main duties include alerting the Web site if the task is delayed and aborting the process if no member can be assigned to the next task.

The duty of the *Implementation Manager* is relatively straightforward: it completes the task assignment. The task can be executed immediately, at a preset time, or after a series of events. When the assignment is completed, the Implementation Manager informs the Process Planner to dispatch a Configure Agent to locate Web site for the next task assignment. However, the Implementation Manager notices the encountered circumstance and needs to consider more factors: in other words, if the information $inf(M)$ is a strictly increasing function of the distance between current belief τ' and original belief τ, then the Implementation Manager activates the Process Manager again, and the business process can be modified accordingly.

Mobile Agent Function

Mobile agents travel around Web sites as messengers or information locators. In the design, a *Configure Agent* locates a candidate Web site for the next process and providing instructions to the new selected member. That is, the Configure Agent takes the blueprint of a business process, the participant list, the data for implementing the task, and the duty and instructions of task assignment to the next Web site. When it arrives at a new Web site, the local Implementation Manager is enacted immediately, at a preset time or when certain events occur.

The second agent is a *Runtime Agent*, which is responsible for supporting the execution of a business process. It is the duty of the Runtime Agent to obtain augmented information to support the execution of the Implementation Manager. In a P2P Semantic Business Process, every participating member relies on the monitoring function.

As the participating members are dynamically selected and the process flow is modifiable, a *Supervise Agent* is used to monitor the activities of the members based on the most current status reported to and stored in the Process Monitor of the initiated Web site. That is, the Supervise Agent is sent by the initiated Web site to the member Web sites periodically (predefined by timers) or actively (triggered by events) to ensure that the business process operates smoothly.

The Advantages of a Semantic Business Process

The semantic business process takes advantage of the Semantic Web to implement business processes. The first advantage of this approach is a flexible data structure. The conventional Web page presents content and links to a database when a large volume of information is associated with it. As the databases are all using the relational data model, the data structure is rigid and it is difficult to provide personalized service. However, this is not the case in Semantic Web, where data is stored in the format of XML/RDF and is suitable for dynamic environments.

The second advantage is that the Semantic Web can act as a medium to support decision-making rather than simply to provide information, as does the conventional HTML Web page. This is because the content that is embedded in the RDF provides additional information in its tag that can be directly employed in user applications.

The third advantage is that the conventional Web allows users to specify keywords for searching relevant content. However, in the Semantic Web, the system knows more about both information providers and requesters, and then matches the information that is most useful for the requesters. For example, when a user searches for "industrial engineering" on the Web, university departments such as "system engineering" may not appear in the results, even though the courses offered are actually close to what the user is looking for. In the Semantic Web, the search can be further conducted against the course descriptions and program tags, and "system engineering" results can also be included.

Figure 3. An illustration of the order fulfillment of one manufacturer

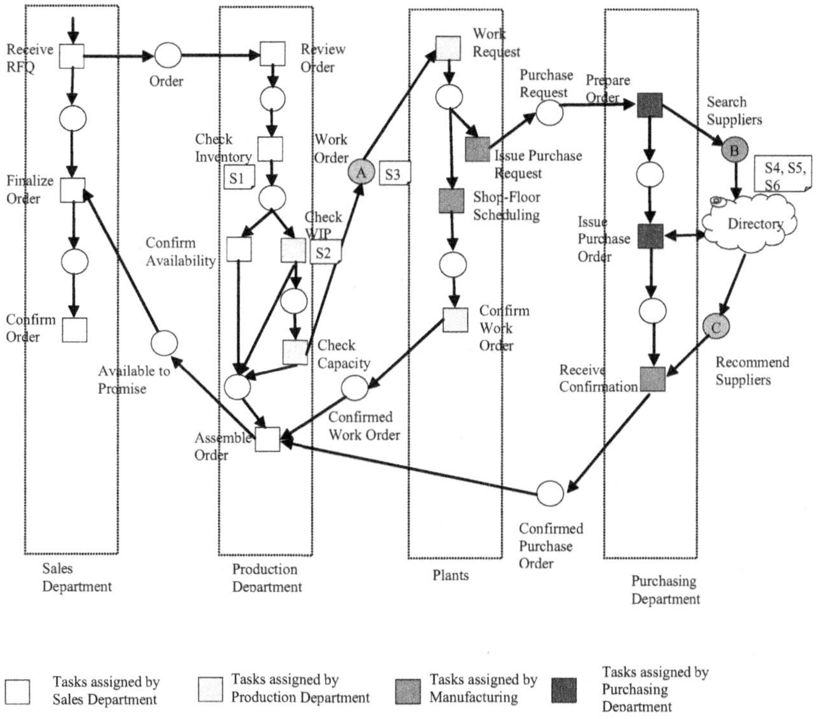

Implementation and Demonstration

This section demonstrates how the business process can be built and expanded in the Semantics Web. The example shown in Figure 3 represents a PC manufacturer receiving orders from buyers. The manufacturer first checks its inventory for finished products, work in process, and the capacity of its own factories. If it cannot fill the orders from its own capacity, then the manufacture outsources all or a part of them to collaborative partners. Depending on the semantic data, such as quality and collaboration history, the system recommends different supplier lists to the manufacturer.

Web Ontology and Semantics

The ontology defines the meaning and the relationship of a particular subject area. To implement the Semantic Web, the ontology of the subject area must be predefined.

The resource description framework (RDF) can be used to represent machine-processable information in the World Wide Web using a triple format: subject, predicate, and object (http://www.w3.org/TR/2004/REC-rdf-concepts-20040210/). RDF uses XML to allow users to define their own document formats to represent statements.

In this demonstration, RDF mainly defines database content that stores information about products, suppliers and the community. The content in these files can be embedded into Web pages to create "semantic" Web files. Here, we separate the content into four RDF files for demonstration. All the RDF files have been validated by the W3C RDF validation service at http://www.w3.org/RDF/Validator/. The structure graph of the major data fraction representation is shown in Figure 4.

1.   Storage.rdf stores data about the finished products and work-in-process products that are either current inventory items or available-to-promise items.

2.   DeptN.rdf stores data about manufacturing departments and production capacities in recent weeks.

3.   SupplierN.rdf stores data about collaborative partners, such as locations, prices, specifications, and stocks of different products.

4.   Resource-manager.rdf acts as a coordinator to determine the selection of collaborative partners. The file also contains information that is related to the collaboration history and ratings of the suppliers.

System Development

This system was developed with the following tools: (1) Macromedia Dreamweaver MX for building common HTML files and dynamic JavaServer Pages (JSP) Web pages; (2)

Figure 4. Graphical presentation of four RDF files

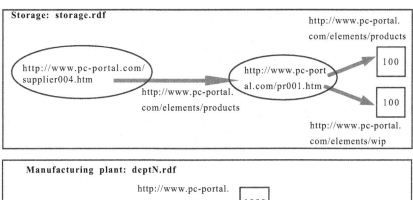

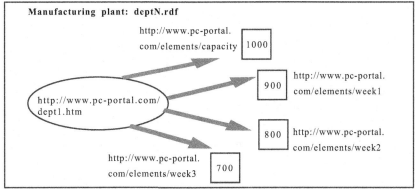

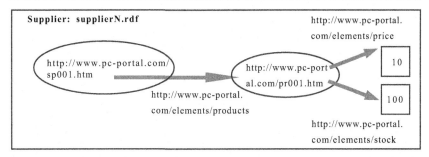

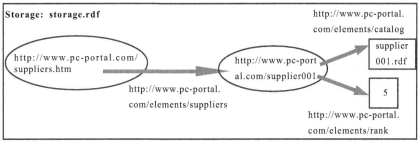

Figure 5. Graphical ontology of the order placing process

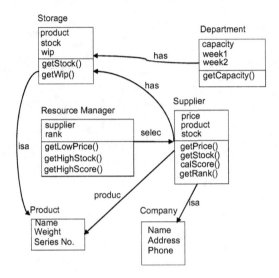

Figure 6. A graphical use case presentation

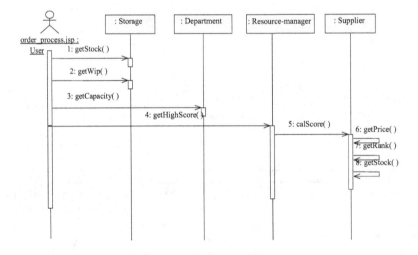

Jbuilder X for building Java files and classes (JSDK 1.4.3 included); (3) Jena 2.1 for building Semantic Web applications, including creating, modifying and querying RDF files, and providing a programmatic environment for RDF, RDFS, and OWL, including a rule-based inference engine; (4) RDQL for querying RDF content; and (5) Tomcat 5.1 for building JSP files to execute on a server.

Four classes with many methods have been built, and the use case is shown in Figures 5 and 6.

1. *Class Storage* is designed to store Information about the product inventory. Two methods are used:

    • getStock(String product): to get the number of finished goods of the specified product in stock; and

    • getWip(String product): to get the number of works in process in stock of the specified product.

2. *Class Department* is designed to store information about manufacturing plants. Two methods are used:

    • getCapacity(String week): to get the capacity of the specified week; and

    • getCapacity(int n): to get the total capacity of n weeks from now.

3. *Class Resource Manager* is designed to store Information about the collaborative partners. One method is used:

    • getHighScore(String product): to find the supplier with the highest score under the current conditions.

4. *Class Supplier* is designed to store information about selected suppliers. Four methods are used:

    • getPrice(String product): to get the price offered by the supplier of the specified product;

    • getStock(String product): to get the stock of the specified product that the supplier owns;

    • getRank(): to get the ranking of the supplier, which is stored on the community page (and thus suppliers are not allowed to modify their own scores); and

    • calScore(String product): to calculate the score for suppliers under different conditions.

Illustration

This section uses the example in Figure 3 for illustration. The scenario is that a manufacturer checks the inventory and work-in-process products to ascertain whether the available-to-promise amount is sufficient when a new order is placed. The manufacturer has three plants, each has a different capacity and inventory. If the internal capacity cannot satisfy the order, the purchasing department of the company will outsource a part or all of the order to collaborative partners. Assuming that the current inventory of available-to-promise finished product is 100 and of work-in-process product is 100, then the manufacturing lead time is one week. In Figure 3, node A represents the Implementation Manager of the manufacturer, node B represents the Resource Manager of the manufacturer, and node C represents the Implementation Manager of suppliers.

Scenario 1: *The order amount is 50 and the delivery date is two weeks from now. After receiving an order, the company first checks whether or not the inventory of finished goods in stock is sufficient. If the finished goods in stock are enough to cover the order, then it will be confirmed. In this scenario, the finished product is sufficient to promise the order, and the order is thus confirmed.*

Scenario 2: *The order amount is 150 and the delivery date is two weeks from now. As the finished product is insufficient, the system will check the work-in-process product. In this scenario, adding the amount of the finished product and work-in-process product is sufficient to promise the order. The order is confirmed.*

Scenario 3: *The order amount is 900 and the delivery date is two weeks from now. As the available-to-promise amount is not enough, the system will check whether the 3 production plants (plants 1-3) are able to produce the outstanding amount within the required delivery time. If they can, then jobs will be assigned to the plants according to their remaining capacities in the required time. That is, the order will first go to the plant with the largest remaining capacity. For example, as shown in Table 2, in the two week period, plant 1 can produce 300, plant 2 can produce 300, and plant 3 can produce 500. As the capacity is sufficient to meet the order, the order is confirmed. The shortage of this order is 700 (order—inventory—work in process), and the order will be spilt into 500 units for plant 3 and 200 units for plant 1.*

Table 2. The capacity and work-in-process of three plants

Plant	Capacity	Week 1	Week 2	Week 3	Week 4	Week 5
1	1000	900	800	700	500	600
2	800	600	700	600	500	400
3	800	500	600	600	400	500

Scenario 4: *The order amount is 1400 and the delivery date is two weeks from now. The demand is larger than the remaining capacities and the inventory of the three plants, so the purchasing department searches for suppliers to outsource the order. The system sends Configure Agents to the community directory to find a list of suppliers that have sufficient stock to cover the outstanding amount (order amount—finished goods— work in process—maximum amount that the departments can produce). As more than one supplier can supply the products, the system will recommend a list of best matching suppliers based on the "semantic" information written in RDF/XML files. For example, there are many factors, such as price, reputation, collaborative history, and current stock, to consider when choosing a supplier. After determining the supplier, the Process Planner of the purchasing department will alter the current business process to include other business processes, such as quality control and delivery service, from the supplier. Again, it is the duty of the purchasing department to check the soundness of the business process. The order is then confirmed.*

Table 3 shows the data that is used in this demonstration. When more than one supplier is qualified, it is the task of Resource Manager to prioritize the suppliers. The algorithm is as follows: if the outstanding amount is less than 10% of the total order, then price will be considered as the most critical factor and given a weight of 50%, with stock given a weight of 30% and reputation given a weight of 20% for selecting the supplier. If the outstanding amount is more than 10% but less than 20% of the total order, then stock is considered to be the most critical factor (50%), followed by price (30%) and reputation (20%). If the outstanding amount is more than 20% of the total order, then reputation becomes the most critical factor (50%), followed by stock (30%) and price (20%). The rational is that when the outsource amount is very large, the manufacturer pays special attention to elements of reputation such as technology level, quality, and experience. The calculation is conducted by assuming that three suppliers all meet the requirements.

The price, stock and reputation of the three suppliers are represented as p1, p2, and p3, s1, s2, and s3, and g1, g2, and g3. The higher score is given to the higher preference, such as low price, high stock, and good reputation. The total score is then multiplied by the weights. In this scenario, as the 1300 units can be produced by the three plants in two weeks, 100 units will be outsourced. Therefore, price is considered to be the most critical factor as the outstanding amount is 7% of the total order. The system thus places supplier 001 at the top of the recommendation list. However, the list is only given to the Resource Manager of the manufacturer as a reference. The Resource Manager should refer to other criteria such as the collaboration history of the suppliers.

Table 3. The price, stock, and reputation of three suppliers

Supplier		Price	Stock	Reputation
1	Product001	10	100	5
	Product002	20	150	
1	Product001	15	200	4
	Product002	25	200	
3	Product001	20	150	4
	Product002	20	200	

Scenario 5: *The order amount is 1500 and the delivery date is two weeks from now. As the outsourced amount is 200 units (13% of the total order), current stock is considered to be the most critical factor. The system thus recommends supplier 002 first.*

Scenario 6: *The order amount is 1700 and the delivery date is two weeks from now. As the outsourced amount is 400 units (23% of the total order), reputation is considered to be the most critical factor. The system thus recommends supplier 001 first.*

Conclusions and Future Study

This study has argued that current business process systems, such as the workflow management system, need to define the whole process before implementing it. This, however, is not suitable for the dynamic business world because collaboration is dynamic. This study has presented a system that uses the Semantic Web to build dynamic business processes. The system is built on top of a P2P architecture that allows each Web site (member) to operate independently and collaboratively through the community directory. In this design, each member has the functions of Process Planner, Resource Manager, Process Monitor, and Implementation Manager. Three mobile agents are used for the communication: a Configure Agent, a Runtime Agent, and a Supervise Agent. The system is illustrated with the case of the order handling process of a manufacturer. The illustration demonstrates that the business process can be extended when necessary, and that the operation of the business processes can take semantics data, defined in RDF and XML, into consideration.

This study does not consider areas of security such as access control. Future studies could address the issues of sharing information when the business process is extended indefinitely. Moreover, the directory service is relatively simple in this study. A related future study on Web service could be used to improve this issue. Another plausible issue is how to select suppliers when thousands of Web sites are qualified or when business processes are interrelated.

References

Aslst, W., & Hee, K. (2002). *Workflow management: Models, methods systems*. Cambridge, MA: MIT Press.

Bellavista, P., Corradi, A., & Stefanelli, C. (2000). An integrated management environment for network resources and services. *IEEE Journal on Selected Areas in Communications, 18*(5), 676-685.

Berners-Lee, T., Hendler, J., & Lassila, O. (May, 2001). The semantic web. *Scientific American, 284*(5), 34-44.

Bertino, E., Jajodia, S., & Smarati, P. (1999). A flexible authorization mechanism for relational data management systems. *ACM Transactions on Information Systems, 17*(2), 101-140.

Cabri, G., Leonardi, L., & Zambonelli, F. (2000, February). Mobile-agent coordination models for internet applications. *IEEE Computer, 33*(2), 82-89.

Castano, S., Fugini, M., Martella, G., & Samarati, P. (1995). *Database security.* Harlow, UK, UK: Addison-Wesley and ACM Press.

Chatzipapadopoulos, F., Perdikeas, M., & Venieris, L. (2000, June). Mobile agent and CORBA technologies in the broadband intelligent network. *IEEE Communication Magazine, 38*(6), 116-124.

Chung, P. W. H., Cheung, L., Stader, J., Jarvis, P., Moore, J., & Macintosh, A. (2003, April). Knowledge-based process management-an approach to handling adaptive workflow. *Knowledge-Based Systems, 16*(3), 149-160.

Cichocki, A., & Rusinkiewicz, M. (2004). Providing transactional properties for migrating workflows. *Mobile Networks and Applications, 9*, 473-480.

Du, T. (2002, June). Techniques and applications of emerging database system architectures. In C. T. Leondes (Ed.), *Database and Data Communication Network Systems.* Burlington, MA: Academic Press.

Du, T., Li, E., & Chang, A.-P. (2003, July). Mobile agents in distributed network management. *Communications of ACM, 46*(7), 127-32.

Jain, A., Aparicio, M., & Singh, M. (March 1999). Agents for process coherence in virtual enterprises, *Communications of the ACM, 42*(3) 62-69.

King, I., Ng, C. H., & Sia, K. C. (2004, July). Distributed content-based visual information retrieval system on peer-to-peer networks, *ACM Transactions on Information Systems* 22, no. 3, 477-501.

Karvounarakis, G., Magganaraki, A., Alexaki, S., Christophides, V., Plexousakis, D., Scholl, M., & Tolle, K. (2003, August). Querying the semantic web with RQL. *Computer Networks* 5, *42*(5), 617-640.

Lange, D., & Oshima, M. (1998). *Programming and deploying java mobile agents with aglets.* Reading, MA: Addison-Wesley.

Rouibah, K., & Caskey, K. (2003, September). A workflow system for the management of inter—company collaborative engineering processes. *Journal of Engineering Design, 14*(3), 273-293.

Sandholm, T., & Huai, Q. (2000, March/April). Nomad: Mobile agent system for an Internet-based auction house. *IEEE Internet Computing, 4*(2), 80-86.

Sandhu, R. S., Coyne, E. J., Feinstein, H. L., & Youman, C. E. (1996, February). Role-based access control models. *IEEE Computer*, 38-47.

Su, S. Y. W., Meng, J., Krithivasan, R., Degwekar, S., & Helal, S. (2003, January). Dynamic inter-enterprise workflow management in a constraint-based e-service infrastructure, *Electronic Commerce Research, 3*(1-2) 9-24.

van der Aalst, W. M. P. (2003, October). Inheritance of interorganizational workflows: How to agree to disagree without losing control. *Information Technology and Management, 4*(4), 345-389.

Wooldridge, M. J., & Jennings, N. R. (1995, February). Agent theories, architectures and languages: A survey. *Lecture Notes in Computer Science, 890*, 1-39.

Zeng, L., Benatallah, B., Lei, H., Ngu, A., Flaxer, D., & Chang, H. (2003, June). Flexible composition of enterprise web services. *Electronic Markets, 13*(2), 141-152.

Zhuge, H. (2003, May). Workflow- and agent-based cognitive flow management for distributed team cooperation. *Information and Management, 40*(5), 419-429.

Chapter IX

An Intelligent Metasearch Engine with Link Prediction and Page Clipping Generation Capabilities

Cheng-Jye Luh, Yuan-Ze University, Taiwan

Lin-Chih Chen,
National Taiwan University of Science and Technology, Taiwan

Abstract

This chapter presents an intelligent metasearch engine that can recommend a user's next hyperlink access and relevant paragraphs extracted from metasearch results. The proposed design is based on the primacy effect of browsing behavior, that users prefer top ranking items in search results. Three search methods were implemented in this engine. First, the search engine vector voting (SVV) method rearranges search results gathered from six well-known search engines according to their weights obtained from user behavior function. The hyperlink prediction (HLP) method then arranges the most likely accessed hyperlinks from the URLs in SVV search results. Finally, the page clipping synthesis (PCS) method extracts relevant paragraphs from the HLP search results. A user study indicated that users are more satisfied with the proposed search methods than with general search engines. Moreover, performance measure results confirmed that the proposed search methods outperform other metasearch and search engines.

Introduction

Internet users generally hope that search engines can locate the exact required information. This task is recognized by search engine designers as difficult (Jansen, Spink, Baterman, & Saracevic, 1998) because the inputs supplied by the users are generally insufficient for collecting suitable data. Literature shows that the Web query averages 2.3 terms long (Spink, Wolfram, Jansen, & Saracevic, 2001). Thousands of results, typically returned for such a short query, generally are arranged in their descending order of relevance using ranking algorithms (Li, 1998). Often the users are concerned with the top ranked URLs, and ignore the rest (Sougné, 2000). Therefore, providing the most relevant Web pages directly to the users would significantly reduce their navigation time on a variety of hyperlinks.

Search engines generally measure the similarity between user query and document contents using information retrieval (IR) techniques including the vector space models, probability models, and fuzzy logic models (Harman, 1992; Yates & Neto, 1999). These models, primarily based on the frequencies of keyword occurrence in documents, are frequently attacked by "keyword spamming" technique. That is, a document's rank can be manipulated by duplicating the same set of keywords in a document (Yates & Neto, 1999). However, search engines can now detect and penalize keyword spamming (Mall-Net, 2001).

Li (1998) developed the HVV method to solve the keyword spamming problem using a SCI (Science Citation Index) like ranking scheme, which ranks each Web page by the number of times other Web pages contain links to it. Thus, a Web page would have a high weight if several hyperlinks point to it. However, this method does not distinguish the ratings given by high-quality Web pages from those given by low-quality Web pages (Henzinger, 2001). Brin and Page (1998) created a PageRank algorithm, which is currently used by the Google search engine, to remedy this problem. The page rank of a page is computed by weighting each hyperlink pointing to the page proportional to the page rank of the referring page containing the hyperlink. However, the PageRank algorithm's recursive nature has raised concern about considerable computing power it needs to analyze the hyperlinks and page ranks (Sobek, 2002).

Collecting search results from search engines is an effective way to collect and rate relevant Web pages. This method is called metasearch (Dreilinger & Howe, 1996; Selberg & Etzioni, 1997). The metasearch approach saves a lot of time by searching only in one place and eliminating the need to use and learn several separate search engines. The quality of metasearch results depends on the search engines used and how the results are organized.

A metasearch method, called search engine vector voting (SVV), was developed in this study to rearrange the search results obtained from several well-known search engines. A Web page wins a vote from a search engine if it is listed on the top 50 items returned for a given query. The weight of a particular Web page is determined by its actual rankings in the search results of search engines from which it wins votes. The SVV method can solve the two problems encountered in using HVV stated above, since well-known search engines are generally recognized as high-quality Web sites, and SVV only considers the top 50 retrieved URLs from each search engine. More importantly, the adoption of SVV would eliminate possible bias of any single search engine.

Web search engines generally respond to user queries with a ranked list of Web page URLs with short description. Users may browse through the URLs to reach the pages most relevant to their queries. Research has been conducted to discover the most relevant Web pages for the users from search results. Nick and Themis (2001) implemented an intelligent agent system that uses a genetic algorithm to recommend Web pages directly to users. The intelligent agent learns a user's interests from Web pages examples submitted by the user in advance. This task is very hard for novice users, even for experienced users, to submit proper examples, which resulting in acceptable outcomes. Thus, a better approach is required to solve the example submission problem.

A hyperlink prediction (HLP) method was then developed to recommend Web pages referred from the URLs listed in search results of any search engine in general and of SVV in particular to the users. HLP is based the assumption that users would follow more hyperlinks on high ranking URLs than on low ranking URLs in search results. HLP starts to collect hyperlinks from the URLs in either SVV or any search results, and applies a tournament competition concept to divide the hyperlinks into "winner" and "loser" sets. The "winner" set contains hyperlinks whose weights are larger than a stated threshold, and the "loser" set consists of the rest. The majority of candidate hyperlinks, which users are most likely to visit, come from the "winner" set, and only a minority comes from the "loser" set. The tournament competition recursively proceeds on the referred Web pages of the candidate hyperlinks to collect more successive hyperlinks until a certain termination condition is reached. The HLP method finally presents a ranked list of hyperlinks to the users.

A page clipping synthesis (PCS) method was also developed to extract relevant paragraphs from search results in a page clipping format. This method is a step toward the design of so-called next generation search engines that use information extraction (IE) to return "things" (like people, jobs, companies, and events), their relations, facts, and trends (McCallum, 2002). PCS uses a genetic algorithm (GA) to generate a set of best fitted paragraphs in a controlled period of time. Genetic algorithms are typically run to a predefined number of generations set by human. A not large enough figure often leads to premature convergence, leaving plenty of room for improvement. On the contrary, an exceedingly large figure would result in the waste of many computational resources in making slightly improvements. Thus, one important design issue of GA is to choose an appropriate threshold about the number of generations to halt the algorithm. Another important design issue is to choose an appropriate fitness function so that GA could terminate in meaningful way. The genetic algorithm used in the PCS method can dynamically determine its termination condition based on the fitness improvement ratio and the standard deviation of the improvement. Consequently, the PCS method can yield cost-effective solutions within controlled amount of time rather than to reach the global optimum.

The rest of this chapter is organized as follows. The second section introduces some related work. The third section presents the system architecture, the user behavior function and the metasearch method SVV. The fourth and fifth sections discuss HLP and PCS in details. The sixth section presents three experiments using the proposed search methods. The first experiment was a user study on the quality of search results for some hot keywords. The second experiment compared SVV with the four best metasearch search engines. The third experiment compared SVV, HLP, and PCS with six well-known search engines. Finally, the last section concludes this chapter and discusses future research.

Background

This section provides literature review of some relevant background, including metasearch, hyperlink exploration, information extraction, question answering, application of genetic algorithms, and genetic algorithm's termination criteria.

Metasearch

Metasearch engines, unlike general search engines, transmit your keywords submitted in its search box simultaneously to several individual search engines, and present the search results in an integrated format (Dreilinger & Howe, 1996; Hai, Meng, Clement, & Zonghuan, 2004; Meng, Clement, & Liu, 2002; Selberg & Etzioni, 1997; Zacharis & Panayiotopoulos, 2002). This format lets the users see at a glance which particular search engine returned the best search results for a query without having to search each one individually. Such finding could be used to adjust the rank order of results. Thus, metasearch can save searching time and eliminate the need to use and learn several separate search engines (Hu, Chen, Schmalz, & Ritter, 2001). The quality of metasearch results depends on the search engines used and how the results are integrated.

Several related studies have been conducted on metasearch engines. Lawrence and Giles (1998) proposed a NECI metasearch engine, which can analyze each document down-loaded and then display results with the query term shown in specific context. This format helps users readily determine whether the document is relevant without having to download each document. Glover, Gordon, and Birmingham, (1998) adopted decision theory to reorder results from a single search engine; thereby capturing more of a user's information need than a text query alone. Glover, Lawrence, Birmingham, and Giles (1999a) described a metasearch engine architecture, which customizes the searching and results ranking strategies based on the user's information need. Compared with a regular metasearch engine, which sends a query to a predefined list of search engines and ranks the results in a predefined order, this method allows much greater personalization by providing customized ranking of search results from a tailored list of search engines. Svidzinska (2001) proposed a two-tier metasearch engine. The first tier collects the required information about topic-specific search engines in advance. The second tier then expands and routes the user queries to a subset of the selected topic-specific search engines through a routing mechanism. Zacharis and Panayiotopoulos (2002) presented a Webnaut metasearch system, which can learn the user's interests and adapt appropriately as these interests change over time. The learning process is driven by a genetic algorithm along with the user feedback to an intelligent agent's filtered selections. Osdin, Ousin, and White (2002) proposed a metaseach system, called HuddleSearch, using a newly developed clustering algorithm to dynamically organize the relevant documents into a traversable hierarchy of general to more specific categories. KartOO (2004), a commercial metasearch engine with visual display interfaces, shows the results with sites being interconnected by keywords. It also presents a thematic map to show the most important sites and the linkage relationships among the various results. Braslavski, Alshanski, & Shishkin (2004) introduced ProThes, a system that combines metasearch engine, graphical user interface for query specification, and thesaurus-based query customization. *ProThes* also provides simple heuristics for results merging and partial re-ranking. Hai et al. (2004) provided an overview of techniques for extracting information from the Web search interfaces of e-commerce search engines, which is useful to construct e-commerce metasearch engines. Hai et al. also presented a tool that can automatically build a unified search interface over multiple heterogeneous e-commerce search engines in the same product domain.

Hyperlink Exploration

Hyperlink exploration is a way of analyzing the hyperlink structures among the Web pages on the Internet (Chakrabarti et al., 1999). The hyperlink analysis results can in turn be used to measure the quality of Web pages. Several researchers have studied new methods to compute the quality of a page by the number of its in-links and the quality of the referring pages containing these links (Brin & Page, 1998; Henzinger, 2001). These methods recursively analyze the hyperlinks and compute the ranks for all the pages starting from a set of source Web pages. Obviously, these methods need huge computing power to be effective (Sobek, 2002).

Several related studies used stochastic methods, such as Markov chains for hyperlink structure analysis and prediction. Lempel and Moran (2000) presented a new stochastic method for hyperlink structure analysis, and claimed that it can discover the most authoritative sites quite effectively and efficiently. Sarukkai (2000) used Markov chains to predict the probability of seeing a link in the future given navigation logs. Chen, LaPaugh, and Singh (2002) presented a two-phase model to predict a user's next access at the category level using temporal and frequency analysis of the user's access pattern. Chi, Pirolli, Chen, and Pitkow (2001) employed information scent to infer a user's information needs from the user's traversal history and then to predict the user's expected surfing patterns. Glover, Lawrence, Gordon, Birmingham, & Giles (1999b) developed a metasearch system, Inquirus 2, which can produce search results tailored to personalized need using utility functions. These studies have two limitations. First, all the proposed methods need training data, either for statistical analysis or to improve the utility functions (Jones, Cunningham, McNab, & Boddie, 2000; Nanopoulos, Katsaros, & Manolopoulos, 2001; Sarukkai, 2000). Second, most of them handle site-specific transition models only, and are not appropriate for multi-site analysis (Gündüz & Özsu, 2003; Sarukkai, 2000).

Information Extraction

Information extraction (IE) aims at transforming a collection of documents into information that could be more readily digested. Information extraction research has attracted increasing attention since the start of the Message Understanding Conferences (MUCs) (DARPA, 1997). Two types of corpus-based IE application systems are available: text mining and Web mining.

Corpus-based text mining systems generally integrate with natural language processing to extract information from unstructured text. Riloff and Lehnert (1994) presented an augmented relevancy signature algorithm that uses linguistic phrases and local context to extract information for high-precision text classification. Nahm and Mooney (2000) described a system, called DiscoTEX, which combines IE and knowledge discovery from database (KDD) methods to perform text mining for discovering prediction rules from natural language corpus. Witten (2004) studied how the adaptive techniques used in text compression can be applied to text mining, and developed several examples including extraction of hierarchical phrase structures from text, identification of key-phrases in documents, and locating proper names and quantities of interest in a piece of text.

Corpus-based Web mining attempts to extract structural information from web HTML documents based on manually generated examples or templates (Lacroix, Sahuguet, & Chandrasekar, 1998). Freitag (1998) presented SRV, a top-down relational algorithm for IE, which uses an extensible token-oriented feature set to provide structural and other information for use in learning extraction patterns. Lin and Ho (2002) developed a method to separate informative news contents from redundant contents such as advertisements- and banners of Web pages from news Web sites. The proposed method, however, is limited to tabular Web pages only. Chang, Hsu, and Lui, (2003) applied several pattern discovery techniques, including PAT-trees, multiple string alignments and pattern matching algorithms to discover extraction patterns from Web pages without user-labeled examples. The proposed method saves human intervention, but works poorly for Web pages with many layout formats.

Question Answering

Question answering (QA), one of IE applications, can bring up the appropriate answers according to the user problem, not documents (Brill, Lin, Banko, Dumais, & Ng, 2001; DARPA, 1997; Kupiec, 1993; Srihari & Li, 2000). Askjeeves (2004) and NECI (Lawrence & Giles, 1998) are two examples of such QA systems. Askjeeves (2004) responds to a user query by bringing up several related questions for user interaction. Then the user clicks on the question most related to his or her query for answers. This approach has two drawbacks: 1) the user needs to evaluate which type of questions is related to his or her query; 2) the user can only get answers for one question at each run, but not all possible answers for a given query. NECI (Lawrence & Giles, 1998) transforms user queries to Specific Express Forms (SEFs). For example, the query "What does NASDAQ stand for?" is transformed into the queries "NASDAQ stands for", "NASDAQ is an abbreviation", and "NASDAQ means". NECI then uses pattern matching to locate documents for the transformed queries. Also, NECI provides query-sensitive summaries, including duplicated context strings, results clustering by sites, and pages that could not be downloaded. Lawrence and Giles (1998) claimed that such query-sensitive summaries help the users find relevant documents faster and perform relevance judgments more accurately. Both Askjeeves and NECI systems are in common to return answers at the level of Web pages only, providing no answers at levels of details.

Several QA systems attempts to generate answers at various levels of details other than Web pages. Salton, Allan, and Buckley (1993) developed a dual text comparison system to verify the global vector similarity between query and document texts as well as the coincidence in the respective local contexts. The documents whose global similarity falls below a stated threshold are therefore rejected. The globally similar text pairs with sufficiently enough locally similar substructures as well are assumed to be related. Hovy, Gerber, Hermjakob, Junk, & Lin (2000) developed a QA system that uses a query created from a given question to retrieve documents. The proposed system then splits the top ranked documents retrieved into segments, and further ranks the resulting segments. Finally, the proposed system generates a list of candidate answers by matching each sentence segment against the question and manually constructed patterns using rules learned from a machine-learning based grammar parser. Radev et al. (2001) presented a question answering using statistical models (QASM) probabilistic algorithm that can learn the best query paraphrase of a natural language question. This proposed algorithm first identifies 10 query modulation operators (INSERT, DELETE, DISJUNCT . . .) from a wide range of training questions, and then determines the best operators tailored to different questions to apply at online question answering. Radev, Fan, Qi, Wu, and Grewal (2002) also developed a process to augment existing search engines to support natural language question answering. This study showed that sentence ranking can improve the performance of question answering.

Application of Genetic Algorithms to Information Retrieval

Genetic algorithms are applied extensively in information retrieval (IR). Gordon (1991; 1998) presented a genetic algorithm based method to document indexing. The proposed method encodes as follows: a keyword represents a gene, a document's list of keywords represents chromosomes, and a collection of relevant documents judged by a user represents the population. The proposed genetic algorithm evolves to find a set of keywords, which in terms of the fitness function best describes the documents. Petry, Buckles, Prabhu, and Kraft (1993) used relevance feedback to develop a genetic algorithm based adaptive retrieval method. The proposed method adapts to produce better solutions. Yang and Korfhage (1993) applied genetic algorithms to modify query term weights for improving recall rate and precision rate of an IR system. Vrajitoru (1997) used a two-point crossover operator instead of a classical crossover operator to avoid generating fewer offspring than their parents, and treated the two selected individuals differently. The study claimed that such modification can improve retrieval performance.

Several studies have used genetic algorithms in Web search systems. Chen, Chung, Yang, and Ramsey (1998) used the best first search algorithm and the genetic algorithm to develop a Web spider system. The study concluded that the genetic algorithm spider did not outperform the best first search spider, but both produced comparable and complementary results. Nick and Themis (2001) used a genetic algorithm to recommend Web pages directly to users in an intelligent agent system. The intelligent agent learns a user's interests from Web page examples the users provide in advance. Picarougne, Monmarché, Oliver, and Venturi (2002) developed a Web spider system, called GeniMiner, and claimed that the genetic search can be valuable when (1) the users can wait for a longer time than they do in using standard search engines; (2) queries are more complex or more precise than a list of keywords. Obviously, the first claim is contrary to what the users generally expect, in other words, quick responses from search engines.

Many studies also adopted GA to resolve relevance user feedback problem in IR applications (Horng & Yeh, 2000; López-Pujalte, Guerrero-Bote, & Moya-Anegón, 2002; 2003). These studies found that the fitness function significantly impacts the precision rate, and therefore suggested that fitness function should consider not only the retrieved documents, but also the order in which the documents are retrieved. These studies claimed that a static ranking function cannot guarantee good performance under all situations, but didn't provide appropriate ranking metrics to resolve this issue. Several studies (Fan, Gordon, & Pathak, 2004a, 2004b; Wang et al., 2003) used genetic programming to develop a so-called ARRANGER technique to automatically discover ranking functions. These studies claimed that the advantage of ARRANGER lies in that it can learn the "optimal" ranking functions for different contexts by effectively combining multiple types of evidence in an automatic and systematic way.

Genetic Algorithm's Termination Criteria

Genetic algorithms are generally terminated once either a predefined objective condition or a predefined maximum number of generations is reached. Previous literature reports that most genetic algorithms are time-consuming in converging to the optimum (Goldberg, 1999; Holland, 1975; Koza, 1992). The majority of recent genetic algorithm research aims at reaching the global optimum in a reasonable amount of time.

Eshelman and Schaffer (1991) suggested using incest prevention with an elitist selection replacement strategy to prevent premature convergence. Rudolph and Sprave (1995) developed a self-adjusting threshold mechanism that chooses offspring for the next generation. This study claimed that the mechanism is convergent to the global optimum if it runs through a predefined maximum number of generations. Sheth (1994) adopted user feedback to adjust the allowable maximum number of generations in newsgroup filtering. Several studies (Aytug, Bhattacharrya, & Koehler, 1996; Greenhalgh & Marshall, 2000) used Markov chains to calculate the smallest number of generations required to guarantee an optimal solution with a fixed probability. These studies claimed in their proof that the genetic algorithm can reach the optimal solution within an upper bound of time. Koza (1992) presented a probability model to minimize the total number of individuals that needs be processed until the predefined maximum number of generations is reached. This study suggested that there is a point after which the cost of extending a given run exceeds the benefits obtained from the increase in the cumulative probability of success. The idea to develop the dynamically terminated genetic algorithm to solve the page clipping generation problem resembles Koza's suggestion.

Metasearch Engine Design

This section presents the proposed intelligent metasearch engine[1], including its system architecture, the underlying user behavior function, and the metasearch method, search engine vector voting (SVV). The advanced search methods, hyperlink prediction (HLP) and page clipping synthesis (PCS) are presented in later sections.

Metasearch Engine Design

The proposed metasearch engine provides three types of search results based on different user requirements:

- **Broad Collection of Data:** This provides the results from an extensive search for data.
- **Deep Collection of Data:** This provides the results of an in-depth search of hyperlinks contained in top ranked Web pages.
- **Content Sampling of Data:** This considers user interests and presents the relevant information in a page clipping format.

The proposed search methods: search engine vector voting (SVV), hyperlink prediction (HLP), and page clipping synthesis (PCS), satisfy the above requirements individually. Of the three search methods, SVV is a metasearch method to collect search results from six well-known search engines. Both HLP and PCS are not metasearch methods. Strictly speaking, they are post search methods to augment search results of any search engines including SVV. Figure 1 illustrates the architecture of the proposed metasearch engine. The following subsections present its external and internal sets of components in more details.

Among the external set, the *search engine set* consists of the metasearch targets used in the SVV method. The *DB* component keeps all previous search results and related information. The *Cached Pages* component stores the pages that have been retrieved in hyperlink prediction. The *Internet connection* component is responsible to fetch specified Web pages from the Internet into the *DB* and *Cached Pages*.

Among the internal set, the *user interface* presents the user with choices of search options. The user may choose any search method based on his or her information needs. The proposed cascading design initially lets the HLP method operate on SVV search

Figure 1. Architecture of the proposed metasearch engine

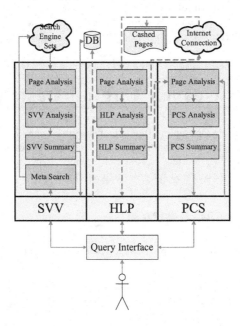

results, and in turn lets the PCS method operate on HLP search results. Thus, an advanced search would invoke a preceding search if required inputs are not available, and would not proceed until the invoked preceding search has been completed. Several analysis modules exist in the internal set. The *page analysis* module analyzes the information required by each method. Specifically speaking, SVV needs the ranks assigned by each search engine to a Web page; HLP needs the hyperlinks found on each Web page; and PCS needs paragraphs extracted from Web pages. The *SVV analysis* module rearranges the rankings of Web pages gathered from various search engines. The *HLP analysis* module chooses and collects hyperlinks which users are most likely to visit. The *PCS analysis* module extracts paragraphs from the Web pages referred by the hyperlinks collected by HLP. Finally, the *summary* modules present the search results in a particular format depending on which search method the user chose.

User Behavior Function

A search engine typically responds to a user query by returning a ranked list of URLs in decreasing order of relevance; that is, the most relevant answers on the top. Consequently, users generally prefer top-ranking Web pages to other Web pages, and this preference gradually decreases. This phenomenon is called primacy effect in

Figure 2. Examples of UBF trajectory

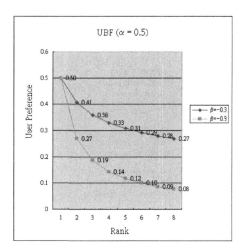

Psychology (Morris, Levine, & Maisto, 2002). Several studies (Lempel & Moran, 2000; Paepcke, Garcia-Molina, Rodriguez-Mula, & Cho, 2000) have observed similar phenomenon in user browsing behavior. Based on the primacy effect, the user behavior function (UBF) for the ith item l_i within an ordered item list l is defined as follows:

$$UBF(l, l_i) = \alpha i^\beta \text{ (where } \beta < 0) \tag{1}$$

where a denotes the user's preference of the first item, which represents the user's first impressions on the item list; β denotes the user preference decay factor. Figure 2 shows the effect of the user preference decay factor for β = -0.3 and β = -0.9. When |β| is small, the UBF value decreases slowly.

Search Engine Vector Voting

SVV is based on the voting concept that a Web page's ranking is dependent on how several selected search engines rank it, rather than its own contents. A Web page wins a vote from a particular search engine if it is listed in the search engine's results to a given query.

Figure 3 shows the flow chart of SVV. SVV currently gathers the top 50 items of search results from each of the following six well-known search engines, Google, Yahoo, AltaVista, Looksmart, Overture, and Lycos. Advertisements and paid placements, which

Figure 3. SVV flow chart

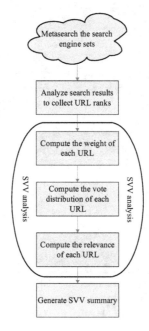

generally show up on the top, are removed before the search results are collected and processed by SVV.

SVV rearranges the returned URLs of Web pages (simply referred as Web pages later) based on their weights. Formally, the weight of a Web page *p* for a user query *q* is defined as follows[2]:

$$w_{p,q} = \sum_{i=1}^{6} \alpha_{i,q} x_{i,p,q}^{\beta} \tag{2}$$

where $\alpha_{i,q}$ denotes the user's preference on the first match (which is generally the most relevant to a user query recommended by the search engine) to a given query *q* returned from search engine *i*, $x_{i,p,q}$ denotes the ranking of Web page *p* in search engine *i*'s results for query q, and b is the user preference decay factor of Web pages (where b<0). According to this definition, a Web page has larger weight if it either wins many votes from search engines or is ranked high in the results of some search engines.

To understand the voting tendency of the six search engines on a particular Web page, a Web page's vote distribution is provided with the following formula:

$$P_{p,q} = w_{p,q} \Big/ \sum_{i=1}^{6} \alpha_i, q \tag{3}$$

where $P_{p,q}$ denotes the vote distribution of Web page p for query q in all six search engines, which is represented as a filled rectangle. A particular Web page, which is ranked #1 at all six search engines, obtains the maximum vote distribution of 1 from equations (2) and (3). However, the vote distribution alone provides insufficient evidence to judge a Web page's relevance to a given query. The fact that two Web pages have the same vote distribution doesn't imply the same relevance to a given query.

Thus, the relevance of a Web page to a given query is also provided as follows:

$$R_{p,q} = \begin{cases} High, & w_{p,q} > \overline{w} + n\sigma_w \\ Middle, & \overline{w} < w_{p,q} \leq \overline{w} + n\sigma_w \\ Low, & otherwise. \end{cases} \tag{4}$$

where $R_{p,q}$ denotes the relevance of a Web page p to a given query q, $\overline{w}$ denotes the average weight of all the Web pages returned in this query, and σ_w denotes the standard deviation of the weights of all the returned Web pages. Here, the probability of the condition $w_{p,q} > \overline{w} + n\sigma_w$, based on Chebyshev's theorem, is less than $1/n^2$ for any population (Walpole, Myers, & Myers, 1998), where n denotes any value greater than 1 (we let $n=3$ in the sample run shown in Figure 4). The Web pages in this category are defined to have high relevance to this query. By contrast, the Web pages whose weights fall below average are considered to have low relevance to the query. Other Web pages whose weights fall between these two categories are considered to have medium relevance to the query. The three relevance categories are indicated by different color balls, namely green, yellow, and red balls for high, medium, and low relevance, respectively.

Figure 4 shows the results of a sample run of the SVV method for the query term "php." The URLs are sorted in a decreasing order of their SVV weights. The SVV method also presents the vote distribution in filled rectangle and the degree of relevance in color balls next to each URL.

Figure 4. A sample run of SVV

Table 1. Rank distribution among six search engines for the query term "php"

Search Engine URL	Google	Yahoo	AltaVista	LookSmart	Overture	Lycos	$w_{p,q}$
http://www.php.net	1	1	1	1	1	1	5.28324
http://phpnuke.org	3	2	3	0	3	4	1.91623
http://php.resourceindex.com	6	5	8	0	5	2	1.41162

*A "0" denotes that the URL cannot be found in the particular search engine.
*The data were collected on 6/2/2004.

Table 2. The range of $\alpha_{i,q}$, β and their initial values

Search Engine Parameter	Google	Yahoo	AltaVista	LookSmart	Overture	Lycos
$\alpha_{i,q}$ range	0.8~0.95	0.8~0.95	0.8~0.95	0.8~0.95	0.8~0.95	0.8~0.95
β range	-1 ~ -0.3	-1 ~ -0.3	-1 ~ -0.3	-1 ~ -0.3	-1 ~ -0.3	-1 ~ -0.3
$\alpha_{i,q}$	0.895259	0.844789	0.811069	0.93683	0.905779	0.889514
β	-0.77304	-0.77304	-0.77304	-0.77304	-0.77304	-0.77304

SVV Examples Illustrated

To show the operations of the formulas related to SVV, a series of examples, based on the SVV search results of the query "php" as shown in Figure 4, appears next.

Example 1. *Table 1 shows the rank distribution among six search engines for the query term "php." To calculate* $w_{p,q}$, $a_{i,q}$ *and b are initially set as two randomly generated numbers[3], each from their own range respectively, as shown in Table 2. As an example, the weight of the URL "http://www.php.net" (the top URL listed in Figure 4),* $w_{p,q}$ =
$0.895259*1^{-0.77304} + 0.844789*1^{-0.77304} + 0.811069*1^{-0.77304} + 0.93683*1^{-0.77304} + 0.905779*1^{-0.77304} + 0.889514*1^{-0.77304} = 5.28324.$

Example 2. *The vote distribution* $P_{p,q}$ *for the URL "http://www.php.net" is 5.28324/ (0.895259+ 0.844789+0.811069+0.93683+0.905779+0.889514) = 1. The rectangle to its left, as shown in Figure 4, is full with color.*

Example 3. *The URL "http://www.php.net" is highly related to query "php", since its* $R_{p,q}$ *is evaluated to be* High *by the following condition 5.28324 > 0.49174555266897 + 3*0.84575553737867, where n=3,* $\bar{w}$ =0.49174555266897, *and* σ_w = 0.84575553737867.

Hyperlink Prediction

As discussed above, users generally favor high ranking Web pages. Users not only spend most time on high ranking Web pages, but also follow the hyperlinks on these pages to find more referred Web pages (Koch, 2003). However, browsing through many hyperlinks is tedious and often distracts users. This study developed the hyperlink prediction (HLP) method to recommend the most valuable hyperlinks to the users. Figure 5 illustrates the flow chart of HLP.

HLP explores the URLs listed in search results of SVV or any other search engines to discover well qualified hyperlinks for the users. For illustration, SVV search results are used as the inputs to HLP in the following subsections. To explore and collect qualified hyperlinks, HLP must recursively answer on the following questions:

1.   Whether a Web page is qualified to have the hyperlinks on it be visited?
2.   Which hyperlinks on a qualified page should be visited to fetch the referred Web pages?
3.   What is the maximum number of successive hyperlinks to be visited?

Figure 5. HLP flow chart

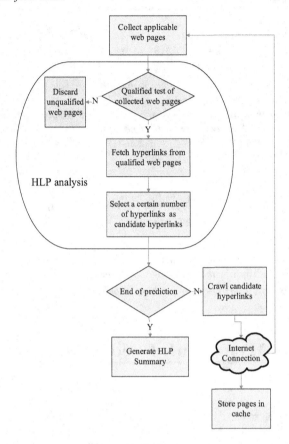

Finding Qualified Web Pages

HLP first determines whether a Web page is qualified for visiting its hyperlinks. Initially, the inputs to HLP, SVV search result pages are recognized as qualified pages by default. The qualification $Q_{p,q}$ of other web pages except SVV result pages are computed individually by the following formula:

$$T_{pc,p} = \begin{cases} \log_2(T_{p,l}), & T_{p,l} > 2 \\ 1, & otherwise \end{cases} \tag{5.1}$$

$$Q_{p,q} = \begin{cases} 1, & if \left\lceil \dfrac{\alpha_{p,q}}{T_{pc,p}} \right\rceil \geq 1 \\ 0, & otherwise. \end{cases} \qquad (5.2)$$

where $\alpha_{p,q}$ denotes the weight of web page p for a given query q, initially set to $w_{p,q}$ obtained from equation 2, $T_{pc,p}$ denotes the penalty cost for page p, and $T_{p,l}$ denotes the total number of successive hyperlinks traversed from a starting URL listed in SVV results to page p. The fact that users often get lost whenever they traverse a large number of successive hyperlinks (Catledge & Pitkow, 1995) suggests that the penalty cost applies to a Web page which is far away from the starting URL. According to equations 5.1 and 5.2, the penalty cost applies when $T_{p,l} > 2$. Finally, qualification value of 1 means a Web page is qualified for having its hyperlinks be visited, and 0 means a Web page is not qualified.

Example 4. *Consider the URL http://www.php.net listed in the SVV result page for query term "php" as shown in Figure 4. Part of its detailed link traversal structure is shown in Figure 6.*

Four cases are examined:

1. The PHP Home Page (http://www.php.net): $T_{p,l} = 1$, $T_{pc,p} = 1$, and its qualification $Q_{p,q} = 1$ since $5.28324 / 1 \geq 1$, where $\alpha_{p,q} = 5.28324$.
2. The PHP Downloads Page (http://www.php.net/downloads.php): $T_{p,l} = 2$, $T_{pc,p} = 1$, and its qualification $Q_{p,q} = 1$ since $5.28324 / 1 \geq 1$, where $\alpha_{p,q} = 5.28324$.

Figure 6. Part of the link traversal structure for http://www.php.net

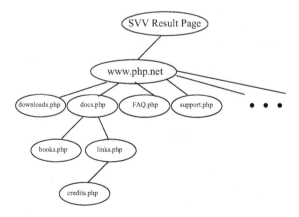

3.   The PHP Books Page (http://www.php.net/books.php): $T_{p,l}=3$, $T_{pc,p}=\log_2(3)=$ 1.58496 and its qualification $Q_{p,q}$ is also 1 since 3.09166 / 1.58496 $\geq$ 1, where $\alpha_{p,q}=$ 3.09166.

4.   The PHP Credits Page (http://www.php.net/credits.php): $T_{p,l}=4$, $T_{pc,p}=\log_2(4)=2$, and its qualification $Q_{p,q}=0$ since 1.80919 / 2 < 1, where $\alpha_{p,q}=1.80919$. $\alpha_{p,q}$ is discussed later in example 5.

Once a Web page is evaluated to be qualified, the HLP analysis process is invoked to fetch all the hyperlinks on this page and compute their individual weights. Then, the fetched hyperlinks are analyzed to determine which ones should be collected as candidate hyperlinks.

Collecting Qualified Hyperlinks

HLP runs tournament competition to collect candidate hyperlinks from the hyperlinks (called applicable hyperlinks) on qualified Web pages. At the start of HLP, the URLs listed in the SVV results are set as the initial applicable hyperlinks. Then the applicable hyperlinks are divided into "winner" and "loser" sets based on their weights. The hyperlinks whose weights are beyond n standard deviation of mean are classified into the winner set, and others are placed into the loser set. The weight of a hyperlink l on a Web page p for a given query q is defined as follows:

$$w_{p,l,q} = \alpha_{p,q} x_{p,l}^{\beta} \tag{6}$$

where $x_{p,l}$ denotes the rank of hyperlink l on page p, β also denotes the user preference decay factor. A hyperlink is assumed to propagate its weight to the referred page. In other words, if the hyperlink l links page p to page p', then $w_{p,l,q}$ becomes $\alpha_{p,q}$, that is, the weight of page p' to a given q.

Example 5. *Tables 3 and 4 show the parameters of the top hyperlinks on URL "http://www.php.net" and its hyperlink http://www.php.net/docs.php, respectively. The value of $\alpha_{p,q}$ for URL http://www.php.net/docs.php used in Table 4 inherits from its corresponding $w_{p,l,q}$ obtained from Table 3.*

Table 3. Parameters of the child hyperlinks on URL "http://www.php.net"

Parameter / URL	$\alpha_{p,q}$	$x_{p,l}$	β	$w_{p,l,q}$
http://www.php.net/downloads.php	5.28324	1	-0.77304	5.28324
http://www.php.net/docs.php	5.28324	2	-0.77304	3.09166

Table 4. Parameters of the child hyperlinks on URL "http://www.php.net/docs.php"

Parameter / URL	$\alpha_{p,q}$	$x_{p,l}$	β	$w_{p,l,q}$
http://www.php.net/books.php	3.09166	1	-0.77304	3.09166
http://www.php.net/links.php	3.09166	2	-0.77304	1.80919

Table 5. Weights of hyperlinks on URL "http://www.php.net"

Parameter / URL	$w_{p,l,q}$	$\overline{w_{p,l,q}} + n^*\sigma_{w_{p,l,q}}$	$in\ V_{p,l,q}$
http://www.php.net/downloads.php	5.28324	1.62713	✓
http://www.php.net/docs.php	3.09166	1.62713	✓
http://www.php.net/FAQ.php	2.25978	1.62713	✓
http://www.php.net/support.php	1.80919	1.62713	✓
http://www.php.net/mailing-lists.php	1.52254	1.62713	✗

The hyperlinks to be collected into the winner set are specified as follows:

$$V_{p,l,q} = \{l \text{ if } w_{p,l,q} > \overline{w_{p,l,q}} + n\sigma_{w_{p,l,q}}, \text{ for } \forall_{p,l,q}\} \tag{7.1}$$

$$V_{p,q} = |V_{p,l,q}| \tag{7.2}$$

where $V_{p,l,q}$ denotes the set of winning hyperlinks on page p for a given query q, $\forall_{p,l,q}$ denotes all the hyperlinks on page p for a given q, $\overline{w_{p,l,q}}$ denotes the average weight of all the hyperlinks on page p for a given q, $\sigma_{w_{p,l,q}}$ denotes the standard deviation of the weights of all the hyperlinks, and $V_{p,q}$ denotes the size of the winner set. Then, the remaining hyperlinks fall in the "loser" set.

Example 6. *Table 5 shows the weights of hyperlinks on the URL "http://www.php.net",* *and indicates which ones are in the winner set* $V_{p,l,q}$, *where* $n = 3$, $\overline{w_{p,l,q}} = 0.472864$, *and* $\sigma_{wp,l,q} = 0.384756$. *Thus, the number of winning hyperlinks* $V_{p,q}$ *is 4.*

HLP then begins to collect the candidate hyperlinks from each of the winner and loser sets. The HLP analysis process first chooses from the winner set the hyperlinks that have not yet been gathered as part of the candidate hyperlinks. To avoid "link spamming", not

Figure 7. Two Web pages have partially identical hyperlinks

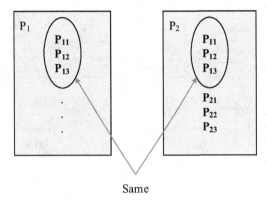

all the winning hyperlinks are chosen. For example in Figure 7, two qualified Web pages, P_1 and P_2 contain some identical hyperlinks as P_{11}, P_{12} and P_{13}. If P_1 is an ancestor Web page of P_2, then these duplicated hyperlinks, P_{11}, P_{12} and P_{13}, should have been collected whenever P_1 is processed. P_2 then gives the opportunity to other eligible hyperlinks that have not been collected. This approach ensures that high-weighted hyperlinks would have chance to be collected, and are only collected once.

HLP then collects candidate hyperlinks from the loser set. Two decisions needs to be made in this step: (1) Determine the collection size, in other words, the number of hyperlinks to collect; (2) determine which hyperlinks to collect. The following two cases are investigated. First, if the current Web page is just a starting SVV result page, then the collection size is determined using the following equation:

$$F_{p,q} = \left\lceil \frac{V_{p,q} \times (1+\beta)}{\log(T_f)} \right\rceil \qquad (8)$$

where $F_{p,q}$ denotes the number of loser hyperlinks on page p for a given query q to be collected, T_f denotes the total number of hyperlinks in the loser set; β denotes the user preference decay factor. Similarly, a large value of T_f makes it difficult for the user to make a decision. Hence, $\log(T_f)$ is defined as the penalty cost. The equation clearly indicates that the number of hyperlinks to be collected from the loser set is proportional to the number of hyperlinks in the winner set, depending on the user preference decay factor, β. The stronger the user prefers the winner set, that is, the smaller β is, the fewer hyperlinks are collected from the loser set of a starting SVV result page.

Example 7. *The collection size from the loser set on the URL "http://www.php.net",*

$$F_{p,q} = \left\lceil \frac{4 \times (1 + (-0.77304))}{\log_{10}(94)} \right\rceil = 1 \text{ , where } V_{p,q} = 4, \beta = -0.77304, \text{ and } T_f = 94.$$

Second, for every Web page except SVV result pages, the collection size is determined using the following equation:

$$F_{p,q} = \left\lceil \frac{\dfrac{\alpha_{p,q}}{\sum \forall_{p,l,q}(w_{p,l,q})} \times T_f \times (1 + \beta)}{\log(T_f)} \right\rceil \tag{9}$$

where $\sum \forall_{p,l,q}(w_{p,l,q})$ denotes the sum of the weight of all the hyperlinks on page p for a given query q. The chance for a hyperlink in the loser set to be collected increases with the page-to-hyperlinks weight ratio of the given page, in other words, $\alpha_{p,q}$ / $\sum \forall_{p,l,q}(w_{p,l,q})$, as shown in this equation.

Example 8. *The collection size from the loser set on the URL "http://www.php.net/downloads.php",*

$$F_{p,q} = \left\lceil \frac{\dfrac{5.28324}{221.48511872068} \times 136 \times (1 + -0.77304)}{\log_{10}(136)} \right\rceil = 1,$$

where $\alpha_{p,q} = 5.28324$, $\sum \forall_{p,l,q}(w_{p,l,q})$ is 221.48511872068, $\beta = -0.77304$, and $T_f = 136$.

Once the collection size is determined, the roulette wheel selection method from genetic algorithms (Goldberg, 1999; Sullivan, 2003; Obitko, 2004) is employed to select hyperlinks from the loser set. The roulette wheel selection offers a higher probability of being selected to those hyperlinks with larger weights even though they fall into the loser set. Once the selection of candidate hyperlinks is finished, the selected hyperlinks are also appended to the candidate hyperlink set. HLP then simultaneously fetches the referred Web pages pointed to by the candidate hyperlinks for the next iteration.

Termination Condition

HLP continues the collection process until the maximum number of successive hyperlinks is reached for each starting URL collected from SVV search results. This constraint lets HLP respond quickly to user queries. Thus, the maximum number of successive hyperlinks to be collected is defined as follows:

$$ML_{p,q} = \left\lceil w_{p,q} \right\rceil \tag{10}$$

That is, the maximum number of successive hyperlinks to be collected from a starting Web page p listed in SVV results for a given query q is determined by the ceiling limit of its own weight.

Example 9. *The maximum number of successive hyperlinks to be collected from the URL* *"http://www.php.net",* $ML_{p,q} = \left\lceil 5.28324 \right\rceil = 6$, *where* $w_{p,q} = 5.28324$.

A Sample Run of HLP

Figure 8 shows the results of a sample run of HLP for the query term "php." The hyperlinks are sorted in a decreasing order of their weights. HLP, similar to SVV, presents the results with the degree of relevance in color balls and the voting distribution in filled rectangles. Notably, the second (http://www.php.net/downloads.php) and the third (http://

Figure 8. A sample run of HLP

www.php.net/docs.php) items are hyperlinks explored from the first-ranked item (http://
/www.php.net), because HLP have explored the inside hyperlinks of the top ranked URLs
in SVV results. Additionally, HLP provides a Cached tag to those pages, which have been
cached for later use, as shown in Figure 8.

Page Clipping Synthesis

Given a ranked list of Web pages produced by a query to a search engine, this study
developed a page clipping synthesis (PCS) method to generate a set of page clippings,
each consisting of paragraphs from these Web pages to provide instructive hints about
the query. Figure 9 shows the flow chart of PCS.

PCS adopts a genetic algorithm to discover and arrange paragraphs extracted from Web
pages. Most paragraphs exhibit the following properties:

Figure 9. PCS flow chart

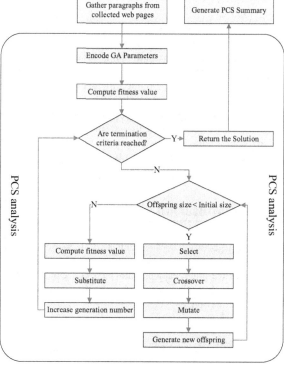

1.   Among the first few paragraphs of a Web page
2.   From the first few Web pages
3.   Matching the query and a special word within the range of three words

Notably, a paragraph, which contains a query term and also a special word occurred within the range of three words, is assumed to be interesting to the user. For example of the query term "php," a paragraph consisting of the phrase "… php is …" might be an answer the user wants. More sophisticated methods to find paragraphs of interest to the user could be easily incorporated into PCS.

Parameter Encoding

PCS encodes the genetic algorithm parameters in the page clippings problem as follows:

- **Population:** For any generation, the population contains all the page clippings produced for a query. The initial population consists of the result web pages returned for a query.

- **Chromosome:** A chromosome, encoded as a sequence of genes, represents one piece of page clipping.

- **Gene:** A gene represents a paragraph in a page clipping. If a paragraph matches one special query phrase pattern, which includes one query term and one special word within the range of three words, then this paragraph is encoded as a gene of "1"; otherwise, it is encoded as "0". The special words notably play an important role in gene encoding. This study counted the occurrences of words nearby the answers to the 500 queries provided in TREC 2002 QA data (2003) to find common used special words. Also, the plural and/or past tense forms of a word are reset to its present singular form. For example, the variant forms of "be" like "*are,*" "*was,*" and "*were*" are conflated to its canonical form "*is.*" Consequently, the 20 most frequently used words were found as follows: *the, in, of, and, to, a, is, on, as, at, by, it, for, that, from, with, have, or, which,* and *about.*

Fitness Value Computation

For each page clipping, in addition to a sequence of "0"s and "1"s representing the sequence of paragraphs, the information about the relative position of each paragraph in its original page and the weight of each original page could be utilized to compute the fitness value. The fitness value of a page clipping *pc* for a query term sequence *ts* is defined in the following equation:

$$f_{pc,ts} = \frac{\sum_{\forall p \ in \ pc} (G_{p,pc} \times W_{p,pc,ts})}{\log T_{pc}} \qquad (11)$$

where "$\forall p \ in \ pc$" denotes all the paragraphs p in pc, $G_{p,pc}$ denotes the gene of p in pc, either "1" or "0", $W_{p,pc,ts}$ denotes the weight of p in pc for query term sequence ts, and is discussed later in equation 13, T_{pc} denotes the total number of paragraphs in pc, and $\log T_{pc}$ denotes the penalty cost.

The initial weight of a paragraph p in page clipping pc, similarly based on the user behavior function, is defined as follows:

$$w_{pc,p} = \alpha_{pc} x_{pc,p}{}^{\beta_1} \qquad (12)$$

where α_{pc} denotes the initial weight of the first paragraph in pc, which is set to the weight of the original Web page containing the fist paragraph, $x_{pc,p}$ denotes the sequential order of p in pc, and β_1 is the user preference decay factor on the paragraphs in pc.

Example 10. *Table 6 shows the initial weights of the top 20 paragraphs in the page clipping shown in Figure 12, where $\alpha_{pc} = 5.28324$, and $\beta = -0.77304$.*

The actual weight of a particular paragraph in a piece of page clipping must consider which query terms and their relative positions in a query term sequence the paragraph matches. Given a query term sequence, users generally expect that a paragraph matching more leading terms has a higher weight. Let $w\{ts\}$ be the weight of a paragraph matching the term sequence ts. For example of query term sequence "php mysql apache", users

Table 6. Initial weights of top 20 paragraphs in a sample piece of page clipping

Paragraph($x_{pc,p}$)	$w_{pc,p}$	Paragraph($x_{pc,p}$)	$w_{pc,p}$
1st	5.28324	2nd	3.091663
3rd	2.259782	4th	1.809189
5th	1.522539	6th	1.322386
7th	1.173831	8th	1.058707
9th	0.966569	10th	0.890964
11th	0.827679	12th	0.773838
13th	0.727407	14th	0.686906
15th	0.651231	16th	0.619537
17th	0.591172	18th	0.56562
19th	0.542466	20th	0.521377

would expect $w_{\{php, mysql, apache\}} > w_{\{php, mysql\}} > w_{\{php, apache\}} > w_{\{php\}}$. The user behavior function again applies to this situation. The weight of paragraph p in page clipping pc for a query with term sequence ts is adjusted as follows:

$$W_{p,pc,ts} = \sum_{\forall t \text{ in } ts} w_{pc,p} x_{p,t,ts}^{\beta_2} \qquad (13)$$

where "$\forall t$ *in ts*" denotes all the query term t in ts, $w_{pc,p}$ denotes the initial weight of paragraph p in pc, $x_{p,t,ts}$ denotes the rank of term t in ts, which is defined as 0 if p does not match any phrase pattern of t, and b_2 is the user preference decay factor on the relative positions of the terms in ts. For example, let $ts = \{php, mysql, apache\}$ again, the case that a paragraph p contains phrase patterns matching "php" and "apache" has $x_{p, php, \{php, mysql, apache\}} = 1$ and $x_{p, apache, \{php, mysql, apache\}} = 3$.

Example 11. *Table 7 shows the final weight of the top 20 paragraphs in the page clipping shown in Figure 12, where $b_2 = -0.77304$.*

Finally, the fitness value of the sample page clipping is computed as follows:

Example 12. *The fitness value of the first page clipping, $f_{pc,ts} = 12.34182$ by Equation 11, where $\{G_{p,po}\} = (1, 1, 0, 1, 1, 1, 0, 0, 1, 0, 1, 1, 0, 1, 1, 0, 0, 0, 0, 0, 0, 1, 0, 0, 0, 1, 1, 0, 0, 0, 1, 0, 1, 1, 1, 1, 1, 0, 0, 1, 0, 0, 1, 0, 0, 1, 0, 1, 1, 0, 1, 1, 0, 0, 0, 0, 0, 0, 0, 1, 1, 1, 0, 0, 0, 0, 0, 0, 0, 1, 0, 0, 0, 1, 1, 0, 0, 0, 0, 1), \{W_{p,pc,ts}\} = (5.28324, 3.091663, 0, 1.809189, 1.522539, 1.322386, 0, 0, 0.966569, 0, 0.827679, 0.773838, 0, 0.686906, 0.651231, 0, 0, 0, 0, 0, 0.484344, 0, 0, 0, 0.425666, 0.413427, 0, 0, 0, 0.371551, 0, 0.35402, 0.345944, 0.338278, 0.330991, 0.324054, 0, 0, 0.305101, 0, 0, 0.288512, 0, 0,*

Table 7. Final weights of top 20 paragraphs in the sample page clipping

$w_{pc,p}$	$x_{p,t,ts}$	$W_{p,pc,ts}$	$w_{pc,p}$	$x_{p,t,ts}$	$W_{p,pc,ts}$
5.28324	1	5.28324	3.091663	1	3.091663
2.259782	0	0	1.809189	1	1.809189
1.522539	1	1.522539	1.322386	1	1.322386
1.173831	0	0	1.058707	0	0
0.966569	1	0.966569	0.890964	0	0
0.827679	1	0.827679	0.773838	1	0.773838
0.727407	0	0	0.686906	1	0.686906
0.651231	1	0.651231	0.619537	0	0
0.591172	0	0	0.56562	0	0
0.542466	0	0	0.521377	0	0

0.273856, 0, 0.264993, 0.260802, 0, 0.25286, 0.249093, 0, 0, 0, 0, 0, 0, 0, 0.223007, 0.220175, 0.217425, 0, 0, 0, 0, 0, 0, 0, 0.195796, 0, 0, 0, 0, 0.185762, 0.183894, 0, 0, 0, 0, 0.175164), and T_{pc} = 82.

Genetic Operators in PCS

Three genetic operators, selection, crossover, and mutation were performed on the chromosomes as follows:

- **Selection:** The Roulette Wheel selection (Austin, 1990; Goldberg, 1999; Lin & Ho, 2002; Obitko, 2004) was used to randomly choose two chromosomes from the current generation. The higher the fitness value of a page clipping, the higher its chance of being chosen to participate in crossover and mutation operators.

- **Crossover:** Two random numbers are first generated from the range [0..1]. If the first random number is less than the second one, then crossover takes place. The length of the two selected chromosomes may not be identical, since any two page clippings may differ in the number of paragraphs they contain. Thus, the shorter chromosome must be padded with Xs (Don't Care) to make its length equal to that of the other chromosome. All the Xs are erased later. The crossover operator exchanges and swaps the genes in between two randomly chosen crossing points from one chromosome to the other. As shown in Figure 10, the chromosomes 110011110111 and 01011101011100110010 are selected for crossover on genes in between positions 7 and 9 (as indicated with the vertical bars '|').

- **Mutation:** The normal bit inversion mutation is not applicable for the page-clipping problem, since a gene represents whether a particular paragraph contains special phase patterns matching at least one query term. This study defined the mutation operator to reverse the order of some genes to achieve fitness improvements. Similar to the crossover operator, two random numbers are generated from the range [0..1]. If the first random number is less than the second one, then mutation takes

Figure 10. Example of crossover of two strings with different length

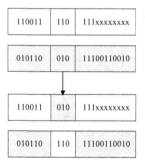

Figure 11. Example of two-point mutation

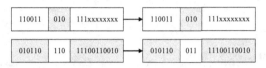

place. A two-point mutation operator is applied individually to the two chromosomes generated after crossover to reverse the order of genes between two randomly chosen positions. For example, each of the two chromosomes shown in Figure 11 has reversed the order of its genes between positions 7 and 9 after mutation.

Termination Criteria in PCS

Most users generally expect quick responses, which may not be globally optimal or suboptimal, from search engines. These responses must be cost effective in a sense that further computation could not yield comparable improvements in the solution. The genetic algorithm adopted in this study is terminated when either the global best-fit solution or the maximum number of generations is reached. These two situations are discussed herein.

First, the number of all the "best fit" page clippings C is defined as follows:

$$C = \left\| \{ pc \mid f_{pc,ts} > \overline{f} + n\sigma_f \} \right\|$$ (14.1)

where $\| \ \|$ denotes the number of elements in a set, $\overline{f}$ denotes the average fitness value of the initial population, σ_f denotes the standard deviation of fitness values of the initial population, n denotes a positive integer, and currently $n=3$. A page clipping satisfying the "best fit" condition $f_{pc,ts} > \overline{f} + n\sigma_f$ is considered as a very good solution. At a given generation, slim chance of further improvement remains once all chromosomes have evolved into very good solutions. Thus, the global best-fit solution of the page clipping problem is defined as follows:

$$C = \text{initial population size}$$ (14.2)

Second, the maximum number of generations is usually set as a fixed figure through experiments. To claim what the maximum number of generations should be is quite difficult. On the one hand, running a large number of generations may waste a significant amount of computing resources on slim improvement. On the other hand, running a small number of generations may result in premature convergence. A cost effective approach dynamically determines the maximum number of generations based on the status of fitness value progress at each generation.

To define the section termination condition, several assumptions are first given as follows. A generation is considered to make *no improvement* if the maximal fitness value of chromosomes at this generation doesn't exceed that at the previous generation. The fact that a large number of consecutive generations without improvement occur implies a slim chance of further improvement.

For a given generation g, the improvement ratio I_g is defined as follows:

$$I_g = \frac{\bar{f}_g - \bar{f}_{g-1}}{\bar{f}_{g-1}} \quad (g > 1) \tag{15}$$

where $\bar{f}_g$ and $\bar{f}_{g-1}$ denote the average fitness value of all page clippings at generations g and $g-1$, respectively.

Generation g is said to make "*no significant improvement*" if its improvement ratio doesn't exceed the average improvement ratio of all generations up to now. Formally, the definition is given as follow:

$$I_g \leq \bar{I}_g \tag{16}$$

where $\bar{I}_g$ denotes the mean of all $I_j, 1 \leq j \leq g$.

Then, the *allowable number of consecutive generations without significant improvement* for generation g is defined as follows:

$$MG_g = \left\lceil \frac{I_g}{\bar{I}_g} \times Pop\_size \times \frac{\sigma_g}{\bar{\sigma}_g} \right\rceil \quad where \quad I_g > 0, \sigma_g > 0 \tag{17}$$

where *Pop_size* denotes the initial population size, σ_g is the standard deviation of all I_j, $1 \leq j \leq g$, $\bar{\sigma}_g$ denotes the mean of all $\sigma_j, 1 \leq j \leq g$. As shown in the definition, the allowable number of consecutive generations without significant improvement is dynamically determined based on the improvement at the current generation and improvement progress history. A large value of either $I_g / \bar{I}_g$ or $\sigma_g / \bar{\sigma}_g$ implies a significant progress at generation g. This progress in turn implies that the probability of further progress is high, and the probability of having reached the optimal solution at this generation is low. Consequently, the second termination condition is refined as follows. The number of consecutive generations without improvement exceeds its allowable number of generations without significant improvement at the current generation. This occurrence is a sign

Figure 12. A sample piece of page clipping

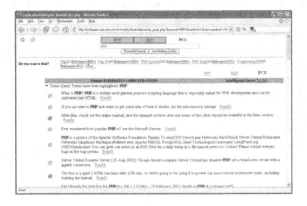

that further computation could not yield much progress, and the genetic algorithm should be terminated immediately.

A Sample Run of PCS

A sample run of PCS was conducted to create a number of page clippings for the query term "php." Figure 12 shows a sample piece of page clipping with the query term marked with different color and the genes represented in green (for "1") and red (for "0") balls. For example, the top six except the third paragraphs are relevant answers to the user query. By contrast, the third and seventh paragraphs are not relevant to the user query. Additionally, the "IntelligentGuess" term, which appears at the right-hand side of the horizontal bar, indicates that more than half of the paragraphs in this page clipping are selected from the same Web page. In such a case, the user can click on the *"TryIt"* link to look at that Web page directly.

Appropriateness Verification of Termination Criteria

Two simulation runs were conducted to demonstrate that the proposed genetic algorithm is terminated properly when either 1) the global best-fit solution is reached, or 2) the number of consecutive generations without improvement exceeds its allowable number of consecutive generations without significant improvement. The following parameters were randomly chosen: the number of chromosomes, the number of genes in each chromosome, the value ("1" or "0") of each gene, and the number of matched query terms contained in each gene.

Table 8 shows the simulation results of the first criterion, where *MaxGen* denotes the maximum number of generations set by humans, *SystemRunGen* denotes the current generation highlighted, *Gen#* denotes the generation number, and *ConseGen* denotes the number of consecutive generations without improvements. This simulation was run with *MaxGen*=200 and a randomly chosen population size *Pop_size*=71. As highlighted in Table 8, the global best-fit solution (*C*=71) has been reached at generation 36. The simulation run instead of being terminated immediately, continued to execute for additional generations on purpose to demonstrate that continued computation after generation 36 wastes computing resource for no improvements on *C* at all.

Table 8. Simulation results of reaching the global best-fit solution: C=Pop_size

				MaxGen = 200 SystemRunGen = 36						
Gen#	Pop_size	$\overline{f_{g-1}}$	$\overline{f_g}$	C	l_g	$\overline{l_g}$	σ_g	$\overline{\sigma_g}$	MG_g	ConseGen
27	71	141.30377	150.67259	53	0.0663	0.10901	0.0371	0.04087	40	16
28	71	150.67259	160.73373	55	0.06677	0.1075	0.03727	0.04074	41	17
29	71	160.73373	170.8358	57	0.06285	0.10596	0.03753	0.04063	39	18
30	71	170.8358	181.501	59	0.06243	0.10451	0.03772	0.04054	40	19
31	71	181.501	193.07562	61	0.06377	0.1032	0.0378	0.04045	42	20
32	71	193.07562	204.95651	63	0.06153	0.1019	0.03791	0.04037	41	21
33	71	204.95651	217.72415	65	0.06229	0.10069	0.03794	0.04029	42	22
34	71	217.72415	230.68797	67	0.05954	0.09948	0.03803	0.04023	41	23
35	71	230.68797	244.3312	69	0.05914	0.09833	0.03808	0.04017	41	24
36	**71**	**244.3312**	**258.55654**	**71**	**0.05822**	**0.09722**	**0.03812**	**0.04011**	**41**	**25**
37	71	258.55654	272.60726	71	0.05434	0.09606	0.03824	0.04006	39	26
38	71	272.60726	287.19611	71	0.05352	0.09494	0.03835	0.04001	39	27
39	71	287.19611	302.1749	71	0.05216	0.09384	0.03846	0.03997	38	28
40	71	302.1749	317.21514	71	0.04977	0.09274	0.03859	0.03994	37	29
41	71	317.21514	332.64784	71	0.04865	0.09167	0.03873	0.03991	37	30
42	71	332.64784	348.18768	71	0.04672	0.09059	0.03887	0.03989	36	31
43	71	348.18768	363.33336	71	0.0435	0.0895	0.03907	0.03987	34	32
44	71	363.33336	378.86113	71	0.04274	0.08844	0.03926	0.03985	34	33
45	71	378.86113	393.92343	71	0.03976	0.08736	0.03948	0.03984	33	34
46	71	393.92343	408.90864	71	0.03804	0.08628	0.03971	0.03984	32	35
47	71	408.90864	423.8672	71	0.03658	0.08523	0.03994	0.03984	31	36
48	71	423.8672	438.65753	71	0.03489	0.08418	0.04017	0.03985	30	37
49	71	438.65753	454.1956	71	0.03542	0.08318	0.04036	0.03986	31	38
50	71	454.1956	469.14006	71	0.0329	0.08218	0.04057	0.03988	29	39
51	71	469.14006	483.7596	71	0.03116	0.08118	0.0408	0.03989	28	40
52	71	483.7596	497.82824	71	0.02908	0.08017	0.04103	0.03992	27	41

In the second simulation, a large population size, *Pop_size* = 194 was randomly chosen. The second termination criterion was reached at generation 107 as highlighted in Table 9, where the number of consecutive generations without improvements (*ConseGen* = 88) exceeds the allowable number of consecutive generations without significant improvements (MG_g = 87). Similarly, the simulation run continued up to 200 generations on purpose to demonstrate that continued computation after generation 107 also wastes computing resource. The number of best-fit page clippings *C* was found to remain at 192, failing to reach its maximum number 194, at the end of the simulation.

Table 9. Simulation results of reaching the termination criteria: MG_g <ConseGen

				MaxGen = 200 SystemRunGen = 107						
Gen#	Pop_size	$\overline{f_{g\text{-}1}}$	$\overline{f_g}$	C	l_g	$\overline{l_g}$	σ_g	$\overline{\sigma_g}$	MG_g	ConseGen
87	194	284.87309	291.90684	170	0.02469	0.04456	0.02099	0.02221	102	68
88	194	291.90684	299.04971	172	0.02447	0.04433	0.02098	0.0222	102	69
89	194	299.04971	306.26201	174	0.02412	0.0441	0.02097	0.02218	101	70
90	194	306.26201	313.56732	176	0.02385	0.04388	0.02096	0.02217	100	71
91	194	313.56732	320.9603	178	0.02358	0.04365	0.02095	0.02216	100	72
92	194	320.9603	328.4007	180	0.02318	0.04343	0.02094	0.02214	98	73
93	194	328.4007	335.91739	182	0.02289	0.04321	0.02094	0.02213	98	74
94	194	335.91739	343.59833	184	0.02287	0.04299	0.02093	0.02212	98	75
95	194	343.59833	351.32598	186	0.02249	0.04278	0.02092	0.0221	97	76
96	194	351.32598	359.20183	188	0.02242	0.04257	0.02092	0.02209	97	77
97	194	359.20183	367.20819	190	0.02229	0.04236	0.02091	0.02208	97	78
98	194	367.20819	375.32846	192	0.02211	0.04215	0.0209	0.02207	97	79
99	194	375.32846	383.59458	192	0.02202	0.04195	0.02089	0.02206	97	80
100	194	383.59458	391.88046	192	0.0216	0.04174	0.02089	0.02204	96	81
101	194	391.88046	400.25727	192	0.02138	0.04154	0.02088	0.02203	95	82
102	194	400.25727	408.62844	192	0.02091	0.04134	0.02088	0.02202	94	83
103	194	408.62844	417.07735	192	0.02068	0.04114	0.02087	0.02201	93	84
104	194	417.07735	425.42663	192	0.02002	0.04094	0.02088	0.022	91	85
105	194	425.42663	433.69656	192	0.01944	0.04073	0.02088	0.02199	88	86
106	194	433.69656	442.05893	192	0.01928	0.04053	0.02089	0.02198	88	87
107	**194**	**442.05893**	**450.39653**	**192**	**0.01886**	**0.04033**	**0.02089**	**0.02197**	**87**	**88**
108	194	450.39653	458.87073	192	0.01881	0.04013	0.0209	0.02196	87	89
109	194	458.87073	467.4351	192	0.01866	0.03993	0.0209	0.02195	87	90
110	194	467.4351	476.00875	192	0.01834	0.03973	0.02091	0.02194	86	91
111	194	476.00875	484.59132	192	0.01803	0.03954	0.02091	0.02193	85	92
112	194	484.59132	493.2813	192	0.01793	0.03935	0.02092	0.02192	85	93
113	194	493.2813	502.03701	192	0.01775	0.03915	0.02092	0.02191	84	94
114	194	502.03701	510.72948	192	0.01731	0.03896	0.02093	0.0219	83	95
115	194	510.72948	519.58163	192	0.01733	0.03877	0.02094	0.0219	83	96
116	194	519.58163	528.49209	192	0.01715	0.03859	0.02094	0.02189	83	97
117	194	528.49209	537.35253	192	0.01677	0.0384	0.02095	0.02188	82	98
118	194	537.35253	546.19555	192	0.01646	0.03822	0.02096	0.02187	81	99

Justifying Cost Effectiveness of PCS

To justify that PCS yields cost effective solutions, an experiment was conducted to compare the solutions produced by the dynamically terminated genetic algorithm with the solutions produced by a traditional genetic algorithm terminated at predefined numbers of generations. The predefined numbers of generations (*NG*) used in simulation runs are 50, 100, 150, and 200. A thousand simulation runs, each starts with a randomly generated population size, were conducted for each of the four predefined configurations and the dynamically terminated configuration as well. First, the success rate between the real *C* achieved and the global best-fit *C* (*C=Pop_size*) is defined as follows:

$$Success\ Rate = C_{achieved}/C_{best\text{-}fit} \tag{18}$$

The average success rates (*ASR*) obtained from the simulation results for the five cases are 0.7275 (*NG*=50), 0.9331 (*NG*=100), 0.9490 (*NG*=150), 0.9624 (*NG*=200), and 0.9255 (*NG*=System Determined), respectively.

Figure 13 shows the curve of the number of generations (*NG*) achieved over 1000 simulation runs for each case. The curves for cases *NG*=50, 100, 150, and 200 remains constant, since all simulations for each case ran to the same predefined number. By contrast, the curve for the case *NG=System Determined* fluctuates, since each simulation run was terminated at a dynamically determined generation. The average *NG*s (*ANG*s) for the five cases over 1000 simulation runs are 50, 100, 150, 200 and 76.601, respectively.

Figure 13. Number of generations achieved over 1000 simulation runs

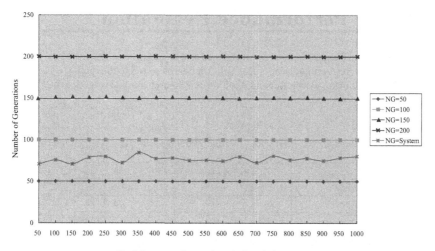

Simulation runs on the second termination criteria

Then, the performance ratio (PR) between $NG=n$ and $NG=m$, *where* $n < m$ is given as follows:

$$PR_{n,m} = Improved\ ASR_{n,m} /\ Improved\ ANG\ Ratio_{n,m} \tag{19}$$

where

$Improved\ ASR_{n,m} = ASR_n - ASR_m$

$Improved\ ANG\ Ratio_{n,m} = (|\ ANG_n - ANG_m\ |)/\ ANG_m$

Table 10 shows the PR values for cases $NG=50, 100, 150,$ and 200 using the *System Determined* case as benchmark. Of the predefined number cases, the case $NG=50$ was notably inferior to the *System Determined* case; other cases slightly improved less than 0.025 in *PR*. This finding reveals that a simulation run can significantly improve before reaching the system determined number of generations, and beyond that threshold, the improvement rapidly decreases to a very slim level at the price of long processing time. For example, the case $NG=100$ took 30.55% more of generations for only about 0.76% improvements in success rate. The figures are even worse for cases $NG=150$ and $NG=200$. As the figures depicts, increasing the number of generations beyond 76.601 does slightly increase the success rate; however, the cost of this increase, as measured by the additional computation time, out-weights its benefits.

According to these results, we conclude that the dynamically terminated genetic algorithm yields cost effective solutions in a comparatively short amount of time.

Performance Evaluation

Three performance experiments were performed on the proposed search methods. First, 23 volunteers were recruited from local bulletin boards to judge the quality of search results for some hot keywords. Second, the SVV metasearch method was compared with

Table 10. PR values for NG=50, 100, 150, and 200 based on NG=System Determined

NG	50	System Determined	100	150	200
Average SR	0.7275	0.9255	0.9331	0.9490	0.9624
Average NG	50	76.601	100	150	200
Improved ASR	-0.1980		0.0076	0.0235	0.0369
Improved ANG Ratio	0.3473		0.3055	0.9582	1.6109
PR	-0.5701		0.0249	0.0245	0.0229

four well-known metasearch engines (Sherman, 2002a, 2002b). Third, SVV, HLP, and PCS were compared with six well-known search engines.

User Study

A user study was performed to determine how users rate the proposed search methods, as compared with other search engines.

A total of 23 volunteers were recruited from local bulletin boards to judge the quality of search results returned by Google, Yahoo, AltaVista, LookSmart, Overture, Lycos, and the proposed search methods, SVV, HLP, and PCS. In this experiment, the search engines adopted for SVV were the preceding six popular search engines. The popularity of Google and Yahoo was emphasized by adjusting their $a_{i,q}$ and b ranges so that our search results would be consistent with general preferences of most users. Additionally, sponsored and banner links at the top of search results from AltaVista, LookSmart, Lycos and Overture were dropped to make SVV rank reasonably without any distortion. HLP and PCS, in principle, can be applied to the search results of any search engine. This experiment applied HLP on the search results of SVV, and in turn applied PCS on the search results of HLP.

The testers were asked to perform queries on each search engine with popular query terms obtained from Lycos 50 (2004) including "Dragonball", "Pamela Anderson", "Britney

Table 11. User study results of SVV, HLP, PCS and other search engines

	Google	Yahoo	AltaVista	LookSmart	Overture	Lycos	SVV	HLP	PCS
Dragonball	4.18	4.23	3.08	3.57	2.25	3.51	4.18	4.33	4.58
Pamela Anderson	3.84	3.51	2.11	3.74	2.90	3.56	3.79	4.04	4.26
Britney Spears	4.09	3.43	2.78	4.02	1.77	3.33	3.93	4.34	4.78
Las Vegas	3.81	4.23	3.36	3.55	1.32	3.74	4.02	4.18	4.01
Harry Potter	3.15	2.69	3.70	3.77	1.33	3.27	3.86	3.77	3.22
Kazaa	4.11	3.86	3.71	3.95	2.34	3.86	4.03	4.07	4.35
WWE	3.97	3.74	3.38	3.73	2.25	3.51	3.95	4.22	4.23
Jennifer Lopez	4.29	3.95	3.02	3.16	2.67	3.66	4.02	3.45	3.71
Final Fantasy	3.51	4.01	3.52	3.66	2.28	3.37	3.83	4.33	4.35
Yu-Gi-Oh!	4.30	4.52	2.41	3.33	2.71	3.29	4.33	4.46	4.66
The Bible	2.73	2.63	2.09	2.86	2.21	2.90	2.57	2.79	3.05
NBA	3.71	3.82	3.77	3.79	1.08	3.35	4.04	4.35	4.54
Average	3.81	3.72	3.08	3.59	2.09	3.45	3.88	4.03	4.15

Spears", "Las Vegas", "Harry Potter", "Kazaa", "WWE", "Jennifer Lopez", "Final Fantasy", "Yu-Gi-Oh!", "The Bible", and "NBA". The testers independently rated the search results of each search engine for a given query term on a score ranging from 1 to 5.

Table 11 shows the experimental results. The number in each cell (except the last row) is the average score of a search engine on a given query term. For example, Google has an average score 4.18 for the query term "Dragonball". The last row in Table 11 shows the average score of each search engine on all testing query terms. Generally, the results were consistent with those expected of the proposed search methods. That is, PCS scored higher than HLP, and HLP in turn scored higher than SVV and other search engines. The scores of PCS and HLP, 4.15 and 4.03 respectively, were significantly better than those of other search engines. The SVV score, 3.88, was close to that of Google (3.81) and Yahoo (3.72), which is consistent with the SVV parameter configuration. The experiment confirmed that users are more satisfied with the proposed search methods than with general search engines.

However, HLP and PCS had lower scores than other methods in some query terms, such as "Jennifer Lopez" and "Harry Potter", because HLP and PCS perform badly on Web pages without description texts or with many non-textual elements such as Flash, Photo, Audio, and Movie. For example, HLP has a hard time predicting hyperlinks from the top returned URL "http://www.jenniferlopez.com", which has no description text, in the case of "Jennifer Lopez." Similarly, PCS has a hard time discovering relevant paragraphs for "Harry Potter" from the top URL "http://harrypotter.warnerbros.com", which includes many photos on its home page.

Notably, the average score of Overture was 2.09, the lowest among all search engines. The reason for Overture's low ranking is that it places many banner links at the top of search results since it is a pay-per-click search engine for hot keywords. Meanwhile, no search engines scored well on the query term "The Bible", because some testers expected to find some "bible" books on programming topics.

Comparisons with Metasearch Engines

SVV were compared with four well-known metasearch engines, Dogpile, Excite, MetaCrawler, and WebCrawler (Sherman, 2002a, 2002b). The mean reciprocal rank (MRR) was used to measure the effectiveness of the metasearch engines. The 500 queries provided in the TREC 2002 QA data (2003) were applied to each metasearch engine. The MRR of each individual query is the reciprocal of the rank at which the first correct answer occurred, or zero if none of the top 10 results contains a correct answer. The score for the 500 queries is the mean of each individual query's reciprocal ranks. Table 12 lists the ranks at which the metasearch engines returned correct answers. For example, Dogpile returned the correct page at rank #1 in 218 out of 500 cases, and returned no answer[4] in 116 out of 500.

Figure 14 shows the MRR values achieved by the five metasearch engines. SVV was found to outperform other metasearch search engines, because it rearranges the metasearch results based on the weights obtained from the user behavior function (UBF), but does not simply group the results together. Therefore, correct answers in the top 10 results of any metasearch engine are very likely to appear in the top 10 results of SVV.

Table 12. Distribution of ranks at which the first correct answer returned by metasearch engines out of the 500 queries

Rank	Dogpile	Excite	MetaCrawler	WebCrawler	SVV
1	218	220	219	220	294
2	96	82	90	90	60
3	28	37	23	23	18
4	10	18	15	19	8
5	11	5	14	12	8
6	5	8	9	11	10
7	3	8	7	3	2
8	11	5	4	2	5
9	1	0	3	3	2
10	1	5	1	6	1
No	116	112	115	111	92

Figure 14. Mean reciprocal rank achieved by the metasearch engines

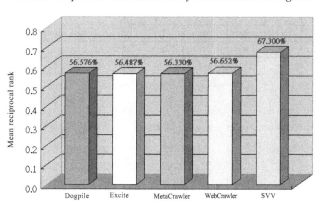

Search results gathered from 04/21/2004 to 05/03/2004

Comparisons with General Search Engines

MRR was used to measure the effectiveness of SVV, HLP, PCS and some well-known search engines. The 500 queries provided in the TREC 2002 QA data (2003) were applied individually to Google, Yahoo, AltaVista, LookSmart, Overture, Lycos, SVV, HLP, and PCS. Table 13 shows the ranks at which the search engines returned the first correct answers.

Figure 15 shows the MRR values achieved by the nine search engines. Google, Yahoo, SVV, HLP and PCS were found to outperform AltaVista, LookSmart, Overture, and Lycos. Most significantly, the proposed search methods, SVV, HLP and PCS performed better than most other search engines, and PCS performed the best. As stated previously, SVV collectively expresses the voting behavior of the six other search engines in terms of correct answers. Therefore, correct answers appearing in any search engine's top 10

Table 13. Distribution of ranks at which the first correct answer returned by search engines out of the 500 queries

Rank	Google	Yahoo	AltaVista	LookSmart	Overture	Lycos	SVV	HLP	PCS
1	262	266	209	115	224	172	277	278	313
2	54	58	71	55	84	74	64	42	39
3	31	34	34	35	33	47	20	27	11
4	19	15	24	33	16	31	11	12	8
5	17	12	22	27	14	17	9	6	3
6	8	8	10	24	8	11	9	3	1
7	5	4	8	9	6	7	2	4	1
8	5	5	7	7	9	10	5	5	5
9	0	1	5	4	4	6	2	6	4
10	4	3	6	4	2	4	2	4	4
No	95	94	104	187	100	121	99	113	111

Figure 15. Mean reciprocal rank achieved by the general search engines

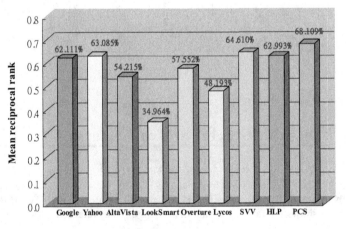

Search results gathered from 03/12/2004 to 03/22/2004

results are highly likely to also appear in SVV top 10 results, but not necessarily the other way around. HLP further expands the inside links of the top ranked URLs in SVV results into its top 10 results, and possibly pushes correct answers out of the top 10. Thus, HLP performed slightly worse than SVV. However, HLP performed better than SVV in some cases, in which the correct answer appears inside a hyperlink of a top ranked URL in SVV results, but does not appear in the URL itself. For example, SVV cannot find a correct answer for Qid=1562 (Q: Where did the U.S. Civil War begin? Answer: Fort Sumter). However, HLP found the correct answer at rank #7 URL http://www.plainfield.k12.in.us/hschool/webq/webq44/HISTORY.HTM, which is a referred link from http://www.plainfield.k12.in.us/hschool/webq/webq44/civwar.htm (a URL which appeared at rank #3 in SVV). Finally, PCS gathers matched paragraphs from the top-ranked Web pages. PCS can possibly move paragraphs containing correct answers into its top 10 results, even though the paragraphs' original Web pages are not in the top 10 results of SVV or HLP. Thus, PCS is very likely to surpass SVV and HLP. For example, PCS found the correct answer for Qid=1507 (Q: What is the national anthem in England? Answer: God Saves the Queen) at rank #1 of its results; while SVV and HLP found the same answer at ranks #2 and #4 of their results, respectively.

Finally, the search results of the most popular search engines, Google and Yahoo, were taken as the inputs to HLP and to PCS to demonstrate that HLP and PCS can be used to improve the search results of any search engines. The combined search engines were designated Google_HLP, Yahoo_HLP, Google_PCS, and Yahoo_PCS, respectively. Figure 16 shows the MRR achieved by Google (62.716%), Google_HLP (66.241%), Google_PCS (67.857%), Yahoo (62.473%), Yahoo_HLP (66.103%), and Yahoo_PCS (67.860%). Obviously, Google_HLP, Yahoo_HLP, Google_PCS, and Yahoo_PCS outperformed their respective originating search engines, Google and Yahoo. Similarly, HLP and PCS could be used to improve the results of AltaVista, LookSmart, Overture, and Lycos.

Figure 16. Mean reciprocal rank achieved by Google, Google_HLP, Google_PCS, Yahoo, Yahoo_HLP, and Yahoo_PCS

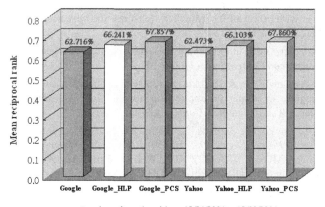

Search results gathered from 12/24/2004 to 12/30/2004

Conclusions and Future Directions

This study developed SVV, a metasearch method, and HLP and PCS, two post-search methods in an intelligent metasearch engine. These methods working together can recommend a user's next hyperlink access and relevant paragraphs in a page-clipping format from metasearch results. The proposed design is based on the primacy effect of browsing behavior, that users favor the top ranking items in search results. This approach is unbiased of any search engines and needs no training data as well. A user study showed that users are more satisfied with the proposed methods than with general search engines. Moreover, two performance measures confirmed that the proposed search methods outperform other metasearch and search engines. Finally, a performance measure also demonstrated that the proposed HLP and PCS methods can improve the search results of any search engines.

Future work is planned along several directions. First, the search methods implemented are primarily based on the keyword match between the contents of Web pages and the user query items. Using the semantic Web in recommending concepts or items relevant to the user query might help finding the exact contents required by users. This approach is particularly helpful when the users lack sufficient knowledge about the domains they are searching for. Second, several advanced pattern matching techniques used in PCS gene encoding are investigated to improve the precision rate of the retrieved paragraphs. Third, further user feedback is needed to fine-tune the search parameters, including a and b, to improve the performance of the proposed methods. Finally, the proposed methods should be compared with the best systems participating TREC question answering track to show the differences between the proposed methods and related work.

References

Austin, S. (1990). An introduction to genetic algorithms. *AI Expert, 5*(3), 48-53.

Aytug, H., Bhattacharrya, S., & Koehler, G. J. (1996). A Markov chain analysis of genetic algorithms with power of 2 cardinality alphabets. *European Journal of Operational Research, 96*(1), 195-201.

Aytug, H., & Koehler, G. J. (1996). Stopping criteria for finite length genetic algorithms. *ORSA Journal on Computing, 8*(2), 183-191.

Braslavski, P., Alshanski, G., & Shishkin, A. (2004). ProThes: Thesaurus-based meta-search engine for a specific application domain. In *Proceedings of the 13th International World Wide Web Conference* (pp. 222-223).

Brill, E., Lin, J., Banko, M., Dumais, S., & Ng, A. (2001). Data intensive question answering. In *Proceedings of the 10th Text REtrieval Conference (TREC 2001)*, Gaithersburg, MD (pp. 183-189). NIST. Retrieved from http://www.ai.mit.edu/people/jimmylin/publications/Brill-etal-TREC2001.pdf

Brin, S., & Page, L. (1998). The anatomy of a large-scale hypertextual Web search engines. In *Proceedings of the 7th World Wide Web Conference* (pp. 107-117).

Catledge, L. D., & Pitkow, J. E. (1995). Characterizing browsing strategies in the World-Wide Web. *Computer Networks and ISDN Systems, 27*(6), 1065-1073.

Chakrabarti, S., Dom, B. E., Kumar, S. R., Raghavan, P., Rajagopalan, S., Tomkins, A., et al. (1999). Mining the Web's link structure. *IEEE Computing, 32*(8), 60-67.

Chang, C. H., Hsu, C. N., & Lui, S. C. (2003). Automatic information extraction from semi-structured Web pages by pattern discovery. *Decision Support Systems, 35*(1), 129-147.

Chen, H., Chung, Y., Yang, C., & Ramsey, M. (1998). A smart itsy bitsy spider for the Web. *Journal of the American Society for Information Science and Technology, 49*(7), 604-618.

Chen, M., LaPaugh, A. S., & Singh, J. P. (2002). Predicting category accesses for a user in a structured information space. *Proceedings of the 25th Annual International ACM SIGIR Conference on Research and Development in Information Retrieval* (pp. 65-72).

Chi, E. H., Pirolli, P., Chen, K., & Pitkow, J. (2001). Using information scent to model user information needs and actions on the Web. *Proceedings of the SIGCHI Conference on Human Factors in Computing Systems* (pp. 490-497).

DARPA (The Defense Advanced Research Projects Agency). (1997). *Proceedings of the 7th Message Understanding Conference.* Retrieved May 3, 2006, from http://www.itl.nist.gov/iaui/894.02/related_projects/muc/proceedings/muc_7_toc.html

Dreilinger, D. & Howe, A. (1996). *An information gathering agent for querying Web search engine.* Technical Report CS-96-111, Computer Science Department, Colorado State University.

Eshelman, L. J., & Schaffer, J. D. (1991). Preventing premature convergence in genetic algorithms by preventing incest. In *Proceedings of the 4th International Conference on Genetic Algorithms* (pp. 115-122).

Fan, W., Gordon, M. D., & Pathak, P. (2004). A generic ranking function discovery framework by genetic programming for information retrieval. *Information Processing and Management, 40*(4), 587-602.

Fan, W., Gordon, M. D., & Pathak, P. (2004). Discovery of context-specific ranking functions for effective information retrieval by genetic programming. *IEEE Transactions on Knowledge and Data Engineering, 16*(4), 523-527.

Freitag, D. (1998). Information extraction from HTML: Application of agGeneral learning approach. *Proceedings of the 15th National Conference on Artificial Intelligence* (pp. 517-523).

Glover, E. J., Gordon, M. D., & Birmingham, W. P. (1998). Improving web search using utility theory. *Proceedings of the 1st International Workshop on Web Information and Data Management* (pp. 5-8).

Glover, E. J., Lawrence, S., Birmingham, W. P., & Giles, C. L. (1999). Architecture of a metasearch engine that supports user information needs. *Proceedings of the 8ᵗʰ International Conference on Information Knowledge Management* (pp. 210-216).

Glover, E. J., Lawrence, S., Gordon, M. D., Birmingham, W. P., & Giles, C. L. (1999, August). Recommending web documents based on user preferences. In *ACM SIGIR '99 Workshop on Recommender Systems*, Berkeley, CA.

Goldberg, D. E. (1999). *Genetic algorithms in search, optimization and machine learning*. Redwood City, CA: Addison-Wesley.

Gordon, M. D. (1991). User-based document clustering by redescribing subject descriptions with a genetic algorithm. *Journal of the American Society for Information Science and Technology, 42*(5), 311-322.

Gordon, M. D. (1998). Probabilistic and genetic algorithms for document retrieval. *Communications of the ACM, 31*(10), 1208-1218.

Greenhalgh, D. & Marshall, S. (2000). Convergence criteria for genetic algorithms. SIAM *Journal on Computing, 30*(1), 269-282.

Gündüz, S., & Özsu, M. T. (2003, June 26-29). Recommendation models for user accesses to Web pages. In *Proceedings of Joint International Conference ICANN/ICONIP 2003*, Istanbul, Turkey (LNCS 2714, pp. 1003-1010).

Hai, H., Meng, W., Clement, Y., & Zonghuan, W. (2004, May 19-21). Automatic extraction of Web search interfaces. In *Proceedings of the 13ᵗʰ International World Wide Web Conference*, New York (pp. 414-415).

Harman, D. (1992). *Information retrieval data structure and algorithm*. Englewood Cliffs, NJ: Prentice-Hall.

Henzinger, M. R. (2001). Hyperlink analysis for the Web. *IEEE Internet Computing, 5*(1), 45-50.

Holland, J. (1975). *Adaptation in natural and artificial systems*. Ann Arbor: University of Michigan Press.

Horng, J. T., & Yeh, C. C. (2000). Applying genetic algorithms to query optimization in document retrieval. *Information Processing and Management, 36*(5), 737-759.

Hovy, E., Gerber, L., Hermjakob, U., Junk, M., & Lin, C. Y. (2000). Question answering in webclopedia. In *Proceedings of the 9ᵗʰ TREC Conference*. Retrieved May 4, 2006, from http://trec.nist.gov/pubs/trec9/papers/webclopedia.pdf

Hu, W. C., Chen, Y., Schmalz, M. S., & Ritter, G. X. (2001, July 22-25). An overview of the World Wide Web search technologies. In *Proceedings of the 5ᵗʰ World Multi-Conference on System, Cybernetics and Informatics (SCI2001)*, Orlando, FL. Retrieved from http://webminer.mis.yzu.edu.tw/ref/hu01overview.pdf.

Jansen, B. J., Spink, A., Bateman, J., & Saracevic, T. (1998). Real life information retrieval: A study of user queries on the Web. *SIGIR FORUM, 32*(1), 5-17.

Jones, K. S. (1972). A statistical interpretation of term specificity and its application in retrieval. *Journal of Documentation, 28*(1), 11-21.

Jones, S., Cunningham, S. J., McNab, R. J., & Boddie, S. (2000). A transaction log analysis of a digital library. *International Journal on Digital Libraries, 3*(2), 152-169.

KartOO (2004). *KartOO visual metasearch engine*. Retrieved May 4, 2006, from http://www.kartoo.com/

Koch, R. (2003). *The 80/20 individual: How to build on the 20% of what you do best*. London: Doubleday & Company.

Koza, J. R. (1992). *Genetic programming: On the programming of computers by means of natural selection*. Ann Arbor, MI: University of Michigan Press.

Kupiec, J. (1993, June 27-July 1). MURAX: A robust linguistic approach for question answering using an on-line encyclopedia. In *Proceedings of the 16th Annual International ACM SIGIR Conference on Research and Development in Information Retrieval*, Pittsburgh, PA (pp. 181-190).

Lacroix, Z., Sahuguet, A., & Chandrasekar, R. (1998, June). Information extraction and database techniques: A user-oriented approach to querying the Web. In *Proceedings of the 10th International Conference on Advanced Information Systems Engineering (CAiSE '98)*, Pisa, Italy (LNCS 1413, pp. 289-304).

Lawrence, S., & Giles, C. L. (1998). Context and page analysis for improved Web search. *IEEE Internet Computing, 2*(4), 38-46.

Lempel, R., & Moran, S. (2000). The stochastic approach for link-structure analysis (SALSA) and the TKC effect. *Proceedings of the Ninth International World Wide Web Conference*, New York (pp. 387-401). Elsevier Science.

Li, Y. (1998). Toward a qualitative search engine. *IEEE Internet Computing, 2*(4), 24-29.

Lin, S. H., & Ho, J. M. (2002, July 23-26). Discovering informative content block from Web documents. In *Proceedings of the Eighth ACM SIGKDD International Conference on Knowledge Discovery and Data Mining*, Edmonton, Alberta, Canada. Retrieved May 4, 2006, from http://citeseer.ist.psu.edu/lin02discovering.html

López-Pujalte, C. V., Guerrero-Bote, P., & Moya-Anegón, F. de. (2002). A test of genetic algorithms in relevance feedback. *Information Processing and Management, 38*(6), 795-807.

López-Pujalte, C. V., Guerrero-Bote, P., & Moya-Anegón, F. de. (2003). Order-based fitness functions for genetic algorithms applied to relevance geedback. *Journal of the American Society for Information Science and Technology, 54*(2), 152-160.

Lycos50 (2004). *Lycos50 with Aaron Schatz — Lycos.com*. Retrieved from http://50.lycos.com/

Malerba, D., Esposito, F. & Ceci, M. (2002, March 24-28) Mining HTML pages to support document sharing in a cooperative system. In *Proceedings of the EDBT 2002 Workshops XMLDM, MDDE, and YRWS*, Czech Republic (LNCS 2490, pp. 420-434).

Mall-Net. (2001). *Web site design to sell*. Retrieved from http://www.mall-net.com/se_report/

McCallum, A. (2002). Information Extraction from the World Wide Web. Retrieved from http://www-2.cs.cmu.edu/Web/Groups/NIPS/NIPS2002/nips-tutorials.html

Meng, W., Clement, T. Y., & Liu, K. L. (2002). Building efficient and effective metasearch engines. *ACM Computing Surveys, 34*(1), 48-89.

Morris, C. G., Levine, A., & Maisto, A. A. (2002). *Psychology: An introduction*. NJ: Prentice-Hall.

Nahm, U. Y., & Mooney, R. J. (2000). Using information extraction to aid the discovery of prediction rules from text. In *Proceedings of the 6th ACM SIGKDD International Conference on Knowledge Discovery and Data Mining*. Retrieved from http://www-2.cs.cmu.edu/~dunja/KDDpapers/Nahm_TM_IE.ps

Nanopoulos, A., Katsaros, D. & Manolopoulos, Y. (2001). Exploiting Web Log Mining for Web Cache Enhancement. In *Proceedings of the 3rd International Workshop on Mining Web Log Data Across All Customers Touch Points* (pp. 68-87).

Nick, Z. Z., & Themis, P. (2001). Web search using a genetic algorithm. *IEEE Internet Computing, 5*(2), 18-26.

Obitko, M. (2004). *Introduction to genetic algorithms with Java applets*. Retrieved from http://cs.felk.cvut.cz/~xobitko/ga/

Osdin, R., Ounis, I., & White, R. W. (2002). Using hierarchical clustering and summarisation approaches for Web retrieval: Glasgow at the TREC 2002 Interactive Track. In *Proceedings of the 10th Text Retrieval Conference (TREC-2002)*.

Paepcke, A., Garcia-Molina, H., Rodriguez-Mula, G. & Cho, J. (2000). Beyond document similarity: Understanding value-based search and browsing technologies. *SIGMOD Record, 29*(1), 80-92.

Petry, F., Buckles, B., Prabhu, D., & Kraft, D. (1993). Fuzzy information retrieval using genetic algorithms and relevance feedback. In *Proceedings of the ASIS Annual Meeting* (pp. 122-125).

Picarougne, F., Monmarché, N., Oliver, A., & Venturini, G. (2002). Web mining with a genetic algorithm. *Proceedings of the Eleventh International World Wide Web Conference*, http://www2002.org/CDROM/poster/58/

Radev, D. R., Fan, W., Qi, H., Wu, H., & Grewal, A. (2002). Probabilistic question answering from the web. In *Proceedings of the 11th WWW Conference*. Retrieved from http://www2002.org/CDROM/refereed/19/

Radev, D. R., Fan, W., Qi, H., Zheng, Z., Goldensohn, S. B., Zhang, Z., & Prager, J. (2001). Mining the web for answers to natural language questions. In *Proceedings of 2001 International Conference on Information and Knowledge Management* (pp. 143-150).

Riloff, E., & Lehnert, W. (1994). Information extraction as a basis for high-precision text classification. *ACM Transactions on Information Systems, 12*(3), 296-333.

Rudolph, G., & Sprave, J. (1995). A cellular genetic algorithm with self-adjusting acceptance threshold. In *Proceedings of the 1st IEE/IEEE International Conference on Genetic Algorithms in Engineering Systems: Innovations and Applications* (pp. 365-372).

Salton, G., Allan, J., & Buckley, C. (1993). *Approaches to passage retrieval in full text information systems*. ACM SIGIR conference on R&D in Information Retrieval (pp. 49-58).

Sarukkai, R. R. (2000). Link prediction and path analysis using Markov chains. *Computer Networks, 33*, 377-386.

Selberg, E. & Etzioni, O. (1997). The MetaCrawler architecture for resource aggregation on the Web. *IEEE Expert, 12*(1), 8-14.

Sherman, C. (2002). *SearchDay—The Best and Most Popular Meta Search Engines*. Retrieved from http://searchenginewatch.com/searchday/article.php/2160791

Sherman, C. (2002). *SearchDay—The Big Four Meta Search Engines*. Retrieved from http://searchenginewatch.com/searchday/article.php/2160781

Sheth, B. D. (1994). *A learning approach to personalized information filtering*. Unpublished master thesis at MIT. Retrieved from http://citeseer.ist.psu.edu/sheth94learning.html

Sobek, M. (2002). *Additional factors influencing PageRank*. Retrieved from http://pr.efactory.de/e-further-factors.shtml

Sougné, J. P. (2000). *Short term memory in a network of spiking neurons*. Technical report, University of Liège. Retrieved May 4, 2006, from http://www.ulg.ac.be/cogsci/jsougne/TR2000-1.pdf

Spink, A., Wolfram, D., Jansen, B. J., & Saracevic, T. (2001). Searching the Web: The public and their queries. *Journal of the American Society of Information Science, 53*(2), 226-234.

Srihari, R., & Li, W. (2000). A question answering system supported by information extraction. In *Proceedings of ANLP-NAACL 2000 and the Student Research Workshop* (pp. 166-172).

Sullivan, M. (2003). *An introduction to genetic algorithms*. Retrieved May 13, 2004, from http://www.cs.qub.ac.uk/~M.Sullivan/ga/ga_index.html

Svidzinska, R. (2001). *A World Wide Web Meta Search Engine using an automatic query routing algorithm*. Master thesis at Auburn University. Retrieved May 4, 2006, from ftp://ftp.eng.auburn.edu/pub/techreports/csse/01/CSSE01-06.ps.gz

TREC 2002. (2003). *TREC 2002 QA data*. Text Retrieval Conference. Retrieved May 4, 2006 from http://trec.nist.gov/data/qa/t2002_qadata.html

Voorhees, E. M. (2003). Overview of the TREC 2002 question answering track. In *Proceedings of the 11th Text Retrieval Conference (TREC 2003)*, Gaithersburg, MD. Retrieved from http://trec.nist.gov/pubs/trec11/papers/VIDEO.OVER.pdf

Vrajitoru, D. (1997, June 23-26). Genetic algorithms in information retrieval. In *Proceedings of the 7th Conference of the International Association for the Development of Interdisciplinary Research (AIDRI '97). Learning: From Natural Principles to Artificial Methods*, University of Geneva.

Walpole, R. E., Myers, R. H., & Myers, S. L. (1998). *Probability and statistics for engineers and scientists*. Englewood Cliffs, NJ: Prentice-Hall.

Wang, L., Fan, W., Yang, R., Xi, W., Luo, M., Zhou, Y., & Fox, E. A. (2003). Ranking function discovery by genetic programming for robust retrieval. *Proceedings of the 12th TREC Conference*. Retrieved May 4, 2006, from http://trec.nist.gov/pubs/trec12/papers/vatech.robust.pdf

Witten, I. H. (2004). Adaptive text mining: Inferring structure from sequences. *Journal of Discrete Algorithms*. Retrieved May 4, 2006, from http://www.cs.waikato.ac.nz/~ihw/papers/01IHW-Adaptivetextmining.pdf

Yang, J., & Korfhage, R. R. (1993). Effects of query term weights modification in document retrieval: A study based on a genetic algorithm. In *Proceedings of the 2nd Annual*

Symposium on Document Analysis and Information Retrieval, Las Vegas, NV (pp. 271-285).

Yao, Y. Y. (1995). Measuring retrieval effectiveness based on user preference of documents. *Journal of the American Society for Information Science, 46*(2), 133-145.

Yates, R. B., & Neto, B. R. (1999). *Modern information retrieval.* Redwood City, CA: Addison-Wesley

Zacharis, N., & Panayiotopoulos, T. (2002, April 11-12). SpiderServer: The MetaSearch Engine of WebNaut. In *Proceedings of the 2ⁿᵈ Hellenic Conference on Artificial Intelligence*, Thessaloniki, Greece (pp. 475-486).

Zipf, G. K. (1949). *Human behavior and the principle of least effort: An introduction to human ecology.* Redwood City, CA: Addison-Wesley.

Endnotes

[1]   The proposed metasearch engine is available at: http://webminer.mis.yzu.edu.tw/i_metasearch.

[2]   Inverse document frequency (IDF) (Jones, 1972) is a popular measure of a word's importance used in information retrieval. The fact that IDF treats all the texts that contain a certain term equally makes it inappropriate to express the primacy effect, which users prefer the front terms in a term list to the rear ones. Thus, the user behavior function (UBF) instead of IDF was adopted to define term weights.

[3]   Literature suggests that the human behavior is a random process (Zipf, 1949; Malerba, Esposito, & Ceci, 2002) and moreover, human preferences are values ranging from lower bound to upper bound (Yao, 1995). Thus, the values of ± and ² are randomly generated to simulate the user behavior. The ranges of ± and ², which are initially obtained from our own evaluation experiments and mining of the user access log, are subject to change based on user feedback.

[4]   In this experiment, "no" answer denotes one of the situations:

   •   The TREC-2002 provides no answer.

   •   No correct answer appeared in a given search engine's top 10 results.

   •   A dead link, e.g., 404 not found, 403 Forbidden, was found.

Chapter X

Access Control for Web Service Applications:
An Example in Collaborative Auditing

Timon C. Du, The Chinese University of Hong Kong, Hong Kong, China

Richard Hwang, California State University at San Marcos, USA

Charles Ling-yu Chou, The Chinese University of Hong Kong, Hong Kong, China

Abstract

Given the rapid changes in the information technologies, the issue of information securities and company's internal controls has become very critical to both internal and external auditors. Recently, external auditors are under pressure to provide real-time assurance. Movement of this kind has complicated as to when and how to grant the access privileges to external auditors. In addition, when there is a high degree of collaborative relationship among organizations, the collaborators need to establish policies of auditors' access controls and set up conditions and constraints for security and confidentiality reasons. Since auditors among the collaborators have different seniority, the access privileges should be granted based on the seniority of the auditors in the collaborative team members. In contrast, the growth of Web service becomes a new paradigm to provide collaborative auditing service via Web. The access control issue is a crucial issue for the future collaboration. In this study, we propose a role-based Chinese Wall model, which organizes the corporate data into four different types of control groups with different access control policies, for the auditors to access the data among collaborating enterprises. Using the vendor-managed inventories (VMI) example, the study discusses how auditing tasks can be performed under the proposed access control environment. To ensure the functionality of the proposed framework, the study uses Oracle software to demonstrate the feasibility of the model.

Introduction

To respond to the fast-changing environment, corporations are under pressure to form collaboration within and among organizations. Workflow collaboration is a typical example of intra-organizational collaboration where tasks are organized in such a way that they can be implemented collaboratively inside an entity. Another instance of collaboration is concurrent engineering where a firm organizes a team of its own employees with different expertise so that lead-time and cost of product development can be reduced. Supply chain management, on the other hand, is a popular form of an among-organization collaboration in which an organization structures a supply chain relationship with the suppliers as well as the buyers. Such collaboration improves the performance of the whole chain and diminishes the results of the bullwhip effect. For example, organizations such as O_{11}, O_{12}, O_{21}, O_{22} O_{31}, and O_{32} shown in Figure 1 form a supply chain where O_{11} and O_{12} are the retailers, O_{21} and O_{22} are the wholesalers, and O_{31} and O_{32} are the manufacturers. The supply chain links organizations together to share information, products, funds, and other activities in order to efficiently fulfill the pull-type demands. Built on a supply chain, collaborative commerce allows a degree of collaboration at the level of product development, similar to concurrent engineering, where the development team may comprise members from different organizations. When the collaborative network shares data, it could include business transaction data, as well as the product development information such as product data definition (PDM). As illustrated in Figure 1, the lines between O_{11} and O_{12}, between O_{21} and O_{22}, and between O_{31} and O_{32} extend the relationship beyond a supply chain into the format of collaborative commerce.

There are many reported examples of how collaborative commerce can be implemented. One of the most mentioned cases is the vendor-managed inventories (VMI) model that moves the duty of product replenishment from the retailers to the wholesalers or from the

Figure 1. A collaborative network, where O_{11} and O_{12} are the retailers, O_{21} and O_{22} are the wholesalers, and O_{31} and O_{32} are the manufacturers

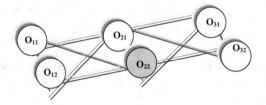

wholesalers to the manufacturers, by allowing the vendor (the wholesalers or the manufacturers) to manage the inventories for the buyers (the retailers or the wholesalers). Under the system, a continuous replenishment program (CRP) allows the suppliers to regularly monitor the point-of-sales (POS) data and determine the replenishment period. To facilitate the collaboration, it is essential to share the ERP data or warehouse data among organizations. Of course, organizations may decide to deepen the degree of collaboration by adopting advanced planning and scheduling (APS) which takes the plant capacity and material availability of both the suppliers and the manufacturers into collaborative scheme. Similarly, managers could consider using collaborative forecasting and replenishment (CFAR) so that the demands of retailers and wholesalers can be examined to trig the production activities. Moreover, an integrated approach of APS and CFAR, called collaborative planning, forecasting, and replenishment (CPFR) allows collaborators to manage simultaneously the relationships between retailers and wholesalers and between wholesalers and manufacturers.

Internal auditors appraise the level of efficiency of a firm's operations and the level of its compliance to the existing regulations. On the other hand, external auditors provide assurance to the reliability of a client's financial and nonfinancial information reported in the quarter and annual financial statements. To fulfill their responsibilities, both internal and external auditors need to evaluate the efficiency and effectiveness of an organization's internal controls. Since internal auditors involve in the entity's daily operations and are independent of business activities, they are the most qualified groups of individuals who can assist the external auditors to conduct an audit engagement. Regardless which format chosen, internal and external auditors of collaborative organizations should have access to the data stored in (and owned by) the various organizations. In this case, it is apparent that an access control to an organization's data is critical to protect the integrity and proprietary information among collaborators. As one may aware, the roles and tasks performed by internal and external auditors are quite different. To the external auditors, their primary responsibility is to examine whether a company's financial statements (balance sheet, income statement, and statement of cash flows) are prepared based on generally accepted accounting principles (GAAP). As part of professional responsibilities, external auditors need to develop a high-level understanding of client's operations, so they can express a professional opinion on a client's financial statements objectively and confidently. On the other hand, internal auditors are in charge of the operational audit and the compliance audit. When performing an operational audit, internal auditors review the efficiency and effectiveness of a firm's operational procedures. Such an audit includes, but is not limited to, an examination of transactions process and the evaluation of less quantifiable information like the degree of customer satisfaction. Moreover, internal auditors are responsible for compliance audit to determine whether the company practice follows the regulations promulgated by authorities such as the Environmental Protection Agency (EPA) and Federal Depository Insurance Commission (FDIC).

Traditionally, the external auditors examine the historical data periodically. Since the growth of information technology and the dynamics of the business world, external auditors have gradually shifted their focuses from periodical examination to real-time assurance. Since most internal auditors perform operational and compliance audits on continuous basis, their inputs to the external audit processes are imperative to yield high quality financial audit reports. Therefore, it is essential for the external auditors to work closely with a company's internal audit department during the course of an audit engagement. While working closely, both internal auditors and external auditors share the same concern over the implementation of computer control and information security under the real-time and continuous assurance environment when data is transferred electronically (Rezaee, Sharbatoghlie, Elam, & McMickel, 2002; Elliot, 2002; Daigle & Lampe, 2002).

The Web services provide a new paradigm of reusing and sharing available online resources. The resources provided online for reuse and sharing include not only the process logic for delivering specific functionality but also the implementation. The adoption of this new paradigm in may change the ways of auditing in several ways: (1) the service is online; (2) a new approach to solve problems; and (3) a new model of electronic business. We all aware the existence of information risk when one makes decisions under uncertainty. Such a risk may have indeed increased in an electronic business environment. For example, the bullwhip effect may exist in the supply chain, where the information could be twisted during propagation (Chopra & Meindl, 2001). Moreover, the biases of the information provider and complex data exchanges in the corporate collaboration may raise the level of information risks. To alleviate such a risk and to provide timely information to the public, all audits, including operational, compliance, and financial, have to be conducted on a continuous and real-time basis, particularly when an organization engages in collaborative commerce. Such an inter-organization arrangement leads to the need for designing access controls for auditors. The purpose of the study is to propose a model of data access control for external auditors when clients involve in the corporate collaboration.

In the next section, the study reviews the access control models and introduces the access control mechanism to auditors. Using a role-based Chinese Wall Model, the study illustrates how the access control for auditors can be implemented. Then, we demonstrate how a VMI model can be implemented under the Oracle system. Finally, conclusions and discussions are presented in the last section.

Access Control for Auditors

In an organization, there are several data security concerns. As summarized by Castano, Fugini, Martella, and Samarati (1995), these concerns can be classified into the following groups:

1. protecting data from improper access;

2. protecting confidential data that can be inferred from non-confidential data;

3. protecting data from unauthorized access that could damage the contents of the data,

4. providing for the operational integrity of the data;

5. ensuring the logical consistency of any modified data by specifying integrity constraints;

6. providing accountability and auditing;

7. identifying unique user authentication for access to the database;

8. managing sensitive data;

9. providing multilevel protection to data according to their classification; and

10. avoiding undesired information transfer between system programs.

Essentially, these concerns can be grouped into four categories of security problems (Elmasri & Navathe, 2000): (1) data security problems, such as security policy, authorization rules, legal and ethical issues; (2) information flow control problems, such as the prevention of unauthorized persons from accessing the system; (3) control of the statistical database, such as providing statistical information or summaries of values without revealing the individual information; and (4) data encryption, such as protecting sensitive data from being transmitted via communications networks. Normally, access control involves the first two categories, in other words, the data security and information flow control. Access control regulates the access privileges (read, write, run, append, etc.) that subjects (users, programs, roles, etc.) can operate on the objects (data, programs, documents, etc.) by specifying a set of access policies and a set of control procedures. The third category, control of the statistical database, allows the authorized users to access data in statistical formats, not the individual data, while data encryption focuses on the protection of data transmission.

The conventional access control models are grouped into discretionary access control models (DAC), mandatory access control models (MAC), and flow control models. As implied by the name, DAC explicitly specifies the discrepancy of subjects to objects using an access matrix. In contrast, MAC models identify the multilevel security of both subjects and objects, and the granting of access privileges is determined by the relative security levels. The most famous DAC models are the HRU (Harrison-Ruzzo-Ullman) model and Action-Entity model. The major concern for DAC is the Trojan Horse problem, which happens when an intruder uses macro facilities to gather unauthorized information, such as passwords, even though the DAC is upheld (Bosworth & Kabay, 2002). The model proposed by Bell and Lapadula in 1973 is the earliest and the most famous model in MAC (Sandhu, 1993). The model adopted multilevel security and classified both subjects and objects into different security levels. A subject cannot access an object unless its security level is dominant (higher). Unlike DAC and MAC, which manage direct access to information and which are primarily concerned with confidentiality and integrity, the flow control models make sure that higher-secured information does not flow explicitly or implicitly into less protected objects that can be easily accessed by the lower security level subjects. The well-known flow control models include the lattice model, Chinese Wall model and Role-based access model. The earliest lattice model managing information flow was proposed by Denning in 1975 and involved flow relations that are organized into classes (Sandhu, 1993). The data are allowed to flow from one class to another class explicitly or implicitly under constraints. Similarly, Chinese Wall model, proposed by Brewer and Nash in 1989, organizes the company data into mutually disjoint conflict-of-interest classes (Sandhu, 1993). Users cannot access the data of a class if they have accessed the data belongs to conflict-of-interest classes. (This model will be explained in detail later.) The role-based access control model (RBAC) is probably the most popular one for information flow control (Sandhu & Goyne, 1996; Zhang & Yang, 2002). The RBAC regulates the information flow by separating the role from the user. That is, a user is a subject to implement a job while a role is a function with authority and responsibility to execute the job. In the RBAC, the privilege to access data objects is assigned to the roles instead of the users. This provides the flexibility to assign system users to more than one role with different privileges.

Before deciding which model is the best to address the issue discussed in this study, it is important to understand the roles of internal auditors and external auditors in the U.S. business and legal environment. In the U.S., a publicly-traded company is required to establish an audit committee. An independent director in the Board of Directors chairs such a committee. Both internal and external auditors report to the chair, who has substantial experience in finance and accounting, of the audit committee. As discussed earlier, the primary responsibilities of internal auditors are to appraise the level of operational efficiency and effectiveness and evaluate the degree of compliance of a company's operations to the existing regulations. To conduct these tasks, internal auditors need to evaluate a firm's internal controls. In general, a firm's internal controls are evaluated based on whether controls in place can (1) provide reasonable assurance that the goals of each process are being achieved, (2) alleviate the risk that the enterprise will be exposed, and (3) provide reasonable assurance that certain legal obligations are being met (Gelinas & Sutton, 2002). As to the external auditors, their main duties are to assure that the company is a going-concern and to attest the reliability of a firm's set of financial statements. When recommending external auditors (an accounting firm) to the Board of Directors, the chair of the audit committee needs to ensure the external auditors are competent to conduct a high quality audit. In this regard, the appointed external auditors should demonstrate their expertise in auditing the industry to which the client belongs. To accomplish their assigned tasks, both internal and external shall have rights to request and to review the data and documents of the company (client) as well as of those companies having collaborative relationships with the client.

For the following discussion, we will focus on the functions and tasks of external auditors and illustrate how access control can be established in a collaborative commerce environment. For external auditors to conduct an audit engagement, it is common that an audit team comprises of auditors with various numbers of years of experiences. Table 1 shows the task descriptions based on the different levels and roles in a team for a typical audit engagement. According to the Generally Accepted Auditing Standards (GAAS), lower-level auditors should be closely supervised by those with higher ranks to ensure the audit quality. Given the hierarchical structure in accounting firm, an entry-level audit professional normally starts as an assistant and performs most of the detailed (and routine) audit tasks (procedures). As time passing, the level of professional knowledge and experience can be enhanced by in-house and on-job training. Thus, auditors should be gradually promoted to senior auditor, manager, and partner who have an ultimate responsibility to the audit report.

Table 1. The task descriptions of auditors based on different levels and roles in an auditing team

Staff Level	Budgetary Weight	Average Years of Experience	Primary Responsibilities
Partner	10% of budget	10+ years	• Review the overall audit work. • Meet with client and the partners of the client to discuss any unsolved issues from last year's audit. • Review audit results of current year. • Formulate opinion of this year's audit. • Draft and issue report.
Manager	10% of budget	6-10 years	• Help senior auditor to manage the audit. • Manage the relationship with the client and the partners of the client. • Propose this year's audit budget. • Appraise overall audit risk. • Estimate level of materiality. • Develop overall audit plan. • Make final assesment of interal control. • Obtain representations from management, attorneys, and others. • Review audit results. • Formulate opinion.
Senior auditor	20% of budget	3-6 years	• Coordinate the audit field work. • Propose this year's audit budget. • Perform prelimary analytical review at planning stage. • Review client's internal controls. • Determine optimal reliance on internal controls. • Design tests of the internal controls. • Design substantive test procedures. • Write/revise audit program. • Conduct post balance sheet review procedures. • Evaluate results of substantive procedures • Review audit results.
Assistant	60% of budget	0-2 years	• Perform most of the detailed audit work. • Conduct detailed tests of transactions in the accounting cycles. • Conduct detailed tests of the account balances in the accounting cycles.

In order for the external auditors to perform their jobs, the company needs to allow them to have read privileges (SELECT privilege in SQL) on all the data to the highest level. In fact, access control for the auditors is simple—the auditors must be able to read whatever data necessary to perform their duties, but auditors are not allowed to write data to the system. Since an accounting firm specializes in certain types of industries, which gives the professionals a greater advantage of gaining a deeper understanding of the client's business, the access control for the auditors is necessary when collaborative network exists. It is also likely that an accounting firm could be the auditors for multi companies in the collaborative team. Using the auditors of O_{11} in Figure 1 as an example, assume an accounting firm has expertise in a specific industry, say the IT industry, and was hired by O_{11} as the external auditor. Since the firm may have many clients, it normally groups its auditors into auditing teams. In this case, the firm that has expertise in the IT industry may have the same team worked for companies who are in the same industry, such as O_{12} to O_{11}. Again, when the auditing team performs its duties, it should have the highest privileges to read all the data in order to confirm the reliability of the financial statements. The privileges should be granted to the all the team members since a duty of proxy may be possible during the course of an audit. Moreover, the team should be granted privileges to review the data related to the collaborative activities with organizational partners. For example, assume retailer O_{11} implements the collaboration of continuous replenishment programs (CRP), which allows wholesaler O_{22} to replenish the inventory for retailer $O_{11,}$ based on the POS data of O_{11}. During the implementation, O_{22} delivers physical goods, such as scanners, to O_{11} as well as transferring essential data, such as dollar amount, cost, and date of a particular shipment to O_{11}. For the O_{11} auditor, it is necessary to check the accuracy of the data and this need is not limited to O_{11}, but also necessary to O_{22}. Therefore, the access control mechanism of O_{22} should allow the auditors of O_{11} to read the data related to O_{11} stored in O_{22}. Therefore, O_{22} should manage various access controls for the different collaborative users, including the auditors of the collaborators. Since the auditors of the collaborators have obligations to collect evidence confirming the financial statements as well as the going-concern status, they should be allowed to examine data at more than just the operational level in O_{22}. It is reasonable to assume that it may be the best interest of O_{22} not to allow all auditing team members of O_{11} to access highly sensitive data. Instead, O_{22} will only allow the higher-ranking auditors to see the secured data. For example, the senior auditor can see the data for controlling purposes and the manager or firm partners can see the data related to corporate strategies. This explains why an organization needs to have segmentation of data access for the auditors.

For managing access control, the corporate data can be divided into two categories, general data and confidential data. Examples of general data are product specifications with performance indices, new product development plans, pro forma financial statements and analyses, updates and announcements, management discussions and analyses, and so on. Only the other hand, confidential (proprietary) data are available to the members of specific communities, such as the buyer or supplier communities, but not to the public. Data can be divided further into operational data, control data, and strategic data. The operational data record the daily operations of the company and are only available to specific collaborators. The control data maintain the data for operational control and financial control. The data are normally aggregated and are presented in a statistical format, such as the reviewer can see the statistics, but not the individual data. Examples of control data include rejection rates of products, inventory checks, and others. The data are only open to senior members. The strategic data are highly abstract and can be used to depict the future direction of the company. This data is normally maintained in the form of documents and is only available to the highest executives. Therefore, different types of data should be managed by different access control polices (refer to Figure 2).

Figure 2. A role-based Chinese Wall model with different access control polices for four different types of data

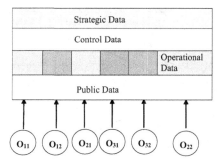

Role-Based Chinese Wall Model for Auditors

To maintain various access control policies for the auditors of collaborators, a role-based Chinese Wall model that integrating a Chinese Wall policy and a role-based access model is used. The role-based Chinese Wall model uses discretionary control (DAC) to moderate the general data level modified Chinese Wall model which manages the confidential data at operational, control and strategy levels. Note that Trojan Horses should not be of concern to the model since the auditors have read-only privileges. That is, they have no privileges to write any data to the system. In general, the data at the control level are managed by a statistical database and the data at a strategic level are managed by a document system.

The Chinese Wall model was derived from the British law for stockbrokers consulting different firms (Sandhu, 1993). The policy prevents information from flowing to the consultants who belong to groups having a conflict-of-interest (COI). The dynamic assignment of consultants was changed to the affiliated workers of an organization to solve the decentralized workflow problem (see Atluri, Chun, & Mazzoleni, 2001). Since the workflow depends on the flows, tasks, and objects, the study distributes the workflow across the organization without violating the dependency rules. In the design, the data are categorized as sensitive data and nonsensitive data. The sensitive data of one company cannot be read, evaluated, nor written by workers who belong to different companies of a COI group.

The privileges are assigned according to roles, not users, in the role-base security model. This assignment provides better flexibility and is a better reflection of real-world implementation. The role-based Chinese Wall model should consider roles, users, permissions, constraints, and role-hierarchy. The relationships between roles and users are many-to-many. The constraint limits the privileges assigned to roles and the role

Figure 3. The access control procedure in the role-based Chinese Wall model for auditors

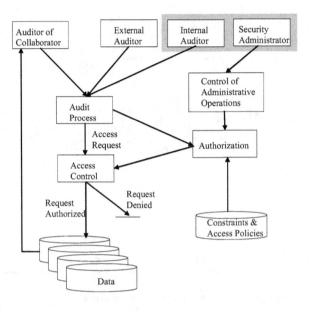

hierarchy structures the roles to reflect an organization's assignment of authorization and responsibility.

In summary, the role-based Chinese Wall model integrates the advantages of both the Chinese Wall model and the role-based model. Figure 3 shows the authorization process for the authorizing of the auditors. The audit requests issued by an auditor will be checked against the constraints and access policies. An auditor can access the data only if a privilege is granted. The *subjects* are the auditors who have read privileges only. The subject can read all the data maintained by its clients, but only a part of the data maintained by the client's collaborators. The subjects can serve any of the companies in the collaborative network, including the client's competitors. The *objects* are the data stored by the organizations, including transactional data, document files, audio/video files, programs, and statistics. The *access mode* of the subject is the read privilege to the data. The auditor has the highest security level, but is limited to read privileges, unlike the system administrator. However, the data of an organization are protected from the auditors of collaborators based on the access control mechanism. Again, only a read privilege is given. Moreover, such privileges are granted based on two principles, (1) the auditors of the collaborators should not be able to read detailed information belongs to other collaborators, and (2) the auditors of the collaborators are allowed to read data with different degrees of sensitivity based on their seniority.

The Chinese Wall policy puts the data into mutually disjoint classes, in which the auditing teams of the collaborative partners can only access the data related to their own organization. An *access matrix* is used to maintain the privileges of subjects against the objects. Notice that the subject in the matrix is the role of the auditors, not the users. The roles include all roles in the role hierarchy, in other words, partners, managers, senior auditors, and assistants. Since auditors have only read privileges, there is no ownership problem, and privilege propagation is not allowed, either.

Using VMI as an Example

This section uses vendor-managed inventories (VMI) to illustrate how the access control can be implemented in a corporate collaboration. The implementation platform is the Oracle database management system. Since the VMI allows the suppliers to manage the inventory of their buyers, a part of the data in the buyers' databases should be accessible by the suppliers so that the suppliers can manage the inventory promptly and properly. To do the auditing task, the auditors of the suppliers should be allowed to access the data owned and managed by the buyers. The following will use the tasks of the senior auditor, manager, partner, and assistant to illustrate the duty and access controls.

Senior Auditor

Using the relationship between O_{22} and O_{31} in Figure 1 as an example, an auditor-in-charge (senior auditor) of O_{31} needs to establish a clear understanding of the internal controls and be aware of whether there are changes in the business activities of the collaborator, O_{22}. Therefore, to obtain this understanding, the auditor-in-charge of O_{31} should first read last year's working papers and evaluate whether any major changes have been made that may affect key areas in the inventory management of O_{22}, and hence need special attention. For example, if there are major advancements in technology which could cause the knowledge of O_{22} to be obsolete, the auditor needs to discuss these issues with O_{22} before moving on to a test of controls or a test of details. The auditor-in-charge should also conduct some analytical procedures, cross-sectional and/or time series analysis, on O_{22}'s financial data (e.g., compare this year's ending inventory with last year's figures, compare the relationship with total sales, or cost of goods sold to see whether these ratios are reasonable). When evaluating whether the relationship between inventory items is reasonable, the auditor needs to develop benchmarks for comparisons. Some relationships between financial and nonfinancial data are also important.

The auditor-in-charge should coordinate with the personnel of O_{22}, such as the internal audit department, for the current year's audit. During the coordination with the internal auditing department personnel of O_{22}, some activities can be assigned to the internal auditors of O_{22}. For example, internal auditors can prepare a list of inventory items at year-end, or identify whether there are consignments that may have been mistakenly included

Table 2. Audit responsibilities and tasks in an inventory cycle

Level	Major Audit Tasks Performed
Partners	o Evaluate the possible threats from external forces (competition, technological advancement, obsolete inventory) which may cause problems to a going-concern. o Evaluate whether the client's R&D activities are sufficient to sustain the level of competition in the industry. o Evaluate whether the client's strategic alliance is strong enough to meet the external forces in the industry. o Evaluate the validity of the assumptions made by the client regarding its business risks and financial risks. o Evaluate whether the design of the control framework established by the client adequately addresses the business and financial risks. o Evaluate whether the client has sufficient control to monitor and react to the significant risks in order to achieve its strategic intent. o Determine the overall effects of the client's strategy on audit. o Evaluate whether there are proper links between strategic, control and operating activities that result in a reliable set of financial statements. o Determine the sufficiency of audit evidence to support audit opinions.
Managers	o Understand the client's business philosophy and detail, and assess the appropriateness of the management processes. o Evaluate the client's internal control framework. o Evaluate the client's detailed monitoring process. o Evaluate the client's underlying accounting choices and financial statement disclosures. o Understand client's estimates and valuations. o Determine whether the client's estimates and valuations properly reflect the client's business risk and financial risks. o Determine how the client's strategic intents and control framework affect the company's operating activities. o Establish a level of materiality for audit testing. o Assess whether there is additional audit work, related to the client's business process and transactions, not in the original audit plan, that needs to be conducted.
Senior s (In charge)	o Establish a clear understanding of the relationship between the client's internal controls and its business activities. o Review last year's working papers to identify key areas for planning and focusing on the current year's audit. o Conduct audit planning. o Coordinate with the client's personnel, such as the internal audit department, for the current year's audit. o Assign audit tasks to the audit team. o Document the client's internal control framework and activities using DFD. o Assess the strengths and weaknesses of client's internal controls. o Revise the internal control questionnaires to evaluate the control framework and processes. o Determine the level of reliance on the client's internal controls. o Design sampling plan and determine the proper sampling methods. o Identify benchmarks for comparisons. o Build relationships between financial and non-financial data. o Perform analytical procedures (cross-sectional and time series) on client's financial data. o Evaluate whether it is necessary to adjust the level of materiality and its effect on the budget and audit tasks. o Review working papers prepared by audit team members and clients.

Table 2. continued

Senior s (In charge)	o Review working papers prepared by audit team members and clients.
	o Communicate and discuss with the client's management any issues encountered during the auditing processes.
	o Review working papers completed by assistants to ensure audit quality.
Staffs (assistants)	o Update the client's DFD from the last audit period.
	o Test of internal controls based on the client's internal control framework and control activities documented in DFD.
	o Complete the internal control questionnaires.
	o Conduct audit sampling based on the acceptable audit risk, inherent risk and control risk.
	o Report the results of the tests of controls to in-charge auditors.
	o Print listing of off-premises inventory for confirmation, and print confirmations.
	o Conduct physical counts of the client's inventory.
	o Tally perpetual inventory records in descending order by dollar amount to select target items for test counting.
	o Access and print year-end receipts and shipments for agreement with cutoff information with cutoff information obtained during the physical inventory observations.
	o Trace details in perpetual records to machine-readable source documents (e.g., receiving reports, production records etc.).
	o Verify footing, cross-footing, and extensions of final priced inventory and/or perpetual accounting records.
	o Trace details in final priced inventory to perpetual inventory records.
	o Select inventory items for price testing using internally stored random number generators and perpetual inventory records.
	o Perform price tests.
	o Compare charges/credits in perpetual records with purchases/sales master files.
	o Examine the condition of the inventory and determine whether inventories are obsolete.
	o Merge physical inventory counts with perpetual inventory records.

into the inventory records of O_{22}. The internal auditors can also assist the external auditors to identify whether there are slow-moving items in the inventory.

Then, the auditor-in-charge of O_{31} will assign audit tasks to the audit team members. It is typical for detailed testing of inventory, such as inventory observations (i.e., taking a physical count of inventory at the end of year) and some price-testing tasks to be assigned to less experienced auditors. The senior auditor documents and updates the client information system using a DFD (data flow diagram) and identifies whether there are weaknesses/problems in the internal controls of O_{22} following a control framework and a system flowchart. This assessment should based on control objectives, such as the ACID test (accounting, custody of assets, independent review, and decision-making authority), which are then used to determine the types of errors that may occur if the internal controls are not followed by the personnel of O_{22}. Then auditor-in-charge should also determine whether the control procedures of O_{22}, as they are currently implemented, are sufficient to assure the integrity of the internal controls.

While assessing the strengths and weaknesses of the internal controls of O_{22}, the auditor-in-charge will use an internal control questionnaire to go over the key areas of the controls. Such a questionnaire is subject to revision after the assessment of the control framework described in the previous paragraph. At the end of this process, the auditor-in-charge should determine whether the internal controls of O_{22} are reliable. With a clear understanding of the internal controls, a senior auditor is responsible for designing a sampling plan and for determining the proper sampling methods. The auditor-in-charge also needs to supervise the sampling process to make sure that the assistants have drawn the samples according to the sampling plan. Of course, the discrepancies form controls, which should be clearly defined so that the assistants can decide whether certain procedures are not strictly followed.

Based on the results of the test of internal controls, the auditor-in-charge needs to evaluate whether it is necessary to adjust the level of materiality and determine the level of the effect of the internal controls on the budget. Since additional tasks may be needed for an O_{22} with weak internal controls, the auditor-in-charge should also adjust the engagement budget so that additional audit tasks can be conducted. The senior auditor is also responsible for reviewing the working papers prepared by the audit team members and O_{22} and communicating and discussing with the O_{22} management any issues encountered during the auditing processes. A detailed description of the audit tasks is provided in Table 2.

To implement the role-base Chinese Wall model in a VMI, the system will have roles, users, auditing activities, and privileges granting. Note that both discretionary access control and mandatory access control are allowed in Oracle. However, the mandatory access control, conforming to U.S. B1 TCSEC criteria and the E3 assurance level for the European ITSEC standard, only works on operating systems with similar security standards, not on the World Wide Web (Muller, 1999). Therefore, the following will mainly use the discretionary access control functions of Oracle for demonstration purposes. The privileges of the discretionary access control of Oracle are INSERT, DELETE, SELECT, UPDATE, REFERENCE, and USAGE. The privileges can be granted to either roles or users, where the roles are a named collection of privileges and the users are authorization identifiers, called *user name* in Oracle. Different privileges are assigned to different roles, and then the roles are assigned to users. In this study, as in most similar designs, a user represents a human being, in other words, an auditor. Oracle provides several default roles when the database is built, CONNECT, RESOURCE, DBA (version 6 and after), SYSDBA, SYSOPER, EXP_FULL_DATABASE, IMP_FULL_DATABASE (version 7.1.6 and after), DELETE_CATALOG_ROLE, EXECUTE_CATALOG_ROLE, SELECT_CATALOG_ROLE (version 8 and after), and PUBLIC. The privileges of these default roles are to the system, not the data objects. Therefore, the database administrators should create the auditor roles them-selves. For example, to create the roles of a senior auditor and an assistant auditor for O_{31} by O_{22} the commands are:

```
CREATE ROLE Assistant_O₃₁;
CREATE ROLE Senior_O₃₁;
```

We can also grant roles to roles to form a role hierarchy. For example, the privileges of assistants are granted to senior auditors using the command:

```
GRANT Assistant_O₃₁ TO Senior_O₃₁;
```

In this way the privilege of *Assistant_O$_{31}$* can also be propagated to *Senior_O$_{31}$*. In Oracle, some user accounts are automatically created, sys, system, dbsnmp, scott, demo, and po8. The default user accounts are mainly created for testing and demonstration purposes. They should be removed or renamed after the system installation is fully installed. For example, to create a user *Mary* with password *hamster* for O$_{31}$ in O$_{22}$ the commands are:

CREATE USER Mary
IDENTIFIED BY hamster
DEFAULT TABLESPACE users
TEMPORARY TABLESPACE temp;

Oracle provides *view* to present data retrieved from one or more tables without storing it. It is a good mechanism for managing data security since the view encapsulates the references to the tables used. Moreover, the row-level security, specifying the qualification in the *WHERE* clause in SQL, can limit the results so that they only appear to the authorized person (Theriault & Heney, 1998). The constraints, such as the Chinese Wall model, can be applied to view by simply setting up disjoint views for roles belong to different organizations and hierarchies. For example, to sample the transfers of raw materials from internal controls, a senior auditor can trace approved materials requisitions, transfer to work-in-process perpetual records, compare quantities and unit costs, and summarize the transfer entries in the general ledger control accounts.

Again, it should be noted, that most of the control data are only revealed to the collaborator in a statistical form if the data includes more than one collaborator. An example of a view, created in Oracle, for the senior auditor of O$_{31}$ in O$_{22}$ to see product name, averaged sales quantity, averaged sale price, and unit cost is:

```
CREATE OR REPLACE VIEW con_O3 AS
SELECT p.product_name, avg(s.sales_quantity), avg(s.sales_price), p.unit_cost
FROM sales s, product p, supplier b
WHERE p.product_name = b.product_sell
AND  s.product_num=p.product_num
AND b.rank='senior' AND b.organization='O_31'
AND b.employee_num IN
(SELECT employee_num
FROM employee
WHERE loging_name =user);
```

Note that the additional attribute, *loging_name* of employee, is added into the employee table for access control purposes.

There are other roles in the auditing team of O$_{31}$, such as managers, firm partners, and assistant auditors. Both the managers and firm partners are responsible for evaluating the strategic plan of the collaborators.

Manager

Since the managers are the most experienced audit assistants (all audit professionals who have not yet reached the partner level are assistants according to GAAS), their responsibilities are to understand the business philosophy of O_{22} and to assess the appropriateness of the management processes. For instance, an audit manager could be the individual, except the audit partner, in the engagement team who have knowledge of the best practices in the industry and understand what are the industry norms. An audit manager should be in the position to evaluate the full picture of the competition and be ready to identify possible solutions for O_{22} in dealing with financial and business risks. In addition, the audit manager of O_{31} needs to evaluate the internal control framework of O_{22} and assess whether O_{22} has a proper (sufficient), detailed monitoring process of internal controls. In particular, the manager should understand whether the information systems of O_{22} are sophisticated enough to support the intended internal controls.

Where the financial statements are concerned, an audit manager is responsible for evaluating the underlying accounting choices and the financial statement disclosures of O_{22}. By assessing the accounting choices, the manager gauges whether the accounting choices made truthfully represent the company's economic activities and the industry norms. Financial disclosures should be sufficient so that the users of the financial statements are able to retrieve the underlying economic activities. In addition, the management of O_{22} also makes numerous estimates and valuations of its inventories. The audit manager should discuss these issues with the proper personnel of O_{22}. An audit manager also needs to determine whether the estimates and valuations of O_{22} properly reflect the business risks and financial risks of O_{22}.

Finally, the manager should determine how a client's strategic intents and control framework affect the company's operating activities and concurrently determine the level of materiality for audit testing. An audit manager assesses whether there is an additional audit work, not in the original audit plan, relating to the business process and transactions of O_{22} that needs to be carried out.

Partner

What the partners are concerned about is whether the opinion expressed by the accounting firm truly represents the financial condition of the client, and that there is no immediate risk to the going-concern of the client (i.e., the client is not headed for bankruptcy). To ensure that the possibility of bankruptcy is very low, a partner needs to discuss with the client's top management, including the internal audit department, the possible threats from external forces (competition, technological advancement, and inventory obsolete). Moreover, the partner will pay attention to evaluating whether the client's R&D activities are sufficient to sustain the level of competition in the industry. This assessment is critical, particularly for clients who are engaged in complex, dynamic, and technology sensitive industries. Many clients will leverage their strategic alliance (partners) to ensure they are strong enough to meet the external forces in the industry. The audit partner also evaluates the validity of the assumptions made by the client regarding its business risks and financial risks. Since fraudulent activities may occur, due to poorly designed internal controls, the audit partner may discuss these issues with the client's management, the head of the internal audit department, and the chair of audit committee (an independent director on the board). While assessing these risks (concerns), the partner also evaluates whether the client has sufficient controls to monitor and react to any significant risks in order to achieve its strategic intent.

Many accounting firms take a strategic view in determining the overall effects of the client's strategy on the client's business activities, and the auditors need to evaluate whether there are proper links between strategic, control and operating activities that result in a reliable set of financial statements. Before rendering an audit opinion, the audit partner also determines whether the audit evidence is sufficient to support the intended audit opinion.

The information for strategic planning is normally maintained in a document format, which is managed by the document system (Eloff, Holbien, & Teufel, 1996). To build a view for both the audit manager and audit partner to see these strategic documents of O_{22}, the following statement is required:

```
CREATE OR REPLACE VIEW str_O AS
SELECT strategy_document.content_name, strategy_document.content
FROM strategy_document, supplier
WHERE strategy_document.access_list =supplier.name
AND supplier.rank='manager'AND supplier.organization='O_31'
AND supplier.employee_num IN
(SELECT employee_num
FROM employee
WHERE loging_name =user);
```

Assistant

The audit assistant is the person who performs the detail work of an audit. Based on the assignments given by the senior auditor in charge, the assistants conduct an audit sampling based on the acceptable audit risk (calculated based on the audit risk model which includes inherent risk, control risk, and detection risk). According to the results of the test, the assistants will tally the discrepancies and make projections about the population (cost of goods sold, finished goods inventory, etc.) and report the results to the senior auditor-in-charge. Assistants also are responsible for conducting inventory observation (i.e., counting inventory) under the supervision of senior auditor-in-charge. The inventory observation is arranged by mutual agreement between the in-charge auditor and the management of O_{22}, as discussed before. Before conducting these procedures, assistant auditors should obtain a list of the inventory items (without quantity) and distinguish whether the items are on or off the premises. For the off-premises inventory, arrangements can be made with a reliable third party to count the inventory on behalf of the engagement auditors. If items are currently on consignment with other entities (such as 7-Eleven sells products on commission for Pepsi), confirmations of the inventory should be sent to verify the existence and quantity of the products.

While conducting physical counts, the quantity information of the client's inventory is available on the firm's perpetual inventory records. Assistants need to make sure they have good internal controls on inventory movements while they are conducting the inventory observation, especially movement between O_{31} and O_{22}. In other words, all movements, in or out, should be recorded for reconciliation purposes. Assistants also need to make sure that all items counted belong to O_{22} (i.e., there are no consignments made by outside parties to the audit client).

Assistants need to print year-end receipts and shipments for reconciliation with the cutoff information obtained during the physical inventory observations. Upon completion of the inventory observations, the assistants are required to trace the details in the perpetual records to machine-readable source documents, such as receiving reports, production records, and so on. In addition, a price list of inventory records is also important to verify the value of the inventory. Using quantity from inventory observations and price information on the client's internal records, assistants can verify the quality by footing (i.e., adds up) and extension (multiplying) of the final priced inventory and/or the perpetual accounting records. Assistants also need to trace the details of the final priced inventory in the perpetual inventory record.

To test the validity and completeness of the price listing, the assistants need to randomly select inventory items from O_{22} for price testing using internally stored random number generators and perpetual inventory records. Finally, the auditors should compare the charges/credits in the perpetual records with the purchases/sales master files for possible returns and discounts. Finally, the auditors need to randomly examine the condition of the inventory and determine whether any of the inventory is obsolete. For example, to sample purchases of raw materials, compare the quantities and unit costs from vendor invoices with perpetual inventory records, a view can be created for the assistant auditor of O_{31} in O_{22} to see product name, quantity, and price.

```
CREATE OR REPLACE VIEW inv_O31 AS
SELECT p.product_name, p.product_qualtity, p.product_price
FROM   product p, supplier b
WHERE p.product_name = b.product_sell
AND b.organization='O31'
AND b.employee_num IN
(SELECT employee_num
FROM employee
WHERE loging_name =user);
```

The data dictionary views provided by Oracle can also be used for security purposes. For example, ROLE_ROLE_PRIVS can be used to observe the roles granted to roles; ROLE_SYS_PRIVS shows the system privilege granted to roles; ROLE_TAB_PRIVS provides the information about tables granted to roles; USER_ROLE_PRIVS maintains the

Table 3. A role-object access matrix manages the access rights granted to the collaborators in O_{22}. Note—√: the SELECT priviledge to the views.

Role Name/ View Name	pub_O_1	pub_O_2	pub_O_3	inv_O_{11}	inv_O_{12}	inv_O_{21}	inv_O_{31}	inv_O_{32}	con_O_1	con_O_2	con_O_3	str_O
Assistant O_{11}	√			√								
Senior O_{11}	√			√					√			
Manager O_{11}	√			√					√			√
Partner O_{11}	√			√					√			√
Assistant O_{12}	√				√							
Senior O_{12}	√				√				√			
Manager O_{12}	√				√				√			√
Partner O_{12}	√				√				√			√
Assistant O_{21}		√				√						
Senior O_{21}		√				√				√		√
Manager O_{21}		√				√				√		√
Partner O_{21}		√				√				√		√
Assistant O_{31}			√				√					
Senior O_{31}			√				√				√	√
Manager O_{31}			√				√				√	√
Partner O_{31}			√				√				√	√
Assistant O_{32}			√					√				
Senior O_{32}			√					√			√	√
Manager O_{32}			√					√			√	√
Partner O_{32}			√					√			√	√

information about roles granted to users, etc. To see the roles granted to users and other roles, the following query can be issued:

```
SELECT *
FROM dba_role_privs;
```

After creating a view, it should be granted to the role.

```
GRANT SELECT ON inv_O_{31} To Assistant_O_{31};
```

It should be noticed that since the role *Assistant_O$_{31}$* has been granted to *Senior_O$_{31}$* to form a role-hierarchy, the senior auditors, having the privileges of *Senior_O$_{31}$*, could also access *inv_O$_{31}$*. Then, the users who implement the auditing work should be assigned the role.

```
GRANT Assistant_O_{31} TO Mary;
```

Finally, a role-object access matrix can be used to manage the access rights granted to the collaborators, as shown in Table 3. The matrix should be carefully designed, maintained, and examined regularly.

Conclusion

When a company has collaborative relationships with other organizations, the appropriate design of data access controls is important. This is particularly true in the Web service arena. The access controls should specify various control policies to collaborators for different purposes. Depending on the type of collaboration, the access controls can be very complicated. For example, if the collaboration is on product development, the access control on the product definition data should includes intricate formats of read and write privileges. However, the access control for auditors is relatively straightforward, read-only privileges are given. The access control for the auditor to the client data is the highest read privilege since all data are subject to audit. When the company forms a collaborative network with collaborators, the access control should consider giving different access control policies to the auditors of different collaborators. This study demonstrates a role-based Chinese Wall model which organizes the corporate data into four different types of control groups using different access control policies. In short, the general data is maintained by DAC while the operational data, control data (normally presented in statistical form), and strategic data (normally presented as documents) are managed by the role-based Chinese Wall model. A thorough discussion of the auditing tasks of senior auditors, managers, partners, and assistants illustrated in the VMI is provided. Finally, Oracle is used to demonstrate the feasibility of implementing the model.

Reference

Atluri, V., Chun, S. A., & Mazzoleni, P. (2001, November 6-8) A Chinese Wall Security Model for decentralized workflow. In *Proceedings of the 8th ACM Conference on Computer and Communications Security (CCS '01),* Philadelphia (pp. 48-57). ACM Press.

Bosworth, S., & Kabay, M. E. (2002). *Computer security handbook* (4th ed.). Danvers, MA: John Wiley & Sons.

Castano, S., Fugini, M., Martella, G., & Samarati, P. (1995). *Database security.* Harlow, UK: Addison-Wesley Longman Limited.

Chopra, S., & Meindl, P., (2001). *Supply chain management: Strategy, planning, and operation.* Upper Saddle River, NJ: Prentice Hall.

Daigle, R., & Lampe, J. (2002, September/October). Continuous online assurance: Expanding internal audit's scope. *Internal Auditing, 17*(5), 8-17.

Elliott, R. (2002), Twenty-First Century Assurance. *Auditing: A Journal of Practice & Theory, 21*(1), 139-146.

Elmasri, R., & Navathe, S. (2000). *Fundamentals of database systems* (3rd ed.). Reading MA: Addison-Wesley.

Eloff, J. H. P., Holbein, R., & Teufel, S. (1996). Security classification for documents. *Computers & Security, 15*(1), 55-71.

Gelinas, U., & Sutton, S. (2002). *Accounting information systems* (5th ed.). Cincinnati, OH: South-Western, Thomson Learning.

Muller, R. (1999). *Oracle developer starter kit.* Berkeley, Osborne: McGraw-Hill.

Rezaee, Z. A, Sharbatoghlie, A. R., Elam, R., & McMickle, P. (2002). Continuous auditing: Building automated auditing capability. *Auditing: A Journal of Practice & Theory, 21*(1), 147-163.

Sandhu, R. S. (1993, November). Lattice-based access control models. *IEEE Computer, 26*(11), 9-19.

Sandhu, R. S., & Goyne, E. J. (1996, February). Role-based access control models. *IEEE Computer, 29*(2), 38-47.

Theriault, M., & Heney, W. (1998). *Oracle security.* Sebastopol, CA: O'Reilly.

Zhang, C., & Yang, C. (2002). Information flow analysis on role-based access control model. *Information Management & Computer Security, 10*(5), 225-236.

Endnote

[1]   The short version of this chapter was presented in IRMA2006 in Washington, DC, USA.

Chapter XI

Semantics and the Medical Healthcare Search

Amanda Spink, Queensland University of Technology, Australia

Robert M. Wolfe, Northwestern University, USA

Bernard J. Jansen, The Pennsylvania State University, USA

Abstract

This chapter discusses issues related to semantics and the medical Web. Much health information is available on the Web, but not always effectively found by users. Studies examining various aspects of medical Web searching show that searchers' do not always use correct medical terminology. This chapter reports results from a longitudinal study of medical/health related searches using commercial Web search engine query data from 1997 to 2004.

Introduction

Web studies are a major interdisciplinary area of research, including user behavior modeling and Web search engine performance (Spink & Jansen, 2004). Since the 1990s Web search engine crawling and retrieving studies have evolved as an important area of Web research.

The Web also provides growing opportunities for people to learn more about medical and health. This chapter provides an overview of the research into the current state of Web searching for medical/health. A major problem for the Web and medical industry, and medical consumers, is the effective access to health care information. There exist a growing number of identified problems in managing the complex relationships inherent in medical semantics and the semantic Web (Berners-Lee, Hendler, & Lassila, 2001). In the U.S., The National Library of Medicine's (NLM) long-range plan includes the need to promote the use of health information by both the public and health professionals. The NLM influences the public indirectly by making current authoritative information available. Their proposed strategy may narrow the knowledge gap between consumers and health professionals. Identifying the use of controlled medical terminology by commercial Web search engines user is inherently useful for training programs, access portals, and scalable information resources that are accessible to people of disparate cultures, languages, and knowledge levels. The use of evidence-based medicine in US healthcare means the need to educate consumers within the health care system.

As we move towards more effective medical/health information access via the Web, we need to know more about consumer use of the medical Web: how are they searching and how often? Medical and health information seeking constitutes an important use of the Web. The Pew Internet Project (2002a, 2002b) one of the largest national surveys accomplished to date, estimates that 62% of Internet users (some 73 million people living in the United States) search the Web for health information. Results from the Pew study indicated that 93% of health information seekers surveyed looked for information about a specific illness or condition, 65% sought information on exercise, nutrition or weight control, 64% for prescription drugs, and 33% for sensitive health information. More than half the respondents reported using the Web for health information every few months or less frequently. Clearly, many American are using the Web for medical and health information, often as a supplement to seeking help from medical providers.

However, Phillipov, and Phillips (2003) recently reported that health queries accounted for fewer than 1% of the top 300 queries on the Internet (excluding pornography), and they concluded that information on both general health and specific disorders have a very low priority for people using Internet search engines. We believed that the authors' methods failed to account for the magnitude and variety of Internet searches, and thus did not give an accurate estimate of the overall number of health-related Internet searches performed in the sample time period. To address this, we analyzed the frequency of use of Web search-engine keywords for health-related subject matter in several large databases of Web queries from the Excite and AltaVista search engines.

In the next section of the chapter we first provide an overview of the recent research studies examining medical/health Web searching.

Related Studies

Web search studies are growing in importance. The Pew Internet and American Life Project (2005) recently showed that many people do not understand Web search engines capabilities. Some 84.1% of people online use a Web search engine every month to find information. According to the Pew Internet Study Web searching is also the second most popular online activity, behind e-mail (Pew Internet and American Life Project, 2005).

Medical use of the Web is increasing among physicians as well as consumers. A study by Chen and Siu, (2001) found that Internet searching for medical information was common among Canadian cancer patients. A recent study by the American Medical Association (2002) reported an increase in the use of the Internet by physicians. Patients further seek medical advice from physicians via email (Borowitz & Wyatt, 1998; Speilberg, 1998) and from the Web (Ferguson, 1998; O'Connor & Johanson, 2000). As both patients and providers begin to share common information, this may become the basis for shared communication and decision-making as well. In addition to seeking factual or general information on medical and health issues, people may use Web search engines to seek advice on personal problems, where related queries may be very detailed and solicit specific medical or health information.

In this growing shared decision making medical environment, the quality of Web-based information retrieved by the patient becomes of growing importance to the provider (Impicciatore, Pandolfini, Casella, & Bonati, 1997). Many studies have examined aspects of consumer-health related Web use, including Web sites and electronic lists (Barnas & Kahn, 1999; Jones et al., 2001; McCray et al., 2000; Pandolfini, 2002; Rozic-Hristovski, Hristovski, & Todorovski, 2000).

Studies have evaluated the accuracy, quality, and reliability of medical information on the Web (European Commission Information Society, 2001; Fallis & Fricke, 2002; McLeod, 1998; Pandolfini, 2002). McCray, Loane, Browne, and Bangalore (1998) studied users' queries on the National Library of Medicine Web site. Some 94% of terms submitted were medical terms covering a broad range of medical topics. Many medical terms were misspelled and most medical queries were short (less than four words). Many users also asked specific questions whose complexity went beyond the scope of the general public portal of the National Library of Medicine (NLM) Web site.

Medical Web site quality is being tested through the URAC (http://webapps.urac.org/websiteaccreditation/default.htm) accreditation process, "health on the Net" logo program, and the HI Ethics project. As part of the European Union's eEurope: Health Online actions, Member State representatives and experts have agreed to establish a set of guidelines for quality criteria for health-related Web sites. Such criteria are designed to increase user confidence in the use of such sites and foster best practices in the development of sites. However, whether these criteria are practical or usable, or even do more harm than good, is not known (Jadad & Gagliardi, 1998).

Medical/Health Related Searching

Researchers have studied users' medical searching and information retrieval (IR) within complex abstracting systems such as MEDLINE (Hersh et al., 2002). Hersh and Hickham (1999) found that medical and nurse practitioner students were moderately successful at answering clinical questions correctly when searching MEDLINE. In the Web context, Eysenbach and Kohler (2002) found that for 21 consumer Web users, searching for health information was suboptimal, but users nevertheless found health information successfully. Atlas (2001) found that first-year medical students reported that general Web search engines produced better results than meta-medical Web sites and medicine-specific search engines. Many researchers have called for a new generation of Web-based medical information retrieval tools (Rogers, 2000; Suarez, Hao, Chang, & Masys, 1997).

Studies on health information seeking on the Web also indicate that lay terminology is only partly successful for effective searches that locate useful health (Bin & Li, 2001), and often yields misleading or unrelated information for the lay health consumer. Berland, Elliot, Morales, Algazy, Kravits, and Broder (2002) likewise concluded that accessing health information using search engines and a simple search term was not efficient, since high reading levels are required to comprehend Web-based health information.

McLeod (1998) summarized the limitations of the Web as an electronic consumer resource: "while immediate access to such information has been of great benefit to health care professionals and patients, there is growing concern that a substantial proportion of clinical information on the Web might be inaccurate, erroneous, misleading, or fraudulent, and thereby pose a threat to public health…" (McLeod, 1998). For example, a study by Bichakjian, Schwartz, Wang, Hall, Johnson, and Bierman (2002) found that, of 74 Internet sites containing information about melanoma, found using general Internet search engines, the majority lacked complete basic melanoma information and 14% of the sites contained inaccuracies.

Often, then, the Web-enabled health information seeker must know, within the realm of language, the near-specific location of the knowledge they seek. When an exact clinical term is not known, most laypersons will resort to their only available resource, the popular/lay terminology for the concept, illness, or subject of interest. While the capacity of the patient to gather and collect such information remains a matter for the clinician to assess, it is undeniable that Internet-derived information can serve as a powerful catalyst for seeking health services (Faxon & Lenhant, 2001; Muhlhauser & Berger, 2000; Rivera, Kim, Garone, Morgenstern, & Mohsenifar, 2001).

Recent studies by and Spink, Jansen, Wolfram and Saracevic (2001) and Spink and Jansen (2004) show that users general Web search engine sessions are usually short and contain few search terms or queries. Medical and health related topics generated approximately 9.5% of Excite Web searches in 1997, 7.8% in 1999 and 7.5% in 2001. Spink and Ozmutlu (2002) found that 11.5% of Ask Jeeves question queries were medical- or health-related.

Spink et al., (2004) also found also that a small proportion of searching on commercial Web search engines, in the United States and Europe, are medical or health related. Despite the large percentage of Internet users who conduct medical or health searchers reported by the Pew Internet Project survey, examination of large-scale commercial Web query logs suggest that medical or health Web searching is a small proportion of Web searches on general search engines. This finding suggests an ongoing shift in Web users' search topics. From 1997 to 2001, queries related to entertainment or recreation and medicine or health, have declined proportionally as the queries related to e-commerce, travel, employment or economy and people, places, or things have increased. This proportional shift may also reflect a shift by Web users to more specialized medical or health Web sites, such as WebMD, and a shift towards more e-commerce Web sites and Web searching.

In this chapter we report findings from a large-scale study of medical and health related Web querying on different commercial Web search engines. These results are also compared to previous findings from Spink, Jansen, Wolfram and Saracevic (2002) and Spink et al. (2004) who examined medical and health query trends from 1997 to 2001.

To further address the issue of medical/health Web searching the next sections of the chapter outlines our research goals and research design.

Research Goals

The major research goal of our study was to assess the state of medical/health Web searching. Our specific research goals were to examine:

1. The proportion of Web searches related to medical/health related issues.
3. Implications for the semantic Web and more effective medical Web search.
4. Areas for future research

Research Design

Data Collection

We analyzed the following user Web query data, including sessions, queries, and terms.

The queries we used for this research were submitted to two major Web search engines, on four separate dates over a five year period. Three of the transactions logs are from Excite, each holding a large and varied set of queries. The transaction logs spanned several hours of user searching on the following dates: September 16, 1997 (Tuesday, midnight to 8 a.m.), December 1, 1999 (Wednesday, 9 a.m. to 1 p.m.), and April 30, 2001 (Monday, midnight to midnight). The fourth transaction log is from the AltaVista search engine, collected on September 8, 2002 (Sunday, midnight to midnight). Each transaction log record contains a variety of fields, including the query exactly as entered by the user.

Data Analysis

The combined set of transaction logs contained over four million queries, which was too many for qualitative analysis. Therefore, we utilized only those queries that occurred more than four times, resulting in just under a million queries. We qualitatively analyzed approximately 35,000 of these queries, evaluating each query as either health-related or not. Using the queries annotated as health-related, we then extracted all identical queries from all four transactions logs, culling a subset of queries pertaining to health and health-related information using a modified snowball sampling technique.

More specifically, we started with several seed terms (i.e., health, medical, illness) that are central indicators of health-related searching. Using this set of terms, we extracted all records from the transaction logs that contained these terms. We then reviewed the extracted records identifying other terms that frequently appeared. These new terms were then combined with the set of original terms, and from the original transaction log we extracted all records that contained these terms.

We repeated the process until the addition of new terms to the set added less than 10 new queries. We then reviewed all the queries extracted to ensure they were health-related. We also extracted several thousand queries at random from each data set to identify health related queries that we may have missed, adding these to the subsets. Overall, we feel confident that the queries we extracted are solely health-related queries, and if anything we are under-counting.

Results

The key results are reported in Table 1. Our results show that health searches on the Internet account for 1.9-2.5% of all Internet queries. It should be noted that the database in our study includes all queries made, including pornographic queries, whereas Phillipov and Phillips' (2003) database excluded them. Although pornographic queries have been estimated to account for 20-25% of all Internet queries, one study of Web queries found that the category of "sex, pornography, [sex] preferences" accounted for 16.8% of all Web queries (Spink & Jansen, 2004; Spink, Jansen, Wolfram, & Saracevic, 2001).

Eysenbach and Köhler (2002) recently reported 3.5-4.5% incidence of health-related terms, which was higher than our results. The difference could be due to their selection

Table 1. Analysis of health related queries

Analysis of Health Related Queries.			
Transaction Log	Number of Queries	Health-Related Queries	Percentage of Total
Excite (1997)	107,084	2,430	2.3%
Excite (1999)	439,742	8,279	1.9%
Excite (2001)	90,604	2,278	2.5%
AltaVista (2002)	322,109	6,741	2.1%

of MetaCrawler, a relatively low-traffic search engine, and the smaller number of queries used, less than 3,000, whereas we used 35,000 queries, and larger numbers are preferred for nonparametric data. We should add that studies have shown a steady increase in the use of the Internet to access health information. For example, a recent Harris Interactive poll reported that between 2000 and 2004, the percentage of Americans polled who reported that they used the Internet to obtain information about health or disease "very often" or "often," went up eight points, from 13% to 21% (Harris Poll, 2004a). It is possible that the more recent data of Eysenbach and Köhler reflects this trend.

Interpreting these results requires putting it into the context of other studies of the use of the Internet for health information. Pew Internet studies have shown that, on a typical day, about 7% of the American online population seeks health information (Pew Internet & American Life, 2002a, b). The percent of Americans who report using the Internet to access health information varies in different studies from 40% to about 80% (Baker, Wagner, Singer & Bundorf, 2003; Pew Internet & American Life, 2003). How does this correlate with only 2 to 2.5% of queries being health-related? Perhaps we can understand this better if we think of each Web query as a telephone call. Counting the number of phone calls made and their destinations will not necessarily tell us how long the calls lasted, nor will it tell us the importance or impact of those calls.

For example, if each of 100 Web users makes 10 queries in one day (1000 total queries), and seven of these users search for health information, using three of their 10 queries for health information, then 21 of the 1000 total queries, or 2.1%, would be health-related, even though 7% of all the users made health-related searches. Furthermore, it is reasonable to assume that the three health-related searches took more time in reading and consideration, and perhaps had a deeper impact, than the other seven searches, which statistically would be about news, or commerce, such as checking a stock quote.

Phillipov and Phillips (2003) draw essentially two conclusions from their data: (1) "health-related terms are uncommon as search terms for Internet queries…", and (2) "information on both general health and specific disorders has a very low priority for people using Internet search engines…" (p. 2258). In their first conclusion, calling health-related terms "uncommon" uses a term that is quite relative: a study of a 2001 Excite user query sample showed a high rate of terms regarding commerce/economy/employment/travel (24.7% of all terms) and people/places/things (19.7%). After that, the numbers drop rapidly: 9.6% Computers or Internet; 8.5% Sex and pornography; 7.5% Health or sciences; 6.6% Entertainment or recreation; 4.5% Education or humanities; 3.9% Society, culture, ethnicity, or religion (Spink, Jansen, Wolfram, & Saracevic, 2001). None of the latter categories cited in the survey above could be considered "uncommon," even though they approach near the 2.5% frequency of health terms we found in our study.

Regarding the second statement, that health information has a "low priority" for Internet users: this comment is subjective. Significance is a personal thing, and must be measured, and this is surely a measure where quantity does not equal quality. The American public consistently ranks healthcare as a top priority and has shown an increasing interest in using the Internet as a resource for health information (Harris Poll, 2004a, Harris Poll, 2004b). Giving a weight to this use will require further research.

Discussion

Findings from our analysis suggest that, despite the large percentage of Internet users who conduct medical or health searchers reported by the Pew Internet Project (2002a, b) survey, such searches on large-scale commercial Web query logs in the United States and Europe may be a small proportion of Web searches. As stated previously, Pew (2003) does not compare health searching with other topics.

Our findings also suggest an ongoing shift in Web users' search topics. From 1997 to 2001, queries related to entertainment or recreation and medical or health, have declined proportionally as the queries related to e-commerce, travel, employment or economy and people, places or things have increased (Spink, Jansen, Wolfram, & Saracevic, 2002). This proportional shift may also reflect a shift by Web users to more specialized medical or health Web sites, such as WebMD (http://www.webmd.com/), and a shift towards more e-commerce Web sites and Web searching.

Medical or health Web queries and sessions are short and equivalent in length to nonmedical or health querying. Users' also do not reformulate their medical or health searches to a great extent. Thus, they express medical and health issues succinctly. Few people create long medical or health queries that include synonyms or alternate terms. Few users look beyond the first or second page of Web sites retrieved in response to their queries. Users' may be finding the information they seek in the first 10 to 20 Web sites.

The analysis of advice seeking and personified Web queries suggests that when seeking medical and health information, most consumers fail to understand the limitations of the Web search process. Many also ascribe human and advice-seeking abilities to Web search engines, such as Ask Jeeves, that go beyond the system's current capabilities. Many users do not really understand how a Web search engine works in conjunction with their own information seeking and searching processes. Users are often frustrated and emotional during their Web search engine interactions. They wish to engage in an advice seeking interaction, but they may be frustrated by the inability of the search engine to respond to their personal medical and health needs and concerns.

Commercial Web search engines were designed to help people use natural language expressions and formulate searches as readable and understandable queries. When seeking medical information, such technologies have the potential to make medical language, terms, and expressions understandable in searching for help and asking opinions from the search engine. This technology could offer more humanlike communication, and it is often marketed and promoted as a health information service. Such context, however, is problematic when the use of precise clinical terms, descriptions, or concepts is called for.

Current search technologies are becoming more akin to natural language communication, and are being used more frequently by users for health information retrieval, health services, or the sharing of health experiences. Most users may still lack the specialized vocabulary needed to effectively retrieve the information relevant to their condition. Most studies to date have presupposed that people are able to reach (arguably) credible clinical or health information through commercial Web search engines. However, for many people, the operation and outcomes of the commercial Web search engine still pose a significant barrier to usable health information. Research is needed to explore the limitations of Web search engines and Web sites for medical or health information seeking.

The purpose of the Semantic Web is to bridge the gap between the language of the lay person and the technical language of medicine. In essence, an advanced Semantic Web would serve the function of a physician-facilitator, who could translate lay language into an intelligent query that could accurately locate the information desired. A logical algorithm, perhaps aided by "machine-processable evaluation and trust-data" (Eysenbach, 2003) could choose information of high quality and recognize and exclude of poor quality. An even higher level function might allow translation of the retrieved information back into lay terminology, as a physician would do with a patient during a consultation. Eysenbach (2003) suggested the possibility of: "journals publishing electronic supplements online which contain the description of clinical trials in a machine-processable format using metadata language... As these research results are represented as 'knowledge' rather than as text, they may also be automatically tailored for different target audiences, for example translated into a consumer-friendly language by replacing medical terminology with lay terminology."

To do this will require that artificial intelligence be programmed into the Web using logical inference rules and structured collections of information. Furthermore, those structured information sets will need a common logical language. (Berners-Lee, Hendler, & Lassila, 2001). Ultimately, such a development could improve the accuracy of medical Web searches, and enhance the quality of information retrieved, as well as facilitate communication between healthcare consumers and providers.

Large-scale studies of Web queries, as outlined in this chapter, have strengths and weaknesses. Such studies using real data from Web search engines can show large-scale patterns and trends. Frequently, however, they lack demographic data on individual users and their Web search effectiveness.

In an era of health consumerism, evidence-based medicine, and growing shared decision making between patients and providers, it becomes imperative to provide consistent, reliable, health information via the Web. People expect and require information they can trust, delivered in a format that is understandable and usable. Further research is underway that examines the characteristics of medical or health related queries and sessions using query data from other Web search engines.

Conclusion

This chapter has provided an overview of research into medical Web search. Many studies have examined aspects of controlled medical vocabulary, as well as various aspects of medical Web searching. The Web provides growing opportunities for laypersons to gain knowledge about specific health conditions. In this context, there is a growing need to examine more closely how well laypersons' Web queries match controlled medical vocabularies that serve well the needs of medical professionals. Few studies have examined the use of controlled medical vocabulary by Web search engine users. Ultimately, the average consumer of Web health services is not always able to use correct medical terminology, and may not be able to choose analogous or synonymous terms from a search result list. The development of the Semantic Web, using a common logical language linked to artificial intelligence via inference rules, will go a long way toward resolving such difficulties.

References

American Medical Association. (2002). *Study on physicians' use of the World Wide Web*. Chicago: AMA Press.

Atlas, M. C. (2001). First-year students' impressions of the Internet. *Medical Reference Services Quarterly, 20*(1), 11- 25.

Baker, L., Wagner, T. H., Singer, S., & Bundorf, M. K. (2003). Use of the Internet and e-mail for health care information. Results from a national survey. *Journal of the American Medical Association, 289*(18), 2400-2406.

Barnas, G. P., & Kahn, C. E. (1999, November 6-10). Assessing consumers' interest in Internet-based health information. In *Proceedings of the American Medical Informatics Association (AMIA'99)*, Washington, DC.

Berland, G. K., Elliot, M. N, Morales, L. S. Algazy, J. I, Kravitz, R. L., & Broder, M. S. (2002). Health information on the Internet: Accessibility, quality, and readability in English and Spanish. *Journal of the American Medical Association, 285*(20), 2612-2621.

Berners-Lee, T., Hendler, J., & Lassila, O. (2001, May). The semantic Web, a new form of Web content that is meaningful to computers will unleash a revolution of new possibilities. *Scientific American, 284*(5), 25-35.

Bichakjian, C. K, Schwartz, J. L, Wang, T. S., Hall, J. M., Johnson. T. M. & Bierman, J. S. (2002). Melanoma information on the Internet: Often incomplete: A public health opportunity. *Journal of Clinical Oncology, 20*(1), 134-141.

Bin, L., & Li, K. C. (2001). The retrieval effectiveness of medical Information on the Web. *International Journal of Medical Information, 62*(2-3), 155-163.

Borowitz, S. M. & Wyatt, J. C. (1998). The origin, content, and workload of e-mail consultations. *Journal of the American Medical Association, 280*(15), 1321-1324.

Chen, X., & Siu, L. L. (2001). Impact of the media and the Internet on oncology: Survey of cancer patients and oncologists in Canada. *Journal of Clinical Oncology, 19*, 4291-4297.

European Commission Information Society. (2001, September). Guidelines for quality criteria. In *Workshop on Quality Criteria for Health Related Web sites* (Workshop Report). Retrieved from http://europe.eu.int/information_society/eeurope/ehealth/quality/workshop_report/index_en.html

Eysenbach, G. (2003). The semantic Web and healthcare consumers: a new challenge and opportunity on the horizon? *International Journal of Healthcare Technology and Management, 5*, 194-212.

Eysenbach, G., & Kohler, C. (2002). How do consumers search for and appraise health information on the World Wide Web? Qualitative study using focus groups, usability tests, and in-depth interviews. *British Medical Journal, 324*(9), 573-577.

Fallis, D., & Fricke, M. (2002). Indicators of accuracy of consumer health information on the Internet: A study of indicators relating to information for managing fever in children in the home. *Journal of the American Medical Informatics Association, 9*(1), 73-79.

Faxon, D., & Lenfant, C. (2001). Timing is everything: Motivating patients to call 9-1-1 at onset of acute myocardial infarction. *Circulation, 104*, 1210-1211.

Ferguson, T. (1998). Digital doctoring: Opportunities and challenges in electronic patient-physician communication. *Journal of the American Medical Association, 280*(15), 1361-1362.

Harris Poll #68. (2004b, September 23). *War on terror and economy continue to dominate election issues but health care moves up, according to latest Harris Poll.* Rochester, NY: Harris Interactive.

Harris Poll #98. (2004a, December 15). *Email, research, news and weather, information about hobbies or special interests top the list of how people use the Internet as it continues to grow.* Rochester, NY: Harris Interactive.

Hersh, W. R., Crabtree, M. K., Hickman, D. H., Sacherek, L., Friedman, C. P., Tidmarsh, P., et al. (2002). Factors associated with success in searching Medline and applying evidence to answer clinical questions. *Journal of the American Medical Informatics Association, 9*, 283-293.

Hersh, W. R., & Hickam, D. H. (1999). How well do physicians use electronic information retrieval systems? A framework for investigation and systematic review. *Journal of the American Medical Association, 280*, 1347.

Impicciatore, P., Pandolfini, C., Casella, N., & Bonati, M. (1997). Reliability of health information for the public on the World Wide Web: A systematic survey of advice and managing fever in children at home. *British Medical Journal, 314*, 1875-1881.

Jadad, A. R., & Gagliardi, A. (1998). Rating health information on the Internet: Navigating to knowledge or to Babel? *Journal of the American Medical Association, 279*, 611-614.

Jones, R. B., Balfour, F., Gillies, M., Stobo, D., Cawsey, A. J., & Donaldson, K. (2001). The accessibility of computer-based health information for patients: Kiosks and the Web. *Medical Information, 10*(2), 1469-1473.

McCray, A. T., Dorfman, E., Ripple, A., Ide, N. C., Jha, M., Katz, D. G., et al. (2000). Usability issues in developing a Web-based consumer health site. In *Proceedings of the Annual Fall Symposium of the American Medical Informatics Association* (AMIA'00, pp. 556-561).

McCray, A. T., Loane, R. F., Browne, A. C., & Bangalore, A. K. (1998). Terminology issues in user access to Web-based medical information. In *Proceedings of the American Medical Informatics Association* (pp. AMIA'98).

McLeod, S. D. (1998). The quality of medical information on the Internet: A new public health concern. *Archives of Ophthalmology, 116*(12), 1663.

Muhlhauser, I., & Berger, M. (2000). Evidence-based patient information in diabetes. *Diabetic Medicine, 17*(12), 823-829.

O'Connor, J. B., & Johanson, J. F. (2000). Use of the Web for medical information by a gastroentology clinic population. *Journal of the American Medical Association, 284*(15), 1902-1904.

Pandolfini, C. (2002). Follow up of quality of public oriented health information on the World Wide Web: Systematic re-evaluation. *British Medical Journal, 324*(7337), 582-583.

Pew Internet & American Life. (2002a, June). *Search engines: A pew Internet project* [Data memo].

Pew Internet & American Life. (2002b). *Vital decisions: How Internet users decide what information to trust when they or their loved ones are sick.* Pew Internet & American Life Project Report.

Pew Internet & American Life. (2003). *Internet health resources: Health searches and email have become more commonplace, but there is room for improvement in searches and overall Internet access.* Pew Internet & American Life Project Report.

Pew Internet & American Life. (2005). *Search engine use report.* Pew Internet & American Life Project Report.

Phillipov, G., & Phillips, P. J. (2003). Frequency of health-related search terms on the Internet. *Journal of the American Medical Association, 290*(17), 2258-9.

Rivera, S., Kim, D., Garone, S., Morgenstern, L., & Mohsenifar, Z. (2001). Motivating factors in futile clinical interventions. *Chest, 119*(6), 1944-1947.

Rogers, R. P. (2001). Searching for biomedical information on the World Wide Web. *Journal of Medical Practice Management, 15*(6), 306-313.

Rozic-Hristovski, A., Hristovski, D., & Todorovski, L. (2000). Users' information seeking behavior on a medical library Website. *Journal of the Medical Library Association, 90*(2), 210-217.

Spielberg, A. R. (1998). Sociohistorical, legal and ethical implications of e-mail for patient-physician relationship. *Journal of the American Medical Association, 21*(1), 1353-1359.

Spink, A., & Jansen, B. J. (2004). *Web search: Public searching of the Web.* Springer: Berlin.

Spink, A., Jansen, B. J., Wolfram, D., & Saracevic, T. (2002). From e-sex to e-commerce: Web search changes. *IEEE Computer, 35*(3), 107-111.

Spink, A., & Ozmutlu, H. C. (2002). Characteristics of question format Web queries: An exploratory study. *Information Processing and Management, 38*(4), 453-471.

Spink, A., Yang, Y., Jansen, B. J., Nyganen, P., Lorence, D. P., Ozmutlu, S., et al. (2004). A study of medical and health queries to Web search engines. *Health Information and Libraries Journal, 21*(1), 44-51.

Suarez, H. H., Hao, X., Chang, I. F., & Masys, D. R. (1997). Searching for information on the Internet using IMLS and medical world search. In *Proceedings of the Annual Fall Symposium of the American Medical Informatics Association* (pp. AMIA'97, pp. 824-828). Philadelphia: Hanley & Belfus.

Appendix

Terms

Each Dogpile record contains three fields:

- **Session:** entire query sequence by a user
- **Query:** one or more entered terms
- **Term:** any string of characters bounded by white space

Other terms:

- **User Identification:** a user code automatically to identify a particular computer
- **Cookie:** an anonymous cookie automatically assigned by the Dogpile.com server to identify unique users on a particular computer.
- **Time of Day:** measured in hours, minutes, and seconds as recorded by the Dogpile.com server.
- **Query Terms:** terms exactly as entered by the given user.
- **Location:** the geographic location of the user's computer as denoted by the Internet Protocol (IP) address of the searcher's computer.

Chapter XII

Web Mining for Protein-to-Protein Interaction Information

Hsi-Chieh Lee
Yuan Ze University, Taiwan &
National Kinmen Institute of Technology, Taiwan

Szu-Wei Huang
Yuan Ze University, Taiwan

Eldon Y. Li
National Chengchi University, Taiwan, &
California Polytechnic State University, USA

Abstract

This study proposes a mining system for finding protein-to-protein interaction literatures from the databases on the Internet. In this system, we search for discriminating words for protein-to-protein interaction by way of statistics and the results from literatures. A threshold is also evaluated to check if a given literature is related to protein-to-protein interactions. In addition, a keypage-based search mechanism is used to find related papers for protein-to-protein interactions from a given document. To expand the search space and ensure better performance of the system, mechanisms for protein name identification and databases for protein names are also developed. The system is designed with a web-based user interface and a job-dispatching kernel. Experiments are conducted and the results have been checked by a biomedical expert. The experimental results indicate that by using the proposed mining system, it is helpful for researchers to find protein-to-protein literatures from the overwhelming pieces of information available on the biomedical databases over the Internet.

Introduction

In recent years, due to advances in information technology, more and more biomedical-related information is available electronically on the Internet. For example, the MEDLINE database contains over 12 million citations dating back to the mid-1960's. Therefore, it has become an important issue for mining valuable biomedical information from the literature (Valencia-García, Ruiz-Sánchez, Vicente, Fernández-Breis, & Martínez-Béjar, 2004; Wang, Kuo, Chen, Hsiao, & Tsai, 2005), especially information on the Internet (Hong & Han, 2002). Expert systems and data mining techniques have been used for years in medical diagnosis domain (Chou, Lee, Shao, & Chen, 2004; Alonso, Caraça-Valente, González, & Montes, 2002).

In the post-genomic era, some scientists focus on finding meaningful information of DNA or try to use the information of gene sequence in solving problems. However, the spirit of post-genomic era can be view broadly in three ways. The first one is the sequences from DNA level, and the second one is the expressed sequence tag (EST) from RNA level. The last one is proteome from the protein level. People can use the analyzed information to understand the interaction between each other and discover the meaning behind it. In other words, after decoding the sequence, scientist can analyze the interaction between gene and protein, and understand the role the gene is playing on an organism. It has been shown that the protein and genomics would become the main issue in the post-genomic era (Eisenberg, Marcott, Xenarios, & Yeates, 2000).

Moreover, scientists try to understand the interaction and relation between proteins from biochemistry and gene-related angles. For example, the database of interaction proteins (DIP) developed in UCLA (Xenarios et al., 2000) has data about over 5900 proteins and 10500 protein-to-protein interactions. Besides DIP, there exist many other databases with the collection of the data regarding protein function and pathway. However, if people want to know the relationship between proteins, they have to search different literatures and try to find some relationships. It is considered mission impossible to check on MEDLINE manually where there exist more than 15 million biomedical citations. It is time-consuming and ineffective. It would be helpful if the job can be processed automatically and the database can be updated as soon as new literatures are available.

Generally, mining the literatures of protein-to-protein interactions requires natural language processing. The literature discussing protein-to-protein interactions does not contain a language that a computer can understand. As a result, there are two typical approaches in solving the problem. The first approach is transferring the format into a way that computer can understand by natural language processing. For example, in Ono, Hishigaki, Tanigami, and Takagi (2001), they brought up an idea to extract biomedical-related information with two steps. The first step is to scan the full document with a protein name dictionary. The second step is to extract content related to protein-to-protein interactions by predefined rules. The second approach is to extract biomedical-related information using statistics. The most typically way of statistics is calculating the frequency of words. In Marcotte, Xenarios, and Eisenberg (2001), they used statistics to find 83 words as discriminative words to check whether a paper is discussing protein-to-protein interaction.

In this study, we integrate both approaches mentioned above. The natural language processing techniques and statistics were utilized to process the biomedical-related literatures. Besides checking whether a paper is discussing protein-to-protein interaction, we also find the probable protein names in the target document and help people in finding other related literatures. The proposed mining system is described in detail in the following section and the experimental results are illustrated subsequently.

The Proposed System

The literature mining procedures of the proposed mining system is illustrated in Figure 1. The system starts by feeding a target document (e.g., a protein-to-protein interaction paper) to the system. The first step of the mining system is to calculate the frequency of words and decide whether the target document can be classified as a paper related to protein-to-protein interaction. Next, the mining system will identify the potential protein names in the target document. The third step is to identify the category of interaction of the target document according to the frequencies of words in it. The final step is to compose keywords automatically and send the query to the PubMed. Once the query results are ready, the system will then retrieve the related literatures from the Internet (http://www.ncbi.nlm.nih.gov/PubMed/). The detailed description of each step is shown next.

Figure 1. The literature mining procedures of the proposed system

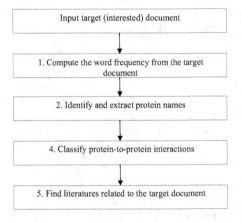

Step 1. Compute the Frequency of the Word Tokens in the Target (Interested) Document

In the proposed mining system, we used 20 words that have the most discriminate capability. To ensure that they are the most discriminate words, we retrieved 2203 abstracts from database of interacting proteins (http://dip.doe-mbi.ucla.edu/) (Xenarios et al., 2000)—a well-known database dedicated for data about protein interaction. We calculated the frequency of the words in these documents and took them as the most discriminating words (stop words were excluded). When the researcher inputs the target document, the system will calculate the frequencies of the 20 words. If the frequencies are high enough, this target document is considered as discussing protein interactions by the proposed system. In a different study, Marcotte, Xenarios, and Eisenbert (2001) found statistics of 65807 literatures and derived 83 discriminate words.

Step 2. Identify and Extract Protein Names

In the biology domain, it is not uncommon to have new findings everyday. When there is a new finding, the researcher will give it a new name to discriminate it from others. As a result, new protein names are created rapidly which makes it difficult to identify all the protein names. In general, a protein name can be classified into one of the following types of word.

- Single words with upper case letters, numerical figures, and non-alphabetical letters. Mostly derived from gene name.
- Compound words with upper case letters, numerical letters, and non-alphabetical letters.
- Single word with only lower case letters.

The first two types of protein names are more commonly found in research papers while protein names of type 3 are rarely found (Fukuda, Tsunoda, Tamura, & Takagi, 1998).

Another difficulty with identifying a protein name is the inconsistency of naming convention. It is also not uncommon to find the same protein being expressed differently by different researchers, depending on the researchers' styles. For example, the term "epidermal growth factor receptor", some researchers describe it directly while others use abbreviations as "EGF receptor" or "EGFR". That is, even the abbreviation might be expressed differently. The following example demonstrates some variation of expression for a protein function (Fukuda, Tsunoda, Tamura, & Takagi, 1998).

- the Ras guanine nucleotide exchange factor Sos
- the Ras guanine nucleotide releasing protein Sos
- the Ras exchanger Sos

Figure 2. Identification and extraction of protein names from a document

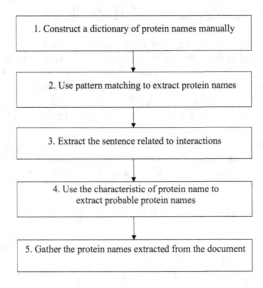

As mentioned above, protein names and their expressions are mainly decided by researchers' style. Therefore, it becomes a challenge to find them in the literature. The general way of finding protein names is constructing a dictionary of protein names manually and uses the dictionary for pattern matching (Thomas, Milward, Ouzounis, Pulman, & Carroll, 2000). Another way of finding the protein names is to check the words that are used often around the literature. In addition, it is also applicable to analyze the characteristics of words and try to find protein names in the literature. In the proposed system, we integrate the three approaches mentioned above for identifying the protein names in the literature. The detailed process of extracting protein names is shown in Figure 2 and the discussion follows.

1.   To construct a dictionary of protein names for the system, we retrieve the protein names from Protein Name Abbreviation Dictionary, (http://pnad.ontology.ims.u-tokyo.ac.jp/search/php/ search.php) and then add other known protein names manually.

2.   Using pattern-matching approach to compare every word in the literature and extract the protein names from the literature.

A set of word patterns is commonly used for recognition of protein-to-protein interaction, namely, "interact", "bind", "associate", and "complex". Unfortunately, they might appear in different forms. As a result, we try to extract these word patterns using regular expression and the rule shown below. In addition, the Brill POS tagger package (Brill, 1994) is used to analyze the target test.

Rule: If the sentence matches the following part-of-speech pattern as indicated by regular expression, it can be extracted.

interact .* | complex .* | bind .* | associate .*

When getting the sentence from the target document, the Brill POS tagger extracts the words which are tagged as NN or NNP (see Table 1). Once the sentence contains word patterns of protein-to-protein interaction, we treat the words that are tagged as NN or NNP in the sentence to be potential protein name. To further eliminate words that are not related, for example, words like "domain", "function", the Porter's Stemming Algorithm (Porter, 1980) is used. This algorithm processes suffix of words. If the word is plurality or other type, it will be transformed back to the original word. We will try to compare the words extracted to those on WordNet and try to eliminate words that are not interested. The Brill POS tagger definition of symbols is shown in Table 1.

Table 1. Definition of symbols

Symbol	Definition
,	Comma
:	Colon
;	Semi-colon
CC	Coordinating conjunction
DT	Determiner
IN	Preposition or subordinating conjugation
JJ	Adjective
NN	Noun, singular or mass
NNP	Proper noun, singular
NNS	Noun, plural
P(1/2)	Phrase
P(3/4/5)	Phrase without verb
VB(1/2)	Verb
VBN	Verb, past participle
VBZ	Verb, 3rd person singular present

3.   In this step, we adopt Fukuda et al.'s (1998) approach to extracting protein names with the following characteristics.

    a.   Based on characteristics of protein name, extract the words with upper cases, numerical figures, and/or special symbols.

    b.   Use the rules listed below to filter out improbable words.

       •   Exclude words whose length is more than nine characters and consists of "-" and lower cases.

       •   Exclude words in which more than half of its character string consists of special symbols.

       •   Exclude words related to numbers such as units. Eight words (aa, AA, fold, bp, nM, microM, %, UV) are registered as units.

       •   Exclude words that agree to the reference template prepared beforehand.

    c.   If extracting words are in common use, they can be filtered out by words in WordNet.

    d.   The words that are left over are the probable protein names.

4.   Integrating the probable protein names found using three different approaches: comparing with database, extracting by regular expression, and extracting by characteristics of protein names.

Step 3. Classification of Protein-to-Protein Interactions

After extracting the protein names, we further try to classify the interaction discussed in the target document into a category. Based on the words commonly used to describe interaction and by checking the words that are discriminated by the statistics, four words (interact, associate, complex, and bind) were used. According to the frequencies of the four words, the highest one will be considered as the category of interaction that is discussed in the target document.

Step 4. Finding Related Literature of the Target Document

Once the protein names and the category of interaction are identified, they will be used as input for search on the search engine of PubMed (URL:) for retrieving the candidate research papers related to the target document which has been entered into the proposed mining system by the researcher. The results from PubMed are URLs of candidate research papers. The system will then retrieve the papers from the Internet and then extracting features from each of them and calculate the similarity with the target document using SimNet's kernel function (Lee, Dagli, Ercal, & Ozbayoglu, 1995). SimNet is a neuro-fuzzy system that integrates the neural network architecture and fuzzy theory. The idea of SimNet was first introduced for character recognition and has later been used for speaker identification. It combines a neural network structure with the subsethood concept of fuzzy logic to produce a rapid data clustering system that works similar to Adaptive Resonance Theory and Self-Organizing Maps. It has two neural network architectures (Lee, Dagli, Ercal, & Ozbayoglu, 1995), namely, a 2-layer unsupervised learning model and a 3-layer supervised learning model. In this study, only the similarity measurement equation is used to compare the similarity of documents. We use the algorithm to calculate similarity of documents and get the most related documents. The similarity measurement equation of SimNet is shown next.

$$MD(I,W) = \sqrt{\frac{(\sum_i \min(I_i, W_i))^2}{(\sum_i W_i)(\sum_i I_i) + \varepsilon}}, \text{ where } \mu \text{ is a non-zero minimal}$$

This procedure turns the keyword-based search into a keypage-based search that reduces the amount of unrelated information significantly.

Illustration of Source Programs

There are a number of program modules in the proposed literature mining system. For instance, the document input module, word frequency counting module, protein name identification module, protein name extracting module, protein classification module, Internet document retrieving module, protein name extracting module, interaction sentence extracting module, and so forth. Four of these modules are illustrated in the Appendix. These include: (1) Extract protein names according to the database, (2) Extract words with protein name characteristics, (3) Retrieve potential protein names using regular expression, and (4) Retrieve similar documents.

Experimental Results

In order to decide whether the target document fell into the category that discussed protein-to-protein interaction, we started by finding the 20 most discriminating words. We downloaded 2203 abstracts from the DIP and then calculated the word frequencies. The average number of words in an abstract was 196 words. The top 20 most frequently used words were found as shown in Table 2. As we could see in Table 2, the word patterns, {interact, binding, complex} that were commonly used in protein-to-protein interaction papers were also included.

Since all the literatures in DIP were considered to have the topic regarding the protein-to-protein interaction. Therefore, we tried to analyze the behavior of the literatures in DIP by calculating the Matching Degree of each abstract in DIP with the overall frequency vector as shown in Table 2. The matching degree (MD) is the kernel function in SimNet

Table 2. The 20 most discriminating words

Discriminating word	Frequency	Discriminating word	Frequency
complex/complexes	1845	binding	1221
interact/interaction /interactions/interacts	2449	component	249
		required	626
two-hybrid	448	suggesting	256
With	3997	From	907
protein/proteins	4434	demonstrate	251
Function	607	Kinase	803
Domain	1039	essential	444

(Lee, Dagli, Ercal, & Ozbayoglu, 1995). The similarity measurement equation MD is shown next.

$$MD(I,W) = \sqrt{\frac{(\sum_i \min(I_i, W_i))^2}{(\sum_i W_i)(\sum_i I_i) + \varepsilon}}, \text{ where } \mu \text{ is a non-zero minimal}$$

In this equation, the vector "*I*" means the word frequency that is shown in Table 2 and notice that it has been normalized. The vector "*W*" means the frequency of 20 discriminate words of each abstract found in DIP. The detailed calculating steps are demonstrated in Figure 3.

The experiment found the Matching Degrees (MDs) of the 2203 abstracts from DIP. The experimental results shown in Figure 4 reveal that the values of MD were in the range between 0.02 and 0.74 and the average value of MD was 0.457. If the threshold was set to 0.02, all the literatures would be accepted as papers of protein-to-protein interaction and the recall rate would be maximized. However, the precision rate did not appear to be good. When we set the threshold to the average value 0.457, 45% of the literatures would be accepted and 55% would be dropped.

To generalize the results for the MD threshold and to find the precision and recall rate with different thresholds, we randomly chose 535 literatures from DIP that represented the research papers of protein-to-protein interaction. Moreover, we used the four keywords, "interact", "associate", "bind", and "complex" as inputs to MEDLINE. There were 30277 abstracts obtained by the MEDLINE search using these keywords as the MeSH terms. With a random selection and a duplication-elimination process, 10531 abstracts were retrieved from MEDLINE. The MDs were calculated from a total of 11066 abstracts, in which, 535 abstracts derived from DIP and 10531 abstracts derived from MEDLINE. The detailed calculating steps were demonstrated in Figure 3 and the MDs

Figure 3. The steps of calculating the matching degrees

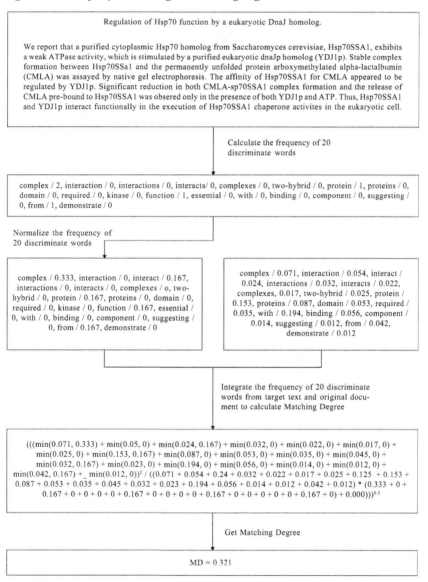

Regulation of Hsp70 function by a eukaryotic DnaJ homolog.

We report that a purified cytoplasmic Hsp70 homolog from Saccharomyces cerevisiae, Hsp70SSA1, exhibits a weak ATPase activity, which is stimulated by a purified eukaryotic dnaJp homolog (YDJ1p). Stable complex formation between Hsp70SSa1 and the permanently unfolded protein arboxymethylated alpha-lactalbumin (CMLA) was assayed by native gel electrophoresis. The affinity of Hsp70SSA1 for CMLA appeared to be regulated by YDJ1p. Significant reduction in both CMLA-sp70SSA1 complex formation and the release of CMLA pre-bound to Hsp70SSA1 was obsered only in the presence of both YDJ1p and ATP. Thus, Hsp70SSA1 and YDJ1p interact functionally in the execution of Hsp70SSA1 chaperone activites in the eukaryotic cell.

Calculate the frequency of 20 discriminate words

complex / 2, interaction / 0, interactions / 0, interacts/ 0, complexes / 0, two-hybrid / 0, protein / 1, proteins / 0, domain / 0, required / 0, kinase / 0, function / 1, essential / 0, with / 0, binding / 0, component / 0, suggesting / 0, from / 1, demonstrate / 0

Normalize the frequency of 20 discriminate words

complex / 0.333, interaction / 0, interact / 0.167, interactions / 0, interacts / 0, complexes / o, two-hybrid / 0, protein / 0.167, proteins / 0, domain / 0, required / 0, kinase / 0, function / 0.167, essential / 0, with / 0, binding / 0, component / 0, suggesting / 0, from / 0.167, demonstrate / 0

complex / 0.071, interaction / 0.054, interact / 0.024, interactions / 0.032, interacts / 0.022, complexes, 0.017, two-hybrid / 0.025, protein / 0.153, proteins / 0.087, domain / 0.053, required / 0.035, with / 0.194, binding / 0.056, component / 0.014, suggesting / 0.012, from / 0.042, demonstrate / 0.012

Integrate the frequency of 20 discriminate words from target text and original document to calculate Matching Degree

$$(((\min(0.071, 0.333) + \min(0.05, 0) + \min(0.024, 0.167) + \min(0.032, 0) + \min(0.022, 0) + \min(0.017, 0) + \min(0.025, 0) + \min(0.153, 0.167) + \min(0.087, 0) + \min(0.053, 0) + \min(0.035, 0) + \min(0.045, 0) + \min(0.032, 0.167) + \min(0.023, 0) + \min(0.194, 0) + \min(0.056, 0) + \min(0.014, 0) + \min(0.012, 0) + \min(0.042, 0.167) + \_ \min(0.012, 0))^2 / ((0.071 + 0.054 + 0.24 + 0.032 + 0.022 + 0.017 + 0.025 + 0.125 + 0.153 + 0.087 + 0.053 + 0.035 + 0.045 + 0.032 + 0.023 + 0.194 + 0.056 + 0.014 + 0.012 + 0.042 + 0.012) * (0.333 + 0 + 0.167 + 0 + 0 + 0 + 0 + 0.167 + 0 + 0 + 0 + 0 + 0.167 + 0 + 0 + 0 + 0 + 0 + 0.167 + 0) + 0.000)))^{0.5}$$

Get Matching Degree

MD = 0.321

Figure 4. The Matching Degree (MD) of literatures in DIP

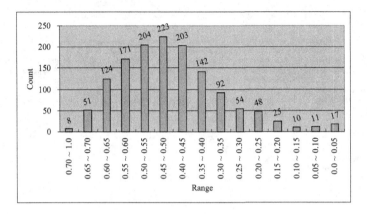

Figure 5. The Matching Degree (MD) of 11066 abstracts

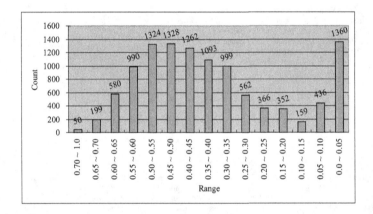

of these abstracts were shown in Figure 5. It could be observed that the test results of the 11066 abstracts shown in Figure 5 looked similar to the test results of the 2203 abstracts in Figure 4.

To test if the MD thresholds could be applied to those literatures that were not included in the set of the 11066 abstracts, a new experiment was conducted and the results for the precision and recall rate were verified by an expert of protein chemistry. This expert was a physician from a local hospital who held a PhD degree from an institution in the U.S. and specialized in protein chemistry, matrix biology, and glycobiology. A total of 740

Figure 6. The matching degree (MD) of 740 abstracts

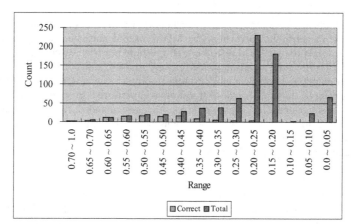

Figure 7. Precision-recall chart with different thresholds

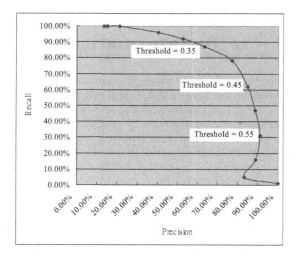

abstracts were used for calculating the Matching Degree. Out of the 740 abstracts, 100 of them were selected randomly from DIP, and the rest of them were selected randomly from MEDLINE that were considered not literatures of protein-to-protein interaction. The experimental results of the 740 abstracts were shown in Figure 6.

The experimental results for the 740 abstracts were transformed into the precision-recall chart as shown in Figure 7. When the MD threshold was set to 0.35, 87% abstracts would be correctly classified as papers of protein-to-protein interaction. However, the precision rate was not as high.

There was a tradeoff between the recall rate and the precision as shown in Figure 7. In other words, to get higher precision, the MD threshold must be higher than 0.45. Conversely, to get higher recall rate, the MD threshold must be lower than 0.35. The selection of MD threshold mainly depended on the purpose of using the proposed mining system. For example, to retrieve more protein-to-protein interaction papers that were related to the target document, a lower threshold was preferred. In contrast, higher MD threshold was suggested if less but accurate results were demanded. Note that the mining job requested in this study was a nontrivial computation-intensive and communication-demanding task. The main reason was that the proposed system needed to analyze the target document in order to find the probable protein names and then send the query to the Internet search engines. In addition, each and every document found should also be retrieved from the Internet and the analysis process would be applied to each and every document again. Finally, computation for MDs between the target document and the documents retrieved from the Internet should be done to find the similarity. Fortunately, this time-consuming process could be resolved using a parallel and distributed environment proposed in Chen and Lee (2002).

Managerial Implications to Bioinformatics

As human's genetic disease has been proven to relate to gene variation, genomic sequence has been used for searching the genetic sequence of disease, researching the way of prevention, diagnosis, and treatment. It also helps people in understanding the relation between environment and evolution by comparing cross gene of species. Besides analyzing the gene, the analysis of protein is another important approach. Moving the research from the one dimension of DNA into the three dimension of protein, people can understand the protein's structure and function. We can also use this information to develop new medicine or new prevention mechanism for diseases. During the course of this research, we must understand the interaction and relation between proteins in biochemistry and gene-related ways. In order to conserve the resources demanded by experimental studies, we can find the related experimental outcomes published in the literature. However, the information available on the extant literature is overwhelming. For example, just the MEDLINE (see http://www.ncbi.nlm.nih.gov/Literature/) alone contains over 15,000,000 biomedical journal citations. Likewise, Database of Interaction Proteins (Xenarios et al., 2000) alone contains over 5,900 proteins and 10,500 interactions data about protein-to-protein interaction. It is impossible for a human being to search through all these pieces of data. Therefore, our proposed mining system will help researcher in finding related papers of protein interactions from the literatures available over the Internet, with a simple input of an interested document. The proposed mining system is expected to reduce the time and effort significantly for researchers in the stage of literature review.

Conclusion

In this study, a mining system has been proposed for finding protein-to-protein interaction literatures from the database on the Internet. Through this system, we found discriminating words for protein-to-protein interaction by way of statistics and results from literatures. A threshold was also evaluated using the MD function of SimNet to check if a given literature was related to protein-to-protein interactions. In addition, a keypage-based search mechanism was used to find papers related to protein-to-protein interactions from a given document. Moreover, to expand the search space and ensure better performance of the system, both mechanisms for protein name identification and databases for protein names were used. Experiments were conducted and the results were checked by an expert of protein chemistry.

The findings of the study suggest that to get precision as high as 90%, the MD threshold can be adjusted to a value higher than 0.45. In addition, to get recall rate as high as 90%, the MD threshold can be adjusted to be lower than 0.35. These indicate that by using the proposed mining system, it is helpful for researchers to find protein-to-protein literatures from the overwhelming amount of information available on the biomedical database over the Internet. Moreover, because of the nature of the architecture, the results can be derived in a reasonable time with the help of the parallel and distributed mechanism.

Finding related literature of protein interactions from the Internet using simply an interested document is the major contribution of this study. It keeps the researchers from inputting many possible keywords and check hundreds and thousands of results returned from general search engines. However, there are two major concerns in this research which needs further investigation and study in the future. The first one is the prediction of protein names. As long as there exists no "golden" standard for protein naming convention, there exists the problem of "guessing" protein name available in the literatures. The second concern for implementing such a mining system is the performance of the system which is usually measured by precision and recall rate. To measure the performance, one may build a benchmarking database in any target domain (e.g., DIP for protein interactions) which is a job requires considerably involvement of domain experts.

Acknowledgment

This research is supported partially under the grants of NSC91-2745-P-155-003 and NSC93-2745-E-155-010-URD, Taiwan, R.O.C. The earlier version of this chapter was published in *Expert Systems with Applications* (Lee, Huang, & Li, 2006).

References

Alonso, F., Caraça-Valente, J. P., González, A. L., & Montes, C. (2002). Combining expert knowledge and data mining in a medical diagnosis domain. *Expert Systems with Applications, 23*(4), 367-375.

Brill, E. (1994). A report of recent progress in transformation-based error-driven learning. In *Proceedings of Human Language Technology Workshop* (ARPA-94), Princeton, NJ.

Chen, P. W., & Lee, H. C. (2002, September 23-25). C^2AS: An agent-based distributed and parallel processing virtual machine. In the *7th International Conference on Applications of High-Performance Computers in Engineering (HPC 2002)*, Bologna, Italy.

Chou, S. M., Lee, T. S., Shao, Y. E., & Chen, I. F. (2004). Mining the breast cancer pattern using artificial neural networks and multivariate adaptive regression splines. *Expert Systems with Applications, 27*(1), 133-142.

Eisenberg, D., Marcott, E. M., Xenarios, I., & Yeates, T. O. (2000). Protein function in the post-genomic era. *Nature, 405*(6788), 823-6.

Fukuda, K., Tsunoda, T., Tamura, A., & Takagi, T. (1998, January 4-8). Toward information extraction: Identifying protein names from biological papers. In *Proceedings of the Pacific Symposium on Biocomputing* (PSB'98, pp. 707-718), Maui, HI.

Hong, T., & Han, I. (2002). Knowledge-based data mining of news information on the Internet using cognitive maps and neural networks. *Expert Systems with Applications, 23*(1), 1-8.

Lee, H. C., Dagli, C. H., Ercal, F., & Ozbayoglu, A. M. (1995). SimNet: A parallel neuro-fuzzy paradigm for data clustering. *OAI Neural Networks Symposium and Workshop (OAINN '95)*, Athens, OH.

Lee, H. C., Huang, S. W., and Li, E. Y. (2006) Mining protein-protein interaction information on the Internet. *Expert Systems with Applications, 30*(1), 142-148

Marcotte, E. M., Xenarios, I., & Eisenberg, D. (2001). Mining literature for protein-to-protein interactions. *Bioinformatics, 17*(4), 359-363.

Ono, T., Hishigaki, H., Tanigami, A., & Takagi, T. (2001). Automated extraction of information on protein-to-protein interactions from the biological literature. *Bioinformatics, 17*(4), 155-161.

Porter, M. F. (1980). An algorithm for suffix stripping. *Program, 14*(3), 130-137.

Valencia-García, R., Ruiz-Sánchez, J. M., Vicente, P. J. V., Fernández-Breis, J. T., & Martínez-Béjar, R. (2004). An incremental approach for discovering medical knowledge from texts. *Expert Systems with Applications, 26*(3), 291-299.

Thomas, J., Milward, D., Ouzounis, C., Pulman, S., & Carroll, M. (2000, January 4-9). *Automatic extraction of protein interactions from scientific abstracts.* In R. B. Altman, A. K. Dunker, L. Hunter, K. Lauderdale, & T. E. D. Klein (Eds.), *Pacific*

Symposium of Biocomputing 2000, Honolulu, HI (pp. 541-552). World Scientific Publishing Company.

Wang, H. C., Kuo, H. C., Chen, H. H., Hsiao, Y. Y., & Tsai, W. C. (2005). KSPF: Using gene sequence patterns and data mining for biological knowledge management. *Expert Systems with Applications, 28*(3), 537-545.

Xenarios, I., Rice, D. W., Salwinski, L., Baron, M. K., Marcotte, E. M., & Eisenberg, D. (2000). DIP: The database of interacting proteins. *Nucleic Acids Res, 28*(1), 289-91.

Note

This chapter was adapted from Lee, H. C., Huange, S. W., Li, E. Y. (2006). Mining protein-protein interaction informationo n the Internet. *Expert Systems with Applicatioins, 30*(1), 142-148.

Appendix:
Illustration of Source Programs

In this section, the source codes for four important modules of the proposed literature mining system are provided and commented accordingly. These include (1) Extract protein names according to the database, (2) Extract words with protein name characteristics, (3) Retrieve potential protein names using regular expression, and (4) Retrieve similar documents.

1.   Extract protein names according to the database

```
//Try to find protein name in the target document according to the data in the database.
    pSet = new CProtein;
    ASSERT_VALID( pSet );
    pSet->Open();
    for( i=0; i<(DWORD) pKeyWord->GetCount(); i++)
    {
        pSet->m_strFilter.Format("%s%s%s","protein='",(*pKeyWord)[i],"'");
        if(!pSet->Requery())
            break;
        if( !pSet->IsEOF() )
        {
            pProteinName->Add( (*pKeyWord)[i]);
        }
    }
    pSet->Close();
    delete pSet;

//Add the protein found into variable m_sDatabaseProtein.
    for( i=0; i<(DWORD)pProteinName->GetCount(); i++)
    {
        for ( bResult=TRUE, ListProteinIterator = m_lpProtein.begin(); ListProteinIterator !=
m_lpProtein.end(); ++ListProteinIterator )
        {
            if ( (*ListProteinIterator)->szProteinName == pProteinName->GetAt(i) )
            {
                bResult = FALSE;
                pProtein = (LPPROTEIN) (*ListProteinIterator);
                break;
            }
        }

        if ( bResult )
        {
            pProtein = new PROTEIN;
            ASSERT( pProtein != NULL );
            pProtein->szProteinName = pProteinName->GetAt(i);
            pProtein->dwCount = 1;
        }
        else
            continue;
        for( bResult=TRUE, j=0; j<(DWORD)m_sProteinName.GetCount(); j++ )
        {
            if( pProteinName->GetAt(i) == m_sProteinName.GetAt(j) )
            {
                bResult = FALSE;
```

```
                        pProtein->dwCount++;
                        break;
                }
        }
        if( bResult )
        {
                m_sDatabaseProtein.Add( pProteinName->GetAt(i) );
                m_sProteinName.Add( pProteinName->GetAt(i) );
                m_lpProtein.push_back( pProtein );
        }
}

//Extract words that contains uppercase letter, "/" sign, or "-" sign.
for( i=0; i<(DWORD)pKeyWord->GetCount(); i++)
{
        bResult = TRUE;
        TRACE( "%s\n", pKeyWord->GetAt(i) );
        for( j=0; j<(DWORD)pKeyWord->GetAt(i).GetLength(); j++)
        {
                if(pKeyWord->GetAt(i).GetAt(j) >= 'A' && pKeyWord->GetAt(i).GetAt(j) <= 'Z')
                {
                        bResult = TRUE;
                        break;
                }
                else if( pKeyWord->GetAt(i).GetAt(j) == '/')
                {
                        bResult = TRUE;
                        break;
                }
                else if( pKeyWord->GetAt(i).GetAt(j) == '-')
                {
                        bResult = TRUE;
                        break;
                }
                else
                        bResult = FALSE;
        }
        if( !bResult )
        {
                pKeyWord->RemoveAt(i);
                i--;
        }
}

//Remove words without required characteristics using filter.
for( i=0; i<(DWORD)pKeyWord->GetCount(); i++)
{
        bResult = TRUE;
        dwCount = 0;
        if( pKeyWord->GetAt(i).GetLength() > 9)
        {
                for( j=0; j<(DWORD)pKeyWord->GetAt(i).GetLength(); j++)
                {
                        if( pKeyWord->GetAt(i).GetAt(j) == '-')
                        {
                                bResult = FALSE;
                                break;
                        }
                }
                if( !bResult )
                {
                        for( j=0; j<(DWORD)pKeyWord->GetAt(i).GetLength(); j++)
                        {
                                if( pKeyWord->GetAt(i).GetAt(j) >= 'A' && pKeyWord->GetAt(i).GetAt(j) <=
'Z')
                                {
                                        bResult = TRUE;
                                        break;
```

```
                                    }
                            }
                    }
                    if( !bResult )
                    {
                            pKeyWord->RemoveAt(i);
                            i--;
                    }
            }
            else
            {
                    for( j=0; j<(DWORD)pKeyWord->GetAt(i).GetLength(); j++)
                    {

//Count the numbers of special characters.
                        switch( pKeyWord->GetAt(i).GetAt(j) )                    {
                        case '<':case
',':case'?':case'~':case'!':case'@':case'#':case'$':case'^':case'&':case'*':
                        case '(':case ')':case '+':case '|':case '{':case '}':case'>':case'-':case'\n':
                                dwCount++;
                                break;
                        case'%':
                                bResult = FALSE;
                                break;
                        case'1':case'2':case'3':case'4':case'5':case'6':case'7':case'8':case'9':case'0':
                                dwNumber++;
                                break;
                    }
                    if( pKeyWord->GetAt(i).GetLength() > 3
&&pKeyWord->GetAt(i).Find("aa",pKeyWord->GetAt(i).GetLength()-2) != -1)
                            bResult = FALSE;
                    if( pKeyWord->GetAt(i).GetLength() > 3 &&
pKeyWord->GetAt(i).Find("AA",pKeyWord->GetAt(i).GetLength()-2) != -1)
                            bResult = FALSE;
                    if( pKeyWord->GetAt(i).GetLength() > 5 &&
pKeyWord->GetAt(i).Find("fold",pKeyWord->GetAt(i).GetLength()-4) != -1)
                            bResult = FALSE;
                    if( pKeyWord->GetAt(i).GetLength() > 3 &&
pKeyWord->GetAt(i).Find("bp",pKeyWord->GetAt(i).GetLength()-2) != -1)
                            bResult = FALSE;
                    if( pKeyWord->GetAt(i).GetLength() > 3 &&
pKeyWord->GetAt(i).Find("nM",pKeyWord->GetAt(i).GetLength()-2) != -1)
                            bResult = FALSE;
                    if( pKeyWord->GetAt(i).GetLength() > 7 &&
pKeyWord->GetAt(i).Find("microM",pKeyWord->GetAt(i).GetLength()-6) != -1)
                            bResult = FALSE;
                    if( pKeyWord->GetAt(i).GetLength() > 3 &&
pKeyWord->GetAt(i).Find("UV",pKeyWord->GetAt(i).GetLength()-2) != -1)
                            bResult = FALSE;
                    if( dwCount > (DWORD)pKeyWord->GetAt(i).GetLength()/2 || bResult == FALSE ||
dwNumber > (DWORD)pKeyWord->GetAt(i).GetLength()/2)
                    {
                            pKeyWord->RemoveAt(i);
                            i--;
                    }
            }
    }

//Transfer words into their origins using porter stemmer.
symbol sBuffer[1024] = {0};
TCHAR   sBufferFinish[1024] = {0};
SN_env * pSNenv = NULL;
    pSNenv = porter_create_env();
    for ( i=0; i<(DWORD)pKeyWord->GetCount(); i++ )
    {
            ::FillMemory( sBuffer, 1024, 0 );
            CopyMemory( sBuffer, (LPCTSTR)
```

```
              pKeyWord->GetAt(i).GetLength() > 1023 ? 1023 : pKeyWord->GetAt(i).GetLength() );
                TRACE( "orig = %s ", pKeyWord->GetAt(i) );
                SN_set_current( pSNenv, pKeyWord->GetAt(i).GetLength() > 1023 ? 1023 :
      pKeyWord->GetAt(i).GetLength(), sBuffer );
                porter_stem( pSNenv );
                ::FillMemory( sBufferFinish, 1024, 0 );
                CopyMemory( sBufferFinish, pSNenv->p, pSNenv->l > 1023 ? 1023 : pSNenv->l );
                TRACE( "%s\n", sBufferFinish );
                (*pKeyWord)[i] = sBufferFinish;
        }

        porter_close_env( pSNenv );

    //Remove words that can be found in WordNet.
        pNoun = new CNoun;
        ASSERT_VALID( pNoun );
        pNoun->Open();
        for( i=0; i< (DWORD)pKeyWord->GetCount(); i++)
        {
                if( !pKeyWord->IsEmpty() && pKeyWord->GetAt(i).Find("'") == -1)
                {
                        szTemp = (*pKeyWord)[i];
                        szTemp.Trim( );
                        szTemp.Trim(",%&.@#*!~?");
                        pNoun->m_strFilter.Format("%s%s%s","noun='",szTemp.MakeLower(),"'");
                        if(!pNoun->Requery())
                                break;
                        if( !pNoun->IsEOF() )
                        {
                                pKeyWord->RemoveAt(i);
                                i--;
                        }
                }
        }
        pNoun->Close();
        delete pNoun;

    //Add the protein found into variables m_sCProtein and m_sProteinName.
        for( i=0; i<(DWORD)pKeyWord->GetCount(); i++ )
        {
                for ( bResult = TRUE, ListProteinIterator = m_lpProtein.begin(); ListProteinIterator !=
      m_lpProtein.end(); ++ListProteinIterator )
                {
                        if( (*ListProteinIterator)->szProteinName == pKeyWord->GetAt(i) )
                        {
                                bResult = FALSE;
                                pProtein = (LPPROTEIN) (*ListProteinIterator);
                                break;
                        }
                }
                if( bResult )
                {
                        pProtein = new PROTEIN;
                        ASSERT( pProtein != NULL );
                        pProtein->szProteinName = pKeyWord->GetAt(i);
                        pProtein->dwCount = 0;
                }
                for(bResult = TRUE, j=0; j<(DWORD)m_sProteinName.GetCount(); j++ )
                {
                        if( pKeyWord->GetAt(i) == m_sProteinName[j] )
                        {
                                bResult = FALSE;
                                pProtein->dwCount++;
                                break;
                        }
                }
```

```
                  if( bResult )
                  {
                         m_sProteinName.Add( pKeyWord->GetAt(i) );
                         pProteinName->Add( pKeyWord->GetAt(i) );
                         m_sCProtein.Add( pKeyWord->GetAt(i) );
                         m_lpProtein.push_back( pProtein );
                  }
           }
```

2.   **Extract words with protein name characteristics**

   //Extract words that contain uppercase letter, "/" sign, or "-" sign.

```
     for( i=0; i<(DWORD)pKeyWord->GetCount(); i++)
     {
            bResult = TRUE;
            TRACE( "%s\n", pKeyWord->GetAt(i) );

            for( j=0; j<(DWORD)pKeyWord->GetAt(i).GetLength(); j++)
            {
                   if(pKeyWord->GetAt(i).GetAt(j) >= 'A' && pKeyWord->GetAt(i).GetAt(j) <= 'Z')
                   {
                          bResult = TRUE;
                          break;
                   }
                   else if( pKeyWord->GetAt(i).GetAt(j) == '/')
                   {
                          bResult = TRUE;
                          break;
                   }
                   else if( pKeyWord->GetAt(i).GetAt(j) == '-')
                   {
                          bResult = TRUE;
                          break;
                   }
                   else
                          bResult = FALSE;
            }
            if( !bResult )
            {
                   pKeyWord->RemoveAt(i);
                   i--;
            }
     }
```

   //Remove atypical words using filter.

```
     for( i=0; i<(DWORD)pKeyWord->GetCount(); i++)
     {
            bResult = TRUE;
            dwCount = 0;
            if( pKeyWord->GetAt(i).GetLength() > 9)
            {
                   for( j=0; j<(DWORD)pKeyWord->GetAt(i).GetLength(); j++)
                   {
                          if( pKeyWord->GetAt(i).GetAt(j) == '-')
                          {
                                 bResult = FALSE;
                                 break;
                          }
                   }
                   if( !bResult )
                   {
                          for( j=0; j<(DWORD)pKeyWord->GetAt(i).GetLength(); j++)
                          {
```

```
                                if( pKeyWord->GetAt(i).GetAt(j) >= 'A' && pKeyWord->GetAt(i).GetAt(j) <=
'Z')
                                {
                                    bResult = TRUE;
                                    break;
                                }
                            }
                        }
                    if( !bResult )
                    {
                        pKeyWord->RemoveAt(i);
                        i--;
                    }
                }
            else
            {
                for( j=0; j<(DWORD)pKeyWord->GetAt(i).GetLength(); j++)
                {
//Count the numbers of special characters.
                    switch( pKeyWord->GetAt(i).GetAt(j) )
                    {
                    case '<':case
',':case'?':case'~':case'!':case'@':case'#':case'$':case'^':case'&':case'*':
                    case '(':case ')':case '+':case '|':case '{':case '}':case'>':case'-':case'\n':
                        dwCount++;
                        break;
                    case'%':
                        bResult = FALSE;
                        break;
                    case'1':case'2':case'3':case'4':case'5':case'6':case'7':case'8':case'9':case'0':
                        dwNumber++;
                        break;
                    }
                }
                if( pKeyWord->GetAt(i).GetLength() > 3
&&pKeyWord->GetAt(i).Find("aa",pKeyWord->GetAt(i).GetLength()-2) != -1)
                    bResult = FALSE;
                if( pKeyWord->GetAt(i).GetLength() > 3 &&
pKeyWord->GetAt(i).Find("AA",pKeyWord->GetAt(i).GetLength()-2) != -1)
                    bResult = FALSE;
                if( pKeyWord->GetAt(i).GetLength() > 5 &&
pKeyWord->GetAt(i).Find("fold",pKeyWord->GetAt(i).GetLength()-4) != -1)
                    bResult = FALSE;
                if( pKeyWord->GetAt(i).GetLength() > 3 &&
pKeyWord->GetAt(i).Find("bp",pKeyWord->GetAt(i).GetLength()-2) != -1)
                    bResult = FALSE;
                if( pKeyWord->GetAt(i).GetLength() > 3 &&
pKeyWord->GetAt(i).Find("nM",pKeyWord->GetAt(i).GetLength()-2) != -1)
                    bResult = FALSE;
                if( pKeyWord->GetAt(i).GetLength() > 7 &&
pKeyWord->GetAt(i).Find("microM",pKeyWord->GetAt(i).GetLength()-6) != -1)
                    bResult = FALSE;
                if( pKeyWord->GetAt(i).GetLength() > 3 &&
pKeyWord->GetAt(i).Find("UV",pKeyWord->GetAt(i).GetLength()-2) != -1)
                    bResult = FALSE;
                if( dwCount > (DWORD)pKeyWord->GetAt(i).GetLength()/2 || bResult == FALSE ||
dwNumber > (DWORD)pKeyWord->GetAt(i).GetLength()/2)
                {
                    pKeyWord->RemoveAt(i);
                    i--;
                }
            }
        }

//Transfer words into their origins using porter stemmer.
symbol sBuffer[1024] = {0};
TCHAR   sBufferFinish[1024] = {0};
SN_env * pSNenv = NULL;
```

```
        pSNenv = porter_create_env();

        for ( i=0; i<(DWORD)pKeyWord->GetCount(); i++ )
        {
                ::FillMemory( sBuffer, 1024, 0 );
                CopyMemory( sBuffer, (LPCTSTR) (pKeyWord->GetAt(i)), pKeyWord->GetAt(i).GetLength() >
1023 ? 1023 : pKeyWord->GetAt(i).GetLength() );
                TRACE( "orig = %s ", pKeyWord->GetAt(i) );
                SN_set_current( pSNenv, pKeyWord->GetAt(i).GetLength() > 1023 ? 1023 :
pKeyWord->GetAt(i).GetLength(), sBuffer );
                porter_stem( pSNenv );
                ::FillMemory( sBufferFinish, 1024, 0 );
                CopyMemory( sBufferFinish, pSNenv->p, pSNenv->l > 1023 ? 1023 : pSNenv->l );
                TRACE( "%s\n", sBufferFinish );
                (*pKeyWord)[i] = sBufferFinish;
        }
        porter_close_env( pSNenv );

//Remove words that can be found in WordNet.
        pNoun = new CNoun;
        ASSERT_VALID( pNoun );
        pNoun->Open();
        for( i=0; i< (DWORD)pKeyWord->GetCount(); i++)
        {
                if( !pKeyWord->IsEmpty() && pKeyWord->GetAt(i).Find("'") == -1 )
                {
                        szTemp = (*pKeyWord)[i];
                        szTemp.Trim( );
                        szTemp.Trim(",%&.@#*!~?");
                        pNoun->m_strFilter.Format("%s%s%s","noun='",szTemp.MakeLower(),"'");
                        if(!pNoun->Requery())
                                break;
                        if( !pNoun->IsEOF() )
                        {
                                pKeyWord->RemoveAt(i);
                                i--;
                        }
                }
        }
        pNoun->Close();
        delete pNoun;

//Add the protein found into variables m_sCProtein and m_sProteinName.
        for( i=0; i<(DWORD)pKeyWord->GetCount(); i++ )
        {
                for ( bResult = TRUE, ListProteinIterator = m_lpProtein.begin(); ListProteinIterator !=
m_lpProtein.end(); ++ListProteinIterator )
                {
                        if( (*ListProteinIterator)->szProteinName == pKeyWord->GetAt(i) )
                        {
                                bResult = FALSE;
                                pProtein = (LPPROTEIN) (*ListProteinIterator);
                                break;
                        }
                }
                if( bResult )
                {
                        pProtein = new PROTEIN;
                        ASSERT( pProtein != NULL );
                        pProtein->szProteinName = pKeyWord->GetAt(i);
                        pProtein->dwCount = 0;
                }
                for(bResult = TRUE, j=0; j<(DWORD)m_sProteinName.GetCount(); j++ )
                {
```

```
                    if( pKeyWord->GetAt(i) == m_sProteinName[j] )
                    {
                        bResult = FALSE;
                        pProtein->dwCount++;
                        break;
                    }
                }
            if( bResult )
            {
                m_sProteinName.Add( pKeyWord->GetAt(i) );
                pProteinName->Add( pKeyWord->GetAt(i) );
                m_sCProtein.Add( pKeyWord->GetAt(i) );
                m_lpProtein.push_back( pProtein );
            }
        }
```

2. **retrieve potential protein names using regular expression**

```
  if( pszText != NULL && pszText->IsEmpty() == FALSE )
      {
            ProcessFullStop( pszText );
            file.Open("c:\\text.txt",CFile::modeCreate | CFile::modeReadWrite);
            file.WriteString( (LPCTSTR) (*pszText) );
            file.Close();
            dwResult = system( "D:\\ProteinInteraction\\POStagger\\mytagger.exe
            D:\\ProteinInteraction\\POStagger\\LEXICON.BROWN.AND.WSJ c:\\TEXT.TXT
            D:\\ProteinInteraction\\POStagger\\BIGRAMS
            D:\\ProteinInteraction\\POStagger\\LEXICALRULEFILE.WSJ
            D:\\ProteinInteraction\\POStagger\\CONTEXTUALRULEFILE.WSJ > C:\\res.txt ");
            file.Open("C:\\res.txt",CFile::modeReadWrite);
            pszText->Empty();
            szTemp = (LPTSTR) ::GlobalAlloc( GPTR,(SIZE_T) file.GetLength()+1 );
            ASSERT( szTemp!=NULL );
            file.Read( szTemp ,(UINT)file.GetLength());
            file.Close();
            *pszText = szTemp;
            ::GlobalFree( szTemp );
            szTemp = NULL;
            MakePause( pszText, &saSentence);
      }
```

```
  //Find sentences with interaction keywords and extract those with NN tag using regular expression
      RE.SetExpression("interact.*|bind.*|associat.*|complex.*|two-hybrid.*|protein.*|domain.*|require.*|kina
se.*|function.*|essential.*|component.*|suggest.*|demonstrate.*");
      for( i=0; i<(DWORD)saSentence.GetCount(); i++)
      {
            RE.SetStringToMatch(saSentence.GetAt(i));
            if( RE.Grep() == 0 )
            {
                saSentence.RemoveAt(i);
                i--;
            }
            else
            {
                TRACE("The sentence =%s\n",saSentence[i]);
                for( dwFind = 0;dwFind< (DWORD)saSentence[i].GetLength(); )
                {
                    bResult = FALSE;
                    dwFind = saSentence[i].Find("/NN",dwFind);
                    if( dwFind != -1 )
                    {
                        for( j=dwFind; j>0; j--)
                        {
```

```
if( saSentence[i].GetAt(j) == '>')
{
    k = j;
    while( k > 0)
    {
        if( saSentence[i].GetAt(k) != '<')
            k--;
        else
        {
            bResult = TRUE;
            break;
        }
    }
}
if( saSentence[i].GetAt(j) == ' ' && j!=dwFind )
{
    if( bResult )
    {
        szMid = saSentence[i].Mid(j,dwFind-k).Trim();
        szMid.Trim(_T("?!'[]*,.();<>^|\""));
        TRACE( "rexrexrex %s\n", szMid );
        saTempWord.Add( szMid );
        break;
    }
    else
    {
        szMid = saSentence[i].Mid(j,dwFind-j).Trim();
        szMid.Trim(_T("?!'[]*,.();<>^|\""));
        TRACE( "rexrexrex %s\n", szMid );
        saTempWord.Add( szMid );
        break;
    }
}
                    }
                    dwFind = dwFind + 5;
                }
            }
        }
    }

//Find word frequency related to the word "interact."
    for( i=0; i<(DWORD)saSentence.GetCount(); i++ )
    {
        for( dwResult=0; dwResult<(DWORD)saSentence[i].GetLength(); )
        {
            dwResult = saSentence[i].Find("interact",dwResult);
            if( dwResult != -1)
            {
                dwInteract++;
                dwResult = dwResult + 8;
            }
        }
    }

//Find word frequency related to the word "associate."
    for( i=0; i<(DWORD)saSentence.GetCount(); i++ )
    {
        for( dwResult=0; dwResult<(DWORD)saSentence[i].GetLength(); )
        {
            dwResult = saSentence[i].Find("associat",dwResult);
            if( dwResult != -1)
            {
```

```
dwBind++;
                                dwResult += 4;
                        }
                }
        }

//Find word frequency related to the word "complex."
        for( i=0; i<(DWORD)saSentence.GetCount(); i++ )
        {
                for( dwResult=0; dwResult<(DWORD)saSentence[i].GetLength(); )
                {
                        dwResult = saSentence[i].Find("complex",dwResult);
                        if( dwResult != -1)
                        {
                                dwComplex++;
                                dwResult += 7;
                        }
                }
        }
        m_dwWordCount.Add( dwAssociate );
        m_dwWordCount.Add( dwBind );
        m_dwWordCount.Add( dwComplex );
        m_dwWordCount.Add( dwInteract );

//Remove words from stop word dictionary.
        pSet = new CWordsnot;
        ASSERT_VALID( pSet );
        pSet->Open();
        for( i=0; i<(DWORD)saTempWord.GetCount(); i++ )
        {
                if( !saTempWord.IsEmpty() && saTempWord[i].Find("") == -1)
                {
                        szMakelower = saTempWord[i];
                        pSet->m_strFilter.Format("%s%s%s","wordsnot='",szMakelower.MakeLower(),"'");
                        if( !pSet->Requery() )
                                break;
                        if( !pSet->IsEOF() )
                        {
                                saTempWord.RemoveAt(i);
                                i--;
                        }
                }
        }
        pSet->Close();
        delete pSet;

//Remove words that can be found in WordNet.
        pNoun = new CNoun;
        ASSERT_VALID( pNoun );
        pNoun->Open();
        for( i=0; i<(DWORD)saTempWord.GetCount(); i++)
        {
                if( !saTempWord.IsEmpty() && saTempWord[i].Find("") == -1)
                {
                        szMakelower = saTempWord[i];
                        szMakelower.Trim();
                        szMakelower.Trim("[]\"<>,%&.@#*!~?");
                        pNoun->m_strFilter.Format("%s%s%s","noun='",szMakelower.MakeLower(),"'");
                        if( !pNoun->Requery())
                                break;
                        if( !pNoun->IsEOF() )
                        {
                                saTempWord.RemoveAt(i);
                                i--;
                        }
                }
        }
        pNoun->Close();
        delete pNoun;
```

```
//Remove plurality.
    pPlurality = new CPlurality;
    ASSERT_VALID( pPlurality );

    pPlurality->Open();
    for( i=0; i<(DWORD)saTempWord.GetCount(); i++)
    {
        if( !saTempWord.IsEmpty() && saTempWord[i].Find("") == -1)
        {
            szMakelower = saTempWord[i];
    pPlurality->m_strFilter.Format("%s%s%s","word='",szMakelower.MakeLower(),"'");
            if( !pPlurality->Requery())
                break;
            if( !pPlurality->IsEOF() )
            {
                saTempWord.RemoveAt(i);
                i--;
            }
        }
    }
    pPlurality->Close();
    delete pPlurality;

//Remove suffix using porter.stem2.
symbol sBuffer[1024] = {0};
TCHAR   sBufferFinish[1024] = {0};
SN_env * pSNenv = NULL;
    pSNenv = porter_create_env();
    for ( i=0; i<(DWORD)saTempWord.GetCount(); i++ )
    {
        ::FillMemory( sBuffer, 1024, 0 );
        CopyMemory( sBuffer, (LPCTSTR) (saTempWord.GetAt(i)), saTempWord.GetAt(i).GetLength()
> 1023 ? 1023 : saTempWord.GetAt(i).GetLength() );
        TRACE( "orig = %s ", saTempWord.GetAt(i) );
        SN_set_current( pSNenv, saTempWord.GetAt(i).GetLength() > 1023 ? 1023 :
saTempWord.GetAt(i).GetLength(), sBuffer );
        porter_stem( pSNenv );
        ::FillMemory( sBufferFinish, 1024, 0 );
        CopyMemory( sBufferFinish, pSNenv->p, pSNenv->l > 1023 ? 1023 : pSNenv->l );
        TRACE( "%s\n", sBufferFinish );
        saTempWord[i] = sBufferFinish;
    }

    porter_close_env( pSNenv );

//Remove words that can be found in WordNet again.
    pNoun = new CNoun;
    ASSERT_VALID( pNoun );
    pNoun->Open();
    for( i=0; i<(DWORD)saTempWord.GetCount(); i++)
    {
        if( !saTempWord.IsEmpty() && saTempWord[i].Find("") == -1)
        {
            szMakelower = saTempWord[i];
            pNoun->m_strFilter.Format("%s%s%s","noun='",szMakelower.MakeLower(),"'");
            if( !pNoun->Requery())
                break;
            if( !pNoun->IsEOF() )
            {
                saTempWord.RemoveAt(i);
```

```
                                i--;
                        }
                }
        }
        pNoun->Close();
        delete pNoun;

    //Add protein name found using regular expression into variables sREProtein and
    m_sProteinName.
        for( i=0; i<(DWORD)saTempWord.GetCount(); i++)
        {
                for( bResult = TRUE, ListProteinIterator = m_lpProtein.begin(); ListProteinIterator !=
        m_lpProtein.end(); ++ListProteinIterator)
                {
                        if( (*ListProteinIterator)->szProteinName == saTempWord.GetAt(i) )
                        {
                                bResult = FALSE;
                                pProtein = (LPPROTEIN) (*ListProteinIterator);
                                break;
                        }
                }
                if( bResult )
                {
                        pProtein = new PROTEIN;
                        ASSERT( pProtein != NULL );
                        pProtein->szProteinName = saTempWord.GetAt(i);
                        pProtein->dwCount = 0;
                }
                for( bResult = TRUE,j=0; j<(DWORD)m_sProteinName.GetCount(); j++)
                {
                        if( saTempWord.GetAt(i) == m_sProteinName.GetAt(j) )
                        {
                                bResult = FALSE;
                                pProtein->dwCount++;
                                break;
                        }
                }
                if( bResult )
                {
                        m_sREProtein.Add( saTempWord[i] );
                        m_sProteinName.Add( saTempWord[i] );
                        m_lpProtein.push_back( pProtein );
                }
        }
```

4.   Retrieve similar documents from the Internet

```
    //Organize query string and submit the URLs.
    qsort(FindKeyWord, 20, sizeof(KEYWORD), CPreprocess::compare );
        for( i=0, ListProteinIterator = m_KI.m_lpProtein.begin(); i<3 &&
    ListProteinIterator!=m_KI.m_lpProtein.end(); i++,++ListProteinIterator )
        {
                saKeyword.Add( (*ListProteinIterator)->szProteinName );
        }
        szURL = "http://www.ncbi.nlm.nih.gov/entrez/query.fcgi?db=PubMed&orig_db=PubMed&term=" +
    (*FindKeyWord[0].sKeyword);
        szURL = szURL + "AND";
        szURL = szURL + FindKeyWord[1].sKeyword + "AND";
        szURL = szURL + FindKeyWord[2].sKeyword + "OR";
        szURL = szURL + saKeyword[0] + "OR";
        szURL = szURL + saKeyword[1] + "OR";
        szURL = szURL + saKeyword[2] + "&dopt=DocSum&dispmax=";
        szTemp.Format("%d", m_dwSetCount);
        szURL = szURL + szTemp;
        ::AfxMessageBox( szURL,MB_OK);
        m_szTempURL = szURL;
```

```
//Retrieve the web content according to the URL provided by the user and save it in m_pszBuffer.
    m_szURL = url;
    if ( m_pszBuffer )
    {
        delete m_pszBuffer;
        m_pszBuffer = NULL;
    }
    m_pszBuffer = new CString;
    ASSERT( m_pszBuffer != NULL );
    pCurl = curl_easy_init();
    curl_easy_setopt(pCurl,CURLOPT_URL,m_szURL);
    curl_easy_setopt(pCurl,CURLOPT_WRITEFUNCTION,CallbackWrite);
    curl_easy_setopt(pCurl,CURLOPT_WRITEDATA, (LPVOID) m_pszBuffer);
    res = curl_easy_perform( pCurl );
    curl_easy_cleanup( pCurl );

// Retrieve corresponding URLs for the similar documents.
    for( dwFind=0; dwFind<(DWORD)pszText->GetLength(); )
    {
        dwStart = pszText->Find( "PMID:", dwFind);
        if( dwStart == -1)
        {
            dwEnd = pszText->Find( "[PubMed - in process]", dwStart);
            szTemp =
"http://www.ncbi.nlm.nih.gov/entrez/query.fcgi?cmd=Retrieve&db=PubMed&list_uids=" +
pszText->Mid(dwStart+5,dwEnd-(dwStart+5)) + "&dopt=Abstract";
            TRACE("URL:%s \n",szTemp);
            m_sListURL.AddTail( szTemp );
            dwFind = dwEnd + 22;
        }
    }
    if( m_sListURL.IsEmpty() == FALSE)
    {
        if( pSet )
        {
            delete pSet;
            pSet=NULL;
        }
        pSet = new CSimurl;
        ASSERT_VALID( pSet );
        pSet->Open();
        for( pos = m_sListURL.GetHeadPosition(); pos != NULL; )
        {
            pSet->AddNew();
            pSet->m_profile = (*pszProfile);
            pSet->m_favname = (*pszFavname);
            pSet->m_urladr = m_sListURL.GetAt(pos);
            pSet->m_ntchk = '2';
            pSet->Update();
            m_sListURL.GetNext(pos);
        }
        pSet->Close();
    }
    delete pSet;
    pSet = NULL;

//Calculate the similarity.
    for( i=0; i<20; i++)
    {
        dNormalize = dNormalize + FindKeyWord[i].dCount;
    }
```

```
//Normalization process.
    for( i=0; i<20; i++)
    {
         FindKeyWord[i].dCount = FindKeyWord[i].dCount / dNormalize;
    }

    for( i=0; i<20; i++)
    {
         dSumFind = dSumFind + FindKeyWord[i].dCount;
         dSumOrig = dSumOrig + OrigKeyWord[i].dCount;
    }
    for( i=0; i<20; i++)
    {
         if( OrigKeyWord[i].dCount < FindKeyWord[i].dCount )
              dSum = dSum + OrigKeyWord[i].dCount;
         else
              dSum = dSum + FindKeyWord[i].dCount;
    }
    dMD = pow((dSum * dSum )/((dSumFind*dSumOrig)+0.0001),0.5);
    m_dSimilarity = dMD;
```

Chapter XIII

SWAP:
A Framework for Ontology Support in Semantic Web Applications

Arijit Sengupta, Wright State University, USA

Henry Kim, York University, Canada

Abstract

We present SWAP (Semantic Web application pyramid), a framework for incorporating ontologies in data-oriented semantic Web applications. We have implemented this framework with a measurement ontology for a quality management Web service. This quality management Web service is built on top of a set of XML Web services implementing agents representing quality management clients, quality management servers, and vendors. SWAP facilitates data exchange between these Web services with vendor data stored in databases, and the processing of the data using a combination of RuleML and SQL. The testbed implementation demonstrates the feasibility and scalability of the framework for any type of three-tier ontology-based semantic Web applications involving low to moderate data exchange. We discuss methods for improving this framework for high data exchange volumes as well. The primary contribution of this framework is in the component-based implementation of real-world semantic Web applications.

Introduction

The semantic Web, introduced by Berners-Lee (Berners-Lee, Hendler, & Lassila, 2001) opens the door to intelligent Web applications. The concept of the semantic Web is still evolving, and needs the integration of several key technologies such as databases, XML Web services, and ontology theory and its applications. We present SWAP (Semantic Web application pyramid)—a framework with a three-tier architecture for developing ontology-based semantic Web applications. To demonstrate the applicability of this framework, we present a measurement ontology to create a quality management Web service for the semantic Web using this framework.

Ontologies from the applied AI field are useful for semantic Web applications. A kind of ontology is an explicit representation of shared understanding. In order to represent a shared understanding, a model of a domain must minimize ambiguity in interpretation by those who are using it to share data. Ontology use minimizes interpretation ambiguity because proper ontology construction requires a thorough and systematic analysis of a domain. Specifically, a domain's key assumptions, vocabulary, and principles must be made explicit, represented, and generalized. This explication of what is often implicitly held then reduces the possibility of ambiguity, which is further minimized if the ontology is expressed in a formal language with limited syntax and semantics, then that limits possible interpretations of a given ontology expression. Smith and Poulter (1999) posit that terms and business rules common to trading partners in an electronic market can be represented in shared ontologies. Software agents representing trading partners then can communicate and share data without ambiguity, thus automating rote transactions between partners. VerticalNet (2005) uses ontologies to represent domain knowledge of vertical industries for which it creates business-to-business markets. An interesting extension is described by Glushko, Tenenbaum, and Meltzer (1999) who use generic XML-based ontologies, called the common business library. These library objects are used to construct a translation layer so that the supplier and customer can use their own terms and business rules in conducting online transactions, yet still be able to communicate intended meanings to each other. For the distributed intelligent Web applications, the customer and supplier in distinct organizations on the Web specially need use the ontology to interchange their own vocabulary and business rules while ensuring that intended meanings are communicated. So it is quite understandable that ontologies are very useful for the intelligent Semantic Web applications. However, there is not a consensus characterization for ontologies. For some, it is a set of terms organized in an is-a hierarchy. For others, it is a set of agreed-upon XML data definitions. Yet for others, it is a rich set of terms and axioms represented in an expressive formal language like first-order logic. So there is a need to set forth a rigorous methodology that can be used to systematically design an appropriate ontology for a Web application. Here we use the TOVE ontological engineering methodology to generate the TOVE measurement ontology, which is a solid theoretical core of the SWAP framework.

The TOVE ontological engineering methodology is a structured design methodology for systematically and rigorously engineering ontologies. In the methodology, motivating scenarios of enterprises are analyzed to explicate informal competency questions for an ontology. These questions are analyzed to explicate terminology, and assumptions that bound the scope of an ontology. From these, formal competency questions expressed using the terminology are stated. Then, axioms that define and constrain the interpretation of the terminology are engineered. By reasoning using these axioms, the formal competency questions are answered; this is the demonstration of competency of the ontology. Augmentation or creation of new motivating scenarios then initiates another iteration of the TOVE Ontological Engineering Methodology to augment the ontology, or to engineer a new one. Since quality control is the primary concern in our SWAP framework, we apply the TOVE ontological engineering methodology to construct the TOVE measurement ontology, which is one of several ontologies for enterprise modeling for quality management (Kim, 1999).

This chapter serves the dual purpose of presenting the SWAP framework as well as its prototypical application. The rest of this chapter is organized as follows: first, we explore some background in quality management, measurement ontologies and semantic Web architectures. Second, we present the TOVE Ontological engineering methodology and the measurement ontology that we use. Third, we present the SWAP framework and the process of integrating databases into the framework. Fourth, we describe experiments with the framework, in particular our testbed application using the presented measurement ontology. Finally, we conclude in last section.

Background and Literature Review

Because of the length restriction, a full-length literature review is not included in this article. Here we summarize some of the current efforts in software development protocols for the semantic Web, and on the development of quality measurement ontologies.

An application protocol for semantic Web is not a highly researched topic. The most important problem in this domain which is actively researched is metadata management. Shah and Seth (1999) propose a model for managing metadata in a distributed environment. Interoperation across ontologies is also heavily researched and implemented (Mena, Kashyap, Sheth, & Illarramendi, 1996). We concentrate on a framework for appropriately and meaningfully distributing both data and metadata in SWAP, thereby creating a full environment where distributed semantic Web applications can be developed. OWL (ontology Web language) (McGuinness & van Harmelen, 2003) is the culmination of W3C and other researchers' efforts at developing a standardized ontology language for the semantic Web. SWRL (Semantic Web rule language) (Horrocks, Patel-Schneider, & van Harmelon, 2003) combines the frame-based approach to knowledge representation of OWL with the rule-based approach of RuleML (Rule Markup Language) (Boley, Tabet, & Wagner, 2001) for the semantic Web. Unfortunately, automatic inference engines explicitly for these ontology languages are not as well-developed as XML query engines (Lee & Sohn, 2003), thus making the use of a hybrid approach such as SWAP pragmatic.

Though not specifically designed for the semantic Web, there are ontologies that support day-to-day business decisions such those made for quality control. These ontology-based enterprise modeling projects are the Enterprise (Uschold, King, Moralee,

& Zorgios, 1998) and TOVE projects (Fox, 1992). The Enterprise Ontology is comprised of ontologies of activity, time, organization, strategy, and marketing. A "building block" approach is taken in the TOVE project to construct ontologies of higher-level core concepts such as product, activity, state, causality, and time, resource collectively called the activity-state ontology (Grüninger & Fox, 1994). A fundamental domain necessary to execute ontology-based Web services is measurement, and a measurement ontology (Kim & Fox, 2002) is built from the TOVE core ontologies. Though other measurement ontologies do exist (e.g., Heflin, 2001), they are not developed to support enterprise activities as would be required for quality management Web services.

The TOVE Ontological Engineering Methodology and Measurement Ontology

By employing the steps shown next, the TOVE Ontological Engineering Methodology is used to develop and generate measurement ontology, and performs ontology-based analysis.

Step 1: Motivating Scenario

The motivating scenario is a detailed narrative about the application, where emphasis is placed on problems that the application is facing, or the tasks it needs to perform. Ultimately, an application built using an ontology is used to solve this problem.

Figure 1. Methodology for developing ontology representations

```
 Motivating Scenarios

        │ through Analysis, explicate:
        ▼
 Informal Competency Questions ────through Analysis, explicate:───► Terminology
 Competency
 Questions                      with Terminology, state:                        Ontology
 Formal Competency Questions ────can answer Formal────► Axioms
                                  Competency Questions with:

                                      show Formal Competency Questions
                                      are answerable through:
                  Demonstration of Competency
 Evaluations of
 Ontology
```

Step 2: Analysis

Generic concepts independent of reference to a specific Web application are abstracted by analyzing the motivating scenario. An ontology is comprised of explicit and formal representations of these concepts. For example, the customer's motivating scenario highlights its need to model measurement to address product quality. This scenario then compels explication of design issues about what concepts are made explicit: e.g. how to define and represent measurement, and how to represent attributes of an entity that needs to be measured. This analysis leads to representing concepts related to measurement assessment in the TOVE Measurement Ontology.

Step 3: Informal Competency Questions

The analysis leads to asking of competency questions. A key validation of a software application constructed using ontology representations as underlying data and logical models is the capability to answer these questions. Since the terms required to pose the questions as formal queries in the ontology's language have yet to be developed, these questions are inherently informal, asked in English using vocabulary and semantics familiar to the users of the ontology. For representing measurement assessment concepts, some of these questions are:

*   What are the physical characteristics that are measured?
*   What ought to be the measured value; that is, what is the expected value for that physical characteristic?

Step 4: Terminology–Using Representations from Other Ontologies

Terms with which competency questions can be posed formally are identified and then organized in a data model. In most ontological engineering efforts, the first step in constructing the ontology's terminological, or data, model is the organization of representations from other ontologies used to construct a given ontology. Thus the TOVE Measurement Ontology is constructed with representations from the TOVE Ontological engineering methodology.

The TOVE measurement ontology is designed explicitly with quality control in mind, rather than only the basic process of measurement. A complete discussion of the measurement ontology is out of the scope of this chapter; here we only present some of the most important terms and axioms.

TOVE Measurement Ontology terms are defined with propositions (or Boolean terms) from the TOVE Core Ontologies. The TOVE measurement ontology consists of 19 core terms, 16 terms and 3 axioms. Table 1 shows some of the main terms and their descriptions.

Table 1. TOVE measurement ontology: Salient terms and axioms

	Expression	Description
Term-1	*quality_requirement(Qr)*	*Qr* is a quality requirement
Term-2	*measured_attribute(At)*	*At* is a measured attribute
Term-4	*has_sample_sizing(At, Sz)*	Measured Attribute *At* has sample sizing plan *Sz*
Term-8	*has_unit_of_measurement(At, U)*	*At* is measured using unit *U*
Term-9	*measuring_resource(R)*	Measurement performed by resource *R*
Term-10	*primitive_measure(A)*	*A* is a primitive measure activity
Term-11	*measure(A)*	*A* is primitive or collection of primitive measure activities
Term-12	*inspect_and_text(A)*	*A* is an inspect and test activity
Term-13	*measurement_pt(Rt, At, Mp, Tp)*	Attribute *At* of a batch *Rt* measured using measurement point *Mp* at time point *Tp*
Term-14	*conformance_pt(Q, Rt, At, Tp)*	Measurement of attribute *At* of a batch *Rt* taken at time *Tp* shows that the batch conforms to the quality requirement *Q*.
Term-15	*nonconformance_pt(Q, Rt, At, Tp)*	As above, does not conform
Term-16	*conforming_quality(X, Qr)*	*X* has a quality requirement *Qr*

The SWAP Framework

One of the most crucial parts of a semantic Web application is the automation of the processing of ontologies. We now present an architecture that supports one way of processing ontologies in a semantic Web application. This framework also has a three tier structure as shown in Figure 2.

1. The top tier is the client tier, consisting of clients or client agents, which are capable of sending requests to the next tier. Clients can be users interacting with a user interface, or automated intelligent software agents (ISAs). At this tier, clients pose queries using client ontologies and submit them to the next tier.

2. The next tier is the ontology processing tier. This tier uses the ontology, as well as any available mapping techniques to process the queries coming from the client tier. All rules and axioms are available at this layer for processing. Facts are retrieved as needed by sending appropriate queries to the data layer. The retrieved facts can then be processed for the purpose of answering the client queries.

3. The data layer consists of all the facts included in the knowledge base. The ontology processing layer decides on which facts need to be retrieved, and sends appropriate queries to the data layer. The queries are processed at the data layer using any necessary mapping methods, and resulting facts are sent back to the ontology processing layer.

Figure 2. The SWAP pyramid showing the client, ontology and data layers, and the quality management

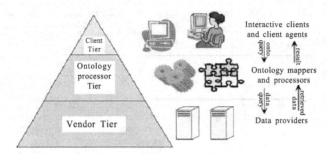

Figure 3. A simple family tree facts and rules

```
Person ('Joe')
hasSex ('Joe', 'male').
Person ('Jill')
hasSex ('Jill', 'female').
hasChild ('Joe', 'Mike'). Father (X, Y) :- hasChild (X, Y), hasSex(X, 'male').
hasChild ('Jill', 'Mike')  Mother (X, Y) :- hasChild (X, Y), hasSex(X, 'female').
Person ('Mike')        Spouse (X, Y) :- hasChild (X, Z), hasChild (X, Z).
hasSex ('Mike', 'male'). ancestor (X, Y) :- hasChild (X, Y).
hasChild ('Joe, 'Lucy'). ancestor (X, Y) :- hasChild (X, Z), ancestor (Z, Y)
hasChild ('Jill', 'Lucy') descendant (X, Y) :- ancestor (Y, X).
Person ('Lucy').
Person ('Lucy', 'female')
Person ('Tim').
hasSex ('Tim', 'male')
```

As an illustration of the above framework, let's consider a simple ontology for processing family trees. This sample ontology consists of a single class Person, having properties hasSex, and hasChild. Represented in a prolog-like format, a sample set of facts and rules in this ontology are shown in Figure 3.

In our framework, the client will issue a query such as ancestor(X,'Mike'), and would expect a response from the ontology processor returning all possible substitution for the variable X. The ontology processor has all the rules, and the data tier has all the facts. During the processing of the rules at the ontology processor, whenever facts are needed, they are retrieved from the data tier. For example, in processing the above query, the system will need to send the following fact queries to the data layer: (1) hasChild(X,'Mike'), (2) hasChild(X, 'Joe') and (3) hasChild(X, 'Jill').

Integrating Databases

In the above discussion, we have not made any specific assumption about the data tier. Typically organizational data is stored in relational databases, and agents in this tier would need to translate the fact retrieval queries into SQL. This process is fairly trivial, since a fact retrieval can be translated into SQL by simply placing constants in the query in the WHERE clause of the SQL statement. For example, in the above example, a fact retrieval such as hasChild(X,'Mike') translates to the SQL query SELECT * from hasChild WHERE col2='Mike' (assuming that the database has the hasChild stored in a table hasChild with columns col1 and col2).

Integrating databases into the data tier enables the use of database query optimization techniques to speed up the retrieval of the facts, which helps in the overall performance of the system in general. As shown in the measurement ontology case above, the use of multiple agents at one or more levels also increases the scalability of the system. Databases can be distributed over different agents and can be merged during the post retrieval process. All of these advances are possible because of the separation of the different tiers, enabling a form of data independence in semantic Web applications.

Experiments with the SWAP Framework

We have implemented the SWAP Framework on several ontology-based applications, including test applications like the simple family tree ontology above, as well as a complex quality management Web service using the measurement ontology discussed above. Here we describe our primary prototype case with a quality management Web service.

A Quality Management Web Service Using SWAP

A prototype application for simulated quality mediation between organizations has been developed, completely using SWAP. The readers should note that the functionality of the mediation system was less critical than the applicability of SWAP in its development, and as a generalized semantic Web application development protocol. In this section, we present a scenario that explains how the ontology and data queries flow between the different layers. In the prototype system, we implemented all the SWAP layers using agents implemented using J2EE Web services, with two independent producer agents comprising the data tier, the customer agents at the client tier, and the QM agent is at the ontology tier.

Information flow between SWAP Layers First the customer agent sends the quality requirements for a receiving product to the Quality Management (QM) agent. The QM agent then classifies and stores these requirements along with other customers. The QM agent can then play the role of a third-party responsible for independent quality auditing, assurance, and control for the customer, automatically working with producer agents to ensure compliance to quality requirements. The following provides a detailed excerpt of this scenario.

1. The customer agent, org1, sends its quality requirements to the QM agent, qm0:

    agent_sends(org1,qm0,q_requirement_bundle_from_org1).
    q_requirement_bundle_from_org1 is a pointer to a hierarchy of quality sub-requirements.

2. The QM agent represents a hierarchy of requirements in the following exemplar way:

    quality_requirement(q_requirement_bundle_from_org1),
    has_requirement(q_requirement_bundle_from_org1,qreq1),
    has_requirement(q_req1,q_req1_1).

3. If a requirement has no sub-requirements, e.g., q req1 1, then the QM agent translates the contents of the requirement in the following exemplar way:

    primitive_requirement_measures_attribute(q_req1_1,widget_length),
    has_standard_value(widget_length,15),
    has_specification_set(widget_length,[14.5,15,5]),
    has_unit_of_measurement(widget_length,cm).
    Standard value is akin to mean; specification set, tolerance specifications.

4. These requirements are sent to producer agents, and results of their quality control measurements are sent back to the QM agent:

    measurement_point(batch22,widget_length, 14.8,10), where 14.8cm is the value of the measurement and 10s the time of measurement.

5. Each measurement point is assessed by the QM agent as a conformance or nonconformance point, *e.g., conformance_pt(q_req1_1,batch22,widget length, 10).* Reports of conformance are sent to the customer agent for immediate action or periodic reporting.

Conclusion and Future Work

As shown in the quality management Web service, the framework can be easily augmented with agents to automate the process of exchange and retrieval. These experiments show the applicability of this framework as a generalized method for implementing semantic Web applications, with or without major data retrieval tasks. We believe a generalizable framework for ontology and data-oriented semantic Web applications is a basic necessity for efficient and organized development, and SWAP is an ideal step towards that direction. The SWAP layers can be extended and merged to fulfill most multitiered business applications using ontologies and web service integration. Detailed analysis of merging layers in SWAP for different business needs is part of the ongoing and future research. We intend to develop other testbed applications using SWAP, and run empirical studies to determine its effectiveness.

References

Berners-Lee, T., Hendler, J., & Lassila, O. (2001). The Semantic Web. *Scientific American, 284*(5), 34-43.

Boley, H., Tabet, S., & Wagner, G. (2001, July 31-August 1). Design rationale of RuleML: A Markup Language for Semantic Web Rules. In *Proceedings of the 1st Semantic Web Working Symposium (SWWS'01)*, Stanford, CA.

Fox, M. S. (1992). The TOVE Project, towards a common sense model of the enterprise. In C. Petrie (Ed.), *Enterprise integration*. Cambridge, MA: MIT Press.

Glushko, R. J., Tenenbaum, J. M., & Meltzer, B. (1999). An XML framework for agent-based e-commerce. *Communications of the ACM, 42*(3), 106+.

Grüninger, M., & Fox, M. S. (1994, April). *An activity ontology for enterprise modelling* [Technical report]. Toronto, Ontario, Canada: Department of Industrial Engineering, University of Toronto. Retrieved May 11, 2006, from http://www.eil.utoronto.ca/enterprise-modelling/papers/gruninger-wetice94-act.pdf

Heflin, J. (2001). *Towards the Semantic Web: Knowledge representation in a dynamic, distributed environment*. University of Maryland, College Park.

Horrocks, I., Patel-Schneider, P. F., & van Harmelen, F. (2003). From SHIQ and RDF to OWL: The making of a web ontology language. *Journal of Web Semantics, 1*(1), 7-26.

Kim, H. M. (1999). *Representing and Reasoning about Quality using Enterprise Models*. Doctoral thesis, Department of Industrial Engineering, University of Toronto.

Kim, H. M., & Fox, M. S. (2002). Towards quality management Web services: An ontology of measurement for enterprise modeling. *Lecture Notes in Computer Science* (2348), 230-44.

Lee, J., & Sohn, M. (2003). The eXtensible Rule Markup Language. *Communication of the ACM, 46*(5), 59-64.

McGuinness, D. L., & van Harmelen, F. (2003, August 18). *OWL Web Ontology Language Overview*. CR-owl-features-20030818, W3C, Boston.

Mena, E., Kashyap, V., Sheth, A. P., & Illarramendi, A. (1996, June 19-21). OBSERVER: An approach for query processing in global information systems based on interoperation across pre-existing ontologies. In *Proceedings of the International Conference on Cooperative Information Systems,* Brussels, Belgium, (pp. 14-25).

Shah, K., & Sheth, A. (1999). Infoharness: Managing distributed, heterogenous information. *IEEE Internet Computing, 3,* 18-28.

Smith, H., & Poulter, K. (1999). Share the ontology in XML-based trading architectures. *Communications of the ACM, 42*(3), 110-111.

Uschold, M., King, M., Moralee, S., & Zorgios, Y. (1998). The enterprise ontology. *Knowledge Engineering Review, 13*(1), 31-89.

Verticalnet. (2005). Verticalnet. Retrieved October 30, 2005, from http://www.vertical.net

About the Authors

Eldon Y. Li is university chair professor in the College of Commerce, National Chengchi University, Taiwan. He was the chair professor and dean of the College of Informatics at Yuan Ze University, Taiwan. He is on leave from the Orfalea College of Business, California Polytechnic State University, San Luis Obispo. He was the founding director of the Graduate Institute of Information Management at the National Chung Cheng University, the president of the Western Decision Sciences Institute (WDSI), and the founding executive director of the International Consortium for Electronic Business (ICEB). He holds MS and PhD degrees from Texas Tech University. He has published more than 100 papers in the areas of human factors in information technology (IT), strategic IT planning, software engineering, quality assurance, information management, and business management. He is the founding editor for the *International Journal of Electronic Business, International Journal of Information Policy and Law, International Journal of Information and Computer Security, International Journal of Internet and Enterprise Management*, and *International Journal of Internet Marketing and Advertising*.

Timon C. Du is a professor of decision sciences and managerial economics with the Faculty of Business Administration, The Chinese University of Hong Kong. He also serves as director of master of sciences in e-business management. He earned his MS and PhD degrees in industrial engineering from Arizona State University. Currently, his research interests are business intelligence, RFID privacy and security, e-logistics, culture and e-commerce, and the Semantic Web. He has published papers in many leading international journals such as *International Journal of Production Research, Communications of the ACM, IIE Transactions, International Journal of Computer-Integrated Manufacturing, Decision Support Systems, Omega, Information System Technology*, and others. He was executive editor for the *International Journal of Internet and Enterprise Management*. Currently, he is executive editor for the *International Journal of Electronic Business* and president-elect of the International Consortium for Electronic Business (ICEB).

* * * * * *

Sinuhé Arroyo is a PhD researcher at DERI in the area of Semantic Web services. He earned his MS in computer science at the Universidad de Málaga, Spain (2000) and his BS in software engineering from the University Complutense de Madrid, Spain (1997). Arroyo has published numerous peer-reviewed papers in international conferences and has extensive teaching experience. While with DERI (Australia), he has been a project manager of the EU-funded projects Esperonto and DIP, and contributed to numerous funded proposals under the EU-framework 6 program. He was previously the project leader at iSOCO in Madrid.

Lin-Chih Chen earned his PhD in information management from the National Taiwan University of Science and Technology. His research interests include Web mining and distributed system applications.

Hui Siu Cheung is an associate professor in the School of Computer Engineering at Nanyang Technological University, Singapore. His current research interests include data mining, Internet technology, and multimedia systems. Previously, he worked for IBM China/Hong Kong as a system engineer (1987-1990). He earned his BSc in mathematics (1983) and a DPhil in computer science (1987) from the University of Sussex, UK. Dr. Hui is a member of IEEE and ACM.

Charles Ling-yu Chou earned his BS and master's degree in mechanical engineering from National Taiwan University, Taiwan (1990 and 1995, respectively). Currently, Mr. Chou is a PhD student at The Chinese University of Hong Kong. His research interests include virtual enterprise management, computer assisted auditing model, e-commerce, product data management, Web services, Semantic Web technologies, and electronic business.

Suo Cong earned a BS in EE from the University of Electronic Science and Technology of China (UESTC) (1992), an MS in EE from UESTC (1995), and a PhD in CS from Fudan University, Shanghai, China (2000). Since 2000, he has been a postdoc with the Department of Informatics, University of Zurich, Switzerland.

Daniela E. Damm studied computer science with a minor topic in medicine at the University of ULM before taking a position as a research assistant at the University of Zurich in 1998. She finished her PhD studies in the area of IS-architecture to support cooperative inter-organizational network organizations. Since January 2004, she has been working for Zuhlke Engineering Ltd., London, as an IT consultant and software engineer. Her main subjects include project management, requirements engineering and software architecture design with a focus on the telecommunications area.

A. C. M. Fong is an assistant professor in the School of Computer Engineering at Nanyang Technological University, Singapore. His research interests include various aspects of Internet technology, information theory, and video and image signal processing. He was educated at the University of Auckland and Imperial College, London. Dr. Fong is a member of IEEE and IEE, and is a chartered engineer.

Farshad Hakimpour is a visiting scholar at LSDIS at the University of Georgia (USA). He earned his PhD from the University of Zurich (2003) and worked as a research fellow at the Open University, UK, until the end of 2004. He earned an MSc from ITC, The Netherlands, in integrated map and geoinformation production. He also earned a BSc in software engineering from Tehran University. Hakimpour Web site is http://www.hakim pour.com.

Shiu-Li Huang earned his PhD from the Department of Information Management, National Sun Yat-sen University (2005). He is currently an assistant professor in the Department of Information Management, Ming Chuan University, Taiwan. His research interests are mainly in intelligent agent, electronic commerce, and data mining. He is a member of the Phi Tau Phi Scholastic Honor Society.

Szu-Wei Huang was a graduate student of Yuan Ze University, Taiwan, in the Department of Information Management. She earned her MS in June 2003. She is currently an employee of Twinhead International Corporation.

Richard Hwang earned a BBA in accountancy from National Cheng-Kung University, Taiwan (1980). He also earned a master's degree and a PhD degree in accountancy from the University of Missouri-Kansas City and Saint Louis University, respectively. Currently, Dr. Hwang is an associate professor at California State University at San Marcos, USA. Recently, he has focused his research effort in issues relate to accounting firm operations in an IT environment.

Bernard J. Jansen is an assistant professor in the School of Information Sciences and Technology at The Pennsylvania State University, USA. His research focus is at the convergence of people, information, and technology, with the overall goal of improving the effectiveness and efficiency of human-system interaction during information searching. His research projects have dealt with agents, information retrieval, human-computer interaction, and computational intelligence. Dr. Jansen's current research projects are exploring the process in which real users interact with Web information systems and devising new development strategies to build advanced information systems.

Henry Kim is an associate professor of information systems at the Schulich School of Business, York University in Toronto, Canada. He is interested in information systems that facilitate data and knowledge for enterprise modeling, knowledge management, and e-commerce. His articles have appeared in journals such as the *Communications of the ACM, Internet Research, BT Technology Journal, Business Process Management*

Journal, and *Operational Research: An International Journal*. He has consulted to industries and researched in laboratories in Canada, the U.S., UK, and Australia. He earned a PhD in industrial engineering from the University of Toronto

Irwin King earned a BSc in engineering and applied science from California Institute of Technology, Pasadena (1984). He earned an MSc and PhD in computer science from the University of Southern California, Los Angeles (1988 and 1993, respectively). He is a member of ACM, IEEE Computer Society, International Neural Network Society (INNS), and Asian Pacific Neural Network Assembly (APNNA). Currently, he is serving the Neural Network Technical Committee (NNTC) under the IEEE Computational Intelligence Society (formerly the IEEE Neural Network Society). His research interests include content-based retrieval methods for multimedia databases, distributed multimedia information retrieval in peer-to-peer systems, and statistical learning theory

Tak-Pang Lau is currently a master of philosophy student in the Department of Computer Science and Engineering, The Chinese University of Hong Kong. He earned a BEng in computer engineering from the same university in 2004. He is now a team member in the Chinese University Plagiarism IDentification (CUPID) project. His research interests include information retrieval, plagiarism detection, document processing, and Chinese text processing.

Hsi-Chieh Lee is an associate professor in the Department of Information Management, Yuan Ze University, Taiwan, and is temporarily transferred to the National Kinmen Institute of Technology where he served as director of the Computer Center and chairman of the Department of Information Management. He earned his PhDs from the University of Missouri-Rolla in both computer science and engineering management. His research interests are in computational intelligence, parallel processing, and computer networks.

Sam Lee is an assistant professor at Texas State University - San Marcos (USA). Before joining Texas State University, he worked in the information technology industry for four years, specializing in the development of e-business systems using the Java 2 Platform, Enterprise Edition. He earned a bachelor of science in applied mathematics from Tatung University, Taiwan and a Master of Science in applied mathematics from National Chiao Tung University, Taiwan. He earned his PhD in industrial engineering from Arizona State University. His research interests are Web application engineering, decision support systems, and supply chain management

Fu-ren Lin earned his PhD in information systems from the University of Illinois at Urbana-Champaign (1996). He then taught with the Department of Information Management, National Sun Yat-sen University, Taiwan. In 2004, he moved to National Tsing Hua University as a professor at the Institute of Technology Management, Taiwan. His research interests include business process innovation, electronic commerce, data/text mining, and knowledge management.

José-Manuel López-Cobo is a PhD researcher at the University of Alcalá de Henares in the area of Semantic Web services and e-learning. He is also working in Atos Origin as technical manager of the Software and Services Unit, developing research projects. He earned his MS in computer science at Universidad de Málaga, Spain (1998). José-Manuel has focused his career in the management and research in EU funded projects, gathering some expertise in the field of the Semantic Web (iBROW), Semantic Web Services (SWWS, DIP, INFRAWEBS) and in the service centric approach (SeCSE).

Cheng-Jye Luh is an associate professor with the Department of Information Management, Yuan-Ze University, Taiwan. His research interests include Web mining, Semantic Web, and e-business applications. He earned a PhD in electrical and computer engineering from the University of Arizona. He is a member of the IEEE.

Michael R. Lyu earned his BS in electrical engineering from the National Taiwan University (1981), his MS in computer science from the University of California, Santa Barbara (1985), and his PhD in computer science from the University of California, Los Angeles (1988). He has participated in more than 30 industrial projects in these areas, and helped to develop many commercial systems and software tools. His research interests include software reliability engineering, distributed systems, fault-tolerant computing, Web technologies, mobile networks, digital video library, multimedia processing, and video searching and delivery

Quan Thanh Tho is a PhD student at the School of Computer Engineering, Nanyang Technological University, Singapore. Mr. Quan earned his BEng in computer engineering at Hochiminh City University of Technology, Vietnam. His research interests include data mining, ontology, Semantic Web and Web services.

Salvador Sánchez-Alonso earned a university degree in computer science from the Pontifical University of Salamanca, Spain (1997), and a PhD in computing from the Polytechnic University of Madrid, Spain (2005). He worked as an assistant professor at the Pontifical University of Salamanca (1997-2000, 2002-2005). He also worked as a software engineer at a software solutions company (2000-2001). Since 2005, he has been a professor in the Computer Science Department of the University of Alcalá. His research interests include learning objects reusability, metadata, object-oriented technologies and Web engineering.

Arijit Sengupta is an assistant professor of information systems and operations management at the Raj Soin College of Business, Wright State University, Dayton, Ohio, USA. He earned his PhD in computer science from Indiana University. Prior to joining Wright State, Dr. Sengupta served as faculty at Kelley School of Business at Indiana University and the Robinson College of Business, Georgia State University. Dr. Sengupta's research areas are in databases and XML, specifically in modeling, query languages, data mining, and human-computer interaction. He has published more than 30 scholarly articles in leading journals and conferences, as well as authored several books and book chapters. He is a member of the information technology committee of the Decision Sciences institute and has led several of the information technology innovation projects for the institute. He has served in the program committee of several international conferences.

Miguel-Angel Sicilia obtained a university degree in computer science from the Pontifical University of Salamanca, Spain (1996), and a PhD in computing from the Carlos III University of Madrid (1999). From 1997 to 1999 he worked as an assistant professor and later on as a part time lecturer with the Computer Science Department of the same university. He also worked as a software architect in e-commerce consulting firms. From 2002 to 2003 he worked as a full-time lecturer at the Carlos III University, after which he joined the University of Alcalá, where he currently leads the Information Engineering Research Unit. His research interests are primarily in the areas of adaptive hypermedia, learning technology and human-computer interaction, with a special focus on the role of uncertainty and imprecision handling techniques in those fields.

Amanda Spink is a professor of information technology at the Faculty of Information Technology, Queensland University of Technology, Australia. Her research focuses on theoretical and applied studies of human information behavior and interactive information retrieval (IR), including Web and digital libraries studies, and information science theory. She has published more than 220 journal articles, refereed conference papers and book chapters, with many in the *Journal of the American Society for Information Science and Technology, Information Processing and Management, Journal of Documentation, Interacting with Computers, IEEE Computer, International Journal of Information Management, Information Research* and *Internet Research*.

Robert M. Wolfe, MD, is an assistant professor in the Department of Family Medicine at Northwestern University's Feinberg School of Medicine in Chicago, USA. He has a particular interest in the Internet and its impact on healthcare and health education. He has published several studies concerning the use of the Internet by antivaccination groups to spread misinformation about childhood vaccination programs, and has also written articles about the history and philosophy of the antivaccination movement. He is a member of the steering committee of the Group on Immunization Education of the Society of Teachers of Family Medicine, and is also a member of the Medical Informatics Committee of Evanston-Northwestern Healthcare in Evanston, Illinois.

Wan-Yeung Wong is currently an analyst of the IT Department of Chow Sang Sang Holdings International Limited. He is an experienced software engineer in the financial industry, especially for developing securities trading systems. In the past, he also worked as a software engineer in a mobile application company. He was responsible for developing several Web and WAP products, and messaging systems for mobile handsets. In addition, he earned his MPhil from the Department of Computer Science and Engineering, The Chinese University of Hong Kong. His research involved Web technologies, information retrieval, and peer-to-peer networks.

Index

F

factual statements 10
fail 162
fault diagnosis 96
FDIC 247
Federal Depository Insurance Commission
    (FDIC) 247
first-order logic 311
FOAF 117
formal language 7, 8
formal logic 14
friend of a friend (FOAF) 117
functional properties 48
fuzzy logic models 200

G

GA 201
GAAP 247
GAAS 250
gene 222
generally accepted accounting principles
    (GAAP) 247
generally accepted auditing standards
    (GAAS) 250
genetic algorithm (GA) 201
GeniMiner 206
global best-fit solution 226
Google 3
grammar rules 9
grounding 76

H

HLP 199, 201
HTML 2, 181, 189
HTTP 2, 34, 77
HuddleSearch 203
human agents 32
HVV method 200
hyperlink exploration 203
hyperlink prediction 201
hyperlinks 200
hypertext markup language 181

I

IE 201
IEEE 143
implementation manager 185
incorporation 8
inductive reasoning 9
information representation 5
information retrieval 200
information risks 248
input 48
Inquirus 2 203
instances generation 102
intelligent software agents (ISAs) 315
internal auditors 247
Internet queries 272
intranets 181
IOPEs 48
IR 200, 269
ISAs 315

J

J2EE 80
Java Message Dervice (JMS) 77
Java RMI 34
JavaServer Pages 190
Jbuilder 192
Jena 125
JMS 77, 80
JSP 190

K

k-nearest neighbor (kNN) 111
KDD 204
kernel function 286
key-phrases 204
keyword spamming 200
KM 147
kNN 111
knowledge base 9
knowledge discovery 98
knowledge management 23
Kohonen Self-Organizing Map (KSOM)
    100
KSOM 100

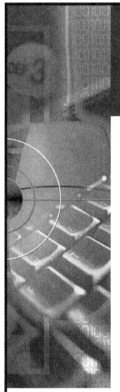